Cultural Politics in Contemporary America

Cultural Politics in Contemporary America

Edited by Ian Angus
and Sut Jhally

Routledge

New York and London

First published in 1989 by

Routledge
an imprint of Routledge, Chapman and Hall, Inc.
29 West 35 Street
New York, NY 10001

Published in Great Britain by

Routledge
11 New Fetter Lane
London EC4P 4EE

Library of Congress Cataloging-in-Publication Data

Cultural politics in contemporary America / [edited by] Ian H. Angus & Sut Jhally.
    p.   cm.
    Includes index.
    ISBN 0–415–90009–3. ISBN 0–415–90010–7 (pbk.)
    1. Mass media—United States.   2. United States—Popular culture—History—20th century. I. Angus, Ian H II. Jhally, Sut
P92.U5C85 1988 302.2′34—dc19 88–20934

British Library Cataloguing in Publication Data

Cultural politics in contemporary America.
   I. United States. Society. Influence of mass media.
   I. Angus, Ian H. II. Jhally, Sut 302.2′34′0973

ISBN 0–415–90009–3
ISBN 0–415–90010–7 Pbk

Dedicated to the memory of
Joe Hill
Wobbly, labor militant,
and genius of cultural politics
Murdered by the Authorities
of the State of Utah
November 19, 1915

Contents

Acknowledgments   xi

Introduction   1

Part I: EMPIRE AND CONSUMPTION

1. Requiem for the American Empire
    Gore Vidal   17

2. The Imperial Cannibal
    Bill Livant   26

3. American Empire and Global Communication
    Eileen Mahoney   37

4. Power, Hegemony, and Communication Theory
    Leslie Good   51

5. The Political Economy of Culture
    Sut Jhally   65

6. Advertising and the Development of Consumer
    Society
    Stuart Ewen   82

7. Circumscribing Postmodern Culture
    Ian H. Angus   96

Part II: DIMENSIONS OF CULTURAL EXPERIENCE

8. In Living Color: Race and American Culture
   Michael Omi   111

9. Cultural Conundrums and Gender: America's
   Present Past
   Jean Bethke Elshtain   123

10. Working Class Culture in the Electronic Age
    Stanley Aronowitz   135

11. Nature in Industrial Society
    Neil Evernden   151

Part III: THEMES IN POPULAR CULTURE

12. Sexual Politics
    Ellen Willis   167

13. Action-Adventure as Ideology
    Gina Marchetti   182

14. Vehicles for Myth: The Shifting Image of the
    Modern Car
    Andrew Wernick   198

15. Advertising as Religion: The Dialectic of
    Technology and Magic
    Sut Jhally   217

16. The Importance of Shredding in Earnest: Reading
    the National Security Culture and Terrorism
    James Der Derian   230

17. Television and Democracy
    Michael Morgan   240

18. MTV: Swinging on the (Postmodern) Star
    Lawrence Grossberg   254

Part IV: THE LOGIC OF CONTEMPORARY CULTURE

19. The Decline of American Intellectuals
    Russell Jacoby   271

20. The Myth of the Information Society
    William Leiss   282

21. Limits to the Imagination: Marketing and
Children's Culture
Stephen Kline   299

22. The Privatization of Culture
Herbert Schiller   317

23. Media Beyond Representation
Ian H. Angus   333

24. Postmodernism: Roots and Politics
Todd Gitlin   347

Notes   361

Contributors   386

Acknowledgments

This project has benefited enormously from the support provided by the Department of Communication at the University of Massachusetts at Amherst, especially W. Barnett Pearce, Chair of the Department, and Vernon Cronen. The hospitable environment of the Department, and continuing discussions with faculty and graduate students, has encouraged the establishment of a "critical cultural studies" approach to communication. This book is one result of this continuing dialogue. We thank Glen Gordon, Dean of Social and Behavioral Sciences, for his support of the project at a crucial stage. We are also thankful to our colleagues in the University community for engaged interdisciplinary inquiry, some of which is reflected in the contributions to the collection.

We would like to thank David Maxcy for his valuable help in the preparation of the manuscript. Sut Jhally extends special thanks to Eileen McNutt.

For both editors, this collaboration has been a very enjoyable and fruitful experience of cooperative work, which is at the very heart of socialist practice.

Introduction

Ian H. Angus and Sut Jhally

In societies where modern conditions of production
prevail, all of life presents itself as an immense
accumulation of spectacles. Everything that was
directly lived has moved away into a representation.

Guy Debord

Image and Identity

We live in a world continually transformed by a proliferation of
images. Media representations substitute for the social action needed
to address "real life" concerns. Violence against women intensifies and
the response by right-wing fundamentalists and left-wing feminists is
to unite to remove the images of pornography from the iconography
of our culture. Polls indicate that most Americans want to maintain
the Welfare State and reduce military spending while a right-wing
Hollywood actor wins the Presidency in a landslide victory on the basis
of his "communication skills." The homeless huddle outside the gates
of the White House and the poverty level rises while the media assure
us that the American Dream is alive and well. Racial tensions increase
and blacks and minorities are subjected to violent physical attacks as
Bill Cosby tops the television ratings. Social commentators bemoan the
general knowledge and literacy skills of the young, as children dutifully
chant advertising jingles and hypnotically watch the space adventures
of characters created by toy manufacturers. The nuclear arsenal builds,
children's nightmares of holocaust intensify, and comic-book fantasies
of protection from space dominate disarmament negotiations. Vietnam
veterans protest intervention in Central America while Hollywood
attempts to convince teenage America that a lost war was in fact
a victory. As Bruce Springsteen sings of alienation and frustration in
the heartland of America and devotes funds to food banks and trade
unions, Chrysler offers him $12 million to use "Born in the USA" as

1

an advertising slogan in a nationalistic campaign to assure us that the "pride is back."

In contemporary culture the media have become central to the constitution of social identity. It is not just that media messages have become important forms of influence on *individuals*. We also identify and construct ourselves as *social beings* through the mediation of images. This is not simply a case of people being dominated by images, but of people seeking and obtaining pleasure through the experience of the consumption of these images. An understanding of contemporary culture involves a focus on both the phenomenology of watching and the cultural form of images.

The essays in this book probe the dimensions of what we call "cultural politics." By this phrase we do not intend a narrow definition of either the realm of culture as referring to artistic production or of politics as referring to the formal electoral process. Instead, we focus on a wider definition of both terms that refers to the complex process by which the whole domain in which people search and create meaning about their everyday lives is subject to politicization and struggle.

The central issue of such a cultural politics is the exercise of power in both institutional and ideological forms and the manner in which "cultural practices" relate to this context. People create their own meaning, but as Marx noted, "not in conditions of their own choosing." Understanding the manner in which institutional and ideological structures act as limits to the possibilities of cultural practices is indispensable to social action directed to our real problems.

The power of representations in the formation of social identity occurs within the broader political economy of culture and society as a whole. The 1980s have been characterized by three related movements regarding the culture industries. First, there has been an increasing integration of the media within the broader control of transnational corporations, such that there is a severe restriction on the autonomy of the media from the influence of business and commerce. Second, there has been an increasing concentration of ownership of the media, such that there are far fewer independent voices available in the United States to contribute to a democratic dialogue. Fewer and fewer companies own more and more media outlets.

Third, power is not only exercised through direct control of the cultural realm by economic force or the state but by blurring the boundaries between the economic and cultural spheres. The media have increasingly become just another sphere of business such that their uniqueness and centrality as cultural forms are submerged beneath their treatment as commodities like any other. As Mark Fowler, Commissioner of the FCC under the Reagan administration remarked, "television is just like any other business . . . it is a toaster with pictures." Commodification is the form that cultural life assumes under these conditions and the goal of critical cultural analysis should be to ask what possibilities this opens up and what forms of expression, activity, and understanding it mitigates against.

On the basis of the first two developments, it is possible to understand the combination of national identity spectacles and secrecy in contemporary American politics. Alexander Cockburn has referred to the increasing presentation of events as a kind of "electronic Nuremberg rally" where only one kind of interpretation is allowed and endlessly repeated.[1] Alternative readings are not presented or allowed to intrude. The media coverage of the invasion of Grenada, the bombing of Libya, and the explosion of the Space Shuttle are examples of this "rally" principle, where rituals of patriotism and national identity whip up popular sentiment against the "enemy other." Simultaneously, whereas once the media were used by the government to report imperial activities, the bulk of these activities have now become covert and secret. For example, the widespread anger and revolt that followed President Nixon's announcement in 1970 of the bombing of Cambodia led to a political opposition around these events that brought to a head several years of development of public opposition to the undeclared war in Vietnam. The murders at Kent State and Jackson State were the culmination of state repression of this opposition. In retrospect, it is important to note that this response was called forth by Nixon himself in the TV broadcast speech that disclosed the military's bombing inside the Cambodian border. What if that announcement had not been made? Government officials and those engaged in putting into practice an imperial foreign policy have learned this lesson. Now the problem is secrecy; the facts are withheld, covered up, and — even if finally exposed — they are distanced from the event and diffused in their effect. At most, the public resents the secrecy; they are at arm's length from any viable response to the events themselves. While nations, especially nations with foreign policies that may be criticized by the population, have always had some tendency to secrecy, this has become much more pervasive since the political right has learned the lessons of protest against the Vietnam war. Oliver North is only the tip of a much deeper program of government and military secrecy, a situation in which the media no longer play the role of assisting informed public discussion. It is this combination of celebration and secrecy that constitutes the main political effect of corporate concentration and control of media production.

However, there are further consequences for cultural politics stemming from the contemporary commodification of culture. In order to understand properly these consequences, we need to clarify the present stage of industrial culture through an account of its historic development.

The Three Stages of Cultural Development

With the onset of industrial capitalist society in the 17th century, the traditional basis of cultural life in feudal political relations and an agrarian economy was gradually eroded. The formation of social identities revolved to an increasing extent around relationships stemming from industrial production. The *first* stage of industrial culture was *class culture* in which the class relations between workers and owners in the factory defined their sense of identity and place in the social world generally. Cultural expressions fit into this divided society through the separation between high culture and popular culture. The former centered on such institutions as concert halls, classical music, novels, and theater, while the latter revolved around taverns, folk music, pamphlets, and union meetings.

At the beginning of the twentieth century a dramatic increase in the concentration of capitalist ownership occurred. From being a system with a large number of separate owners competing for success in a predominantly competitive market, ownership was centralized in fewer and fewer hands and the market was increasingly dominated by large-scale producers. On this basis there was a "rationalization" of production through the meticulous analysis of the production process by time-and-motion studies and so forth. The old trades and their control over the manner of production were broken down and workers were confined to minutely specialized tasks. It was just another step to the assembly line, in which these tasks were performed by machines rather than workers, and the further development of automation.

Alongside this control of the production process, there was also increasing control of the market. In the first place, it was necessary to make sure that the great number of consumer goods produced by automated methods were bought by consumers. Second, it was necessary to ensure that the market became the major arena in which needs and desires aimed at satisfaction. Thus, ethnic, regional, and class allegiances — which aimed at particular and non-market means of satisfaction — were broken down in favor of homogeneous, market-oriented needs. Advertising was a key element in this transition. In the consumer society the main focus is on the realization of investment rather than its production.

From these changes, in the first two decades of this century, emerges the *second* stage of industrial culture — *mass culture*. Culture becomes industrially produced for mass consumption. While there remain differential degrees of access to the goods of mass culture, this is not the same as the totally different spheres of cultural goods present in class culture. Mass culture is in principle available to all; the same type of goods are produced. The only differential is the relative amount of access groups and individuals have to the same sphere of goods. Thus mass culture levels the differences of class culture and projects a totally enclosing sphere in which homogeneous cultural expressions are produced and consumed as commodities. While class differences in production remain, social identity is formed primarily in consumption. Mass culture depends upon, but hides, its production process.

Since the 1960s there has been a further change in industrial culture. This is associated with the shift to a so-called "information society" and is part of a larger transition including the explosion of electronic media, the shift from print literacy to images, and the penetration of the commodity form throughout all cultural production. As in the previous two stages, a transition in production is also underway. Science and technology have become central productive forces so that goods are increasingly distanced from the human work that produces them. Industry has come upon ecological limits not only to capitalism but to industrial production itself. The concentration of ownership has now proceeded to such a vast extent that many transnational corporations are larger than national governments. This third stage of industrialism will require careful political-economic evaluation to assess the exact nature of the change underway. Our book, however, is focused on the cultural dimensions of this *third* stage.

Recent changes in the production and consumption of images have led many commentators to label contemporary society as *postmodern culture* — a society where social identity is formed through mass-mediated images and where culture and economy have merged to form a single sphere. It is a society and culture fundamentally different from the two earlier stages of industrial society and emerges on the basis of the two prior developments.

We suggest that the culture of the information age consists in the production of *staged difference*. Images are consumed as simulations of social identities. They no longer proceed through the homogenization of culture but rather through the simulation of differences overlaid on previous social homogenization. Thus, sex, race, ethnicity, as well as other differences, are no longer suppressed. They are simulated and floated as images in the social imagination. Social identities are constructed through the images on which the desire of audiences temporarily alights. Industrial culture now centers on a politics of images.

Violence, pornography, Reagan's TV politics, are just so many examples of the third stage of industrial culture. Thus the distinction between "images" and "real life," with which we began this introduction, can no longer be regarded as tenable. Social representations constitute social identities. The real is always mediated through images. It is this culture, and this politics, that is discussed under the heading of "postmodernism."

The postmodern stage of industrial culture has also given rise to the argument that we are entering an "information society." Many apologists for industrial capitalism (such as Daniel Bell, Alvin Toffler, and Marshall McLuhan) claim that the information society will remove the toils of industrial work, inequality on both national and international scales, and the separation between work and leisure. However, we may see in these claims merely a continuation of the ideological claims of mass culture: The supposed elimination of differentials stemming from the production process is really just a hiding of these inequalities behind the screen of consumed goods. Moreover, differentials in access to consumption remain. Both of these are issues of the distribution and exercise of social power. They will not disappear in the information age and need to be addressed by critical analysis.

We argue that the postmodern culture of staged difference is *overlaid* on the earlier phases of class culture and mass culture. Class relations in production and mass homogenization have not disappeared; they have simply ceased to be the central phenomenon through which the conjuncture of social relationships in contemporary society is articulated. This leads to a further point about the centrality of cultural dynamics in contemporary society. The dominant cultural articulation can proceed from any of a number of locations in the social body. The stages of industrial society involve just such shifts in the origin of cultural articulations. Culture, in this analysis, should not be thought of as totally dominated by and dependent upon the economic realm. It has to a large degree attained a measure of autonomy and also importance to the survival of the whole social realm. While we cannot say that power has shifted from Wall Street to Madison Avenue, we can say that the power of Wall Street is dependent upon the power of Madison Avenue for its realization and, therefore, the cultural dynamics of contemporary capitalism are not only significant in their own right, but also central to economic dynamics. Thus, cultural politics must address new sources of inequality in postmodern society. The question that poses itself is the extent to which these new conditions allow the possibility of an oppositional or progressive cultural politics.

Mainstream and Alternative Culture

Within the left, it has normally been assumed that mainstream culture offers no openings for a genuine alternative vision and that the creation of an *alternate* sphere is the best way for cultural politics to proceed. This is cultural politics based upon the "sixties" tradition of Joe Hill, Woody Guthrie, Leadbelly, Joan Baez, Phil Ochs, the Weavers, Pete Seeger, and many more. These cultural productions draw on the folk traditions of black, ethnic, and regional music and crafts to articulate an independent version of events, but also and more importantly, of the framework within which events become meaningful and have significance. This is the politics of folk concerts, first-person documentaries, marches, demonstrations, teach-ins, etc. in which culture is created and maintained as an alternative political force. It is the cultural politics of Manhattan Cable's "Paper Tiger" television, for example, where the ordinariness of handheld signs is celebrated as a triumph of authenticity over the technical wizardry that hides the inauthenticity of mainstream culture.[2]

Recently, a critique of this traditional notion of cultural politics has emerged. Jesse Lemisch argues that left culture has failed to engage the mainstream of American life and the vast bulk of the American people.

> Why, at a time when so much avant-garde culture is crossing over toward a mainstream audience, does the left, with more important messages to convey, intentionally remain so isolated? What we have is a culture descended from a noble tradition of popular struggles — one whose public rehearsal is an important ritual of affirmation for those of us who grew up in it — that leaves us speaking a language that more and more Americans don't understand.[3]

Lemisch claims that the left's suspicious attitude toward slick, striking images and pure technique has doomed it to talk in old forms of communication that much of the audience simply finds dated and boring. It is a culture of isolationism where the "converted" reaffirm their conversation — a cultural practice that has abdicated the very cultural domain in which the vast majority of the audience participate in some form or another (even if it is a participation of passivity). Left culture, at its own peril, has refused to play the "numbers game."

Such suspicion of the cultural forces of capitalism raises some interesting issues of what a future "socialist" culture might look like. Marx was clear that he regarded the development of material forces (separate from the relations of production under capitalism) as progressive. Indeed, the socialist economy would be dependent upon the productive capacity unleashed by capitalist forms of production. The deeper question for us here is the extent to which the cultural forces of capitalism can be used to promote a more democratic and egalitarian society. Surely the perceived drabness of the Soviet Union or the Eastern European countries cannot attract anyone's imagination. Lemisch urges the left to adopt the most advanced *forms* of communication of the contemporary marketplace to advance *left* content.

> There are new ways of looking at the world, some from inside the left, some from outside. Say what we will about the values of television advertising and MTV, we recognize their form as distinctly contemporary, and so does much of America. They offer us rapid movement, mobile cameras, quick cutting, excitement, condensed expression, wit, comedy and attractive color. While I hold plenty of reservations about content, anyone who wants to talk to Americans — as the left presumably does — must understand this language.[4]

This critique of traditional left cultural strategies certainly hits at the core of the issues and raises some important questions. However, before we enthusiastically embrace the central tendencies of postmodern culture we need to consider some important reservations. First, what is the relationship of the world of images through which we hope to "speak" to Americans to an alternative political culture? The critique implies that left culture can be created through these images and is not dependent for its success upon the surrounding conditions of reception and experience. Lemisch mentions the "Sun City" video as an example of the success of this type of strategy. This video was produced by Artists United Against Apartheid in order to oppose the racist South African government. However, if the "Sun City" video was successful the real factor is its relationship to an existing and strong anti-apartheid movement in the United States such that the alternative images are both understood and appreciated by the audience. Could the MTV strategy work with an issue that does not already have a developed political base? As a counterexample, Neil Kinnock and the Labour Party of Britain in the election of 1987 put forward a superb media campaign that used the techniques of postmodern imagery but met with giant failure. The whole question of how the reception of this new proposed cultural object is affected by forces from *outside* the object itself remains to be answered.

Secondly, this approach does not investigate the affect of power on the form of culture. What is the effect of the production of culture as a commodity on the image-form? The separation of form and content that Lemisch's approach assumes may not be as simple as it appears.

What if the form affects the experience of the cultural product to such an extent that it alters the content? This, in short, is the "postmodern question." In such a situation, the external context of reception takes on an even greater significance. The tendency of the contemporary commercial form of communication is toward a sequence of juxtaposed images without an explicit internal form of connection. This tendency has been led by ads, but is spreading throughout the media system. The production of cultural artifacts as commodities squeezes the maximum number of images into the shortest space of time — speedup in the entertainment industry — and, in so doing, pushes increasingly more of the context necessary for interpretation to the side of the audience (and away from its provision within the cultural object itself). This has been recognized by advertisers, who direct their messages at specific segments of the market, rather than at the audience as a whole. The representation of people in the ads as similar to the "type" advertisers want to buy the product indicates a recognition of the importance of a context of reception — though, of course, because of the speedup, this context is merely triggered and not developed.

In short, the argument that the left must abandon its traditional preference for small-scale, alternative, "folk" events makes far too many assumptions concerning the benign character of the packaging effect of mass media. First, it ignores the importance of a context of reception within which a message has meaning; and, second, it fails to investigate the connection between the commodity-form and the image-form.

The Possibilities of Intervention:
Lennon and Springsteen

The issues that we have raised in the previous section can be concretized with specific reference to the two most important figures in mainstream culture, from a left perspective, in the last twenty years: John Lennon and Bruce Springsteen.

One reading of Springsteen is that he is a traditional lefty (with ties to the poor, unions, the unemployed, etc.) who despite his best intentions is misunderstood by his fans who do not recognize his political message. But Springsteen is much more ambiguous than this simple reading. The attempt by Ronald Reagan to appropriate "Born in the USA" as a campaign theme in 1984 was met by Springsteen with a kind of bemused bafflement rather than a clear refutation. In part, Springsteen could get away with not reacting because there was no pressure on him to clarify his position. Unlike the 1960s and the early 1970s, the political context did not force him to take sides. There was, in effect, "no pull from the streets" in the vacuum that was left political culture. But as Marshall Berman notes, this situation may change and thus force Springsteen's hand. If the United States invades Central America,

> what will Springsteen do? In the rap that precedes "War," he's pretty well said "Hell no, don't go" already. If he reiterates this, he knows — and the government knows — that it will influence many people to resist. What then? Is he prepared to see his songs pulled off the radio, his records disappear from the stores? The FBI's vendetta against John Lennon could have been just a run-through. Is he ready to head into the storm, and how many of us are ready to go with him?[5]

The "misunderstanding" of Springsteen is then partly of his own creation, which in turn is a reaction to an absent alternative political culture. It is this same absence that contributes to the non-political reading of Springsteen. This issue can be highlighted with reference to the way many people understand "Born in the USA." While for many of us, it rings as a fierce indictment of the Vietnam war, for the majority of those familiar with the song (especially the younger listeners) it is a celebration of American roots and patriotism. Above all it is a celebration of "America." One aspect of Springsteen's huge popularity is indeed this very *populism* that is expressed through the celebration of being American. People tell stories of being in foreign countries where the song brings (young) Americans together. Springsteen's populism however is not the only kind that vies for identity in the 1980s. It combats and finally succumbs to the other great recent populist ideology — Reaganism. Daniel Hallin has perceptively noted that while the network news divisions have not succumbed to Reagan and the causes he has championed, they have succumbed to *Reaganism*, especially the "America is Back," "We're Number One" nationalism.[6] In the battle for the definition of what populism will be defined as, Springsteen's vision has become blurred with the Reaganite one. It is the relationship between populism and authority that is important to understand here. In such a context it is difficult for people to read "Born in the USA," (or at least the slogan) in a critical vein.

In addition to this, there is also the issue of whether there is something *within* the message itself that encourages a non-critical populist reading. For one thing, unless one reads them from the jacket cover, the words are very difficult to understand. All that comes across is the slogan (jingle). (Even if the words could be heard it is possible that they could be given a rightist slant given the celebration of militarism that pervades the culture.) The video for the song, directed by John Sayles (a filmmaker of impeccable political credentials), is highly ambiguous. A stream of images of working-class life, the Vietnam war, and disabled veterans intermingle together, without a clear intended message. The advertising industry has known for a long time that fast moving images work through emotion rather than logic or narrative. Why should these images, using the same techniques be any different? Our young students tell us that they don't pay very much attention to the images that rush before their eyes. This of course is mistaken, but the perception has its basis in the fact that they cannot *distinguish within* the image system. Springsteen merges with Michael Jackson, Madonna, Coke, Miller Beer, and Guess jeans. The image system overwhelms isolated images. Speed and fragmentation are not very good to *think* with. They are good to *feel* with. People can then feel the song while not "understanding" it. In one series of ads for MTV, a teenage boy or girl engages in a continuous monologue of events, characters, feelings, and emotions without any central thread. As the video images mirror the fragmentation of the thoughts, the ad ends with the plug: "Finally a channel for the way you think." In his frustration at the misunderstanding of his art Springsteen responded with the song "War" — as blunt a statement as is possible. There is endless repetition of the same phrase: "War — what is it good for? Absolutely nothing!" It is ironic that Springsteen has drawn upon the *alternate populism* of Woody Guthrie in playing "This land is your land" when his own performances are squarely within the commercial mainstream.

John Lennon suffered from no such ambiguity. In addition to there being no possible misunderstanding of his art, he explicitly articulated his political views. In the situation of the 1960s and the early 1970s, he had to. He could not sit on the fence. He could not passively let a reappropriation of his messages take place. For this he paid, as Marshall Berman noted, a price — political persecution. At the same time, his music had an active political culture to draw upon and which could shape its understanding. He knew "a working class hero is something to be" and he strived, despite his enormous financial success, to become one. Again, unlike the situation that Springsteen confronts, Lennon's music could be separated from the commercial image system. In part, this was because in the early 1970s there still remained some separation between television and rock music. To some degree, the music could stand on its own without having to work against the surrounding image world. Of course this had nothing to do with the music itself but the context. In the postmodern context, "Revolution" turns into an advertising jingle for Nike sneakers (but this may be an anachronism, in a sense, since it is hard to image such a song deliberately being written for an ad — Jackson Browne's "For America" is not being used to sell anything). In the contemporary situation, for a generation that grew up in the absence of an alternative political culture, John

Lennon is simply a Beatle, rather than a figure who was part of an oppositional political culture. In short, the image involves a stripping of its context and a re-immersion in a commercial nexus which is today virtually all-pervasive.

The tendency of the commodity form to decontextualize cultural productions and reinscribe them within a process of exchange cannot be avoided by any cultural producers today. Lennon cannot be insulated from Nike, and his future meaning will become tied up with Nike in the minds of audiences. In the absence of a "pull from the streets," and an alternative political culture, the external conditions of reception will be monopolized by the mainstream. Moreover, the artist will not be pushed to clarify her or his meaning. Consequently, the reception of the most critical content will be ceded to the commercial norm. This situation is even more crucial with the postmodern emphasis on the image, which places an even greater burden on the process of reception.

A Critical Approach to Media and Culture

Mainstream analyses of media have ignored the dimension of power that we have argued is vital to understanding contemporary culture. A critical theory of postmodern culture requires: First, an analysis of the political economy of media and cultural institutions; second, a focus on the form of the cultural commodity; third, a politics of images centering on the experience of viewing.

The starting point for understanding the relationship between economy and culture is the work of Karl Marx. Marx wrote that there is a very close connection between the control of material wealth and the control of ideas and culture, for the ruling class is able to dictate (because of their control of the "means of mental production" such as media) the context within which people think about their daily lives. Consequently, what people accept as "natural" and "self-evident" is exactly what should become problematic and in need of explanation from a critical standpoint. It is characteristic of Marxist thought to place the conscious expressions of social actors within the whole social complex in which those expressions occur. This theoretical framework has generally been described under what is called the "base/superstructure" model. Briefly, this means that the economic base conditions the contents of the superstructure of ideas and beliefs prevalent in everyday life. While in many subsequent strains of "orthodox" Marxism this model has been applied in a very rigid and deterministic manner, the tradition of "Western Marxism" has offered the most sophisticated, elaborate, and thoughtful exploration of this relationship. Seeking to avoid a crude determinism of culture by the economic base alone, this strain of Marxism has approached the analysis of consciousness from the broader and more complex concept of "totality," in which consciousness is seen as interacting with a whole host of important social forces, not simply as the reflection of economic interests. Theodor Adorno and Max Horkheimer in the *Dialectic of Enlightenment* (1946, translated into English in 1972) pioneered the way for this type of analysis. From this point of view, it is not so much the question of determination by the economy that it is important, but rather the imposition of the "commodity form" on cultural productions. The commodity form is imposed whenever production is for the purpose of exchange, rather than use; consequently, political economic forces come to condition the very form of culture.

We place ourselves squarely within the tradition of Western Marxism, in that our central concern is how to theorize about culture without falling into a reductionist mode. We seek to develop an approach which acknowledges the importance of the economics and production, but at the same time places cultural productions within a much broader *totality* of factors. Certainly economic factors are vitally important in understanding the constraints on contemporary cultural production, but we follow Horkheimer and Adorno in attributing general significance to the commodity *form* as analytically distinct from questions of ownership. Furthermore, we argue that a phenomenology of the viewing experience is essential to clarifying the politics of postmodern culture. We must understand the desire for images and the "pleasure" in their consumption, and not see this as merely the imposition of ideology on a passive audience. The attraction of images, combined with the loss of previous cultural forms, puts media productions at the very basis of identity formation.

Cultural Politics

A contemporary cultural politics must recognize not only the power of ownership, but power in the image, power *of* the image; it must refuse celebration, and turn the analysis of new forms toward the external conditions of reception.

The commercial system requires a continuous influx of new cultural commodities. Assimilation of cultural productions into this system strips them of their original context and presses them into an image-form. Without a context for interpretation of images, they all blend into an undifferentiated continuous flow, in which each individual image or set of images, has no particular significance. Thus, they succumb, whatever their intent or content, to the mainstream assumptions of the society at large which dominate the conditions of reception.

A critical democratic and egalitarian strategy must, of course, find itself in conflict with this system. It is certainly true that a hermetic strategy that relies purely on alternative "folk" forms will be irrelevant to the majority of the population, which is thoroughly saturated with mass media productions. As Lemisch argues, some engagement with these forms is definitely called for. Jackson Browne, especially his album "Lives in the Balance" and the video "For America" is an excellent example of such an attempt. But the critical content, as again the case of Jackson Browne indicates, will succumb to these forms if there is no engagement with audience reception as well. The conditions for an alternative reception cannot be separated from the traditional left attempt at an alternative culture, most simply through providing a *context of recognition* of images that are written out of mainstream accounts. An alternative culture provides a *context of interpretation* which is a public pedagogy, and can provide the external conditions for the reception of alternative content when it surfaces in the mass media. Furthermore, it can ground a critical response to the apologetic content that is far more pervasive. In this context, the work of avant-garde artists, such as David Byrne and Laurie Anderson, is important insofar as it disrupts audiences' conventional expectations and motivates self-reflection that may lead to critical readings. One of the most interesting and encouraging features of postmodern media is that such avant-garde works have become widely popular.

We must engage with the media system, but the image-culture cannot provide the basis for its own interpretation. Alternative culture is not a hermetic strategy of self-congratulation, but is the necessary basis for any expansion of critical consciousness into the media system. It is too early, or too late, to throw out Pete Seeger.

PART I

Empire and Consumption

The essays in this section deal with the two most important external conditions influencing the context within which contemporary cultural experience takes place.

The theme of empire is taken up in the first three essays. Gore Vidal offers a history lesson on the foundations of the American empire and how it has guided political life. Vidal ends with the suggestion that the era of uncontested American power is over and that there is renewed international economic competition. Bill Livant examines how the constraining effect of imperial assumptions has limited our understanding of this situation and proposes an alternative way of thinking. Eileen Mahoney shows how American power has been extended globally through control of communication technology and international regulation especially since the Second World War.

The analysis of empire and consumption is bridged by the discussion of hegemony and political economy. Leslie Good introduces several ways of conceptualizing the relationship between power and communication. The notion of hegemony shows how power has been maintained in its established forms by control of the cultural realm. Sut Jhally sketches the specific ways that political-economic power has shaped the development of culture.

The theme of consumption is addressed in the final two essays of this section. The most overt form of commercial influence on culture is advertising, of which an historical sketch is provided by Stuart Ewen. Ian H. Angus pulls together the two themes of empire and consumption and a discussion of the contemporary postmodern situation.

This account of the external conditions influencing culture provides the general framework within which specific cultural analyses take place. However, the notion of hegemony also suggests that culture is a contested terrain in which a struggle over meanings takes place in everyday life. In subsequent sections, the essays take this into account while nevertheless focusing their attention on the establishment of dominant practices.

1.

Requiem for the American Empire

Gore Vidal

On September 16, 1985, when the Commerce Department announced that the United States had become a debtor nation, the American Empire died. The empire was seventy-one years old and had been in ill health since 1968. Like most modern empires, ours rested not so much on military prowess as on economic primacy.

After the French Revolution, the world money power shifted from Paris to London. For three generations, the British maintained an old fashioned colonial empire, as well as a modern empire based on London's primacy in the money markets. Then, in 1914, New York replaced London as the world's financial capital. Before 1914, the United States had been a developing country, dependent on outside investment. But with the shift of the money power from Old World to New, what had been a debtor nation became a creditor nation and central motor to the world's economy. All in all, the English were well pleased to have us take their place. They were too few in number for so big a task. As early as the turn of the century, they were eager for us not only to help them out financially but to continue, in their behalf, the destiny of the Anglo-Saxon race: to bear with courage the white man's burden, as Rudyard Kipling not so tactfully put it. Were we not — English and Americans — all Anglo-Saxons, united by common blood, laws, language? Well, no, we were not. But our differences were not so apparent then. In any

This article first appeared in *The Nation* (January 11, 1986). Reprinted by permission.

case, we took on the job. We would supervise and civilize the lesser breeds. We would make money.

By the end of World War II, we were the most powerful and least damaged of the great nations. We also had most of the money. America's hegemony lasted exactly five years. Then the cold and hot wars began. Our masters would have us believe that all our problems are the fault of the Evil Empire of the East, with its Satanic and atheistic religion, ever ready to destroy us in the night. This nonsense began at a time when we had atomic weapons and the Russians did not. They had lost 20 million of their people in the war, and 8 million of them before the war, thanks to their neoconservative Mongolian political system. Most important, there was never any chance, then or now, of the money power (all that matters) shifting from New York to Moscow. What was — and is — the reason for the big scare? Well, World War II made prosperous the United States, which had been undergoing a depression for a dozen years; and made very rich those magnates and their managers who govern the republic, with many a wink, in the people's name. In order to maintain a general prosperity (and enormous wealth for the few) they decided that we would become the world's policeman, perennial shield against the Mongol hordes. We shall have an arms race, said one of the high priests, John Foster Dulles, and we shall win it because the Russians will go broke first. We were then put on a permanent wartime economy, which is why a third or so of the government's revenues is constantly being siphoned off to pay for what is euphemistically called defense.

As early as 1950, Albert Einstein understood the nature of the rip-off. He said, "The men who possess real power in this country have no intention of ending the cold war." Thirty-five years later, they are still at it, making money while the nation itself declines to eleventh place in world per capita income, to forty-sixth in literacy and so on, until last summer (not suddenly, I fear) we found ourselves close to $2 trillion in debt. Then, in the fall, the money power shifted from New York to Tokyo, and that was the end of our empire. Now the long-feared Asiatic colossus takes its turn as world leader, and we — the white race — have become the yellow man's burden. Let us hope that he will treat us more kindly than we treated him. In any case, if the foreseable future is not nuclear, it will be Asiatic, some combination of Japan's advanced technology with China's resourceful landmass. Europe and the United States will then be, simply, irrelevant to the world that matters, and so we come full circle. Europe began as the relatively empty uncivilized Wild West of Asia; then the Western Hemisphere became the Wild West of Europe. Now the sun has set in our West and risen once more in the East.

The British used to say that their empire was obtained in a fit of absent-mindedness. They exaggerate, of course. On the other hand, our modern empire was carefully thought out by four men. In 1890 a U.S. Navy captain, Alfred Thayer Mahan, wrote the blueprint for the American imperium, *The Influence of Sea Power Upon History, 1660-1783*. Then Mahan's friend, the historian-geopolitician Brooks Adams, younger brother of Henry, came up with the following formula: "All civilization is centralization. All centralization is economy." He applied the formula in the following syllogism: "Under economical centralization, Asia is cheaper than Europe. The world tends to economic centralization. Therefore, Asia tends to survive and Europe to perish." Ultimately, *that* is why we were in Vietnam. The amateur historian and professional politician Theodore Roosevelt was much under the influence of Adams and Mahan, he was also their political instrument, most active not so much during his Presidency as during the crucial war with Spain, where he can take a good deal of credit for our seizure of the Philippines, which made us a world empire. Finally, Senator Henry Cabot Lodge, Roosevelt's closest friend, kept in line a Congress that had a tendency to forget our holy mission — our manifest destiny — and ask, rather wistfully, for internal improvements.

From the beginnings of our republic, we have had imperial tendencies. We took care — as we continue to take care — of the indigenous population. We maintained slavery a bit too long even by a cynical world's tolerant standards. Then, in 1847, we produced our first conquistador, President James K. Polk. After acquiring Texas, Polk deliberately started a war with Mexico because, as he later told the historian George Bancroft, we had to acquire California. Thanks to Polk, we did, And that is why to this day the Mexicans refer to our Southwestern states as "the occupied lands," which Hispanics are now, quite sensibly, filling up.

The case against empire began as early as 1847. Representative Abraham Lincoln did not think much of Polk's war, while Lieut. Ulysses S. Grant, who fought at Vera Cruz, said in his memoirs, "The war was an instance of a republic following the bad example of European monarchies, in not considering justice in their desire to acquire additional territory." He went on to make a causal link, something not usual in our politics then and completely unknown now: "The Southern rebellion was largely the outgrowth of the Mexican War. Nations, like individuals, are punished for their transgressions. We got our punishment in the most sanguinary and expensive war of modern times."

But the empire has always had more supporters than opponents. By 1895 we had filled up our section of North America. We had tried twice

— and failed — to conquer Canada. We had taken everything that we wanted from Mexico. Where next? Well, there was the Caribbean at our front door and the vast Pacific at our back. Enter the Four Horsemen — Mahan, Adams, Roosevelt and Lodge.

The original republic was thought out carefully, and openly, in *The Federalist Papers*: we were not going to have a monarchy and we were not going to have a democracy. And to this day we have had neither. For 200 years we have had an oligarchical system in which men of property can do well and the others are on their own. Or, as Brooks Adams put it, the sole problem of our ruling class is whether to coerce or to bribe the powerless majority. The so-called Great Society bribed; today coercion is very much in the air. Happily, our neoconservative Mongoloids favour only authoritarian and never totalitarian means of coercion.

Unlike the republic, the empire was worked out largely in secret. Captain Mahan, in a series of lectures delivered at the Naval War College, compared the United States with England. Each was essentially an island state that could prevail in the world only through sea power. England had already proved his thesis. Now the United States must do the same. We must build a great navy in order to acquire overseas possessions. Since great navies are expensive, the wealth of new colonies must be used to pay for our fleets. In fact, the more colonies acquired, the more ships; the more ships; the more empire. Mahan's thesis is agreeably circular. He showed how little England had ended up with most of Africa and all of southern Asia, thanks to sea power. He thought that we should do the same. The Caribbean was our first and easiest target. Then on to the Pacific Ocean, with all its islands. And, finally, to China, which was breaking up as a political entity.

Theodore Roosevelt and Brooks Adams were tremendously excited by this prospect. At the time Roosevelt was a mere police commissioner in New York City, but he had dreams of imperial glory. "He wants to be," snarled Henry Adams, "our Dutch-American Napoleon." Roosevelt began to maneuver his way toward the heart of power, sea power. With Lodge's help, he got himself appointed Assistant Secretary of the Navy, under a weak Secretary and a mild President. Now he was in place to modernize the fleet and to acquire colonies. Hawaii was annexed. Then a part of Samoa. Finally, colonial Cuba, somehow, had to be liberated from Spain's tyranny. At the naval War College, Roosevelt declared, "To prepare for war is the most effectual means to promote peace." How familiar that sounds! But since the United States had no enemies as of June 1897, a contemporary might have remarked that since we were already at peace with everyone, why prepare for war? Today, of course, we are what he dreamed we would be, a nation armed to the teeth and hostile to everyone. But what with Roosevelt was a design to acquire an empire is for us a means to transfer money from the Treasury to the various defense industries, which in turn pay for the elections of Congress and President.

Our turn-of-the-century imperialists may have been wrong, and I think they were. But they were intelligent men with a plan, and the plan worked. Aided by Lodge in the Senate, Brooks Adams in the press, Admiral Mahan at the Naval War College, the young Assistant Secretary of the Navy began to build up the fleet and look for enemies. After all, as Brooks Adams proclaimed, "war is the solvent." But war with whom? And for what? And where? At one point England seemed a likely enemy. We had a boundary dispute with it over Venezuela, which meant that we could invoke the all-purpose Monroe Doctrine (the invention of John Quincy Adams, Brooks's grandfather). But as we might have lost such a war, nothing happened. Nevertheless, Roosevelt kept on beating his drum: "No triumph of peace," he shouted, "can equal the armed triumph of war." Also: "We must take Hawaii in the interests of the white race." Even Henry Adams, who found T. R. tiresome and Brooks, his own brother, brilliant but mad, suddenly declared, "In another fifty years . . . the white race will have to reconquer the tropics by war and nomadic invasion, or be shut up north of the 50th parallel." And so at century's end, our most distinguished ancestral voices were not prophesying but praying for war.

An American warship, the Maine, blew up in Havana harbor. We held Spain responsible; thus, we got what John Hay called "a splendid little war." We would liberate Cuba, drive Spain from the Caribbean. As for the Pacific, even before the Maine was sunk, Roosevelt had ordered Commodore Dewey, and his fleet to the Spanish Philippines — just in case. Spain promptly collapsed, and we inherited its Pacific and Caribbean colonies. Admiral Mahan's plan was working triumphantly.

In time we allowed Cuba the appearance of freedom while holding on to Puerto Rico. Then President William McKinley, after an in-depth talk with God, decided that we should also keep the Philippines. In order, he said, to Christianize them. When reminded that the Filipinos were Roman Catholics, the President said, Exactly. We must Christianize them. Although Philippine nationalists had been our allies against Spain, we promptly betrayed them and their leader, Aguinaldo. As a result it took us several years to conquer the Phillipines, and tens of thousands of Filipinos died that our empire might grow.

The war was the making of Theodor Roosevelt. Surrounded by the flower of the American press, he led a group of so-called Rough Riders up a very small hill in Cuba. For this proto-photo opportunity be became a national hero, Governor of New York, McKinley's running mate and when McKinley was killed in 1901, President.

Not everyone liked the new empire. After Manila, Mark Twain thought that the stars and bars of the American flag should be replaced by a skull and crossbones. He also said, "We cannot maintain an empire in the Orient and maintain a republic in America." He was right, of course. But as he was only a writer who said funny things, he was ignored. The compulsively vigorous Roosevelt defended our war against the Philippine population, and he attacked the likes of Twain. "Every argument that can be made for the Filipinos could be made for the Apaches," he explained, with his lovely gift for analogy. "And every word that can be said for Aguinaldo could be said for Sitting Bull. As peace, order and prosperity followed our expansion over the land of the Indians, so they will follow us in the Philippines."

Despite the criticism of the few, the Four Horsemen had pulled it off. The United States was a world empire. And one of the horsemen not only got to be president but for his pious meddling in the Russo-Japanese conflict, our greatest apostle of war was awarded the Nobel Peace Prize. One must never underestimate the Scandinavian wit.

Empires are restless organisms. They must constantly renew themselves; should an empire start leaking energy, it will die. Not for nothing were the Adams brothers fascinated by entropy. By energy. By force. Brooks Adams, as usual, said the unsayable. "Laws are a necessity," he declared. "Laws are made by the strongest, and they must and shall be obeyed." Oliver Wendell Holmes Jr. thought this a wonderful observation, while the philosopher William James came to a similar conclusion, which can also be detected, like an invisible dynamo, at the heart of the novels of his brother Henry.

According to Brooks Adams, "The most difficult problem of modern times is unquestionably how to protect property under popular governments." The Four Horsemen fretted a lot about this. They need not have. We have never had a popular government in the sense that they feared, nor are we in any danger now. Our only political party has two right wings, one called Republican, the other Democratic. But Henry Adams figured all that out back in the 1890s. "We have a single system" he wrote, and "in that system the only question is the price at which the proletariat is to be bought and sold, the bread and circuses." But none of this was for public consumption. Publicly, the Four Horsemen and their outriders spoke of the American mission to bring to all the world freedom and peace, through slavery and war if necessary. Privately, their constant fear was that the weak masses might combine one day against the strong few, their natural leaders, and take away their money. As early as the election of 1876 socialism had been targeted as a vast evil that must never be allowed to corrupt simple American persons. When Christianity was invoked as the natural enemy of those who might limit the rich and their games, the combination of cross and dollar sign proved — and proves — irresistible.

During the first decade of our disagreeable century, the great world fact was the internal collapse of China. Who could pick up the pieces? Britain grabbed Kowloon; Russia was busy in the north; the Kaiser's fleet prowled the China coast; Japan was modernizing itself, and biding its time. Although Theodore Roosevelt lived and died a dedicated racist, the Japanese puzzled him. After they sank the Russian fleet, Roosevelt decided that they were to be respected and feared even though they were our racial inferiors. For those Americans who served in World War II, it was an article of faith — as of 1941, anyway — that the Japanese could never win a modern war. Because of their slant eyes, they would not be able to master aircraft. Then they sank our fleet at Pearl Harbor.

Jingoism aside, Brooks Adams was a good analyst. In the 1890s he wrote: "Russia, to survive, must undergo a social revolution internally and/or expand externally. She will try to move into Shansi Province, richest prize in the world. Should Russia and Germany combine . . ." That was the nightmare of the Four Horsemen. At a time when simpler folk feared the rise of Germany alone, Brooks Adams saw the world ultimately polarized between Russia and the United States, with China as the common prize. American maritime power versus Russia's landmass. That is why, quite seriously, he wanted to extend the Monroe Doctrine to the Pacific Ocean. For him, "war [was] the ultimate form of economic competition."

We are now at the end of the twentieth century. England, France and Germany have all disappeared from the imperial stage. China is now reassembling itself, and Confucius, greatest of political thinkers, is again at the center of the Middle Kingdom. Japan has the world money power and wants a landmass; China now seems ready to go into business with its ancient enemy. Wars of the sort that the Four Horsemen enjoyed are, if no longer possible, no longer practical. Today's conquests are shifts of currency by computer, and the manufacture of those things that people everywhere are willing to buy.

I have said very little about writers because writers have figured very little in our imperial story. The founders of both republic and empire wrote well: Jefferson and Hamilton, Lincoln and Grant, T. R. and the Adamses. Today public figures can no longer write their own speeches or books; and there is some evidence that they can't read them either.

Yet at the dawn of the empire, for a brief instant, our *professional* writers tried to make a difference. Upton Sinclair and company attacked the excesses of the ruling class. Theodore Roosevelt coined the word "muckraking" to describe what they were doing. He did not mean the word as praise. Since then a few of our writers have written on public themes, but as they were not taken seriously, they have ended by not taking themselves seriously, at least as citizens of a republic. After all, most writers are paid by universities, and it is not wise to be thought critical of a garrison state which spends so much money on so many campuses.

When Confucius was asked what would be the first thing that he would do if he were to lead the state — his ever-to-be-fulfilled dream — he said *rectify the language*. This is wise. This is subtle. As societies grow decadent, the language grows decadent, too. Words are used to disguise, not to illuminate, action: you liberate a city by destroying it. Words are used to confuse, so that at election time people will solemnly vote against their own interests. Finally, words must be so twisted as to justify an empire that has now ceased to exist, much less make sense. Is rectification of our system possible for us? Henry Adams thought not. In 1910 he wrote: "The whole fabric of society will go to wrack if we really lay hands of reform on our rotten institutions." Then he added, "From top to bottom the whole system is a fraud, all of us know it, laborers and capitalist alike, and all of us are consenting parties to it." Since then, consent has grown frayed; and we have become poor, and our people sullen.

To maintain a thirty-five-year arms race it is necessary to have a fearsome enemy. Not since the invention of the Wizard of Oz have American publicists created anything quite so demented as the idea that the Soviet Union is a monolithic, omnipotent empire with tentacles everywhere on earth, intent on our destruction, which will surely take place unless we constantly imitate it with our war machine and its secret services.

In actual fact, the Soviet Union is a Second World country with a First World military capacity. Frighten the Russians sufficiently and they might blow us up. By the same token, as our republic now begins to crack under the vast expense of maintaining a mindless imperial force, we might try to blow them up. Particularly if we had a President who really was a twice-born Christian, and believed that the good folks would all go to heaven (where they were headed anyway) and the bad folks would go where *they* belong. Fortunately, to date, we have had only hypocrites in the White House. But you never can tell.

Even worse than the not-very-likely prospect of a nuclear war — deliberate or by accident — is the economic collapse of our society because too many of our resources have been wasted on the military. The Pentagon is like a black hole; what goes in is forever lost to us, and no new wealth is created. Hence, our cities, whose centers are unlivable; our crime rate, the highest in the Western world; a public education system that has given up . . . you know the litany. There is now only one way out. The time has come for the United States to make common cause with the Soviet Union. The bringing together of the Soviet landmass (with all its natural resources) and our island empire (with all its technological resources) would be of great benefit to each society, not to mention the world. Also, to recall the wisdom of the Four Horsemen who gave us our empire, the Soviet Union and our section of North America combined would be a match, industrially and technologically, for the Sino-Japanese axis that will dominate the future just as Japan dominates world trade today. But where the horsemen thought of war as the supreme solvent, we now know that war is worse than useless. Therefore, the alliance of the two great powers of the Northern Hemisphere will double the strength of each and give us, working together, an opportunity to survive, economically, in a highly centralized Asiatic world.

2.
The Imperial Cannibal
Bill Livant

"I grant this food will be somewhat dear, and therefore very proper for landlords, who, as they have already devoured most of the parents, seem to have the best title to the children."

Jonathan Swift[1]

I

Cultural politics in contemporary America; what kind of politics is this? The answer I propose is that it is politics of the passions, And that is why its basic terrain is art. For the practices of the sciences seek to minimize the place of the passions in their methods of work. Love and hate, and the great symbols of love and hate, may and do motivate work in the sciences, but they are filtered out of its tools. But love and hate is precisely what art magnifies; they are at the center of its forms of work and of its great symbols of communion and rejection. And, as Judith Williamson notes, "consuming passions" are at the very center of popular culture.[2]

Passions are stored in the forms of art, passions are moved by the forms of art because there is something in art to be passionate about. Artistic struggles are struggles over the definition of the genuinely human. They are struggles over what counts as human, over who counts as human. "Art," writes the French sociologist Pierre Bourdieu, "is called upon to mark the difference between humans and non-humans."[3] What is the nature of the power of the forms of art that they can mark such a difference? To answer this, we must try to discover the source of the passions stored in them. Even the most elementary tastes are stores of passions, both desires and disgusts. Bourdieu observes that when tastes have to be justified, when they become part of public culture,

26

. . . they are asserted purely negatively, by the refusal of other tastes. In matters of taste, more than anywhere else, all determination is negation; and tastes are perhaps first and foremost distastes, disgust provoked by horror or visceral intolerance ("sick-making") of the tastes of others . . . . Aesthetic intolerance can be terribly violent. (p. 56)

Nowhere is this more powerful than in the domain of food.

And it is probably in tastes in *food* that one would find the strongest and most indelible mark of infant learning, the lessons which longest withstand the distancing or collapse of the native world, and most durably maintain nostalgia for it. The native world is, above all, the maternal world, the world of primordial tastes and basic foods, of the archetypal relation to the archetypal cultural good, in which pleasure-giving is an integral part of pleasure . . . . It is no accident that even the purest pleasures, those most purified of any trace of corporeality . . . . contain an element which, as in the "crudest" pleasures of the tastes of food, the archetype of all taste, refers directly back to the oldest and deepest experiences . . . . (p. 79)

Food, feeding, eating. The taste, the distaste of food; this is the physical root of the metaphor for all our varied activities of discrimination, of finding value in things. Hunger, the physical root of the metaphor for all deep desiring. Feeding, the physical root of the metaphor for all helping, all aid-giving, all sustaining activity. Eating, the physical root of satisfaction. Good contains it all; the archetypal object of passion.[4] With this passion in mind, we want to look at the Empire. What is its food, how does it eat? Whom does it feed . . . . to whom?

II

"Why is there so much vacillation while we in southern Africa are suffering and dying? *Our lives are food for apartheid.*" This is the Minister of Information from Mozambique speaking.[5] Strange food, strange eater, strange appetite. This is quite different from the maternal pleasure-giving world of feeding. But it draws upon the same passion, though hideously transformed. The minister from Mozambique has identified precisely the central feature of the Empire; the empire is an eater, a consumer of lives and much else besides. It is only when we listen to those *being eaten*, eaten alive, that the essence of the empire is revealed: *consumption.* The empire is something that eats. It does not feed us, it feeds *on* us, feeds *off* us. What and whom it eats, and what it does with what it cannot digest is our task to investigate.

Serious scholars are not afraid of this language either. Geoffrey de Ste. Croix is one of the greatest modern scholars of antiquity. Here is how he concluded his 700 page study of 1400 years of the Greco-Roman world:

> As I see it, the Roman political system . . . facilitated a most intense and ultimately destructive economic exploitation of the great mass of the people, whether slave or free, and it made radical reform impossible. The result was that the propertied class, the men of real wealth, who had deliberately created this system for their own benefit, drained the life-blood from their world and thus destroyed Greco-Roman civilisation over a large part of the empire.[6]

Ste. Croix cites Edward Gibbon on the cause of imperial collapse, that "the stupendous fabric yielded to the pressure of its own weight." To this he adds the opinion of another historian, that "the prosperity of the Mediterranean world seems to have drained to the top." Neither explanation satisfied Ste. Croix. For him these formulations "express the basic idea of something that was essentially either inevitable or fortuitous." Neither expression registers a proper degree or kind of passion:

> If I were in search of a metaphor to describe the great and growing concentration of wealth in the hands of the upper classes, I would not incline towards anything so innocent and so automatic as drainage: I should want to think in terms of something much more purposive and deliberate — perhaps the vampire bat.

Gore Vidal, in "Requiem for the American Empire," (included in this volume) follows Confucius in urging us to "rectify the language." Ste. Croix has done just that here.

Gore Vidal composed a requiem not simply for the American empire but for the Anglo-American empire. From Britain to America there is, he reminds us, a direct historical continuity of capital and culture. Thus the empire that is ending is not just America's but Britain's as well. It would do well, in this light, to consider the words of one who long ago identified the operations of the Anglo empire: Jonathan Swift, Dean of St. Patrick's Cathedral, Dublin, and a great "rectifier of the language." Two hundred and sixty years ago, he wrote A Modest Proposal, "for preventing the children of the poor in Ireland from being a burden to their parents or country, and for making them beneficial to the public." In it he contemplated the condition of the first imperial conquest of the British Empire, Ireland. Swift found it to be a "melancholy object" to walk in the Irish towns or countryside and see the streets, the roads and cabin-doors crowded with beggars of the female sex, followed by three, four or six children, all in rags, and importuning every passenger for an alms.

And therefore whoever could find out a fair, cheap, and easy method of making these children sound and useful members of the commonwealth would deserve so well of the public as to have his statue set up for a preserver of the nation.

How shall these children be made into useful members of the commonwealth?

I have been assured by a very knowing American of my acquaintance in London, that a young healthy child well nursed is at a year old a most delicious, nourishing and wholesome food, whether stewed, roasted, baked or boiled, and I make no doubt that it will equally serve in a fricasee or a ragout . . . . [And they may] be offered in sale to the persons of quality and fortune, through the kingdom, always advising the mother to let them suck plentifully in the last month, so as to render them plump, and fat for a good table.

Furthermore,

Those who are more thrifty (as I confess the times require) may flay the carcass; the skin of which artificially dressed, will make admirable gloves for ladies, and summer boots for fine gentlemen.

Waste not want not. It appears that the Irish babies are to be made useful *members* of the commonwealth by being *dis*membered. Quite a commonwealth.

Notice that Swift calls his proposal a *modest* one. How can this be? It certainly doesn't seem modest but rather outrageous, disgusting. In Bourdieu's words, it is "sick-making," it fills us with "visceral intolerance." But Swift is not lying. His proposal *is* modest, and not merely because he "reasonably" understates a monstrous thing. The modesty is not just a flourish thrown into the title; it is there in the logic of the proposal he unfolds. To discover the nature of its modesty is to discover how the empire works.

First, who are these "fine gentlemen," these persons of "quality and fortune"? Swift tells us in his masterstroke, the passage I quoted at the beginning of this essay. They are the English landlords who,

as they have already devoured most of the parents, seem to have the best title to the children.

Lo and behold, it is the *same* group of people. How have they devoured the parents? Here, Swift very well knows the history of the subjugation of Ireland. The parents have been devoured by conquest; by expropriation of their lands; by the appropriation of all the material conditions necessary for them to produce their existence, for them to feed themselves and their children. As a result they have no land, no tools, no work, no money. And no food. As a result, Swift finds them "importuning every passenger for an alms."

But the appetite of the fine gentlemen for all these means of existence is different from their appetite which Swift modestly proposes to satisfy. The appetite of the individual physical human body for baby stew is satiable. It has a limit. There is only so much baby stew a person of quality can eat, only so many boots he can wear. But this is not true of the appetite for devouring . . . accumulating . . . the conditions of existence. This appetite is *insatiable*. For it is an appetite of this same group of people constituted as an imperial class. It is a *class appetite* — an appetite not for *personal consumption* but for *class exploitation* (recall Ste. Croix).

In his key sentence, Swift writes of the same class in a double manner. He presents them both as an aggregate of individual consumers and as a class of exploiters. And in both capacities, this class *"eats people"* (recall the minister from Mozambique). If the appetite of an individual member of this class for baby stew were indeed insatiable, if it behaved as their class appetite behaves, we would have no trouble diagnosing an addiction, a disease. We would have the horribly swollen body of a patient to deal with. Certain lesions made in the brain of a rat will cause him to eat and eat and eat without end; he becomes an animal hideous to behold. The class appetite is such an addiction. It is the appetite for endless accumulation.

It is the imperial class appetite, which by devouring, exploiting, the parents *produces* the "melancholy" condition of the Irish babies in a particular form. They are *waste*. They are the garbage from the exploitation of the parents. Garbage, filth, refuse, shit. These are indeed the words of visceral intolerance. They get in the way, they are an eyesore, they clutter the streets, they stink. Human garbage. Humans-*as*-garbage. The parents are the food for the appetite of the imperial class, the children are its garbage. The class appetite always requires such food, always produces such garbage.

So Swift's scheme is not based upon something which does not yet exist; it is based upon something which *already* exists. It proposes nothing new. It is not radical, it is modest. It will not disturb the existing order of things in Ireland. In fact, as we shall see, quite the contrary. It will extend them. Something must be done with this garbage, as with all garbage. Shall it be buried, burnt, towed out to sea and dumped off the

Irish coast? These solutions are possible, but they have their problems. The parents might have some objections; such measures make for hard feelings. Can we find a better way than garbage disposal? Yes, thanks to Swift. Why not *recycle* it! It puts a little money in the hands of the parents which they badly need; that should take care of their objections. It puts a new food on the table for persons of quality. Instead of waste disposal, waste re-use. An "ecological" solution, no less. Turn the waste into food.

In fact, having discovered this solution, Swift now requires a steady supply of such garbage. Once a taste, a market for the new product is developed, the supply must be reliable.

> I do therefore humbly offer it to public consideration, that of the hundred and twenty thousand children already computed, twenty thousand may be reserved for breed, whereof only one fourth part to be males, which is more than we allow to sheep . . . that the remaining hundred thousand be offered in sale to the persons of quality and fortune . . . .

With this step, Swift is recycling more than waste. He is *recycling the process of exploitation* that produced the waste. See how modest this is. The class exploitation of the Irish parents has produced a problem. Swift *solves* the problem by *reproducing the problem on an expanded scale*. Not only is this no departure from what already exists, this is its "creative" development. Now, Swift has opened up a new market for personal consumption of a new food. And now that we know how this food was made, we can look at its consumer qualities. These new Irish baby "McNuggets" are not to everyone's taste. To whom are they likely to appeal?

A number of studies of the history of advertising in the twentieth century have found a curious fact. The *first* information about products for personal consumption to *disappear* from the ads was information about how the product was made, by whom under what conditions. Swift has resurrected this bloody information — the insatiable class appetite for the imperial exploiting class. How is this reflected in the features of the new food Swift offers for its personal consumption?

A consumer who will eat *this kind* of object for food will eat *anything and everything*. The *quality* of this new food on the table of the fine gentlemen is an accurate expression of the *class appetite* through which it was produced. This is the class that "devours the parents," the class that will eat everything, turn everything to money, the insatiable appetite. This new food embodies in its physical form-for-consumption the exploitation-in-production, through which it came to be. And these babies, what are they themselves but the class-*future* of the class being eaten, devoured?

It is the great power of Swift's proposal that he puts the central process of exploitation right on the table in the form of an object to eat. He holds before the imperial class merely *its own class nature*. Here's the secret of your empire; eat it if you dare! What could be more modest than that?

III

Swift found the garbage in the empire of his time. An empire can be known by the nature of the garbage it produces. What drives the empire is its basic garbage-making process. It is this process that we must find in Empire 1980s U.S.A. The economic form of this empire is capitalist; accumulation of capital is its fundamental principle. The food for this process is human beings' power to work. And most of us work for a wage; very few of us live mainly from another source of income.[7]

As Karl Marx pointed out, under capitalism my power to work, whatever work I may do, is a peculiar thing. I must sell it to get the wage to buy the food to live. It is a commodity. But if it behaved like any other commodity I could stay in bed in the morning and send it off to work for me. No such luck. Because my power to work is part of a real bodily person, because it is embodied in me, when I sell it, it "drags me along" to *do* it. But all the rest of me that gets dragged along is not what capital uses, not what it eats, not its food, not what it wants to pay for. It is the activity of capital that divides the working person into the useful (to capital) and useless parts of me, into the food (for capital) and the waste, into forces of production and garbage.

This garbage must not be allowed to get in the way of the accumulation of capital. Like any garbage, it must be disposed of, rejected, or, if necessary, ejected. Or it must be somehow recycled into food for capital accumulation. From the division into food-for-capital and garbage-from-capital flow two kinds of relations; they are the basic relations of the empire. All those relations centering on the food-for-capital are relations of *exploitation*. All the relations of the disposal of the garbage-from-capital are relations of *oppression*.

Both these fundamental forms of relation are class-*produced*, although they are not both class-*expressed*. Relations of oppression, and the struggles against oppression, center around all those features of life which at a particular time are *not* food for capital, all those aspects of collective culture and personal identity which are irrelevant or detrimental to capital accumulation. These relations do not appear in class form, they appear first in the form of *anything but* class. They appear to lie outside the process of exploitation. But they don't just lie outside "naturally"; they have been cast out. For capital, they are garbage. The relation between oppressive relations and exploitative relations is constantly changing. If I am automated out of a job, the work my hands once did, food for capital, have now been turned to garbage. Conversely, Swift already showed us how garbage can be turned to food.

These relations shape the culture of the capitalist empire, most of all in its imperial center, the United States. Now that Kentucky Fried Chicken has opened its largest world outlet in Beijing, and MacDonalds is sweeping Japan, it should not be too difficult to identify the core of this culture. It is consumption. In *A Modest Proposal*, Jonathan Swift located an object for personal consumption which captured the appetite of the imperial class in his time. Can we find, such an object in the culture of mass consumption today? Perhaps it lies in the process of consumption itself.

If so, we must examine its features carefully. A number of analyses of consumer culture have singled out its perpetual instability. Some have gone so far as to say that this culture reproduces in its own image the very identity of the people who inhabit it. They have pointed to the perpetual dissatisfaction of personal consumption, the perpetual "disappointment" experienced by its members. Commodities consumed satisfy only for an instant, to be quickly replaced by a longing for yet "something else" to eat. These treatments locate the source of this perpetual dissatisfaction in the relentless circulation of commodities, the constant breakup of their material features into attributes, and their constant recombination. This produces continual instability of needs, produces a personal identity which is a mirror of what Todd Gitlin has called a recombinant culture.[8]

Simply because they are commodities, "things come alive." This is said to be the core of commodity fetishism. This notion is used by William Leiss, Stephen Kline and Sut Jhally to survey the history of advertising in North America since the beginning of the twentieth century.[9] They find, that over the course of the century, advertising is marked by a progressive disintegration of the physical world — above all physical products — into floating sensuous qualities, pure signs, images which incite to dreams and nightmares. These signs appear to be possessed of magical powers of movement, appearance and disappearance; they coalesce from the mist, walk, talk, and dance with us. They appear to move us; they seem to possess us and in the moment of possession melt away. They are sensuous fetishes which reconstruct the consumer.

In these accounts, the endemic dissatisfaction in consumer society is produced by the power of commodities *as such*. But there is one commodity of which almost everybody seems not to have enough, and that is money. Money has a power which does indeed reconstruct the passions. One of the mental oppressions of being poor is that one is forced to think, minute by minute, about a thing which is *intrinsically boring*. For money itself has no qualities — no sunset colors, no warmth, no flavor. It is pure quantity, pure "more and less."

And yet money seems to devour all qualities. We can see this in our language. It devours the language of living things. The business sections of our papers tell us what "seed money" to invest, what "yield" it will bring as if it were a harvest. It devours the language of labor. "Put your money to work for you," but just what kind of "work" does "it" do? Does it work up a sweat? It devours the language of language itself. "Money talks" but with what tongue?

There is something about money which appears to devour everything. And we members of consumer culture can never get enough; appetite for it seems insatiable. This dissatisfaction in personal consumption reflects a *particular form* in which money exists, a form in which *by its very nature* it can *never* eat enough, in which it *inherently must be* perpetually dissatisfied. And that is Capital. Capital is the commodity which embodies the passion for more and only more. In the culture of capitalism, consumer culture, the various commodities for personal consumption *mediate* the insatiable appetite of capital. Personal consumption tends to be driven by capital, not simply into continual variation but continual accumulation of commodities, which mirrors in personal consumption the accumulation of capital. And so what we call a consumer society seems more to resemble a *consumed* one.

If we think about consumer culture, and isolate commodities from capital, we will mistakenly attribute to the commodity magical powers *in itself, by itself alone* to constitute a culture of consumption, which in fact it does not possess. It is just possible that such an account of Commodity Fetishism as the basis of consumer culture, is itself a theory which is a fetish of the commodity?

The insatiability of appetite in consumer culture never originates in personal consumption, though it is reflected in its objects. It originates in that *class appetite* for the *class-food*, human powers to work. In short, in exploitation. Jonathan Swift is our contemporary. In this setting we must practice cultural politics. What are the prospects?

IV

How is cultural politics to be practiced in 1980s Empire U.S.A.? In fact, we are inhabitants of an empire in decline. Recall that Gore Vidal has even dated its death and written its requiem. At any rate, our present condition is unprecedented. Amid the ups and downs, the booms and busts of the imperial economy, the Empire itself has been expanding since the beginning of the Republic.[10]

It may come as a surprise to some readers that we even live in an empire, much less than it's been going on for so long. This very *invisibility* of the Empire is the main cultural feature of what the historian William A. Williams calls, "Empire as a way of Life."[11] And the main reason for its invisibility is that it has been able, as Williams notes, to "externalize evil." This externalization has a material basis. The empire must be able to dispose of its garbage, the very garbage its own imperial exploitation creates; and above all its human garbage. Dispose of it, or recycle it into its own imperial form. This is getting much harder for the imperial class to do.

Vidal dates the end of the American Empire from that day in 1985 when we became an officially declared debtor nation. If I were to choose a *cultural* marker for the date of death, one which draws upon the passions examined in this paper, I would choose August 1987, when a garbage scow from Islip, Long Island sailed the Eastern seaboard and the Caribbean, looking for a place to unload its stinking mess into the sea. In vain. The garbage backs up, and as it does the empire becomes more and more visible. And more unsettling. Will we go down with it?

Such a condition is the setting for deep passions — visceral desires, visceral disgusts, visceral hopes and fears. The cultural politics of the imperial class will reach for those passions and seek to shape them to its purposes. Since, as a class, *it* cannot do without the empire, it will seek to shape our passions to that belief that *we* cannot; that we cannot live without the empire that has been until now our invisible habitat; that without it we would die. This is the central goal of reactionary cultural politics: there is no life after Empire. The goal is to produce our personal identification with the empire, so that anything else becomes unthinkable. As Williams writes, "The first issue involves the extreme difficulty, even in the abstract, of devising and creating an alternative to empire as a way of life."

In Chinese, the character which means *Crisis* is a combination of the characters which mean *Danger* and *Opportunity*. Perhaps the opportunity for the "garbage" is arising; for the human garbage that pours daily from the Empire is backing up. "From the outhouse to the White House!" — this slogan from the Rainbow coalition makes the point. Much of the content of the various "New Social Movements" center on struggles against oppression; against the imperial reduction of their members, their collective cultures, their personal identities, and their habitats to garbage. As these struggles against oppression connect, as the movements begin to join, they encounter the central condition that *turns* them into garbage; the central process that "devours the parents," which Jonathan Swift already identified: exploitation. As they develop, the *class* content of the struggles against oppression come more and more to the fore.

In this process, Americans will "devise and create an alternative to empire as a way of life" We will discover that there *is* Life After the Empire. We will discover not that we can't live without it but that we can no longer live with it. Its end will come as a liberation. Free at last! Free at last! Thank God Almighty, we're free at last! Why not?

3.

American Empire and
Global Communication

Eileen Mahoney

Today's world, yesterday's institutions. It is all
obvious that the present arrangements for international
cooperation, coordination, and common action are not,
by and large, able to cope. Indeed, since most of the
existing international structures were invented in the
1940s, it would be astonishing if they were adequately
coping with the vastly different circumstances we face
in the 1980s and beyond.

Harlan Cleveland[1]

The old order is unravelling. Political, economic, technological, and
cultural developments throughout the postwar period have outstripped
the existing international political regime. So-called "excesses in
democracy" — that is, the exercise of one nation, one vote —
cripple the operation of the United Nations and thereby call its overall
utility into question. Trade wars strain relations among the advanced
industrial members of the Organization for Economic Cooperation and
Development, while the debt crisis deepens despite — some would say
as a result of — the efforts of the World Bank and the International
Monetary Fund. Rapid technological developments, accompanying
military build-ups, and the transnationalization of economic activity
further complicate matters by introducing products which blur traditional boundaries. Environmental problems escape national borders
and elude international controls as well. And, irrepressible demands for
political and cultural automony continue to reverberate throughout the
international community. Thus, it seems the institutional arrangements
set in place some forty years ago can no longer stand the strain,
or more serious still, they block the development of, in Cleveland's
words, "solutions" to deepening and emerging crises. "Rethinking" is
necessary and adjustments must be made.

Within the context of rethinking, international communications policy-making becomes a central area of attention. Far-reaching adjustments are already underway in the field of international communications. They are illustrative of, and contributing to larger trends promoting the reorganization of the international political economy. These developments, the actors and interests promoting and guiding restructuring, and the potential international and national ramifications of such initiatives are the subject of this essay. To grasp the full significance of the ongoing restructuring of the international political regime in the communications/cultural sphere, a review of crucial postwar developments that contribute to the "vastly different circumstances" described by Cleveland must be undertaken.

Legacy of the Postwar
International Political Economy

With the exception of the International Telecommunication Union (ITU), created some 122 years ago, international policy-making bodies in the field of communications were established during the early postwar period. It was a time in which the United States was the unchallenged military, industrial, financial and political power in the world. In contrast to its allies, not to mention its opponents, America had "won" the war with scant material damage. In fact, the demands of war vastly strengthened the technical (and profit-making) capacity of traditional industries, while setting in motion new technological developments that would come to extend the global reach of American business interests. In short, the United States was well-equipped to spearhead the (re)construction of a "new" international political economic order immediately following the Second World War.

Yet, the postwar world American decision-makers encountered did not present unobstructed or certain success. Political forces in Western Europe struggled for power to determine the direction and character of social and economic reconstruction in those areas. Uncertainty also surrounded the future of the former colonial "holdings" of the then weakened European powers. How would those areas be organized? Too, the emergence of new regimes in Eastern Europe and the consolidation of Soviet power meant that an immense area of the earth's surface would develop outside of the sphere of market relations. Whether the vast industrial and economic power built up in the United States during the Second World War could be sustained without (unrestricted) international expansion was a matter of great concern.

Faced with these and related uncertainties, American government and business leaders undertook a variety of measures — economic, political, and cultural — to spur the reconstruction of a global market economy and to facilitate the continued growth of American business. In general, the programmatic and ideological position of the United States throughout the postwar period advanced unfettered free market enterprise. Concretly, the American government and business sector transferred (and invested) massive amounts of capital in order to reconstruct market economies in Western Europe and to incorporate, wherever possible, new spheres of economic activity. Reestablishment of free market principles and practices at the global level, however, required more than capital flows, important as they were.[2] Precisely because the increasingly transnational expansion of American business (and government) interests took place within an (expanding) system of national states, the creation of *supra*national institutions for "international" policy-making and dispute resolution assumed great significance.

Actually, the political organization of the postwar era received attention even while the war was still being waged, and was the focus of major decisions made at the war's end. The international political regime established in the postwar years was designed to insure the stability and continued functioning of the emerging global market economy. The United Nations and its affiliated bodies, it was hoped, would constitute an overall *political* framework for negotiation and/or dispute resolution. General *economic* policy, which was subsequently extended to the field of international communications and new information technology (IT), was forged with bodies more subject to direct American financial control such as the World Bank and the International Monetary Fund. The *cultural and information* arena, also assigned a major role by the architects of the postwar order, was originally entrusted to the United Nations, and the United Nations Educational, Scientific, and Cultural Organization (UNESCO) in particular.

In communications, an area of growing importance throughout the postwar period, the United States promoted what it called "unrestricted use of and access to international information flows." Specifically, the American government adopted the free flow of information doctrine as a means both to break the British monopoly of global communications so as to facilitate American business expansion (access to raw resources, labor supplies, markets, and audiences) and to disallow any regulation of American information flows. UNESCO played a crucial role during the first decades of its existence as a vehicle for promoting the free flow of information as a universal global communications policy and as a marketing mechanism for Western communication and cultural products. Implementation of the "first-come, first-served" principle to the allocation of the radio spectrum required for international communication, as well as necessary technical coordination matters, was assigned to the International Telecommunication Union (ITU).

In their initial formation, postwar international organizations and policies, by and large, facilitated the expansion of the transnational business system. Indeed, in the first quarter century following the war, American business expansion proceeded at an unprecedented rate. Accepted as a general measure of international expansion, American foreign direct investment (in plants and facilities) rose from $7 billion in 1946 to $78 billion in 1970.[3] By 1969, American multinationals produced nearly $140 billion worth of goods, more than any nation except the United States and the Soviet Union. The early postwar international policies — i.e., free trade and the free flow of information — underpinned this expansion.

Significantly, the same period that experienced transnational corporate expansion, also witnessed the emergence of more than 100 new nations into the international community. The achievement of national status by these developing countries presented both new opportunities and new obstacles to expanding business concerns. On the one hand, national markets previously closed by colonial ties became accessible to U.S. businesses. On the other hand, the existence and entrance of these new national actors into world bodies — carrying with them powerful memories of past dependency, knowledge of existing material inequities, as well as common political linkages — were sources of potential problems for the expansion plans of transnational corporate capitalism.

Accordingly, the impacts of expanding (American) transnational business activities were not without opposition in the early postwar decades — consider, for example, the United Nations Decade(s) for Development, the formation of the Non-Aligned Movement, and the creation of "development communications" as an area of political and academic concern in the United States. Still, the then existing balance of power and the continuing expansion of the overall global economy allowed the United States to utilize the capacities of the early international organizations to meet the requirements of its expanding transnational business complex.

Until the early 1970s, the near continuous expansion of transnational capitalism overshadowed — to some extent — the conflicts between national interests and those of transnational enterprises. In fact, modernization theory and development communications thinking, which guided many international and national development efforts, generally characterized transnational business expansion as synonymous with "national development," especially in the Third World. But, as the period of expansion gave way to one marked by global economic recession and recurring crisis, divergence between the commercial imperatives of transnational enterprises and the interests and political realities of nation states were and continued to be manifest in increasingly contentious debates in international organizations. The first great debate and challenge to the existing international political economic order issued from the developing nations' insistent call for redistribution of the world's resources.

Debates and Shifts in the International Political Regime

Increasingly in the 1970s, international and national political economic agendas were influenced by growing mobilization of Third World nations. Third World demands, first for economic independence and later for cultural autonomy (the basic constituents of genuine political sovereignty), sparked great controversy in the major multilateral international organizations, especially the United Nations and its affiliated bodies.

Two areas of decision-making dominated the international communications agenda at the time. One was the movement for a New International Information Order (NIIO). The other involved the terms which would determine if, and how, new information technologies would be installed in both the advanced and developing countries of the world.

Within UNESCO, the movement for a NIIO called into question the prevailing free flow of information policy, and the preponderant Western control over Third World communications and cultural industries that derived from that flow.[4] While the NIIO drew critical attention to the cultural component of continuing dependency in the Third World, it generally failed to take into account the implications of the new information technologies and the electronic networks that were rapidly being created.

Paralleling the call for a NIIO in UNESCO, Third World nations proposed methods for planning use of resources (radio frequencies and satellite orbital slots) required for international communications. Thus, the "a priori" planning method advanced with the ITU in the late 1970s, seriously challenged another Western-supported policy — i.e., the first-come, first-served approach to resource allocation. Both the call for a NIIO and the planning methods proposed in the ITU represented growing national recognition of the significance of communications/information resources *and* international communications policy-making.

What can now be regarded as a brief shift in the relations of force within international forums, especially UNESCO, made it possible for the free flow of information issue to be subject to debate, negotiation, and possible reformulation. Yet, the centrality of communications to the needs of an emerging expansive international political economy based on information prompted the United States government to stymie any policy-making initiatives that might interfere with the international flow of information. In an effort to placate UNESCO's Third World constituency, the American government proposed a minimal technology transfer program. However, its promotion of the free flow of information — the core issue of the debate — remained undiminished. Yet, even these modest efforts to accommodate developing nations were of brief duration. Third World leverage, such as it was, was being rapidly eroded by a continuing global economic recession, its own deepening debt crisis, and the rapid development of the new information technologies.

The New Realities

Although the rhetoric of the earlier period continues to be employed, far-reaching shifts in international communications institutional arrangements are occurring. Three interrelated sets of developments constitute the new reality: 1) transnationalization of economic activities based on new information instrumentation and international communications; 2) intensifying competition among the advanced market economies in the new information/communications sector and related policy disputes; and 3) international ramifications of American domestic policies, especially deregulation in the telecommunications sector.

The transnationalization of economic activities, set in motion long ago, has proceeded rapidly, driven by the commercial imperatives of the dominant economic institutions — the transnational corporations (TNCs). The full-blown emergence of transnational enterprises engaged in the production and distribution of goods and services on a global scale could not have taken place without accompanying rapid expansion and discovery of increasingly sophisticated means of global information collection, processing, and transmission. Growing business (and government) demand for telecommunications and new information technologies, in turn, fueled the development of a new expansive information-based economic sector of increasing significance to transnational and national economic activities.[5] It is within this expanded communications/information sector, that tensions between transnational business activity, national governance, and international organizations are perhaps most directly manifest.

Telecommunication services, until recently, have been organized and operated by national government administrations (known as Postal, Telegraph, and Telecommunications ministries [PTTs]) in the vast majority of the world's countries — the United States being a significant exception. The technical and political-economic coordination (e.g. rate structures) required for transnational interconnection (communication) have been organized by international organizations, namely, the ITU. Transnational corporations, requiring the use of communications facilities and services in scores of countries, have had to obtain those services on terms established by national authorities and approved in international organizations. As cost economies and operational control over vital communications/information resources are increasingly considered essential to unrestrained ("efficient") transnational corporate activity, big business users of communications services press — at both the national and international levels — for greater autonomy in the development, ownership, and use of telecommunications.

Yet, it is precisely the communication/information sector that is considered by national decision-makers as the key to renewed economic growth and national sovereignty. At the same time, policy-making bodies responsible for national telecommunications policies and information-based industries are subject to mounting pressures by transnational business. These are alluded to by the United States Secretary of State in a 1986 speech. According to George Schultz,

> Across the globe the foreign policy agenda reflects new economic disputes as developing and advanced nations alike struggle to come to grips with transborder data flows, technology transfers, satellite transmissions, and the crowding of the radio spectrum. Some of these disputes are between governments. Others are between governments and private corporations. U.S. computer manufacturers, for example, are now disputing with several European governments over the issue of transborder data transfers. The U.S. companies believe that they should be allowed to compile data and have market access rights, while some governments believe that the data should be centrally controlled.

How these disputes are being handled at the international level is integrally related to political economic developments in the center of the transnational business system, the United States.

The ongoing restructuring and transnationalization of the American economy, fueled by shifting investment strategies that favor growth in certain sectors (e.g., the new information-based services), while precipitating decline in others, requires reorganization in the international political economy as well. This is particularly true in the cultural/informational arena, where the prediction of former RCA president, Robert Sarnoff — that "information will become a basic commodity" and "will function as a form of currency in world trade" — now characterizes *actual* economic activities in the United States and in the transnational commercial system generally.[6]

Accordingly, current American policies of deregulation and privatization of the communications/information sector respond to deep structural and political shifts that portend, and already show, profound transformation of international and national political, economic, and socio-cultural landscapes.

The new realities confronting U.S. world power, marked by intensifying struggles between transnational business and national interests for control over vital communications/information resources, demand that the international institutions that once served American interests become targets for reorganization and/or elimination. An analysis of the still to be resolved transborder data flow debate is illustrative of this development. *ideological disputes in the international sector demand loss of national sovereignty for resolution,*

Transborder Data Flows (*TDF*): From Policy to Privatization

Technically defined as the transfer of machine readable data across national borders, TDFs carry information (such as production schedules, inventory and personnel records, tax and legal information, currency transactions, engineering designs, ad campaigns) that is vital to the basic operation of the transnational business system. Transnational corporations, as well as entire service industries, are totally dependent on TDFs which allow businesses to take advantage of international wage and tax differentials and resources and market availabilities. Global distribution of cultural products increasingly relies on these flows as well. It is this enhanced mobility of capital (largely derived from transnational corporate use of TDFs and the new information instrumentation that carries them) that has led to deep and growing concern in much of the world over *national* jurisdiction and well being.

In its largest dimension, unrestricted use of international information flows challenges national prerogatives in economic decision-making, cultural production, and political independence. This was acknowledged by Louis Joinet who framed the core issues regarding transborder data flow in terms of power. Speaking in 1977, he offered the following argument:

Information is power, and economic information is economic power. Information has economic value and the ability to store and process certain types of data may well give one country political and technological advantage over other countries. This in turn may lead to a loss of national sovereignty through supranational data flows.[7]

The debate, initiated in Western Europe and soon thereafter involving Third World nations as well, over the actual and potential ramifications of transborder data flows marked the reappearance of concern regarding national sovereignty. This was no different in its essentials from that expressed in the NIIO, but was also tied to the vastly more important arena of the international political economy of electronically transmitted information.

Challenges to the emergent transnational political, economic, and technological hierarchies based on unrestricted transborder data flows (i.e, the free flow of information) found their earliest expression in national policy statements/studies and soon thereafter in international forums. The production of national government reports in the late 1970s, especially in France and Canada, documented sharply divergent views on national and international communications/information policies.[8] Arguing that their national sovereignty and well-being were integrally tied to control over communications and information resources, these reports called for the establishment of national policies to facilitate the development of national industries in this vital sector as a means to insure economic independence and cultural autonomy.

Discussion in the Third World also considered alternatives to the United States-promoted free flow of information policy. Brazil, for example, adopted a national policy to spur development of its national computer-communications industry and to govern the flow of transborder data. In order to create conditions that would allow for the development of national industries capable of competing with powerful transnational corporations within *domestic* as well as international markets, national policy-makers sought the formation of international agreements.

Filling the Vacuum in
International organization

Growing attention to the significance of transborder data flows for national development and transnational business revealed an organizational vacuum in the international political regime. Neither UNESCO, nor the ITU identified the computer-communications sector as a powerful dynamic in the rapidly emerging international political economy. And, although early Western European and Canadian concerns were registered within the Organization for Economic Cooperation and Development (OECD), limited membership and the forceful American presence in that organization made a wide-ranging and genuine international policy debate an unlikely outcome. The absence of a truly international forum in which these emerging issues could be addressed and decisions taken prompted the creation of new bodies.

Most notable among the new institutions chosen to fill this void was the Intergovernmental Bureau for Informatics (IBI). Although in existence since 1951, the IBI did not enter international communications policy-making until the late 1970s when it cosponsored an international meeting with UNESCO. The enhanced awareness of communications issues created by the NIIO debate in UNESCO, and the emergence of "new" issues regarding the use of new information technologies (i.e, TDF) created space for an organization promising to bridge the gap between old and new issues, between advanced and developing nations.

The IBI advertised and promoted new information technology as the means for both advanced and developing nations to transcend structural realities impeding their economic growth. Developing nations, in the IBI's view, could overcome the obstacles to their development — including those addressed in the NIIO — through the acquisition and application of new information technology. Adoption of the new IT in the Third World, would in turn, reasoned the IBI, create new markets for competing interests in the advanced market economies. In short, the IBI attempted to fuse the commercial imperatives of the TNCs and advanced market economies with the development goals of the Third World.

Intensifying concern over transborder data flow in Western Europe and the Third World for a brief time afforded this little known organization a world platform to review core issues of the emerging international political economy of information. The IBI held international meetings, issued ambiguous policy statements, and provided a forum in which divergent views regarding principles and policies for governing international communications and new information technology were expressed. Although the IBI attempted to "harmonize" the conflicting positions, the inescapable polarization between calls for national and international policy formation to govern TDF issued from Third World nations (and some second-tier advanced industrial countries) and the implacable opposition of the transnational business sector and its governmental representatives to any limits on the free flow of information finally undercut its position.

Shifting Terrain in International
Communications Politics

The great expansion of the transnational business system and its deepening reliance on unrestricted utilization of computer-communication networks might have been expected to generate positive support for an international organization that could defuse Third World resentment and channel Third World government policies into full acceptance of, and participation in, the new information technologies. Yet, a countervailing development interceded.

In the United States, a powerful movement to deregulate the corporate sector, and the communications component in particular, succeeded. Quickly thereafer the movement traveled overseas to Western European industries and beyond. In addition to dismantling what were the means of insuring social accountability, deregulation politically meant an assertion of unilateralism and an unwillingness to accept any kind of multilateral forums and decision-making that might inhibit corporate activity.[9]

In this new climate, international and national policy-making in the field of transborder data flow (which could be regarded as *the* vital issue in the electronic international information order) were considered intolerable by the transnational corporate order. American opposition to TDF policy-making prompted efforts to move policy discussions out of larger, multilateral political forums and into more restricted trade-orientated institutions. In 1980, for example, Harry DeMaio, IBM director of data security and regular IBM representative at TDF meetings, called for "putting aside purely national concerns of protecting native DP (data processing) and telecommunications industries and restricting data flows to counter perceived threats to national sovereignty." A more productive approach, according to DeMaio, would be to focus on "overall economic policies." Efforts to separate *certain* economic interests from broader socio-political concerns informed the political maneuvering by the American government throughout the early 1980s.

This strategy aimed both at establishing new, circumscriptive parameters in the TDF debate which would be more amenable to private sector interests while at the same time narrowing the range and number of national actors able to participate in policy negotiations. Ambassador Diana Lady Dougan, U.S. State Department Coordinator on International Communication and Information Policy, speaking before an OECD sponsored symposium in 1983, offered this rationale for the shifts underway: "If the countries who are first to experience the implications and impact of the new technologies cannot resolve their differences, there is little reason to hope that these issues can be successfully dealt with in other arenas." A different analysis suggests that transnational companies and their government representatives wish to maintain transborder data flows "as a private preserve, shielded from scrutiny and accountability, engaging the attention of a small number of policy makers in the developed market economies."10

Strategic Intervention:
Privatizing the TDF Debate

Within the context wherein international communications issues were also being addressed in "other arenas," reestablishing exclusive control over policy negotiations required significant recasting of just what activities transborder data flows represented and how they should be categorized. Arguing that TDFs entail the rendering of "services" (i.e, data processing, software, data storage and retrieval, telecommunications) those with the predominant interests in transnational business effectively redefined transborder data flows as trade in data services. In doing so, transnational policy strategists have shifted both the terms *and* the terrain for international communications policy-making.

Accompanying redefinition of international communications as a "trade" issue, the United States and its transnational allies, junked the IBI and mobilized two institutional mechanisms — the Organization for Economic Cooperation and Development (OECD) and the General Agreement on Tariffs and Trade (GATT) — to manage the general interests of the advanced market economies. The "free flow of information" declaration proposed by the United States and adopted by members of the OECD was designed to "promote access to data and information and related services, and to avoid the creation of unjustified barriers to the international exchange of data and information." Initial discussion of the American proposal within OECD circles led one participant to observe critically that "the economic and trade dimensions of these [TDF] issues have squeezed out the human rights, legal and policy aspects."11 This, of course, was one of the central objectives of American strategy.

The greater significance of the OECD Declaration on Transborder Data Flow however, lay in its utility as an initial step toward an even more far-reaching initiative intended to "improve the U.S. competitive posture" in the international political economy. In this effort, the United States lobbied intensely and successfully for the extension of the GATT — which until recently only covered trade in goods — to include trade in services, including telecommunications. Accordingly,

G. Russell Pipe reports, that in the current GATT negotiations, "the U.S. is seeking a binding agreement that will proscribe acceptable practices for trade in services and a mechanism for settling any conflicts that may arise."[12] "Acceptable practices," as defined by American negotiators, would allow American businesses to gain "greater access to foreign telecomm[unications] markets, more investment opportunities, and fewer restrictions on users of information-based services." If implemented, such an agreement would severely undercut public sector involvement in telecommunications and new information-based services at the national and international level.

While other advanced market economies, even those moving towards more "liberalized" telecommunications policies, remain wary of American free trade initiatives, the most significant impact will fall on the weaker national economies of the Third World. "The U.S. effort to bring 'service' into GATT by prefixing 'trade' before it," argues C. Raghavan, "is really aimed at reducing, if not eliminating, Third World options in these [sectors]."[13] Development of the "relatively weak" service industries currently existing in developing nations, would require, in his view, "active state involvement" which the GATT agreement aims to prohibit. Moreover, maintains Jan Pronk, under the proposed agreement "the main victims of protectionism in the 1980s [third world countries] would have to open up their markets for new products in new sectors — service sector, high technology — which industrialized countries consider their best chance to enter a new era" of growth.[14] In effect, the agreement would obtain for transnational corporations the full freedom to invest and disinvest without the government of the host country being able to exercise any effective control.

Conclusion

The agreements recently worked out in the organizations that the transnationalists find more congenial represent apparently successful efforts of United States power and transnational corporate interests to outmaneuver efforts made throughout the postwar period to establish some measures of accountability in transnational business practices. Attempts by national principals — especially in, but not limited to, the Third World — to advance policy measures (in UNESCO, the United Nations, the International Telecommunications Union, the IBI) that would protect their national sovereignty and to create conditions wherein they could participate as fully recognized sovereign nations in the international political economy have precipitated Western initiatives to undercut multilateral decision-making.

widespread evidence - Canada FTA
England (EC)
economic factors move countries to surrender sovereignty (Br. in EPM), sometimes —

While battles still brew in the ITU, and more may be expected to erupt in other places, it appears that United States attempts to supplant "yesterday's institutions" (by according ever greater power over "today's world" to transnational corporations) have prevailed. Whether this is a workable arrangement given the existence of more than 160 nation states, remains to be seen. What is clear at this point, however, is that wherever possible — and especially in the communications/informational sectors — transnational corporations will try to bypass any and all forms of international and national oversight.

— and nations won't try to stop them.

4.

Power, Hegemony, and Communication Theory

Leslie T. Good

But anyway, on this particular summer day Bernabé
Montoya walked out of Rael's just as Onofre's mottled-
green, 1953 Chevy pickup with the three-legged dog
on top hiccupped to a stop at the town's lone parking
meter and, with a dispirited — call it a lonely —
"*Ai, Chihuahua!*" the sheriff reached for his citation
pad. Bitterly he began to write, thinking as he did
so that if ever all the cantankerous streaks in people
like Amarante Córdova, Joe Mondragón and Onofre
Martíneze were united behind a common cause, there
would be much more than all hell to pay.

John Nichols, *The Milagro Beanfield War*

Introduction

Shortly after the airing of the ABC mini-series polemic, *Amerika*, a
viewer wrote to the *TV Guide* editor: "*Amerika* was thought-provoking,
challenging and debate-inspiring. . . . Unfortunately, one of the premises of democracy is that people not only be able but *willing* to think about
and discuss things for themselves. If this is an unrealistic expectation,
then the best we can hope for is an efficient and relatively enlightened
tyranny, whether of the right or the left. The point of the show, after all,
is that we get the government we deserve."[1]

This viewer, probably innocently and unwittingly, in just these few
simple sentences, provides a theory of "power," one which is strikingly
close to what Martin Carnoy has called the "official ideology of capitalist
democracies" — pluralism.[2] Put briefly, the pluralist thesis of power says
that power is a diffuse and empirically verifiable outcome of healthy
conflict among competing interest groups, usually manifested as individual consumer-like decisions; and even though based on "conflict,"

power-as-pluralism works for the "common good," integrating us into our social environment, ultimately producing social stability by easing social tensions. In the absence of overt conflict, consensus reigns in a state of equilibrium, and "power" becomes irrelevant. Power simply exercises itself out of business.

At the same time, embedded in the viewer's letter are statements that might, at first blush, look like critiques of that pluralist ideology, but which are actually *qualified* criticisms that ultimately form an ironic articulation of apology for a "common good" view of power. The viewer betrays one of the uncritical biases of pluralism — that we can unproblematically "choose" our own relations of power, or we can at least identify the manifest obstacles to our participation in the system. By extension, we deserve what we get if our apathy prevents us from attempting to exercise the power of choice that we all have at our disposal. Hence, while we might criticize our failure to take control of the process, criticism of the process *itself* is rendered inapposite.

In contrast to general "common good" notions of power — either in pure or apologetic form — of which pluralism is exemplar, are views of power that question the notion of social integration as social "stability." Instead, they interpret stability as *control*, and provide a critical opening for examining the nature of domination and struggle. This general contrast forms the basis for a number of parallel and ongoing debates within the social and behavioral sciences, most explicitly within social and political theory. The debate over contrasting conceptions of power is also found in communication theory in the form of the conventional contrast made between "mainstream" (i.e., common good) and "critical" approaches to communication studies. While one might quarrel with the wisdom of reducing the underlying debate to method or research purpose, the implicit *substantive* debate is one grounded in the nature of the concept of "power." In particular, the debate rests on ways that the intimately related notion of "consensus" becomes implicated and interpreted by competing theories of power.

What are generally taken to be "mainstream" approaches to communication include those views that argue or assume that communication plays a socially integrating role. Power is seen as an ultimately integrative force, and communication is functional in not only exercising power, but also, in turn, in producing and maintaining social stability. Traditional development communication campaigns and the field of journalism, for example, make such functional, integrative assumptions. To some extent, those views do not test or even acknowledge their own theories of power, but simply take them as given. The assumptions they make about the nature of power are often quite opaque — only implicit in their theories of communication.

At the same time, ironically, their assumptions about power suggest that power itself is transparent. That is, their embedded, hidden theories of power assume that power is essentially a phenomenon that can somehow be made empirically available for our inspection and criticism — power is something that cannot hide from us. And since power is potentially transparent to all, perhaps that is why such "mainstream" approaches to communication studies do not perform a thoroughgoing *explicit* analysis of the nature of social power and the role that communication plays in creating and sustaining certain forms of power.

More explicit are criticisms from within what I call a "politic" tradition of communication theory, in which one might locate many — though certainly not all — contemporary American academic communication studies, as well as a number of recent European studies. Such criticisms of the role that communication plays in power relations are still rather genteel in that they amount to a bemoaning of the *failure* of social integration. Those polite critiques essentially languish for power-as-pluralism as an ideal model, and note the failure of communication — for example, the failure of the news or the dearth of public debate — to perform its consummate functional, integrative, socially stabilizing work.

Though system *grievances* are systematically exposed, their theories are not theories of social *control* — they remain implicit theories of social integration and contain biases in favor of social "stability." Their analyses are analyses — indeed, critiques — of relations of communication, but fall short of being thoroughgoing, explicit analyses and critiques of the nature of power relations by extension. Their assumptions about the nature of power remain relatively opaque while still implying that power is relatively transparent. So, while ostensibly "critical" in their approach, they tend to be located within the broadly defined "mainstream" category of communication studies by virtue of their implicit apologetic stance toward power as a functional "common good" force in society.

"Critical" communication studies, on the other hand, make few apologies for the nature of power relations, and also make explicit their complex assumptions about power. In fact, a "critical" approach to communication is critical largely because it assumes that social relations of communication are inseparable from social relations of power. The "integrative" role of communication in the exercise of power is analyzed and critiqued as a form of social *control*, rather than stability, partly in an effort to create the possibility for process and social change.

Furthermore, I argue that critical approaches to communication also assume that all theories of social relations — whether political, social, economic, social-psychological, cultural, etc. — are also theories of power, explicitly or implicitly. The buried assumptions about power found in more traditional approaches are excavated and laid bare. Hence, the "critical" purpose of such broadly defined critical approaches to communication is not only to analyze and critique — in short, to demystify — the nature of power relations as social control and the role of communication in creating and sustaining those relations, but also to demystify *theories* of social relations. While more traditional approaches to communication presume a kind of apolitical objectivity or autonomy from the social practices they examine, critical studies presume a "moral" imperative of demystification as creating "possibility" — that is, as creating a climate of questioning all that is otherwise taken for granted about social action. Such a climate of questioning potentially opens sites for struggle to break the stasis of social control.

The three very general views about power and communication that I have introduced above — the thoroughly integrative view, the apologetically integrative view, and the critical view — are reflected historically within political theory in Stephen Lukes's classic treatise, *Power: A Radical View*.[3] In that work, Lukes defines three basic views of power essentially in terms of three dimensions of opacity: (1) the one-dimensional view — a pluralistic view of entirely transparent decision-making behavior: (2) the two-dimensional view — a qualified critique of the overt behavioral focus of pluralism; and (3) the three-dimensional view — a thoroughgoing critique of pluralism, where power is assumed to be quite opaque, found, for example, in latent, and thus unobservable, conflict. Below, I use Lukes's three categories of the concept "power" not to define, but to help elaborate the assumptions of the three general approaches to the study of communication and (thus) power that I have described. I provide several general examples as illustrations.

Communication as Social Integration: The Thoroughly Integrative View

> I didn't know why I done it, and I don't know what good it would have done me if I had. Knowing wouldn't have made it any less done. (Molly, in Larry McMurtry's *Leaving Cheyenne*)

The first model of power described by Lukes is what he calls a one-dimensional view that focuses on overt decision-making behavior as the principle manifestation of power. This ideal model of "pluralism" assumes that the important social issues are those key issues clearly on the public agenda. Power is defined by overt, manifest conflicts over those issues — as, for example, with traditional political participation in public debate and elections and other ballot measures. According to this view, power is evenly diffused throughout society and citizens rule as consumers within the free marketplace of ideas. Historically, this general pluralist model (as well as other "common good" conceptions of power and the State) has taken (and continues to take) the individual as the focus of it analysis.[4] As empirically verifiable behaviors — i.e., conscious, intentional decisions that express policy preferences — power is an option that is assumed to lie transparently on the surface of social action in the face of overt conflict. Consensus and inaction render power irrelevant, since power requires easily seen conflict.

Implicit within the model of power-as-pluralism is the assumption that the decision-making process described above works for the "common good." Power is thus functional for preserving the general stability of the system — where stability is viewed as highly desirable. The notion of stability, or social integration, enjoys a long history in traditional American communication theory within its parent disciplines. In many senses, the template was set early in this century when social philosopher, John Dewey, and sociologists, Charles Horton Cooley and Robert Park, argued that communication media could be harnessed for democratic purposes. "Together, they construed modern communication essentially as an agent for restoring a broad moral and political consensus to America . . ."[5] This general integrative vision of power's (and communication's) purpose later made itself evident (if sometimes only implicitly so) in development communication, normative models of the "social responsibility" of the press, and functional studies of media uses and gratifications, all in which the audience ultimately reins as rational, intentional "consumer."

The emphasis on rational, informed decisions, particularly consumer-like "buying" or "adopting" behaviors, has traditionally driven much development, diffusion, and communication-campaign research. In many respects, diffusion and educational communication campaigns are not unlike typical marketing campaigns for commercial products; the objective is generally to persuade individuals to adopt new behaviors (for example, adopt an innovative agricultural practice) or change existing behaviors (stop smoking, for instance). Similar strategies have been used (most often by researchers from highly developed nations) to diffuse innovative forms of political participation in developing nations. Until recently, development communication has concentrated its efforts on "modernization," both economic and political, preferring to diffuse pluralist political structures with their extant "free" economies.[6] Such structures are premised on open debate and conscious decision-making behaviors by individuals.

One of the primary — indeed, "necessary" — vehicles presumed to effect open debate is a "free press." In the United States, the normative model of the "social responsibility of the press" clings tenaciously to pluralist ideals when it holds that it is the job of the press to keep a heterogeneous public informed — to objectively, impartially reflect a pluralist world — so that individual citizens may then participate rationally in an open political system. In its assumptions about diffuse, visible power — following from its presumptions of "objectivity" and "impartiality" — this ideal view of the press disregards the many complexities of the agenda-building process, such as technical and practical newsroom routines, constrained source-reporter relationships, and market pressures, all of which tend to work against less-entrenched opinion. And, as John Westergaard has argued, the notion of "social responsibility" inherently contradicts itself. Journalists deny their own influence, as objective purveyors of the "news," but claim responsibility for public education and, in the end, social integration. That "responsibility" of course, entails some authority.[7]

The integrative flavor of this general implicit model of one dimensional power is perhaps most conspicuous in functional studies of media uses and gratifications. In general, this approach argues that people choose to use media to gratify basic human needs — in particular, the need to be connected with one's social environment. But, as Philip Elliott observes, it considers neither the *source* of those needs nor the peculiar distribution of social power and opportunity. Since needs develop within an *existing* set of social relations, such an approach — based on simply identifying and describing needs and their gratifications — inevitably supports those existing relations, hiding and suppressing alternatives.[8] And by emphasizing *use* (i.e., decision-making), this approach, as with more overt politically pluralist approaches to communication, obscures less obvious covert or latent forms of power and conflict played out through complex social arrangements and "logics" that ultimately define and limit the parameters within which individuals are able to make choices. The following view of power provides at least a limited alternative.

The Failure of Communication as
Social Integration: The Apologetically
Integrative View

A little "confessed" evil saves one from acknowledging a lot of hidden evil . . . . it is well worth the price of an immunization. What does it matter, *after all*, if margarine is just fat, when it goes further than butter, and costs less? What does it matter, *after all*, if Order is a little brutal or a little blind, when it allows us to live so cheaply? (Roland Barthes, "Operation Margarine," in *Mythologies*

The two-dimensional view of power that Lukes describes is represented primarily by Peter Bachrach and Morton S. Baratz's qualified critique of the behavioral fetishism of pluralism.[9] The "second face of power" identified by Bachrach and Baratz is *non*decision-making. What is key to this view is that not all consensus is "real" — some consensus is merely apparent and takes the form of *covert* conflict. In other words, this model of power accounts for the suppression of challenges to the interests of a decision-maker as another important way of exercising power.

When one prevents another from making a decision with regard to a policy grievance, one has gone beyond simple decision-making behavior with regard to explicit, key issues. *Potential* issues are now at stake. And those issues may be kept *off* the public agenda, as when marginal social groups are prevented from gaining access to mass media. Thus, the process of agenda-building, rather than merely the agenda itself, becomes relevant. The "agenda" is no longer presumed to be an unrefractive mirror of a pluralist world, but a more selective representation of that world.

Still, in spite of the added critical complexity, the two-dimensional view of power, according to Lukes, remains merely a qualified critique of the behavioral focus of pluralism because it presents nondecision-making as yet another *form* of decision-making. The individual is thus retained as the unit of analysis. Furthermore, it retains the empirical focus of pluralism in that power continues to be defined in terms of *manifest* conflict — whether overt or covert. By failing to escape the essential limitations of the pluralist model — its individualism and empiricism — this ostensible critical view of power, I argue, ultimately works as an apology for "common good" conceptions of power by first displaying its working inefficiencies and imperfections, but then rescuing the *ideal* model by falling back upon its own limiting assumptions. Michael Shapiro has exposed and critiqued the rhetoric of apology as a genre of discourse, and I extend the analogy here to examine a similar genre of communication and power.[10]

Often, criticisms of a particular mainstream area of communication study come from within its own bounds when historical and material reality motivate researchers to reconsider the questions they ask. For example, although the assumptions and political biases of traditional development and diffusion research have been criticized sharply from outside on both substantive and empirical grounds, scholars working in that tradition have also noted some of the limitations of their earlier work. Everett Rogers, for instance, notes the passing of the older behavior-persuasion paradigm with its built-in assumption that development results in the equitable distribution of resources; in its place, a growing concern with inequitable gaps in knowledge and effects — and how to correct them — has emerged.[11] Still, such criticisms tend to focus on the failure of campaigns due to their incorrect structure or strategy, rather than to provide a thoroughgoing critique of the underlying model of pluralism upon which such campaigns are intimately premised in the first place.

Similarly, recent research areas within journalism and political communication provide challenges to the strictly pluralist bent of traditional ancestors. For example, studies of news "gatekeeping" examine the agenda-building process and consider ways in which issues are prevented — through the editorial process especially — from ever reaching the public agenda.[12] Those studies probe a deeper level of power than do their pluralist progenitors; they excavate "apparent" consensus and expose its grounding in covert conflict.

The suppression of social voices assumes a certain spotlight as an object of study — nondecision-making, in Lukes's terms, is recognized as another face of power. But, as in Lukes's scheme, nondecision-making, such as gatekeeping, is regarded as yet another form (if more complex and hidden) of decision-making. Immanent within this view of power, the active suppression of voices (whether intentional or merely incidental to the exigencies of production) operates much like a "bad apple," spoiling the "barrel" of otherwise pluralist diversity. The barrel provides both the context and limiting assumptions, but the apple becomes the primary object of analysis and critique. The imperfections of the journalistic process are discussed at length, but neither the reasons for those "imperfections" nor the larger paradox of the notion of a "free press" in this society are addressed adequately.

The growing interest in socialization and the construction of social reality (or our image of the social world about us) provides — from within the research "mainstream" — another significant, if sometimes limited, challenge to the static functional, behavioral model of pluralism. This general research area provides a significant corrective for the lack of context of functional "media-use" oriented studies. For example, studies of social identity make an explicit attempt to identify the links between internal psychological processes and external social processes at different levels of analysis.[13] Such an approach potentially provides a way of explaining how needs and wants, expressed socially, come into being within a complex social milieu. Similarly, studies of socialization examine the social process of integrating individuals into a larger "legitimate" role structure. Legitimation — a way of explaining or justifying a given social structure and the ideas that support it — mystifies by preventing people from recognizing the conventional, changeable basis of such a social creation.[14] Hence, power implicitly takes on a form of mediation within this approach that is suggestive of the Gramscian view of "hegemony" (which I discuss below).

Still, many studies of social reality seem reluctant to take the critical step of tackling and analyzing the underlying limiting assumptions of the notion of social integration *itself*. Rather, they often seem content with describing the process and how it can sometimes go wrong. Perhaps "Cultivation Analysis," especially of television violence, provides a notable exception from within the research "mainstream." Cultivation theory turns explicitly the entire notion of "consensus" on its head by arguing that resistance to the system is prevented by the cultivation of fear and acquiescence to authority via symbolic representations of power. In other words, we accept authority in the name of safety.[15] Clearly, the theory reinterprets the notions of "integration" as control and containment of change, and of consensus as *consent*. Thus, the approach opens the door to the analysis of *latent* conflict and the complex exercise of power through social arrangements. In the following section, I present an elaboration of just such a compelling critical alternative to the pluralist thesis and its apologies, which takes a more sophisticated form in the concept of "hegemony."

Communication as Social Control: The Critical View

"Why do you keep telling me that things are going from bad to worse on my estate, my dear fellow?" the landlord says to his steward. "I know it without you; can't you talk about something else? You should let me forget about the state of things, leave me in ignorance of it, then I shall be happy." (Nikolai Vasilievich Gogol, *Dead Souls*)

Critical approaches to communication have in common not merely that all social relations and relations of communication are also relations of power; they also assume that those relations of power take some form of *domination* within a complex contextual social web. In other words, "social integration" is explicitly recast as "social control." But the shapes that social control is presumed to take, and the ways relations of domination are accounted for take many different forms. In other words, there is no single "critical" approach to the study of communication, much less social theory: the many and varied approaches that fall within this rubric have drawn from and built upon a wide range of sometimes deeply conflicting intellectual traditions.

For example, political-economic approaches to media studies are grounded in a long tradition of historical materialism. They search for both direct and mediated connections between economic power and cultural forms, leading to questions of media ownership and the role of cultural production itself. In general, such analyses provide a material context for interpreting the role of culture in reproducing social relations and identities; they provide an explicit account of the dynamics behind the production of ideas and the mystification of the whole production process, as opposed to explaining only content or effects.[16]

A more static, functional approach to explaining the nature of social domination is represented by Structuralist Marxism, associated perhaps most strongly with Louis Althusser and Nicos Poulantzas (in his earlier works). In contrast with the historical focus of political-economic analyses, structural analyses in general search for objective structures (economic, political, ideological) that social action presupposes. According to Althusser's anti-existentialist argument, power is effected through individuals' willing subjugation to ideology, which defines them and locates them within a social structure.[17]

Post-structuralist approaches take a very different tack, preferring criticism of manifest social practices, rather than analysis of the underlying structures that give rise to them. Michel Foucault, for instance, focuses on the relationship between power and knowledge in his criticisms of the privileged discursive practices of institutions (such as medicine) and who gets to "talk" those discourses. Rather than seeking the deep structure of discourse (i.e., language), as a semiotician might, Foucault has stayed with its surface structures, its "rules of formation" at given historical moments. In general, Foucault has been more concerned with criticizing the *use* of power to dominate — where social practices are represented in discursive practices — and less concerned with theorizing about the *origin* of power relations.[18]

All critical approaches to power, such as those illustrated here, cast social relations as relations of domination, thus directly challenging pluralist assumptions about "diffuse" power. Further, all confront more or less directly the notion of "consensus" with, for example, arguments about mystification or willing subjugation to ideology. Since a thoroughgoing critique of "consensus" is *crucial* for a thoroughgoing critique of the inadequacy of the pluralist thesis for explaining power relations, it is important to single out here the critical approach that most explicitly takes apart "consensus" — not only "apparent" consensus, but also "real" consensus — at a useful level of abstraction. Such an approach embraces the Gramscian theory of "consent." Thus, that is the approach on which I focus here. And that is also the critical alternative and thoroughgoing challenge to pluralism reflected in Lukes's third model of power.

Unlike Bachrach and Baratz's "second face of power" (the suppression of grievances), the third dimension of power involves the conditioning of consensus by the *prevention* of grievances in the first place rather than simply the prevention of their expression. This process allows the manipulation of the public agenda by the presentation of a paradigm of society that seems natural, inevitable, and unchangeable. "Decisions are choices consciously and intentionally made by individuals between alternatives, whereas the bias of the system can be mobilised, recreated and reinforced in ways that are neither consciously chosen nor the intended result of particular individuals."[19]

Hence, *latent* conflicts become important foci for the exercise of power, and their suppression is no longer adequately characterized as an individual-level activity, but as "a function of collective forces and social arrangements."[20] The complexity of this view of power lies in its assumptions about the *opacity* of power. Power is relatively hidden because it is not necessarily observable (it may be located in latent conflict) and is exercised through an obscure web of sometimes abstract social relations. Such an argument provides both a penetrating critique of and an alternative to the empiricism and individualism of the pluralist model of power, much more so than the politic criticisms reviewed in the previous section.

Lukes's general three-dimensional view of power is not unlike the complex concept of "hegemony" found in critical social-theoretical literature. "Hegemony," though used by some to refer simply to "ideological domination," is more correctly a conceptual tool for understanding and potentially subverting the "consent" of the masses to their own oppression, especially under late monopoly capitalism. Associated most seminally with Antonio Gramsci, the concept goes beyond both the "liberal" idea of consent as "consensus" and the economistic Marxist notion of consent as "false consciousness."[21] "Antonio Gramsci's major contribution to Marxism is that he systematized, from what is implicit in Marx, a Marxist science of political action."[22] There are two general (intimately related) *uses* of the idea of hegemony by social theorists: (1) as a *theory* of consent, which exposes the process; and (2) as a political *strategy*, a way of searching for access points for struggle.

The first goal of the critical model of power-as-hegemony is the project of demystification by theoretical activity. The theory of hegemony — i.e., of consent — goes far beyond pluralist theories of social integration because it does not stop with the observation that we can, indeed, empirically observe a kind of "consensus." Rather, it poses the problem of how that consensus is produced and who produces it, how it is that governed classes "freely consent" to the rule of more powerful governing classes. As such, the concept of hegemony also recasts the notion of "dominance" no longer as one of coercion, but rather as a much more complex, more subtle and dynamic process. Stuart Hall, most conspicuously identified with British cultural studies, argues that:

Hegemony implied that the dominance of certain formations was secured, not by ideological compulsion, but by cultural leadership . . . . The critical point about this conception of "leadership" — which was Gramsci's most distinguished contribution — is that hegemony is understood as accomplished, not without the due measure of legal and legitimate compulsion, but principally by means of winning the active consent of those classes and groups who were subordinated within it.[23]

Hall also argues that the concept of hegemony became important to communication studies precisely because of the observation that media are neither autonomous social actors nor merely reflective of dominant ideologies or consensus. Instead, *media* are *key actors* in the *production* of consent – at once free of direct control by powerful social groups while also subject to working within limits and conditions neither of their own choosing nor within their direct control. Media tend to give weight to well-established opinion (which they help to establish as well), but not by virtue of force — and not unproblematically.

Todd Gitlin uses the notion of hegemony to explain how the American New Left was both "made" and "unmade" in the news media during the mid-1960s.[24] In the struggle over images, conventional framing devices were used by media to first marginalize and trivialize that political movement, and then later to absorb and domesticate its conflicting values and definitions of reality — a process entered into, in some senses, by the movement itself. Gitlin argues that, in journalism, social conflict is brought into the news and reproduced, but reproduced in terms of prevailing "common sense" definitions of reality. "As the mass media have suffused social life, they have become crucial fields for the definition of social meaning — partially contested zones in which the hegemonic ideology meets its partial challenges and then adapts."[25] And the process of adaptation can be highly contradictory.

The second goal of the model of power-as-hegemony is strategically political, which follows partly from the general "moral," reflexively educational imperative of many critical studies. But it also follows from the interpretation of the concept of hegemony itself — not only from Gramsci's notion of "leadership," but also from the ever-changing, imperfect, contradictory nature of the process of hegemony. The imperfection of hegemony is precisely what opens up sites of access for the struggle over images and discourses in culture. Martin Carnoy argues:

Gramsci, in the last analysis, was, like Marx and Lenin, an *educator*. Yet, unlike Lenin, he believed in the intellectual qualities of the masses and their capability to create themselves the hegemony of their class rather than have it done for them by an elite vanguard party or an elite bureaucracy responsible for revolutionary theory and tactics. The development of a working-class consciousness, such a crucial element in Marxist theory, is for Gramsci the principle moment in explaining both capitalist domination *and* its overthrow.[26]

In particular, Gramsci's ideas on revolution focus on the concept of hegemony — as *counter*hegemony. The struggle against bourgeois dominance requires a strategy by which an alternative concept of society is created — one that assaults bourgeois hegemony in a "war of position."[27] For Gramsci, the key struggle takes place not in the realm of militancy, but, instead, in the realm of ideology. That is, the "hegemonic crisis" leads to a struggle over competing definitions of social reality.

In addition to asking questions about power that refer to its location — "who-whom" questions that get at the ideas of "responsibility" and "gain" — Lukes recently suggested that we might also ask the question "Who can secure the achievement of collective goods?"[28] That question permits us to identify critical access points in the struggle over media images and representations. In communication studies, Hall has long affirmed the importance of the politicizing role of confronting the problem of ideology.[29]

In particular, Hall's "theory of articulation" has political consequences in that it informs us about cultural transformations and the creation of new political subjects through the use of media; an example Hall has given is the Rastafarian movement in Jamaica. Others, too, have attempted to provide strategies for the struggle over meaning and political action, such as Ernesto Laclau and Chantel Mouffe's attempt to find a politics of discourse.[30] In general, the theorist who uses the concept of hegemony tends to be more engaged politically — as self-reflexive "educators" and by virtue of the politicizing nature of the concept itself — than pluralists or other political theorists who tend to presume a certain distance from their subject.

The theory of power-as-hegemony, whose use is illustrated in communication studies, provides a greater complexity of explanation about power in its opacity than do the pluralist thesis and its apologia. But in addition to providing a penetrating critique of pluralism, the complexity of the concept of hegemony also provides a substantive *alternative*. In fact, "hegemony" turns the notion of social integration on its head and escapes pluralism's fetishism of the individual and the observable, allowing us to acknowledge the roles of latent conflict and obscure social actors in power exercised as social control. The concept thus demystifies those roles, potentially opening avenues for access. Further, "hegemony" makes *explicit* its assumptions about the process of power — indeed, the politicizing nature of the concept hegemony is inherent in its use.

In general, using the concept of hegemony allows us to ask questions about power that might be obviated by the use of the pluralist thesis or its politic critiques. Analogously, critical approaches to the study of communication and power carry the same advantages over pluralist and quasi-critical approaches. In general, critical communication studies explicitly conceptualize relations of communication as problematic relations of power — that is, power becomes something more than a state or relation to be taken for granted or merely described. Power becomes the central problem for analysis.

5.
The Political Economy of Culture
Sut Jhally

Introduction

Democracies by definition are fragile and unstable social formations. To remain democratic there must be at all times a vigorous and diverse debate underway concerning social policy over a whole range of subject areas. Without open debate, it is all too easy to lapse into a homogenizing authoritarianism. The diversity and richness of the cultural realm are not merely "ornaments of a democracy but essential elements for its survival."[1] It is for this reason that the First Amendment of the Constitution guarantees freedom of belief, expression, and assembly. For many different reasons the framers of the Constitution recognized that such freedom was a prerequisite for political freedom and a bulwark against centralized control of the social and cultural realm.

However, although freedom can be discussed as an abstract concept, it is always played out in specific historical and material circumstances. The freedom of expression (and the press) that the Constitution guarantees is freedom defined in a particular way — it is freedom from control by *government*. In the American mind freedom is integrally linked with the role of the government (hence the perceived loss of freedom under a centralized authority — Communism). However, this one-dimensional definition of freedom ignores the possibility that freedom can be diminished not simply by government restrictions but also by other factors that prevent freedom of belief, expression, and assembly. In freeing culture from government the Constitution entrusts it to the "marketplace of ideas" which, presumably, ensures freedom. But, we shall be asking ourselves here, is this necessarily the case? Is the "marketplace" a truly democratic site?

The metaphor of "the marketplace of ideas" works in two ways: ideologically and materially. Ideologically, it conveys the notion that ideas battle for people's minds in a realm where competition of belief is encouraged, and that from this free and equal struggle "truth" will emerge as the victor. It is diversity and choice and freedom of speech that is stressed in the ideological reading of the metaphor. The way to ensure this — it is argued by democracies — is to block government interference in the political and cultural realms. There are thus no constitutional *laws* restricting freedom of expression in the United States.

The material interpretation of "the marketplace of ideas" takes the notion of marketplace literally — as a place where ideas are bought and sold. It refers to the concrete framework within which the right of free expression exists. As Supreme Court Justice Walter Brennan says:

> Freedom of speech does not exist in the abstract. On the contrary, the right to speak can flourish only if it is allowed to operate in an effective forum — whether it be a public park, a schoolroom, a town meeting hall, a soapbox, or a radio and television frequency. For in the absence of an effective means of communications, the right to speak would ring hollow indeed. And, in recognition of these principles, we have consistently held that the First Amendment embodies, not only the abstract right to be free from censorship, but also the right of an individual to utilize an appropriate and effective medium for the expression of his views.[2]

However, the courts have never been able to agree whether the First Amendment merely prevents Congress from restricting free expression or whether it implies that Congress should take legislative action to widen and protect free expression.

The question that is left to be answered here is: What is the relationship between these two interpretations of the marketplace of ideas? Is there a contradiction between expecting the marketplace to provide genuine diversity while at the same time treating ideas as economic goods to be bought and sold? What are the implications of expecting the marketplace to work in the *public* interest and at the same time leaving the control of the institutions expected to accomplish this in *private* hands?

This paper examines the economic context of our mass-mediated culture. In the modern era, questions of freedom of expression and culture are intimately and inextricably tied to systems of mass communication. While culture cannot be reduced to mere economic factors, it cannot be understood, either, without understanding the economic context that surrounds and shapes it. Culture is not an abstract phenomenon. The process of consciousness and representation is a real material process that requires material resources for its existence and survival. Within the United States, questions about the provision of material resources for the cultural realm have been given largely *industrial* answers. What we specifically need to focus on then are the workings of the *cultural industries*; we need to ask the heretical question of whether the First Amendment (as presently interpreted) leads to domination rather than freedom.

Consciousness Industry

All societies seek to *reproduce* their constitutive social relations over time. If they cannot accomplish this then a new set of social relations will develop and a new type of society will emerge. All societies are characterized by this constant tension between stability and change. There are no historical laws governing these processes, but, in general, groups that benefit from the existing distribution of power and rewards work for stability, while groups denied access to power and resources work for change. Capitalism is characterized by power and rewards being increasingly concentrated in the hands of those who *own* the means of production at the expense of the much larger group of people who own only their own labor power which they sell in exchange for wages.

For societies, such as capitalism, that are characterized by a wide disparity in the distribution of wealth and power, the vital questions of reproduction concern how a minority but dominant social class (capitalists) can maintain power over the vast majority of the population. There are two ways in which this reproduction can be accomplished. First, by sheer force (the use of the police and military). The ruling elites of nations such as South Africa and Chile rule through this method. Second, reproduction can be accomplished through the *consent* of the dominated, by convincing the majority to identify and support the present system of rewards and power rather than opposing it, in fact to live their own domination as freedom. In this the media are vital institutions that far from providing a free marketplace of ideas work to legitimate the existing distribution of power by controlling the context within which people think and define social problems and their possible solutions.

In one very important variant of critical communications theory the function of the media and the cultural realm in general is to produce the appropriate *consciousness* in the majority of people to ensure the reproduction of what is essentially an exploitative system of social relations. Hans Enzensberger coined the phrase "Consciousness Industry" to describe the media.[3] The media here are literally an industry which attempts to produce a form of consciousness in the audience that benefits the class that controls the media and industry in general.

But why would the media act in this way rather than in the public good? The answer of course is that media are not public institutions but private ones. They are owned and controlled by the corporations who have concentrated wealth and power in their hands. They thus reflect the needs of their owners. Ben Bagdikian writes of this situation: "Today there is hardly an American industry that does not own a major media outlet, or a major media outlet grown so large that it does not own a firm in a major industry. These media report the news of industries in which they either are owners or share directors and policies."[4]

This ownership and control is not merely a structural phenomenon — it effects the everyday operations of media organizations. This control is achieved concretely by means of interlocking directorships, by persons who serve on the board of directors of multiple corporations, and thus can coordinate the various interests they represent. For example in 1983 the Gannett Company (which owns 88 daily newspapers with a daily circulation of 3,750,000) shared directors with Merrill Lynch, Standard Oil, 20th Century Fox, Kerr-McGee (oil, gas, nuclear power, aerospace), McDonnell Douglas Aircraft, McGraw-Hill, Eastern Airlines, Phillips Petroleum, Kellog Company, and New York Telephone Company, among others. The authors of a study that examined interlocking directorships among the 25 largest U.S. newspaper companies reached the following conclusion:

> The directors of these companies, whose dailies account for more than half the circulation of all American newspapers, sit on the boards of regional, national and multinational business corporations . . . Overall the directors are linked with powerful business organisations, not with public interest groups; with management, not labour; with well established think tanks and charities, not their grass-roots counterparts.[5]

These directors are responsible for hiring and firing people in important media posts. That is where their power rests, not on interference with reporters and editors at an everyday level. People, in whatever occupation, normally will not engage in actions that will displease superiors and journalists are no exception to this.

The implications for the cultural realm of such connections between the media and the economy are immense. Take the following three issues for example: (a) The debate concerning *the arms race*. Any of the companies who benefit from huge defense contracts are intimately connected with media. How is the debate going to be effected by that relationship? For example, General Electric is a major defense contractor for the government. GE (through its ownership of RCA) owns and operates NBC. Within this context, how will the SDI (or "Star Wars") debate be framed and structured on NBC? If SDI proceeds, General Electric will reap rewards in the billions of dollars! It is little wonder that serious and informed debate about the arms race is almost totally absent from network television; (b) *The energy crisis* will be one of the most contentious issues facing American society from now to the end of the century. The information presented about the oil companies by media is going to be vital in forming public opinion about these issues. What happens if the oil industry has a deep influence on news media? This is not simply an academic question — oil representatives sit on the boards of all the powerful news media; (c) The reporting of *foreign affairs*. Major media companies themselves have investments around the world and they are interlocked with other companies who have investments around the world. How is the reporting of news affected when media companies own interests (or the interests of their partners) are involved? For example, the major networks have investments in South Africa — how does this effect the way they report struggles against apartheid?

There is a second variation in critical theory to the notion that the media is a Consciousness Industry. This is represented in the work of Dallas Smythe who claims that too much attention has been paid to the way in which media produce ideology. Instead we should focus on what their role is in the economy directly. Viewed from an economic perspective, Smythe claims that the principal product of media is not ideology but *audiences*.

Industrial corporations not only need to produce commodities; they also have to ensure that they are sold. In response to this need, in the nineteenth century, newspapers and magazines underwent a process of modernization whereby they would deliver the appropriate audiences to advertisers. In the twentieth century, the commercialization of radio and television ensured that advertising considerations would become *the* predominant factor shaping the structure of the American media system. Smythe writes:

> The secret of the growth of Consciousness Industry in the past century will be found in (1) the relation of advertising to the news, entertainment, and information material in the mass media; (2) the relations of both

that material and advertising to real consumer goods and services, political candidates, and public issues; (3) the relations of advertising and consumer goods and services to the people who consume them; (4) the effective control of people's lives which the monopoly capitalist corporations dominating the foregoing three sets of relationships try to establish and maintain . . . The commercial mass media *are* advertising in their entirety . . . both advertising and the "program material" reflect, mystify, and are essential to the sale of goods and services.[6]

The mass media then sell audiences which perform three key functions for the survival of the system: audiences market goods to themselves, they learn to vote for candidates in the political sphere, and they reaffirm belief in the legitimacy of the politico-economic system.

Smythe's version of Consciousness Industry differs from Enzensberger's in that he stresses the absolutely fundamental necessity of the consumption of commodities for the survival of the system. The Consciousness Industry "produces a particular kind of human nature or consciousness, focusing its energies on the consumption of commodities . . . for about a century the kind of human nature produced in the core area has, to a large degree, been the product of Consciousness Industry. People with this nature exist primarily to serve the system; the system is *not* under their control, serving them."[7]

Both versions of Consciousness Industry referred to above do have a common characteristic — they are functionalist in their treatment of the cultural realm. The first looks at the role of media in the reproduction of society in general. The second emphasizes the role of media in the reproduction of the economy in general. In both accounts, the attention is not so much on the cultural and media sphere itself, but on what function it plays within the *system as a whole*. While this is not an incorrect way to approach the study of culture, it is an incomplete and partial approach. Focusing on the wider role of the media deflects attention away from what could be learned if one focuses closely on the media themselves.

The Industrialization of Culture

Focusing on the specificity of the cultural realm forces us, in an important sense, to treat it in its own terms, rather than focusing on its relationship to another realm (such as the economic). The first issue to be addressed from such a perspective concerns the nature of the cultural realm under capitalism.[8] There is a wide agreement across the political spectrum that the culture of modern capitalism is a very distinct phenomenon from what preceded it. In the early part of this century, as society was moving from an agricultural to an industrial basis, both right-wing and left-wing writers decried the triumph of "mass culture" over local or high culture.[9]

The move to urban industrialization weakens considerably the traditional cultural influence of the extended family, the community and religion in the everyday lives of people. As a direct result, a cultural void opens up. The marketplace moves in to replace older forms of cultural activity. Culture itself is made into a commodity and is bought and sold in the marketplace. The first body of scholars to write about cultural commodification was the Frankfurt School. Two of its representatives, Theodor Adorno and Max Horkheimer, argued that under capitalism the profit motive is transferred to cultural forms in that more and more artistic products were being turned into a commodity, "marketable and interchangeable like an industrial product."[10] This implied a change in the traditional conception of the artist and of art itself. While in earlier epochs, artists also sold their works, monetary exchanges did not prevent them from engaging in "the pursuit of the inherent logic of each work." Under modern capitalism, however, art is first and foremost a commodity and it is this commodification of art that dominates the logic of cultural forms. Commenting on the work of Adorno and Horkheimer, David Held writes:

> Advertising and banking lay down new aesthetic standards. Even where the culture industry does not directly produce for profit its products are determined by this new aesthetic. The economic necessity for a quick and high rate of return on investment demands the production of attractive packages designed either to sell directly or to create an atmosphere of selling — a feeling of insecurity, or want and need. The culture industry either has to sell particular objects or it 'turns into public relations, the manufacturing of "good will" per se.'[11]

In choosing the term "culture industry," Adorno and Horkheimer wanted to stress that this was not "mass culture" or something that arose from "the masses" themselves but was instead imposed by the dictates of the marketplace. Culture then is not the product of genuine demands — its driving force is the need to sell itself as a commodity. The products of cultural industries are divorced from art and become pure entertainment. Their purpose is to divert, distract, and amuse people away from the alienation and drudgery imposed by capitalist work relations. The culture industry offers an escape through pure illusion.

For Adorno and Horkheimer, there is no variety in mass culture. It is all essentially the same and interchangeable. There is a "ruthless unity," and what differences there do appear to be in terms of types of films or magazines:

> depend not so much on subject matter as on classifying, organizing and labeling consumers. Something is provided for all so that none may escape; the distinctions are emphasized and extended. The public is catered for with a hierarchical range of mass-produced products of varying quality, thus advancing the rule of complete quantification. Everybody must behave (as if spontaneously) in accordance with his previously determined and indexed level, and choose the category of mass product turned out for his type. Consumers appear as statistics on research organization charts, and are divided by income groups into red, green and blue areas; the technique is that used for any type of propaganda."[12]

An important part of the Frankfurt School critique is that the products of the culture industries do not challenge people to think and reflect on the world — instead, as standardized products, the response to them is built into their own structure. In this way cultural meaning is imposed upon the audience rather than being created by the audience.

While there is a sense of "overkill" in their writings, and there is no place for audience resistance and subjectivity to intervene in this process that produces what Herbert Marcuse called "one-dimensional" people, their warnings need to be taken seriously. However, in the critical tradition of cultural studies their work has been (mistakenly) seen as part of the "consciousness industry" approach outlined above. Although there is little doubt that Adorno and Horkheimer see the cultural industries as producers of capitalist ideology, they believe that the dynamic process that is producing this mass production of ideology has not been properly understood. The cultural industries produce ideology not primarily because they are controlled by corporations, but because that is necessarily the result when culture is treated as a *commodity*. It is not conspiracy that is the cause but the logic of industrial production applied to cultural products.

In this what we are witnessing is the movement from the formal subsumption of culture to its real subsumption within the capitalist mode of production. The *formal* subsumption refers to a situation where an area of society becomes vital for the functioning of the economic system without taking on the structures of the economic system. The "consciousness industry" approach analyses media as only formally subsumed. The media are seen as vital for the functioning of the capitalist economy but they are not viewed as principally economic institutions. Investment by capitalists in media is not primarily to make money but is to ensure that the media (by producing the appropriate "consciousness") provide the context within which the whole economic system can survive and expand.

Real subsumption refers to a situation where the media become not ideological institutions but are primarily economic ones. That is, investment in media is not for the purpose of ideological control but is for the purpose of reaping the biggest return. Culture is produced first and foremost as a commodity rather than as ideology. Of course these are not exclusive of each other.[13]

In attempting to formulate the correct relationship between the economy and cultural institutions, we are on the terrain of debate referred to as "the base/superstructure" metaphor within critical cultural studies. The British communications theorist Nicholas Garnham is the most sophisticated of recent scholars to explore the implications that stem from recent movements in the cultural sphere (i.e., treating culture as primarily a commodity to be bought and sold in the marketplace) for the conceptualization of this metaphor. He argues that there are two principal ways in which cultural institutions can be supported. First, they can be supported from revenues that derive from other spheres of the economy. If this is the case then the "superstructures" (such as the media) remain subordinated to the "base" — they are dependent upon surpluses created elsewhere in material production. "Material production in this direct sense is determinate in that it is only the surplus produced by this labour that enables other forms of human activity to be pursued. Thus the superstructure remains dependent upon and determined by the base of material production in the very fundamental sense."[14] Thus either through patronage or public expenditure, cultural activities can be supported. This is at the level of formal subsumption.

Second, the cultural realm can support itself by producing and selling cultural commodities, resulting in surplus being generated internally. Culture here becomes a part of material production, a part of the base itself, and is subject to the same laws of economic production as other industrial spheres. This leads to what is called "the industrialization of culture," a process whereby the superstructures become commodified. Thus the film industry or the record industry does not need to be subsidized from other areas of society — they can function in and of themselves. Control of the cultural realm is achieved not by subsidy but "by extracting surpluses directly by means of economic processes. Thus the developments of the capitalist mode of production and its associated division of mental and manual labour has led to the development of the extraction of the necessary surplus for the maintenance of cultural production and reproduction directly via the commodity and exchange form."[15] The real question that is posed by such a process is what happens to cultural activity within such a context. What constraints are imposed by the logic of commodity production on cultural and artistic activity?

In developing the argument thus far I have contrasted two different approaches to the study of culture. The "consciousness industry" approach stresses that the media are principally ideological institutions, while the "industrialization of culture" approach stresses the expansion of the commodity form that has little to do with ideology. This contrast is not oppositional but should be seen as complementary. Nicholas Garnham writes of this:

> one of the key features of the mass media within monopoly capitalism has been the exercise of political and ideological domination through the economic. What concerns us in fact is firstly to stress, from the analytical perspective, the validity of the base/superstructure model while at the same time pointing to and analyzing the ways in which the development of monopoly capitalism has industrialized the superstructure. Indeed Marx's own central insight into the capitalist mode of production stressed its generalizing, abstracting drive; the pressure to reduce everything to the equivalence of exchange-value.[16]

Advertising and Commodified Culture

Garnham however believes that there is something quite specific about cultural commodities that makes it difficult for cultural industries to operate just like other industries. Problems of copyright, ease of duplication, control over consumption, etc. leads to a "two-way pressure either towards advertising finance or State finance." So, for instance, the videocassettes of the movie *Top Gun* had Pepsi ads on them at the start to defray costs. Indeed, in the United States it is impossible to understand the media and cultural domain without recognizing the role of advertising revenues in the operation of the cultural industries. Broadcasting (television and radio) derive 100% of their revenues from advertisers. Magazines and newspapers draw a large majority of their revenues from advertisers. The movie, music, and sports industries increasingly are coming to rely on advertising expenditures for their profitability. In this section I will examine the role that advertising expenditures play in the structure of our cultural forms.

What advertisers buy with their dollars is access to audiences. If we examined the broadcasting or printing industry in economic terms we would see that what they produce as a commodity are not television programs or newspapers — what they sell are audiences to advertisers. As Smythe was absolutely correct in maintaining, in advertising-supported media audiences are produced as *commodities*.

What cultural implications flow from this seemingly simple fact? The newspaper industry is a good example to highlight these issues. The 1970s and the 1980s have been characterized by two related trends. First, there has been an increasing concentration of ownership in which fewer and fewer corporate chains control large numbers of newspapers across the country. Second, there has been a growth in what are called "one-newspaper towns" where old established newspapers with relatively large circulations are going out of business or are being bought up by their competitors and thus leaving many cities with only one newspaper. For example in 1981, the Washington Star (with a daily circulation of 300,000), the Philadelphia Bulletin (with a daily circulation of 400,000), the Minneapolis Star, and the Cleveland Press all folded.

To understand these events one has to understand the workings of the newspaper industry as an *industry*. Advertisers account for close to 80% of the revenue of newspapers. What they get for their dollars are the audiences and readerships of the newspapers in which they buy space. For advertisers, newspaper advertising is just one component of an integrated marketing strategy. They want to use their advertising dollars in the most cost-efficient manner, i.e. to reach the greatest numbers of people for the least amount of money. Advertisers are not particularly concerned with how much it costs to run an ad in a newspaper, but they are concerned with whether it is a good buy. This is measured in CPM (cost-per-thousand), i.e. how much it costs to reach a 1000 people in the audience. Ben Bagdikian gives the following example from Washington D.C.[17] In 1970 there were three newspapers. The Washington Post had a circulation of 500,000 and charged $16,676 for a large ad. The Washington Star had a circulation of 300,000 and charged $12,634. The Washington News had a circulation of 200,000 and charged $9,676. It may seem from this that the Post was the most expensive of the three papers, but for advertisers it was in fact the cheapest in terms of CPM. Advertising in the Post meant each household could be reached for 3.34 cents while the News cost 4.84 cents per household. In such a situation, even when two newspapers are relatively close in terms of circulation, a disproportionately large share of the available advertising dollars go to the larger circulation newspaper. This puts intense pressure on the lower circulation paper. As a result, in 1972 the Washington News went out of business and in 1981 the Washington Star went out of business, leaving the Washington Post as the only newspaper in a one-newspaper town.[18] Monopoly newspapers are very profitable, for they pick up the audience of the demised competitor. In Washington D.C., two years after the Star folded the Post's ad rates rose 58 per cent.

It is the same logic of profit maximization that has led to concentration of ownership within the field of media in general. It is more profitable to run a newspaper when you also own 50 others. There are large savings to be made in economies of scale in the buying of newsprint, in multiple use of printing presses, and in the number of reporters needed to cover stories. This of course has serious implications in terms of the diversity of views that a democracy needs to survive as a democracy. Ben Bagdikian found that 27 corporations controlled most of the American mass media. As he writes: "This is more than an industrial statistic. It goes to the heart of American democracy."[19] Similarly Rohan Samarajiwa notes that:

> Public-information media are said to be organized in the framework of a private marketplace of ideas so that all viewpoints can be expressed without authoritative selection, especially by government. This system is said to ensure the availability of information from diverse and antagonistic sources. But this justification begins to wear dangerously thin when the last vestiges of choice are disappearing from the newspaper field; when the tentacles of massive conglomerates stretch across media boundaries; and when media content is drawn from an increasingly narrower range of sources reflecting a very limited number of viewpoints.[20]

The range of viewpoints is severely restricted as a result of treating culture as a commodity (especially within the newspaper field).

In addition to this, the actual contents of media products is severely effected by their integration into a commodity marketplace. For instance, in television most programs are produced by independent production companies who then sell their product to the networks. The networks recoup their expenses and derive profit by selling audience time to advertisers for spots within these programs. The content of television programs in this context is structured by at least three considerations. First, the program has been able to attract large numbers of people to watch it. It cannot therefore appeal to too narrow of a minority. Second, the program has to attract the "right" kinds of people. Not all parts of the audience are of equal value to the networks. The programming will have to attract those parts of the audience that advertisers wish to reach (such as appealing specifically to teenagers). The content of programs will have to reflect this targeting. Third, the programs not only have to deliver large numbers of the "correct" type of people to advertisers, but they also have to deliver them in the right "frame of mind." Programs should be designed to enhance the effectiveness of the ads that are placed within them. They thus should emphasize the ethic of salvation through consumption and encourage viewers to emulate lifestyles of the wealthy. "Dallas," "Dynasty," and

"Lifestyles of the Rich and Famous" — rather than the culture of and the real problems and issues facing working-class, lower middle-class, and middle-class people (the bulk of the viewing audience) — predominate in broadcasting.

The logic of commodity production in this realm has another strange cultural effect. Todd Gitlin writes that "hits" are so rare in network television (evidenced by the huge turnover of series) that network executives think that "a blatant imitation stands a good chance of getting bigger numbers than a show that stands on its own." This leads to what he calls a "recombinant culture" in which the same old forms are endlessly repackaged in slightly different combinations. The networks are:

> bureaucracies trying to capitalize on and mobilize demonstrable tastes. If the success rates of recombinants are not very good, what routine procedure stands a better chance of fabricating hits with minimum risk of embarrassing flops? Recombination and imitation seem like low-risk ways of getting by . . . The pursuit of safety above all else makes economic sense to the networks, at least in the short run, but success anxiety reduces many a fertile idea to an inert object, which usually also turns out to be a commercial dud. For all the testing and ratings research and all the self-imitative market calculation in the world does not produce that originality or energy that makes for much commercial success, let alone truth, provocation, or beauty.[21]

One aspect of advertising's importance to the cultural realm, then, has to do with advertisers' revenues setting the context within which popular culture production takes place. In addition to this is, of course, the actual presence of the ads themselves within the contents of the media. In general, people turn on their televisions in order to watch programs (fictive stories, documentaries, sports events, news reportage, so on) and editorial commentary. The time that is sold to advertisers, however, is neither program time nor editorial space. It is advertising time and space that is sold to be filled by ads. These ads are a central part of American culture. People talk about them to their fellow workers, children sing their jingles endlessly, feminists complain about them, etc. They are an all pervasive element of modern culture. Often they are much better produced and more creative than the non-advertising content that surrounds them and indeed the advertising industry that creates them has concentrated within itself some of the best artistic talent of our society. But like all cultural products, advertising is constrained within the confines of a commodity system of production. For instance, the movement to shorter and shorter ads has resulted in part from the networks redividing the time available for them to sell advertisers in a new way.[22] Faced with increasing costs for long ads, advertisers adapted to the shorter time-slots by creating a new type of advertising — what is called the "vignette approach" in which product information and "reason why" advertising are foregone in favor of a rapid succession of lifestyle images, meticulously timed with music, that sell feeling and emotion rather than products directly.

Indeed at every stage of the commercialization of a new media form through the nineteenth and twentieth centuries, advertising adapted itself to the changing commodity environment. One of the results of this has been the movement to *imagistic* modes of communication rather than verbal, audio, and textual ones. These images, many of them moving at an incredibly fast speed, are perhaps the most prominent aspect of modern culture. If advertising is a powerful form of social communication in modern society then that influence is strongly mediated through the logic of a commodified cultural production.[23]

The logic of the commodity form of culture is not limited to any one sphere of social life. Once unleashed it can venture anywhere. For instance, the popular music industry is a commodified industry through and through. It produces and sells records, and the survival of musicians and artists is dependent on whether they can produce profit for record companies. This is dependent upon their success within the commodity marketplace, not just on the quality of their performances. Creativity then is constantly being juggled alongside commercialization, of how well one can fit into the existing radio formats that the marketing of records has created. There is nothing unique here as regards a sphere of the culture industry. However in the 1980s the popular music industry has become inextricably linked with the advertising industry through the success of music video as a marketing tool. With the advent of MTV, a music video is indispensable to the success of a record album. Music videos are made by the advertising industry, utilizing techniques derived and learned from the marketing of products. (Through this century, these techniques have developed as a result of the interaction of the advertising industry with commercialized media forms dealing in the sale of audiences.) In many videos there seems to be little link between the music and the visuals. The visuals are chosen because of their proven ability in another realm to *sell*. There seems to some phenomenological evidence that music videos strongly affect the interpretation that is given to the music when heard later without the visuals. The meaning becomes fixed rather than open to interpretation. The realm of *listening* here is subordinated to the realm of *seeing*, to the influence of commercial images. In this sense popular music as a cultural form stands at the intersection of two realms of cultural commodity production that sets the context for the meaning that the audience derives from it. It does not determine it but it sets the limits within which people can dream — a very powerful influence upon culture.[24]

Similarly, professional sports is a cultural industry that has found it impossible to survive without substantial revenues from the media for the rights to televise their games. The sports industry has become dependent upon the media; the media in turn derive their revenues for the purchase of sports broadcast rights from advertisers who wish to reach the audiences that watch sports. Sports leagues then structure themselves and the rules of their sports to be able to offer the best television package. The sale of audience time as a commodity influences what actually gets defined as sports in a more general sense. The other way in which sports can derive additional revenue is to sell themselves directly to advertisers. The 1984 Olympic Games in Los Angeles are the best example of this commercialization taken to extreme lengths. Sports are undoubtedly a very important and powerful cultural force in contemporary America — they give meaning to the lives of many people. That meaning, though, is mediated through the commodity form of culture.[25]

e.g. Rich Stadium - every minute you are bushed with ads (the loudspeaker + scoreboard become media)

Conclusion

Most critical discussions of the political economy of culture have taken as their starting point Marx's famous comment that:

> The ideas of the ruling class are in every epoch the ruling ideas, i.e. the class which is the ruling *material* force of society, is at the same time its ruling *intellectual* force. The class which has the means of material production at its disposal, has control at the same time over the means of mental production, so that thereby, generally speaking, the ideas of those who lack the means of mental production are subject to it.[26]

The vital issues concern how this control is established. How exactly does a ruling class establish control of the cultural realm? In this paper I have pointed to the major ways in which culture can be materially organized. Nicholas Garnham summarizes the options that are open in a capitalist society. He writes:

> Under developing capitalism the means of cultural production may be provided either in commodity form as part of the accumulation process, e.g. records, or as part of the realization process of other sectors of the capitalist economy, e.g. advertising, or directly out of capitalist revenue, e.g. arts patronage . . . or through the State.[27]

In the United States the major means of control have been organized around the first two options laid out by Garnham: producing culture directly as a commodity and through advertising support. Within this, also, there is a tendency towards relying more and more on advertising revenues. The third option, support through the State, has rarely been exercised, as it has in other countries. What then are the implications of treating culture as a commodity? To answer that we need to ask questions about the nature of commodities in general, and to understand their constitutive features as commodities.

All commodities have two fundamental features: they have an _exchange-value_ (that is, they are worth something and can be exchanged in the marketplace) and they have a _use-value_ (that is, they do something that makes them useful to human beings). What is the use-value of a cultural commodity? Its function, and its importance, stems from the _meaning_ that it generates. Records, films, newspapers, paintings, etc. provide meaning for their consumers. If a cultural commodity did not provide this then it would not be capable of being sold. People buy things for their use-value. Cultural commodities also have an exchange-value within the sphere of the marketplace — that is how profit is generated by the producers of the cultural commodities. The question is what is the _relationship_ between the use-value of a commodity and its exchange-value. Are they of equal importance or is one more important than the other? Within a capitalist economy there is always an unequal balance between the twin features of the commodity in that exchange-value subordinates use-value. Producers of commodities are primarily concerned with the exchange-value of a product. The owner of a factory that makes tables and chairs does not produce them to use them, but produces them to sell them. If they cannot be sold, then they will not be produced. The use-values of things are effected by the dictates of exchange-value. This effects their use-value. Compare hand-crafted tables with mass-produced factory ones.

The same is true in the realm of commodity culture. The system of exchange-value (worth) subordinates use-value (meaning). Television programs look like they do, not because this is the best that the American artistic community can come up with, but because programs have a role to play in the production and exchange of audiences. The exchange side dominates the use side. It does not determine in a one-dimensional way, but it sets the context within which television programs are produced. If you change the context, you change the nature of the programs. The BBC in Britain is a good example of what another context will produce.

Within the United States there has never been any questioning of the domination of use-value by exchange-value. Unlike most other western industrial democracies, there is no developed American debate concerning cultural policy. Indeed, the very term "cultural policy" seems an anathema within an American context. (Compare this to the very developed and complex debate about culture that exists in Canada and France.) The rules of the marketplace have been accepted unquestioningly as also the rules of cultural activity. This should not be too surprising given that it is these very assumptions that are enshrined in the First Amendment. As we have seen, government is not the only enemy of freedom. The marketplace can work through different means towards the same ends. In the United States we call government interference domination, and marketplace governance freedom. We should recognize that the marketplace does not automatically ensure diversity, but that (as in the example of the United States) the marketplace can also act as a serious constraint to freedom. While I have concentrated on the material organization of culture, it is important to stress that all such formations are built upon a specific ideological understanding that accepts culture as an industrial issue. Capital is not powerful in and of itself. It requires the appropriate ideological context. It is only this conception of culture that makes possible the kind of political economy I have described.

These are not simply academic questions, nor do they deal with a realm that is static. More and more areas are being drawn into the sphere of domination by exchange-value so that the cultural realm (where healthy societies think about their past, present, and future) becomes more and more intertwined with narrow economic concerns. Capitalist interests are moving forcefully into the one area of society where there may still exist alternate social visions — a process of increasing colonization and control. As Garnham notes, to understand the structure of our culture, to construct the first stages of an alternative cultural politics, we urgently need to confront these central questions.

[Handwritten margin note beside paragraph: FTA / Canada]

[Handwritten note at bottom of page: Positive freedom v. negative freedom. (there is a profound difference) regarding this subject]

6.

Advertising and the Development of Consumer Society

Stuart Ewen

This essay examines an important type of modern, urban-industrial imagery: advertising. Advertising plays a conspicuous and powerful role in people's lives. Wherever one looks — in the street, in our homes, in theatres — it is there, promoting goods and services, anything that can be sold. Advertising pushes a vision of life which says that satisfaction is available across the retail countertop.

According to the logic of advertising, people are what they own. One's quality as a person is directly proportional to one's ability to buy. In the United States, as in other modern industrial societies, this message is continually reinforced across a broad, seemingly endless, imagistic panorama.

Some products are presented as the symbols by which people achieve financial, professional, or personal power over others: the equation for *success*. Other ads encourage people to focus negatively upon their bodies — every pore, every orifice, every surface, every imperfection — with the promise that if people use *this* or *that* product they will be *improved*. In the visionary world of advertising we see people undergoing magical metamorphoses, transcending their innate limits and achieving projected ideals of femininity, of masculinity, of power, and of pleasure. Some ads promise to carry people forward into some utopian future; others offer a return to a simpler, more pacific past (to the historic campfires of a mythic "old west," to the days of chivalry, away from the ennui of the present). Some ads offer the promise of individuality in a society where conformity and monotony often seem to be the norm. Others offer visions of community in a world where loneliness is often the experience.

82

These kind of images and promises are things that we, in the United States, are used to. On television and radio, in print media and on billboards, the consumable life, the buyable fantasy, continually bombards us. Even if we tend to resist a particular message or promise, everywhere the general message is repeated, inescapable.

We must ask many questions of advertising in order to understand its significance and its roots within our lives. Yet in approaching the phenomenon of advertising imagery we must also be cautious. We are dealing with mesmerizing artifacts and can easily be misled. Within the framework of this essay, therefore, it is necessary to approach the development of advertising as an aspect of the general social history of industrial capitalism and urbanization in twentieth-century American life.

Two pitfalls must be avoided. Most media histories let images speak for themselves. They treat images as if they have the ability to tell their own history, apart from society, apart from the real lives of the people with whom they are engaged. Ultimately their historical approach to advertising amounts to little more than mere chronologies. Their underlying assumption is that ads have a self-enclosed cosmology, not directly engaged with the experience of real people.

The second pitfall to avoid is a particular widely held American perception of *the city*. In the United States, the term "melting pot" has long served as a metaphor for American urban life. Under the rubric of this metaphor lies a particular way of seeing the city: that the social history of American cities has consisted of swallowing up and transforming a continual influx of immigrants and migrants. The outcome of this process is a product: "American." While there is certainly truth to the notion that America has transformed people's lives, it is also necessary to see that people — their experiences, their roots, their concerns, their desires — have also shaped the environment they have entered. Urban imagery — advertising — bears the imprint of the lives of the people that they address. To approach an understanding of urban, commercial imagery, images must be seen as engaged in a social-historical process, responsible to the changing terms of social life, of social institutions. Thus, advertising images, though they lay claim to an enormous sweep of vision, must be placed upon the social and political battleground they often intend to mask.

What is this battleground, this social context? The development of the city, of urban life, provides some important clues. If we look across the historical tableau of the past eighty years of urban existence, there is a recurrent lament which deserves attention. Its voice is often romantic, but its troubled content rings true. Three examples, drawn from across the past century, provide a starting place.

The first voice is that of the German sociologist Georg Simmel, who around 1900 expressed some provocative thoughts on the psychological experience of modern, metropolitan life. Writing on "the metropolis and mental life," and noting the potent role of imagery within the city, Simmel observed:

> The psychological basis of the metropolitan type of individuality consists in the *intensification of nervous stimulation* which results from the swift and uninterrupted change of outer and inner stimuli . . . . Lasting impressions which differ only slightly from one another, impressions which take a regular and habitual course and show regular and habitual contrasts — all these use up, so to speak, less consciousness than does the rapid crowding of changing images, the sharp discontinuity in the grasp of a single glance, and the unexpectedness of onrushing impressions. These are the psychological conditions which the metropolis creates.[1]

Within his vision of the city and its images, Simmel sensed a population ripped from its traditional conventions of perception, unbalanced and unhinged.

Some thirty years later, the Chicago sociologist, Robert Park, expressed similar concerns as he evaluated the legacy of urbanization upon the millions who had migrated from around the world to American cities during the early decades of this century. "(T)he 'cake of custom' is broken," he began, "and the individual is freed for new enterprises and for new associations." Yet lurking within this context of opportunity, there was cause for concern:

> One of the consequences of migration is to create a situation in which the same individual . . . . finds himself striving to live in two diverse cultural groups. The effect is to produce an unstable character . . . . This is the "marginal man." It is in the mind of the marginal man that conflicting cultures meet and fuse. It is, therefore, in the mind of the marginal man that the process of civilization is visibly going on, and it is in the mind of the marginal man that the processes of civilization may best be studied.[2]

Park's urbanite, like Simmel's, is plagued by confusion, caught within a disparity of meanings and understandings. Cultural dislocation, for both, is the central experience of urbanization and modernity. Within the shadows of progress stands the culturally eviscerated individual. Since Park made his observations of 1928, the problem has not gone away. For some, it has become epidemic.

Louis Sass, a psychologist and professor at Holy Cross College, has described similar conditions not just among recent arrivals to the metropolis, but also among their progeny over generations. Writing in the Sunday New York *Times Magazine* recently, Sass noted that:

> . . . . (M)any mental-health professionals believe that we live in an era of borderline pathology. Just as the hysterical neurotic of Freud's time — plagued by conflicts of conscience and desire — exemplified the repressive Western culture at the turn of the century, so certain disturbances in an individual's sense of identity and difficulties in maintaining stable human relationships — characteristics attributed to the borderline personality — may reflect the fragmentation of contemporary society.[3]

What do we see in these examples of this recurrent lament, and what is its relation to our understanding of advertising? First, and very simply, we see a continuum of urban life which, aside from its various benefits, has been marked by social fragmentation and alienation. Without question, many of the messages of American advertising have addressed these problems within their formulae for success or transcendence. According to many advertisements, a sense of balance and belonging, of connectedness and peace of mind, lies at the far end of a purchase.

A second thing worth noting about the three quotes is their language. While each writer speaks of social conditions, their description is decidely psychological. Their discourse is a product of that which they are describing: a fissure between the material conditions of existence and the psychological modes of understanding that existence. This magnification of the individual psyche, a hallmark of modern life, is likewise addressed by advertising. Consumption, it might be argued, is the most widely available mode of psychotherapy. Advertising speaks to emotional hungers, presents its commodities as emotional nourishments. In America it is a cliche to say that the best way to deal with being depressed is to go shopping.

Something which is not directly confronted in these quotes is the way in which these emotional hungers are expressions of disruptions within the material conditions of existence, characteristic disruptions of the urban-industrial milieu. The person who is buffeted by "the unexpectedness of onrushing impressions," the "marginal man," the "borderline personality," is also someone who has experienced a transformation within the terms of survival. This transformation may include a process of proletarianization, one within which an agricultural or artisanal pattern of work has been eclipsed by new forms of labor and new rhythms of production: industrial, regimented, bureaucratic. Another aspect of this transformation has been the rise of consumerism as a social relationship, a mode of daily life. If, in the past, people provided for many of their needs directly and collectively, the modern person lives by wages; needs are increasingly embroiled in a choreography of individual purchases and abstract exchange.

If traditional culture was *dependent* upon bonds of family and community, consumer culture makes many of these bonds ceremonial. In the city, more and more of our interactions are interactions with strangers. Cooperation, insofar as it is fostered in the contemporary world, takes place under the hegemonic rubric of the corporation. Within this changed environment of social connections, many of the bonds between people have been increasingly eroded, made fragile; according to the dominant structures of society, they are defined as "unnecessary." People long for community and for self-determination, but in the modern corporate-industrial world, these are elusive, romanticized memory fragments.

Here, too, advertising figures heavily. It historically addressess the transfiguration of survival. It provides a social commentary, a sympathetic voice, *even a critique*, of the very historical conditions of which it is an inextricable part. While reinforcing the priorities of corporate production and marketing, advertising offers a symbolic empathy to its audience, criticizing alienation and offering transcendent alternatives. Needless to say, these "alternatives" are contained, religiously, within the cosmology of the marketplace.

If urban-industrial life has given rise to a critique of alienation, much corporate advertising can be understood as an attempt to appropriate and channel that critique. A good example of this can be seen in a current advertising campaign being waged by IBM to sell small computers. The ads — both print and broadcast — use the likeness of Charlie Chaplin, and make reference to his scathing film comedy about industrial capitalism, "Modern Times" (1936).

"Modern Times" is a masterful critique of an increasingly regimented industrial society, a bitter and poetic examination of modern life and alienation. In Chaplin's film we confront a factory world which increasingly usurps human initiative; in the factory people lie beneath the thumb of productivity, their bodies and souls shaped and overwhelmed by an assembly line. The priorities of such a world submerge human needs and misery abounds. People are seen as useful only if they can be plugged into the productive apparatus. Otherwise, they are tossed aside, like garbage.

Another theme of the film is the relationship between media and power within the industrial world. Those in authority, those with their hands on the controls, utilize the media of communication to exercise their power. Those who labor, poor folks, remain — within the firm — voiceless.

Yet alongside this grim vision of industrial encroachment, Chaplin's "Modern Times" is also utopian, visionary. Against the robotic rhythms of factory life, it calls for poetry, action, resistance. It offers a critique of work itself, suggesting that pleasure is a more meaningful *telos* for human life. Against the monotony of a mechanical civilization, Chaplin evinces a politics of spontaneity, a manifesto for sensuality and positive disorder. At the film's end, Chaplin — a former factory worker — and his beloved "gamin," take to the road. They walk away from the strictures and disciplines of industrial society.

Today, Charlie Chaplin and "Modern Times" have returned to the public eye. In this incarnation, however, the little tramp is selling computers for IBM. In the IBM ad we once again confront Chaplin as a victim of industrial chaos, overwhelmed by the assembly line. But this time, the solution is different. Beleaguered Charlie is saved by the computer, the quintessential modern instrument of order and control. Here the frenetic conditions of modern life are solved by modern technology. While the film pointed a *way out*, the ad points a *way back in*. The critique has been turned on its head, contained and used against itself. Rather than questioning modern life and work, the ad instructs us into an acceptance of that life.

There are three important aspects of the Chaplin/IBM ads worth mentioning. First, these ads reflect and reinforce the contemporary conditions of labor, the work process, structures of technology. Second, the ads are responsive to the social terms of modern life; they reflect a sense of a world "out of control." Last, the ads offer a symbolic empathy with the critique of alienation and with visions of transcendence through the appropriation of the familiar image of "the little tramp." These three aspects, evident in the IBM ads, are basic components of advertising, and have historically emerged as essential parts within the American urban-commercial vernacular.

The historical development of advertising in the United States, from the late-nineteenth century onward, helps us to understand the contours of an emerging commercial vernacular imagery. By the late-nineteenth century advertising imagery had already developed two important and powerful capacities.

First, advertising made use of techniques which promoted a democratic sensibility. A technique used by more and more advertisers in the late 1800s was chromolithography — color printing which produced lustrous and sumptous results cheaply. Advertising cards, selling everything from patent medicines to farm machinery, were mass produced and distributed throughout the county. If traditional culture defined a world where only the wealthy had access to beautiful color pictures — oil paintings — the proliferation of advertising images put, for the first time, colorful works of art in the hands of the masses. While selling their products, advertisers were also providing people with appealing decorations for their homes, decorations formerly unavailable. Today color lithography is everywhere and appears pedestrian, yet to its first recipients it bore tremendous symbolic power. "Chromos" broke the monopoly over art which was formerly a privilege of wealth. In addition to selling goods, color advertisements offered material evidence of democratic social change. The appeal of advertising, then, was partly rooted in its apparent ability to fulfil ancient utopian desires. It made the symbolic accoutrements of wealth available to everyone, free of charge. For people schooled by an historic scarcity of images, the appearance of chromolithography seemed revolutionary. It portended, one might have surmised, a "world turned upside-down." This can be seen in the words of the great black abolitionist — a former slave — Frederick Douglass. He saw chromolithographs as part of the exodus from slavery to freedom. Speaking particularly of the availability of "chromos" to black Americans, Douglass placed these bright images against the grim backdrop of a recently abolished slavery:

> Heretofore, colored Americans have thought little of adorning their parlors with pictures . . . . Pictures come not with slavery and oppression and destitution, but with liberty, fair play, leisure, and refinement. These conditions are now possible to colored American citizens, and I think the walls of their houses will soon begin to bear evidence of their altered relations to the people about them.[4]

Beyond embodying democratic change, advertising was also a mobile form of imagery; it could reach out to an audience. Printed and dispersed widely in the latter decades of the nineteenth century, advertisements provided a vehicle by which urban life could be presented to the countryside — urban industrial values promulgated among rural folks. A notable example of this was the massive distribution of the Sears-Roebuck Catalogue among American farmers from the 1890s on. Based in Chicago, Sears was a mail-order firm dealing with a primarily rural clientele. For many in the countryside, the advertisements in the Sears catalogue provided a first glimpse of the city. Upon the crowded, densely printed pages of the catalogue — dubbed "America's Wish Book" — rural people saw configurations which contrasted sharply with the open spaces with which they were familiar. Here urban density was depicted not as a condition of poverty and squalor, but as a site of abundance. Against rural traditions of scarcity and self-sufficiency, advertising — like that of the Sears catalogue — projected urban consumption as a route toward cornucopian existence. On each page of the catalogue, people confronted a quantity and variety of material goods that was previously unimaginable. Advertising was a kind of urban map, suggesting a world of streets paved with gold. Beyond its democratic implications, advertising beckoned towards a new way of life.

By the 1920s, in the United States, a national advertising industry was taking hold — an offshoot of mass production consumer goods industries and their continual need for ever-growing markets. Within the nascent advertising industry, a tradition of commercial social thought began to emerge. If modern, urban life generated a population of "marginal" men, advertising spoke to the vacuums within their lives. Advertising sought to reform people's perceptions, to create markets and sell people a new way of life. Within the ads of 1920s the selling of products was increasingly linked to an ongoing commentary on the terms of modern existence. Ads spoke less and less about the quality of the products being sold and more and more about the lives of the people being addressed.

Behind these new images lay the emerging ideas of businessmen interested in establishing a consumption-based cultural stability among a population in crisis. Advertising was seen as a way of habituating people to the terms of the marketplace. Edward A. Filene, a Boston department store magnate, and an early ideologue of mass consumer- ism, put it simply:

> Mass production demands the education of the masses. The masses must learn to behave like human beings in a mass production world . . . .
>
> The time has come . . . when all our institutions . . . must concentrate on the great social task of teaching the masses not what to think but HOW TO THINK, and thus to find out how to behave like human beings in the machine age.[5]

Within Filene's vision of education, the priorities of marketing were a motor force, advertising was an essential teaching tool.

Since the American population of the 1920s was more than half immigrant, or the children of immigrants, the question of educating the masses took on a patriotic flavor. The transformation of heterogeneous communities into a coherent national market was often described in political language. Frances Alice Kellor, an advertising woman who placed ads in the foreign language press, saw advertising as a crucial device of social integration. Speaking to businessmen, Kellor argued that advertising was an imperative of the moment — a way of stabilizing a vast and potentially dangerous immigrant work force:

> National advertising is the great Americanizer. American ideals and institutions, law, order, and prosperity, have not yet been sold to all our immigrants. American products and standards of living have not yet been bought by the foreign born in America . . . . If Americans want to combine business and patriotism, they should advertise products, industry and American institutions in the American Foreign Language press.[6]

Once again, the general priority of market development was fused to notions of social order and the obliteration of customary culture. A population of consumers had to be divorced from those memories and perceptions rooted in older ways of life.

By the late 1920s this thrust towards consumerizing the population took on an evangelical fervour. The physics of modern life was underwritten by a religious faith. This faith can be heard in the words of Christine Frederick, an advisor to businessmen, and a leader in the home economic movement:

> Consumptionism is the name given to the new doctrine; and it is admitted today to be the greatest idea that America has to give to the world; the idea that workmen and masses be looked upon not simply as workers and producers but as consumers.

Addressing a business audience, she elucidated a formula for the future of consumer capitalism: "Pay them more, sell them more, prosper more is the equation."[7]

The translation of this formula into a social strategy can be seen in the advertisements that were produced from the 1920s onwards. Advertising addressed the conditions of urban, industrial life, and expressed a sensitivity to popular discontents. Simultaneously ads offered solutions embedded in the new universe of consumer goods, a universe which reinforced patterns of life and work demanded by an industrial society.

While advertising addressed the modern stress of work, it also shied away from depicting the factory *per se*. Factory life was a widely experienced arena of boredom and disaffection, but advertisers did their best to dissociate their products from their sources. The separation of product from factory has become an earmark of modern advertising; if we hear anything about the origins of goods, it is most likely fanciful. One American baking company claims that its cookies are baked by "little elves in hollow trees." Generally, ads follows the dictum laid out by copywriter Helen Woodward in 1929:

If you are advertising any product, never see the factory in which it was made . . . Don't watch the people at work . . . Because, you see, when you know the truth about anything, the real inner truth — it is hard to write the surface fluff which sells it.[8]

Yet despite this tendency towards mystification, much advertising, from the 1920s on, has — at least subliminally — reinforced the modern imperatives of factory work and mechanized labor. One example appeared in a poster ad for soap in the early 1920s:

A *Clean* Machine Runs Better.
Your Body is a Machine.
KEEP IT CLEAN.

Along with selling soap, the ad was selling a perception of humanity that fit the new dictates of scientific management. Factory management tended to view labor as an abstract, measurable commodity. In the name of efficiency, managers from the turn of the century studied human motion as a mechanical process, encouraging workers to conform to the most methodical fusions of time, motion, and profitability. Textbooks on scientific management were filled with vast amounts of anthropometric data, all of which envisioned the worker as a machine, to be managed and controlled. This ad for cleanliness, for soap, conformed to such a vision.

Another aspect of modern work was the replacement of artisanal skills by the monotony of machine production. Deskilling of labor was part and parcel of factory work and the assembly line. If one's value in the old world was drawn from one's accumulated skill and know-how, the modern modes of production placed little emphasis on skill. Obedience and appearance became, more and more, the categories of success on the job. Numerous ads reinforced, mediated this transformation. One such ad, also for soap, depicted a number of men and women sitting in an employment office, waiting for job interviews. At the top of the page, the question: "Which two would *you* hire?" As we look at the people we see a small notation above each head. One woman, applying make-up, has the word "experienced" above her. Others are without experience. The two for whom the jobs are obviously meant sit placidly waiting. Above their heads, the words: "experienced *and clean*." In a world where skill meant less and less, things like cleanliness were magnified in importance. Soap was more than a matter of good hygiene, it was an essential category of employment. So, too, was the passive posture assumed by the two "lucky" ones.

This instruction of people into the modern terms of work continues today in advertising. We have seen it in the person of Charlie Chaplin, *saved* by the computer. Another, ad appearing in magazines throughout the latter half of 1982, was for the "Rush-Hour Clock," a clock to hang up in the bathroom which was resistant to moisture and fogging. Here a product is offered which will organize life from the moment we get up. Bodily functions will be atuned to the timeclock. If early morning eyes are still groggy, the face of the clock will remain bright and clear. Illustrating the ad is a series of images of people rushing to work. The images, multiple, time-lapse photographs, are very much like the time-motion photographs that were taken of workers to amass anthropometric data. The "Rush-Hour Clock" expands the work-day to encompass the moment of rising.

Another aspect of modern life, addressed by advertising, was the breakdown of traditional social bonds. The city was a world of strangers, and advertising from the 1920s onward, offered instructions on how to negotiate such a world. Basic within this development was the notion that if other people appear to each of us as *distant others*, then we must begin to see ourselves as *distant others* as well. After all, in a world of strangers *everyone* is a stranger. The reinforcement of self-alienation was presented as a survival skill. People were encouraged to view themselves as continually under scrutiny and critical judgment. At the heart of this lay a paranoia about the human body itself. One's body, it was argued, was a decided liability. Odor, appearance, surfaces became fixations. One ad (1933) for Odo-ro-no deodorant, depicted a woman in her home after a day at work. She holds her dress to her nose, and her face reveals an extraordinary displeasure. "Is this the way I smell to others?" she asks. Should the graphic drama not be enough, readers of the ad are encouraged to perform the "arm-hole odor test" upon their own garments. Against this backdrop of self-vilification, there was hope, however; a product, a purchase which would mask the body, make the self more viable. Within the logic of the ad, a viable self was one defined by commodities, a commodity-self. In a world of quick judgments and momentary glances, such solutions made sense.

One of the social bonds which has suffered most in the context of urban industrialism is the family. Kinship was rooted in a pre-industrial past, underscored by the framework of a common culture. The home had been a center not merely of family life, but of production. Within the urban-industrial context, this center began to erode. Production gravitated towards factories; family members were drawn, often individually, to the wage system. While the patriarchal family continued as an ideal, it was an ideal increasingly undermined by the structures of the society that surrounded it. The family in jeopardy or tatters has become a meaningful cliche of modern life. Divorce rates climb; aging parents are tossed into the dust-bin; independent youth, responsible only to itself, permeates the cultural climate.

Advertising has engaged this process from all sides. At the same time that it has been a vehicle for narcissism and individualistic consumption, much advertising has evinced a concern for family life. Many products today offer themselves as the cement by which happy family or group bonds will be achieved. Other advertising has noted the decay of mutual dependency with some concern, offering its product as a surrogate, a life preserver. An example of this latter configuration can be seen in an advertising campaign waged in the 1920s by the Prudential Life Insurance Company.

It should be said, at the outset, that the very existence of Life Insurance is testimony to the breakdown of the customary bonds of family and community. Until this century if a parent died, for example, it was understood that care for children would be passed on to others in the family or community. Bonds of mutual obligation were common understandings of life. Even the first forms of insurance were products of mutuality, instituted by fraternal organizations or cooperative associations. Life Insurance, as a corporate-financial enterprise, is rooted in the dissolution of customary networks of support.

If we look at the Prudential advertising, as it emerged in the 1920s, we see that this dissolution had become the raw material for a marketing strategy. The ads to be described appeared in magazines, separate from one another. Yet viewed together they constitute a moral tale, a narrative, a social cosmology of power. They convey the social logic of a corporate society.

The first ad depicts a man leaving a doctor's office. The picture is a close-up, and his face is clearly worried. We share his intimate emotions of fear, guilt, and despair. The caption reads, "Sick! and I let my Life Insurance Lapse." He is afflicted by some mysterious and terminal illness, and as the traditional bearer of family survival, he has failed.

In another ad we see two children standing at the gates of an orphan asylum. One of the asylum matrons whispers to another, "They said father didn't keep his Life Insurance paid up." In another ad, an older son is standing on a corner, in tattered clothes, selling newspapers in the snow. His father failed to make the essential purchase. Now he stands, alone and destitute. Another ad depicts a mother toiling in a sweat shop, her "needle-scarred fingers" grasping nothing but poverty and hopelessness. Here, once again — we are informed — a husband has "failed in his imperative duty" to buy Prudential Life Insurance. Family breakdown and suffering have been the fruits of his failure.

A last ad stands in stark contrast to the others. It is a magnificent view of the Rock of Gibraltar, the corporate logo of Prudential. Here there is no misery, no weakness, only solidity. The caption reads: "Prudential has the strength of Gibraltar."

While these ads speak, ostensibly, on behalf of the family, they depict a family structure which has been gravely wounded. The father, while symbolically dependent upon his family, is in reality weakened and undependable. Within the modern world, as depicted by the Prudential ads, it is the corporation which has inherited the mantle of responsibility. The father is a vanishing species, while the corporation stands like a rock against the turbulent seas.

Within a context where, as Edward Filene observed, "the head of the family is no longer in control of the economic process through which the family must get its living," the maxims of patriarchal authority had little grounding.[9] While paying lip-service to the conventions of family life, advertising also played the midwife for a new structure, one in which the corporation alone stood upon a firm social bedrock. Beyond selling insurance or other products, advertising offered an imagistic reconciliation between the terms of a modern urban world, and a population which stood — "marginal" and "borderline" — within that world.

If advertising provided a mediation for the new, often disconcerting situations of modern life and work, much of it also acknowledged the sense of alienation and fragmentation endemic to industrial existence. Alongside its reinforcement of corporate priorities, advertising claimed to offer a way out of the industrial malaise. While legitimizing the logic of consumer capitalism, advertising also provided a vision of utopian alternatives. A 1920s ad for Alpine Sun Lamps provides a provocative example.

There are two illustrations to the ad. In the upper right-hand corner there is an etching of a woman: nude, arms outstretched, facing into the sun. The main illustration (at the center of the ad) shows a woman lounging on the edge of her bathtub, rope open, her nakedness revealed, fondled and nurtured by the "vitally interesting message" of her Alpine Sun Lamp. The text of the ad reads as follows:

> If you were free to live . . . . Were you today to throw off the restraints of social conformity . . . would you, too, first satisfy that inborn craving for Ultraviolet? Would you discard the trappings of civilization to spend strenuous health-brimmed days in the beneficent sunlight?
>
> For most convention-ridden people such action is denied. But the vital

> Ultraviolet portion of the sunlight can be brought right into the home by means of the justly famous *Alpine Sun Lamp*.[10]

The realities of urban industrialism raised issues of health, fresh air, and inadequate space. Such critiques were not generated by the desire for sun lamps, but rather by more general and fundamental realities of the industrial context. Here in the Alpine ad, however, the critique reappears, along with a Freudian appeal to pre-civilized urges, yet safely confined within the logical boundaries of the marketing process. Advertising today, whether it sells cars as dream machines for country jaunts or "natural" cereals as a means for transcending the admitted evils of chemically fortified supermarket fare, maintains the same logic — the sense that a product contains the negation of its own corporate origins.

In a century where political, social, and sensual realms have been shaken by revolutionary resistance, "mass culture" is a symbolic acquiescence, by capitalism, to the challenges of its critics. Western civilization in general and capitalist society in particular have maintained their hold on the political and social frontiers of freedom, yet alongside these restrictions advertising has often offered an "escape" from the rules of order. It is not uncommon for advertising to depict an exchange process which, despite its concrete limitations, contains the mortar of gratification. The linking of the marketplace to utopian ideals — community, sensuality, peace of mind, self-determination — represents the spectacle of liberation emanating from the experience of domination, discontinuity, and — for many — denial.

Ultimately, the meaning of advertising must be judged against the backdrop of the world it inhabits. Viewed historically, advertising has offered a mediation of contemporary life; it both transmits the priorities of a corporate consumer economy and speaks to the emptiness and frustration so often felt within that very context.

In a sense, advertising may be seen as capitalism's response to observations raised over the past century by Simmel, Park, Sass, and others. Yet if it is a response, it also tends to reproduce the very terms which they describe. Looking at the world according to advertising, then looking at our own lives, the fissure between appearance and reality is so great that perpetual disorientation may be its most significant product.

7.

Circumscribing Postmodern Culture

Ian H. Angus

"Don't start from the good old things, but the bad new ones."

Bertolt Brecht

Modernity can be defined as the domination of nature in order to produce a wealth of commodities which are intended to sustain a community of mutually recognizing free and equal subjects. Postmodern culture consists not in discarding this project, but in its infinite delay. The apogee of the modern project — the simulation of identities in a consumer society, combined with the permanent threat of an external enemy — short-circuits the mutual recognition of autonomous subjects. The accumulation of greater and greater "means" to the modern goal of security and mutual recognition permanently delays arrival at the end. The end remains as the motive for perpetuation of the means, which in turn delays the end — a vicious dialectic without hope of resolution. The present essay circumscribes the phenomenon of postmodern culture in the complementary figures of simulated identity and the enemy — the self as other and the other as threat.

Identities in Consumption

Walter Benjamin's essay "The Work of Art in the Age of Mechanical Reproduction" (1936) has become, with good reason, an essential reference point for subsequent discussions of mass culture and the industrial production of identity. In it, Benjamin argued that the specific difference between traditional artworks and mechanically reproduced cultural products is the loss of an "aura"; it is this "aura" that attaches to originals and unifies the historical process of reception. Originals radiate an authenticity, an aura, stemming from the origin of art in mythic cult. Aura is a "unique phenomenon of a distance, however close it may be" which is the basis for the empathy of the traditional aesthetic subject with the artwork. The mechanically reproduced artwork put "the public in the place of the critic." Nevertheless, this position is "absent-minded" and requires no attention, it is "consummated by a collectivity in a state of distraction." In traditional aesthetics, the consequences for the audience are derived from the artworks themselves. In contrast, in conditions of mechanical reproduction, reception must be directly theorized — which dovetails with the Marxist stress on the historical and class formation of the audience.

With this convergence of the social and aesthetic dimensions of the artwork, we have the beginning of cultural criticism as the analysis of the formation of (social and individual) subjectivity through the production of meaningful objects. Loss of aura due to mechanization accounted, for Benjamin, for the democratic potential of contemporary politicized art to reverse the entire historical division of labor originating in the mythological power of the shaman. This positive potential is in tension with the other main tendency of mechanical culture — the "aesthetization of politics," regarding politics as a spectator sport for the viewer's pleasure which, Benjamin warned, can lead to war and the fascist manipulation of masses. The cultural object has lost its distance from the viewer and functions directly as a constituent of identity.[1]

For Theodor Adorno, Benjamin erred in describing this momentous cultural shift solely in the mechanical apparatus. Rather, it was the development of the apparatus under the conditions of commodity production that gave rise to the contemporary tension. Aura has not been replaced, but rather shifted to a new mythology produced by the capitalist commodification of culture. Thus, the diagnosis of mass culture was extended from direct fascist manipulation to the generalized and anonymous subjugation of individuals by the cultural apparatus of industrial production for exchange.

> Hence the style of the culture industry, which no longer has to test itself against any refractory material, is also the negation of style. The reconciliation of the general and the particular, of the rule and the specific demands of the subject matter, the achievement of which alone gives essential, meaningful content to style, is futile because there has ceased to be the slightest tension between opposite poles: these concordant extremes are dismally identical; the general can replace the particular, and vice versa.[2]

Industrial homogenization of culture reduces the transcendent experiences of traditional art within a totalizing framework that traps the audience into a "repetition" of experiences and thereby blocks their assimilation and criticism. Adorno proposes a "modernist" defense of avant-garde art as the marginalized site of individual opposition to mass culture. Through its individual "style" avant-garde artworks generate a tension between particular and universal. The methods of transgression and shock transfer this tension to the viewer who can then experience the lack of fit between his or her individual needs and experiences and the total structure of society. Thus the possibility of social criticism is retained.

Film is the litmus test of mass culture, where the total externalization of culture is an index of one's response to the interplay of technology and commodity production. For Adorno film simply repeats psychological mechanisms without leaving any room for distance and critique. While Benjamin saw a tension between the politicizing and aestheticizing tendencies of each medium, due to his emphasis on the technological components of this cultural shift, Adorno situated these tendencies within the commodity-structure of the society as a whole, and thereby circumscribed the possibilities of identity-formation with the polarity of mass culture and the avant-garde. The debate here revolved around the relationship between technology and the commodity-form. Benjamin regarded the technology of mechanical reproduction as tending toward "critical collective abstractedness," though it could be offset by direct fascist manipulation of technology and the masses. For Adorno, the issue is not direct manipulation but production of cultural goods for exchange, which issues in indirect manipulation through the elimination of style. The tendency of technique (if it could be liberated from the commodity form), on the other hand, is toward the expression of the state of freedom in art; but this requires the sophisticated audience of avant-garde works which perceives the *structure* of the works, and is not just affected by them. What is fundamentally at issue between Benjamin and Adorno is the extent to which the new possibilities brought forth by mechanical reproduction tend to become democratized through the mass audience, as Benjamin suggested, or whether they are marginalized by capitalist production processes which also create a "regression" in the perception of the audience.[3] For both it is the "loss of distance" that constitutes mass culture, though the potential of this for a critical audience is analyzed differently.

From the present perspective it is more enlightening, rather than entering this debate directly, to take note of the axes around which it is conducted. It may be that mass culture has passed beyond the initial stage analyzed by Benjamin and Adorno. The following discussion makes two observations — the first concerning technology and the second commodity production — that suggest that this debate must be reformulated to account for a new postmodern stage of mass culture. While the Benjamin/Adorno formulation applies to the *decline* of aura due to the homogenizing effect of introducing industrial production methods into culture, it does not adequately capture the *simulation* of authenticity in fully industrialized cultural production.

Benjamin did not distinguish clearly between the mechanical reproduction of previous artworks, such as the Mona Lisa, and the industrial production of cultural objects itself — which began with photography and now extends through electronic media of communication to permeate the whole of contemporary consciousness and identity-formation. Mechanical *reproduction* is not the same as technical *production*. Where he does note this distinction, it is in order to suggest it is a question of "greater degree," rather than a qualitative difference.

> To an even greater degree the work of art reproduced becomes the work of art designed for reproducibility. From a photographic negative, for example, one can make any number of prints; to ask for the "authentic" print makes no sense. But from the instant the criterion of authenticity ceases to be applicable to artistic production, the total function of art is reversed. Instead of being based on ritual, it begins to be based on another practice — politics.[4]

The primacy of politics indicates that the audience's relation to the artwork has become fully conscious and rational. However, when the cultural world is completely pervaded by "copies" without "originals," it is impossible to regard them as "copies" any longer. We are faced simply with a plurality of images that are not simply identical but refer to each other. The many images of Mickey Mouse refer to each other, but we will not find the original at Disneyland, or at Disneyworld either. Even in the case of a supposed "original," the self-referring set of images precedes it. We recognize the Statue of Liberty because many images of it already pervade our cultural world. The experience of "originality" here has not declined, as Benjamin suggested, but is *simulated*. We can describe this new postmodern experience of culture as follows: Circulation of a self-referring set of images constructs a cultural meaning, such as "liberty" or "Mickey Mouse-ness." We recognize and express our subjectivity as individuals and as groups through our relations to these image-sets. Of course, there are a lot of these. Especially in a consumer-oriented capitalist society, there are new image-sets continually becoming available. Thus, social differentiation within postmodern culture consists in different relations to this plurality of available image-sets. Each such image-set *postulates* an original, an authentic experience, that is not within the image-set itself but is created by it. Thus, the Statue of Liberty is immediately recognized by tourists who see it on the basis of a prior circulation of images. In this moment they confront an original and have an authentic experience of "liberty" — "authentic" in the sense that it is the image inherent in the image-set by which it is constructed. It works the same way with Mickey Mouse. In this sense at *both* Disneyland and Disneyworld one can experience the "real" Mickey Mouse. The singleness of the "original" is no longer important for the experience of authenticity, if it ever was. Authenticity requires "distance," that is, an experience of a cultural object which stands over against the viewer as a *source* of meaning, as not being at the audience's whim. Now, of course, the subject is previously formed by the image-sets and is thereby confirmed in his or her cultural being by touristic pilgrimages to view originals. The closeness of the image-sets constructs the distance of the original; viewing the original confirms the relation of image-sets. It has become a self-confirming cycle.

In short, mechanical reproduction does not simply "copy," which would be merely an acceleration of ancient mimesis and ritual repetition. As Benjamin noted, "In principle a work of art has always been reproducible."[5] Reproduction produces a "second" — another whose likeness to the first is not perfect. Only after the second can there be an issue of determining the "original." The first major diagnosis of mass culture rests on a loss of "authenticity" because industrial reproduction is still seen as mimicking an original — as the Mona Lisa in the subway ad harks back to a Renaissance smile. But now there is no need to reproduce original artworks. Photography, film, all electronic media simply simulate the world. There is no copy, no original, neither firsts nor seconds. Authenticity is not lost, but *staged*.

The second observation is concerned with commodity production and therefore applies more directly to Adorno's position. He argued that industrial production and exchange of commodities produces a homogenized mass of consumers of culture.

> Now any person signifies only those attributes by which he can replace everybody else: he is interchangeable, a copy. As an individual he is completely expendable and utterly insignificant . . . [6]

However, more recently, subjection of the individual has given way to the stimulation of consumer choice from a bewildering array of cultural goods. Subjection has not been entirely replaced, but it has been overlaid by a simulation of the individual through uncoerced and unrelated choices from a plethora of industrially produced commodities. It is not so much goods that are for sale nowadays as lifestyles. And here, it may well be, the inner logic of industrialism reaches its apogee:

not goods *for* individuals, but "individuals" produced *through* the staging of goods. Cultural identities produced industrially and exchanged at will. The earlier cultural homogeneity due to the uniformity of *production methods* has been displaced by a diversity of cultural identities focused on *consumer choice.*

If we put together these two observations, it may be suggested that the new postmodern era of mass culture be called "staged difference." The plurality of image-sets sets the stage for "authentic" experiences; commodities are produced for "individuals" who define themselves through their difference from other consumption groups. It is not so much the loss of distance from the object as the simulation of a distance within the self, of the self as other.

The overlaying of homogenization by staged difference requires that the strategy of the avant-garde be similarly displaced; the avant-garde has become a consumer choice within a fractionated market. The total externalization of cultural and perceptual qualities in film is not simply introjected as a uniformity that can be subverted by the avant-garde, but as the self-recognition of an audience that identifies with this film, and more significantly this genre, *as opposed* to others known to be available. Similarly, the methods of shock and transgression only work if there is a bedrock of cultural identity to be roused to reflection and action. Without such a bedrock, they only reinforce cynicism, which is merely one stage in the cycle of postmodern culture. The general availability and uniformity of production for exchange has been displaced by the reproduction of individuals through simulated identities — the reproduction of the labor force through their time outside it in the specific form of differentiated and mutable identities. This is a labor force suited to perform multifarious roles, including unemployment, in a constantly shifting division of labor, but which does not aspire, in Marx's terms, to become the *subject* of production, or of culture either.

Beyond the first stage of mass culture, postmodern industrial culture is not a *repression* but a *simulation* of identity. There is no "alienation" from an original identity to which one can authentically "return." It is possible to interpret this development as a utopian surpassing of industrial specialization. However, against the ecstacies of Marshall McLuhan, electronic simulations do not "recombine" individuals separated by the division of labor and "mediate" a new face-to-face global village.[7] Identities are no more coherent than a stacked deck of cards; technology and commodity production serve to define the rules by which we shuffle the deck. The dissatisfaction and anxiety produced by seeing one's identity available and increasingly adopted by the many fuels one's attachment to renewed tokens of difference. In postmodern culture pleasure ensues from the release of anxiety in which identity is signaled by the consumption of differences. We desire our tokens of identity; they are not forced on us by industrial uniformity; we *find* ourselves in our simulated difference from others.

The cyclical character of postmodern consumer society can be illustrated through the present articulation of sports, masculinity, and militarism on television.[8] Commercials broadcast during basketball and football games show images of men identified as Army personnel performing athletic-type feats with good cheer. "Be the best you can be in the Army," the jingle goes, as it associates sports stars with army recruits. The selection and combination of these images into a set produces a cultural meaning — a fantasy of masculine control, strength, and success — from whose circulation identities are formed. These identities are constructed through the association of sports and military service. (Though such image-sets are not all-powerful and some audiences may react against this identity, the constructed meaning is the basis from which they react.) This association postulates an original masculinity "beneath" its expressions which serves to transmit meaning to the expressions. Moreover, this postulated original meaning is available for "authentication" through confirming experiences that are apparently outside the image-set, but whose cultural meaning is actually constructed by it. For example, hunting, fishing, drinking and so forth seem to be true expressions of the same masculinity outside the media system. Thus, the media system simply *appears* to be confirming prior authentic experiences. This is, as demonstrated by the present analysis, merely apparent. The postulation of originals is accomplished by the image-set; therefore, the media system provides its own confirming instances.[9]

No sooner does an event occur in advanced industrial culture than it is reproduced, simulated, commodified as an image, devoured, and legitimated. Reproductions attract afficionados whose identity is invested in pleasure directed to simulated events. Through industrial duplication we become fractionated audiences of ourselves, contemplating our identity as we search for a new original to authenticate our choices from the promiscuity of simulations. Thereby we open a distance within the self, regard the self as an "other" to be searched for and authenticated. Postmodern culture thrives on its own uncertainty. Availability reduces identity, fuels the postulation of originals, and allows us to recognize ourselves by bringing them closer, setting the stage for renewed dissatisfaction. The industrial production of identity is a cycle of pleasurable recognition, authentication, cynical dissatisfaction, and despair: reduplicated oscillations of novelty and boredom.[10]

Fear of the Enemy

The system of internal differences in industrial society staged by the world of consumer goods is matched by an external difference from non-consumer industrial society. Encircling the system of simulated internal differences, in which the badge of our freedom is a glut of commodities, is the face of the enemy — the other whose opposition reassures us we are nevertheless in the same camp. Fear of the external enemy exerts a control on the internal system of differences in the form of a global imperial confrontation. Postmodern culture is circumscribed by this unstable synthesis of consumption and empire, pleasure and coercion. As the self becomes other through staged difference, the other becomes enemy due to the threat of war.

In deciphering the present external configuration of postmodern culture, one image shines forth with its own light demanding — and yet resisting — interpretation: The bomb, "Little Boy," that illuminated, photographed, and leveled Hiroshima. This bomb, an image for the age of the nuclear Bomb which it ushered in, had its roots in the modern age and in the immense destructions of the twentieth century which emerged from the nightmare reversals of modernity. But it is itself an institution of postmodernity, of the impossibility of holding to the modern claim that the development of science and technology leads to a society which includes and recognizes all individuals.

The Bomb impacts two relationships which for modernity are in principle separable (even though they may be intertwined in actual historical events) — the interhuman relation of self and other and the technological domination of nature.[11] The Bomb connects friend and enemy through a technology of total destruction; it aims not merely to defeat, but to annihilate the enemy. It is a product of the most advanced science and technological alteration of nature. The massive institutional concentration of resources necessary to deploy this technology was inaugurated under the sign of the enemy, whose external image was necessary for such internal concentration. The Bomb is postmodern because the two affirmations of modernity cannot be held together with its image. The domination of nature now seems to require and extend the dialectic of friend and enemy, to shortcircuit mutual recognition. Or, viewing the external other as not (merely, only, or essentially) an enemy requires a suspicion of destructive technology which issues centrally from contemporary science. The two affirmations of modernity have become unhooked: Either may seem possible now, but together they provoke only bitterness, naivete or, much more hopefully, laughter.

The forces of "day" — that is, hope, growth, and progress — reduce humans to meaningless cogs in a megamachine of war. Jan Patochka, the Socrates of Charter 77, which is the focus of the struggle for human rights in Czechoslovakia, has illuminated this frightful reversal of twentieth-century war.

> Under the new circumstances of nuclear weapons and total destruction, a hot war may turn into a cold war or a smoldering one. . . . war incorporates "peace" within itself, in the form of demobilization. . . . Mankind becomes the victim of a war once unleashed, i.e. of peace and day; peace and day count on death as the means of extreme human unfreedom, as the bond which people prefer to ignore but which is everpresent in the form of a *vis a tergo*, of terror that will drive people even into fire. Through death and fear, man is bound to life and is most manipulable.[12]

The wars of the twentieth century are mobilizations of day, of hope, peace and progress, which have colonized death and the night for their purposes. Without hope, or "meaning," why would so many millions march? Why would bombs be built that can end not only civilization but human, and perhaps terrestrial, life itself?

At the origin of the crisis of civilization stands the First World War. For the first time the conflagration into which Europe plunged the world could not be blamed on "uncivilized" outsiders. It was indicative of a failure within European nations themselves, and in their common claim to civilization. The First World War brought forth the experience of "the front" — the boundary outside which the enemy was held and which was crossed in mortal danger. This front was ended by the tank. In the Second World War the front become moveable; air war is a continuous shifting of fronts such that the military advances and recedes over the civilian population.[13] In the nuclear age, we live with what may be called the "ubiquitous front"; it is everpresent and everywhere. There is no longer any "behind the lines." The line is within each one of us; the enemy is always with us. We are all mobilized and can only avoid the trauma of war by avoiding thinking about the situation. Without Hollywood and the shopping malls, the shell-shocked would line the streets. The front, and now Hiroshima, are public experiences of death — of death which resists incorporation into the machinery that produces it. The end of all things is now a possibility for human action. From these negative oracles produced by imperial consumption, we may glimpse a response to the fear of death that is not a recoil in terror from the other.

For Patochka, any renewal, any real peace that is not a mobilization for another war, must come from the "meaningful apex" of the experience of the front, which sees the limit to meanings in the service of mere, everyday life.

> The solidarity of the shattered — shattered in their faith in day, "life" and "peace" — acquires special significance precisely at times of releasing Force. "Day" and "peace," the human life produced in a world of exponential growth patterns, cannot exist without releasing Force. . . . The solidarity of the shattered can say "No" to mobilizations which eternalize the state of war. It will not offer positive programs but will, as Socrates' *daimonion*, speak in warnings.[14]

The confrontation with death at the front shattered the facade of meaning at "home." The experience has been brought to all of us by the Bomb. Fear of the enemy has constructed a postmodern situation in which we threaten to annihilate ourselves, indeed all life, in the name of security.

Throughout human history death has been given meaning by philosophical, religious, and cultural systems in which individual mortality was placed within a larger context. In many of these systems of belief human life itself was seen as subordinate to the higher realm of nature or God. Even in secular systems, through concepts of "nation," "people," "class," and so forth, the inescapable death of the individual was redeemed by a meaningful context. But in the nuclear age, such meaning-systems are radically undermined. The end of the individual in a nuclear exchange will also be the end of these larger contexts. Destruction will be the product of human action, not a force of God, fate, or nature. The human action that has given us this vision of an end implicates all our systems of meaning. One cannot die for the nation if the nation dies too. Most important, the experience of death has now become public. It is no longer an individual fate to be redeemed by higher meaning, but the death of higher meaning in the social encounter with death. Even nature and God will be burned by the blast. If we are to learn from this age into which we have been thrust, it must be that the self can no longer seek security by instilling fear in the enemy. The safety of the self can no longer be found in the terror of the other. There is a moment of true freedom in knowing that the course of history leads to the Bomb. One can now design new futures free from the imposed meaning of God and nation by seeking encounters with the "other" that do not repress it because of an insecure self. There is no "security"; the self must face this uncertainty, its own wager with death. Once you may die at any second, without reason or notice, why obey the rules, give up what you desire for official acceptance? We are free to create the world we want. In ecology, feminism, Third World liberation we have the possibility of encountering the "other" beyond the destructive immobility of fear. Disarming the nuclear nations is a first vision of how their struggles are our own. In the laughter that releases us from meaning-systems we realize the certainty of our own deaths, but publicly now, and can discover together the festival that gathers the myriad faces of the other in a celebration of the fleeting joy of existence.

End of Modernity

Modernity is defined by two central affirmations: That nature is to be dominated as a means to human ends, and that human ends can be reconciled with each other through mutual recognition of free and equal subjects. If the two affirmations of modernity are questioned radically in the light of twentieth-century experience, the ground for their common articulation is eroded. The domination of nature has led to a profusion of commodities that cannot "fulfill human needs" because it has come to simulate identities. "Needs" simply ask for the system to be extended further. This internal dimension of consumer society is matched by an external one: Scientific-technical domination of nature is entwined with the eradication of the enemy, a fear which has now come to encircle us. Thus, modern hope that the domination of nature would produce a society of autonomous and mutually recognizing subjects is no longer possible. While the central beliefs of modernity serve to extend and develop the system, instead of reaching its avowed goal they fuel the cycle of simulation and destruction. New departures are required.

Postmodern culture is this self-reproducing end-circuit of modernity. It consists of *staged difference*: The self becomes an other as a token authenticated by experiences postulated by image-sets; the other as a fear for the self, seeking security in toying with global destruction. It demonstrates the failure of the modern search for free and equal autonomous subjects and requires a radical investigation of the formation of identity as relations of dependence between self and others.[15]

The metaphysical assumptions of the modern concept of the self can be discerned in two dimensions: Modernity is displacement, from which we project authentic origin — and, thereby, the goal of *reappropriation* of this origin. Also, authentic self as against the difference of the other — and, thereby, the goal of *reconciliation* with this difference. Authenticity attempts to close the pain of displacement within a story of alienation which returns us to our origins and to others. The overcoming of alienation is progress guaranteed by the domination of nature which produces a wealth of commodities. The future path of critical thought is anything but secure, but this option is now closed to us. By circumscribing postmodern culture in the figures of empire and consumption, we may begin to determine the contours of this future path.

Part II

Dimensions of Cultural Experience

This section deals with the way in which the external influences of empire and consumption are mediated through four dimensions of cultural experience: race, sex, class, and nature. These are inescapable aspects of everyone's life, but we do not experience them in a straightforward way. In our culture, all four dimensions operate through a key distinction in which one side is dominant: white/non-white, male/female, capital/labor, and humanity/nature. The dominant side of the distinction is the predominant cultural value.

These unequal distinctions are portrayed in culture, especially by the media. Representations are not merely reflections. They are selected, produced, and distributed by powerful social, political, and economic institutions. These representations affect our cultural experience itself. This double-sided relationship between experience and representation is central in contemporary society due to the predominance of the image.

Michael Omi demonstrates the importance of the color bar as the method by which racial distinctions operate in the United States. The cultural definitions given to gender through the twentieth century are investigated by Jean

Elshtain. Stanley Aronowitz examines the way in which working-class identity is defined now, unlike in the past, almost entirely through its representation in the media.

While race, sex, and class are widely regarded as important dimensions of popular culture, it may seem surprising to include nature here. However, like these other dimensions, some relationship to nature is inherent to human existence. Moreover, images of nature have come to predominate over direct experience. Neil Evernden shows that the environmental problems of industrial society require a new conceptualization to be addressed adequately.

8.

In Living Color: Race and American Culture

Michael Omi

In February 1987, Assistant Attorney General William Bradford Reynolds, the nation's chief civil rights enforcer, declared that the recent death of a black man in Howard Beach, New York and the Ku Klux Klan attack on civil rights marchers in Forsyth County, Georgia were "isolated" racial incidences. He emphasized that the places where racial conflict could potentially flare up were "far fewer now than ever before in our history," and concluded that such a diminishment of racism stood as "a powerful testament to how far we have come in the civil rights struggle."[1]

Events in the months following his remarks raise the question as to whether we have come quite so far. They suggest that dramatic instances of racial tension and violence merely constitute the surface manifestations of a deeper racial organization of American society — a system of inequality which has shaped, and in turn been shaped by, our popular culture.

In March, the NAACP released a report on blacks in the record industry entitled "The Discordant Sound of Music." It found that despite the revenues generated by black performers, blacks remain "grossly underrepresented" in the business, marketing and A & R (Artists and Repertoire) departments of major record labels. In addition, few blacks are employed as managers, agents, concert promoters, distributors, and retailers. The report concluded that:

> The record industry is overwhelmingly segregated and discrimination is rampant. No other industry in American so openly classifies its

operations on a racial basis. At every level of the industry, beginning with the separation of black artists into a special category, barriers exist that severely limit opportunities for blacks.[2]

Decades after the passage of civil rights legislation and the affirmation of the principle of "equal opportunity," patterns of racial segregation and exclusion, it seems, continue to characterize the production of popular music.

The enduring logic of Jim Crow is also present in professional sports. In April, Al Campanis, vice president of player personnel for the Los Angeles Dodgers, explained to Ted Koppel on ABC's "Nightline" about the paucity of blacks in baseball front offices and as managers. "I truly believe," Campanis said, "that [blacks] may not have some of the necessities to be, let's say, a field manger or perhaps a general manager." When pressed for a reason, Campanis offered an explanation which had little to do with the structure of opportunity of institutional discrimination within professional sports:

> [W]hy are black men or black people not good swimmers? Because they don't have the buoyancy . . . . They are gifted with great musculature and various other things. They're fleet of foot. And this is why there are a lot of black major league ballplayers. Now as far as having the background to become club presidents, or presidents of a bank, I don't know.[3]

Black exclusion from the front office, therefore, was justified on the basis of biological "difference."

The issue of race, of course, is not confined to the institutional arrangements of popular culture production. Since popular culture deals with the symbolic realm of social life, the images which it creates, represents, and disseminates contribute to the overall racial climate. They become the subject of analysis and political scrutiny. In August, the National Ethnic Coalition of Organizations bestowed the "Golden Pit Awards" on television programs, commercials, and movies that were deemed offensive to racial and ethnic groups. "Saturday Night Live," regarded by many media critics as a politically "progressive" show, was singled out for the "Platinum Pit Award" for its comedy skit "Ching Chang" which depicted a Chinese storeowner and his family in a derogatory manner.[4]

These examples highlight the *overt* manifestations of racism in popular culture — institutional forms of discrimination which keep racial minorities out of the production and organization of popular culture, and the crude racial caricatures by which these groups are portrayed. Yet racism in popular culture is often conveyed in a variety of implicit, and at times invisible, ways. Political theoriest Stuart Hall makes an important distinction between *overt* racism, the elaboration of an explicitly racist argument, policy, or view, and *inferential* racism which refers to "those apparently naturalized representations of events and situations relating to race, whether 'factual' or 'fictional', which have racist premises and propositions inscribed in them as a set of *unquestioned assumptions.*" He argues that inferential racism is more widespread, common, and indeed insidious since "it is largely *invisible* even to those who formulate the world in its terms."[5]

Race itself is a slippery social concept which is paradoxically both "obvious" and "invisible." In our society, one of the first things we notice about people when we encounter them (along with their sex/gender) is their *race.* We utilize race to provide clues about *who* a person is and *how* we should relate to her/him. Our perception of race determines our "presentation of self," distinctions in status, and appropriate modes of conduct in daily and institutional life. This process is often unconscious; we tend to operate off of an unexamined set of *racial beliefs.*

Racial beliefs account for and explain variations in "human nature." Differences in skin color and other obvious physical characteristics supposedly provide visible clues to more substantive differences lurking underneath. Among other qualities, temperament, sexuality, intelligence, and artistic and athletic ability are presumed to be fixed and discernible from the palpable mark of race. Such diverse questions as our confidence and trust in others (as salespeople, neighbors, media figures); our sexual preferences and romantic images; our tastes in music, film, dance, or sports; indeed our very ways of walking and talking are ineluctably shaped by notions of race.

Ideas about race, therefore, have become "common sense" — a way of comprehending, explaining, and acting in the world. This is made painfully obvious when someone disrupts our common sense understandings. An encounter with someone who is, for example, racially "mixed" or of a racial/ethnic group we are unfamiliar with becomes a source of discomfort for us, and momentarily creates a crisis of racial meaning. We also become disoriented when people do not act "black," "Latino," or indeed "white." The content of such stereotypes reveals a series of unsubstantiated beliefs about who these groups are, what they are like, and how they behave.

The existence of such racial consciousness should hardly be surprising. Even prior to the inception of the republic, the United States was a society shaped by racial conflict. The establishment of the Southern plantation economy, Western expansion, and the emergence of the labor movement, among other significant historical developments, have all involved conflicts over the definition and nature of the *color line*. The historical results have been distinct and different groups have encountered unique forms of racial oppression — Native Americans faced genocide, blacks were subjected to slavery, Mexicans were invaded and colonized, and Asians faced exclusion. What is common to the experiences of these groups is that their particular "fate" was linked to historically specific ideas about the significance and meaning of race.[6] Whites defined them as separate "species," ones inferior to Northern European cultural stocks, and thereby rationalized the conditions of their subordination in the economy, in political life, and in the realm of culture.

A crucial dimension of racial oppression in the United States is the elaboration of an ideology of difference or "otherness." This involves defining "us" (i.e., white Americans) in opposition to "them," an important task when distinct racial groups are first encountered, or in historically specific periods where pre-existing racial boundaries are threatened or crumbling.

Political struggles over the very definition of who an "American" is illustrates this process. The Naturalization Law of 1790 declared that only free *white* immigrants could qualify, reflecting the initial desire among Congress to create and maintain a racially homogeneous society. The extension of eligibility to all racial groups has been a long and protracted process. Japanese, for example, were finally eligible to become naturalized citizens after the passage of the Walter-McCarran Act of 1952. The ideological residue of these restrictions in naturalization and citizenship laws is the equation within popular parlance of the term "American" with "white," while other "Americans" are described as black, Mexican, "Oriental," etc.

Popular culture has been an important realm within which racial ideologies have been created, reproduced, and sustained. Such ideologies provide a framework of symbols, concepts, and images through which we understand, interpret, and represent aspects of our "racial" existence.

Race has often formed the central themes of American popular culture. Historian W. L. Rose notes that it is "curious coincidence" that four of the "most popular reading-viewing events in all American history" have in some manner dealt with race, specifically black/white relations in the south.[7] Harriet Beecher Stowe's *Uncle Tom's Cabin*, Thomas Ryan Dixon's *The Clansman* (the inspiration for D. W. Griffith's *The Birth of a Nation*), Margaret Mitchell's *Gone With the Wind* (as a book and film), and Alex Haley's *Roots* (as a book and television miniseries), each appeared at a critical juncture in American race relations and helped to shape new understandings of race.

Emerging social definitions of race and the "real American" were reflected in American popular culture of the nineteenth century. Racial and ethnic stereotypes were shaped and reinforced in the newspapers, magazines, and pulp fiction of the period. But the evolution and ever-increasing sophistication of visual mass communications throughout the twentieth century provided, and continues to provide, the most dramatic means by which racial images are generated and reproduced.

Film and television have been notorious in disseminating images of racial minorities which establish for audiences what these groups look like, how they behave, and, in essence, "who they are." The power of the media lies not only in their ability to reflect the dominant racial ideology, but in their capacity to shape that ideology in the first place. D. W. Griffith's forementioned epic *Birth of a Nation*, a sympathetic treatment of the rise of the Ku Klux Klan during Reconstruction, helped to generate, consolidate, and "nationalize" images of blacks which had been more disparate (more regionally specific, for example) prior to the film's appearance.[8]

In television and film, the necessity to define characters in the briefest and most condensed manner has led to the perpetuation of racial caricatures, as racial stereotypes serve as shorthand for scriptwriters, directors, and actors. Television's tendency to address the "lowest common denominator" in order to render programs "familiar" to an enormous and diverse audience leads it regularly to assign and reassign racial characteristics to particular groups, both minority and majority.

Many of the earliest American films deal with racial and ethnic "difference." The large influx of "new immigrants" at the turn of the century led to a proliferation of negative images of Jews, Italians, and Irish which were assimilated and adapted by such films as Thomas Edison's *Cohen's Advertising Scheme* (1904). Based on an old vaudeville routine, the film featured a scheming Jewish merchant, aggressively hawking his wares. Though stereotypes of these groups persist to this day,[9] by the 1940s many of the earlier ethnic stereotypes had disappeared from Hollywood. But, as historian Michael Winston observes, the "outsiders" of the 1890s remained: "the ever-popular Indian of the Westerns; the inscrutable or sinister Oriental; the sly, but colorful Mexican; and the clowning or submissive Negro."[10]

In many respects the "Western" as a genre has been paradigmatic in establishing images of racial minorities in film and television. The classic scenario involves the encircled wagon train or surrounded fort from which whites bravely fight off fierce bands of Native American Indians. The point of reference and viewer identification lies with those huddled within the circle — the representatives of "civilization" who valiantly attempt to ward off the forces of barbarism. In the classic Western, as writer Tom Engelhardt observes, "the viewer is forced behind the barrel of a repeating rifle and it is from that position, through its gun sights, that he receives a picture history of Western colonialism and imperialism."[11]

Westerns have indeed become the prototype for European and American excursions throughout the Third World. The cast of characters may change, but the story remains the same. The "humanity" of whites is contrasted with the brutality and treachery of non-whites; brave (i.e., white) souls are pitted against the merciless hordes in conflicts ranging from Indians against the British Lancers to Zulus against the Boers. What Stuart Hall refers to as the imperializing "white eye" provides the framework for these films, lurking outside the frame and yet seeing and positioning everything within, it is "the unmarked position from which . . . 'observations' are made and from which, alone, they make sense."[12]

Our "common sense" assumptions about race and racial minorities in the United States are both generated and reflected in the stereotypes presented by the visual media. In the crudest sense, it could be said that such stereotypes underscore white "superiority" by reinforcing the traits, habits, and predispositions of non-whites which demonstrate their "inferiority." Yet a more careful assessment of racial stereotypes reveals intriguing trends and seemingly contradictory themes.

While all racial minorities have been portrayed as "less than human," there are significant differences in the images of different groups. Specific racial minority groups, in spite of their often interchangeable presence in films steeped in the "Western" paradigm, have distinct and often unique qualities assigned to them. Latinos are portrayed as being prone towards violent outbursts of anger; blacks as physically strong, but dim-witted; while Asians are seen as sneaky and cunningly evil. Such differences are crucial to observe and analyze. Race in the United States is not reducible to black/white relations. These differences are significant for a broader understanding of the patterns of race in America, and the unique experience of specific racial minority groups.

It is somewhat ironic that *real* differences which exist within a racially defined minority group are minimized, distorted, or obliterated by the media. "All Asians look alike," the saying goes, and indeed there has been little or no attention given to the vast differences which exist between, say, the Chinese and Japanese with respect to food, dress, language, and culture. This blurring within popular culture has given us supposedly Chinese characters who wear kimonos; it is also the reason why the fast-food restaurant McDonald's can offer "Shanghai McNuggets" with teriyaki sauce. Other groups suffer a similar fate. Professor Gretchen Bataille and Charles Silet find the cinematic Native American of the Northeast wearing the clothing of the Plains Indians, while living in the dwellings of Southwestern tribes:

> The movie men did what thousands of years of social evolution could not do, even what the threat of the encroaching white man could not do; Hollywood produced the homogenized Native American, devoid of tribal characteristics or regional differences.[13]

The need to paint in broad racial strokes has thus rendered "internal" differences invisible. This has been exacerbated by the tendency for screenwriters to "invent" mythical Asian, Latin American, and African countries. Ostensibly done to avoid offending particular nations and peoples, such a subterfuge reinforces the notion that all the countries and cultures of a specific region are the same. European countries retain their distinctiveness, while the Third World is presented as one homogeneous mass riddled with poverty and governed by ruthless and corrupt regimes.

While rendering specific groups in a monolithic fashion, the popular cultural imagination simultaneously reveals a compelling need to distinguish and articulate "bad" and "good" variants of particular racial groups and individuals. Thus each stereotypic image is filled with contradictions: the bloodthirsty Indian is tempered with the image of the noble savage; the *bandido* exists along with the loyal sidekick; and Fu Manchu is offset by Charlie Chan. The existence of such contradictions, however, does not negate the one-dimensionality of these images, nor does it challenge the explicit subservient role of racial minorities. Even the "good" person of color usually exists as a foil in novels and films to underscore the intelligence, courage, and virility of the white male hero.

Another important, perhaps central, dimension of racial minority stereotypes is sex/gender differentiation. The connection between race and sex has traditionally been an explosive and controversial one. For most of American history, sexual and marital relations between whites and non-whites were forbidden by social custom and by legal restrictions. It was not until 1967, for example, that the U.S. Supreme Court ruled that anti-miscegenation laws were unconstitutional. Beginning in the 1920s, the notorious Hays Office, Hollywood's attempt at self-censorship, prohibited scenes and subjects which dealt with miscegenation. The prohibition, however, was not evenly applied in practice. White men could seduce racial minority women, but white women were not to be romantically or sexually linked to racial minority men.

Women of colour were sometimes treated as exotic sex objects. The sultry Latin temptress — such as Dolores Del Rio and Lupe Velez — invariably had boyfriends who were white North Americans; their Latino suitors were portrayed as being unable to keep up with the Anglo-American competition. From Mary Pickford as Cho-Cho San in *Madame Butterfly* (1915) to Nancy Kwan in *The World of Suzie Wong* (1961), Asian women have often been seen as the gracious "geisha girl" or the prostitute with a "heart of gold," willing to do anything to please her man.

By contrast, Asian men, whether cast in the role of villain, servant, sidekick, or Kung-fu master, are seen as asexual or, at least, romantically undesirable. As Asian American studies professor Elaine Kim notes, even a hero such as Bruce Lee played characters whose "single-minded focus on perfecting his fighting skills precludes all other interests, including an interest in women, friendship, or a social life."[14]

The shifting trajectory of black images over time reveals an interesting dynamic with respect to sex and gender. The black male characters in *The Birth of a Nation* were clearly presented as sexual threats to "white womanhood." For decades afterwards, however, Hollywood consciously avoided portraying black men as assertive or sexually aggressive in order to minimize controversy. Black men were instead cast as comic, harmless, and non-threatening figures exemplified by such stars as Bill "Bojangles" Robinson, Stepin Fetchit, and Eddie "Rochester" Anderson. Black women, by contrast, were divided into two broad character types based on color categories. Dark black women such as Hattie McDaniel and Louise Beavers were cast as "dowdy, frumpy, dumpy, overweight mammy figures: while those "close to the white ideal," such as Lena Horne and Dorothy Dandridge, became "Hollywood's treasured mulattoes" in roles emphasizing the tragedy of being of mixed blood.[15]

It was not until the early 1970s that tough, aggressive, sexually assertive black characters, both male and female, appeared. The "blaxploitation" films of the period provided new heroes (e.g., *Shaft*, *Superfly*, *Coffy*, and *Cleopatra Jones*) in sharp contrast to the submissive and subservient images of the past. Unfortunately, most of these films were shoddy productions which did little to create more enduring "positive" images of blacks, either male or female.

In contemporary television and film, there is a tendency to present and equate racial minority groups and individuals with specific social problems. Blacks are associated with drugs and urban crime, Latinos with "illegal" immigration, while Native Americans cope with alcoholism and tribal conflicts. Rarely do we see racial minorities "out of character," in situations removed from the stereotypic arenas which scriptwriters have traditionally embedded them in. Nearly the only time we see young Asians and Latinos of either sex, for example, is when they are members of youth gangs, as *Boulevard Nights* (1979), *Year of the Dragon* (1985), and countless TV cop shows can attest to.

Racial minority actors have continually bemoaned the fact that the roles assigned them on stage and screen are often one-dimensional and imbued with stereotypic assumptions. In theater, the movement towards "blind casting" (i.e., casting actors for roles without regard to race) is a progressive step, but it remains to be seen whether large numbers of audiences can suspend their "beliefs" and deal with a Latino King Lear or an Asian Stanley Kowalski. By contrast, white actors are allowed to play anybody. Though the use of white actors to play blacks in "black face" is clearly unacceptable in the contemporary period, white actors continue to portray Asian, Latino, and Native American characters on stage and screen. *Miss Saigon - two sides to the controversy*

Scores of Charlie Chan films, for example, have been made with white leads (the last one was the 1981 *Charlie Chan and the Curse of the Dragon Queen*). Roland Winters, who played Chan in six features, was once asked to explain the logic of casting a white man in the role of Charlie Chan: "The only thing I can think of is, if you want to cast a homosexual in a show, and you get a homosexual, it'll be awful. It won't be funny . . . and maybe there's something there. . . "[16]

Such a comment reveals an interesting aspect about myth and reality in popular culture. Michael Winston argues that stereotypic images in the visual media were not originally conceived as representations of reality, nor were they initially understood to be "real" by audiences. They were, he suggests, ways of "coding and rationalizing" the racial hierarchy and interracial behavior. Over time, however, "a complex interactive relationship between myth and reality developed, so that images originally understood to be unreal, through constant repetition began to *seem* real."[17]

Such a process consolidated, among other things, our "common sense" understandings of what we think various groups should look like. Such presumptions have led to tragicomical results. Latinos auditioning for a role in a television soap opera, for example, did not fit the Hollywood image of "real Mexicans" and had their faces bronzed with powder before filming because they looked too white. Model Aurora

Garza said, "I'm a real Mexican and very dark anyway. I'm even darker right now because I have a tan. But they kept wanting to make my face darker and darker."[18]

Historically in Hollywood, the fact of having "dark skin" made an actor or actress potentially adaptable for numerous "racial" roles. Actress Lupe Velez once commented that she had portrayed "Chinese, Eskimos, Japs, squaws, Hindus, Swedes, Malays, and Japanese."[19] Dorothy Dandridge, who was the first black woman teamed romantically with white actors, presented a quandary for studio executives who weren't sure what race and nationality to make her. They debated whether she should be a "foreigner," an island girl, or a West Indian.[20] Ironically, what they refused to entertain as a possibility was to present her as what she really was, a black American woman.

The importance of race in popular culture is not restricted to the visual media. In popular music, race and race consciousness has defined, and continues to define, formats, musical communities, and tastes. In the mid-1950s, the secretary of the North Alabama White Citizens Council declared that "Rock and roll is a means of pulling the white man down to the level of the Negro."[21] While rock may no longer be popularly regarded as a racially subversive musical form, the very genres of contemporary popular music remain, in essence, thinly veiled racial categories. "R & B" (Rhythm and Blues) and "soul" music are clearly references to *black* music, while country & western or heavy metal music are viewed, in the popular imagination, as *white* music. Black performers who want to break out of this artistic ghettoization must "crossover," a contemporary form of "passing" in which their music is seen as acceptable to white audiences.

The airwaves themselves are segregated. The designation "urban contemporary" is merely radio lingo for a "black" musical format. Such categorization affects playlists, advertising accounts, and shares of the listening market. On cable television, black music videos rarely receive airplay on MTV, but are confined instead to the more marginal BET (Black Entertainment Television) network.

In spite of such segregation, many performing artists have been able to garner a racially diverse group of fans. And yet, racially integrated concert audiences are extremely rare. Curiously, this "perverse phenomenon" of racially homogeneous crowds takes place despite the color of the performer. Lionel Richie's concert audiences, for example, are virtually all-white, while Teena Marie's are all-black.[22]

Racial symbols and images are omnipresent in popular culture. Commonplace household objects such as cookie jars, salt and pepper shakers, and ashtrays have frequently been designed and fashioned in the form of racial caricatures. Sociologist Steve Dubin in an analysis of these objects found that former tasks of domestic service were symbolically transferred onto these commodities.[23] An Aunt Jemima-type character, for example, is used to hold a roll of paper towels, her outstretched hands supporting the item to be dispensed. "Sprinkle Plenty," a sprinkle bottle in the shape of an Asian man, was used to wet clothes in preparation for ironing. Simple commodities, the household implements which help us perform everyday tasks, may reveal, therefore, a deep structure of racial meaning.

A crucial dimension for discerning the meaning of particular stereotypes and images is the *situation context* for the creation and consumption of popular culture. For example, the setting in which "racist" jokes are told determines the function of humor. Jokes about blacks where the teller and audience are black constitute a form of self-awareness; they allow blacks to cope and "take the edge off" of oppressive aspects of the social order which they commonly confront. The meaning of these same jokes, however, is dramatically transformed when told across the "color line." If a white, or even black, person tells these jokes to a white audience, it will, despite its "purely" humorous intent, serve to reinforce stereotypes and rationalize the existing relations of racial inequality.

Concepts of race and racial images are both overt and implicit within popular culture — the organization of cultural production, the products themselves, and the manner in which they are consumed are deeply structured by race. Particular racial meanings, stereotypes, and myths can change, but the presence of a *system* of racial meanings and stereotypes, of racial ideology, seems to be an enduring aspect of American popular culture.

The era of Reaganism and the overall rightward drift of American politics and culture has added a new twist to the question of racial images and meanings. Increasingly, the problem for racial minorities is not that of misportrayal, but of "invisibility." Instead of celebrating racial and cultural diversity, we are witnessing an attempt by the right to define, once again, who the "real" American is, and what "correct" American values, mores, and political beliefs are. In such a context, racial minorities are no longer the focus of sustained media attention; when they do appear, they are cast as colored versions of essentially "white" characters.

The possibilities for change — for transforming racial stereotypes and challenging institutional inequities — nonetheless exist. Historically, strategies have involved the mobilization of political pressure against an offending institution(s). In the late-1950s, for instance, "Nigger Hair" tobacco changed its name to "Bigger Hare" due to concerted NAACP pressure on the manufacturer. In the early-1970s, Asian American community groups successfully fought NBC's attempt to resurrect Charlie Chan as a television series with white actor Ross Martin. Amidst the furor generated by Al Campanis's remarks cited at the beginning of this chapter, Jesse Jackson suggested that a boycott of major league games be initiated in order to push for a restructuring of hiring and promotion practices.

Partially in response to such action, Baseball Commissioner Peter Ueberroth announced plans in June 1987 to help put more racial minorities in management roles. "The challenge we have," Ueberroth said, "is to manage change without losing tradition."[24] The problem with respect to the issue of race and popular culture, however, is that the *tradition* itself may need to be thoroughly examined, its "common sense" assumptions unearthed and challenged, and its racial images contested and transformed.

9.

Cultural Conundrums and Gender: America's Present Past

Jean Bethke Elshtain

"There comes a time, Constance, when a man's just got to stick his hand in the fire and see what he's made of."
"What the hell are you talking about?"
— dialogue between McCabe (Warren Beatty) and Mrs. Miller (Julie Christie) in Robert Altmann's "McCabe and Mrs. Miller"

That men and women in America cannot *really* speak to one another; that their conversations are a dreary series of ritualized misfirings, is a truism that echoes through the decades in novels, "women's magazines," gossip and locker room banter, insinuating itself as one of the prime staples of 1970s feminist consciousness-raising and, in more abstract ways, helping to constitute much feminist theorizing. Men and women are construed as inhabiting such different discursive universes, even, or especially, if they share the same house, or social location, or ethnicity, or religion, that each is defined reactively with reference to the other. To put it another way, ours is a culture which has given gender a strong reading, highlighting its many markers, constraining and inciting men and women to characteristic modes of action and reaction.

There is no known society that fails to differentiate male from female. The division of humanity, on the conceptual and symbolic level, into two distinct sexes is an essential aspect of human identity and cultural life. To agree that the sex distinction is ineliminable and important does not mean, however, that one must acquiesce in received constructions of "masculine" and "feminine" and the particular ways they are encoded into any given culture. That, in part, was the point of the move to the notion of *gender*, a term now so ubiquitous it threatens to become banalized. Gender was once a rather modest word referring

123

to each of two or three grammatical kinds, corresponding more or less to distinctions of sex, or absence of sex, into which subjects were discriminated according to the nature of the modifications they required. Contemporary feminism transformed the term, structuring it as an analytic tool useful for distinguishing between sexuality, on the one hand, and that which might be seen as an imposition upon a sexed being of a particular identity from the outside, as it were. Gender has to do with that species of imposition.

In the strongest versions of the feminist story of Gender and Culture (booming words that virtually guarantee overreach), one finds two prevalent narratives. First, there is the script of *sex neutrality* which begins with the presumption that real or presumed sex differences are imposed upon generic human material from birth. Neonates are ungendered, and the social imposition of gender literally engenders maleness, femaleness, and what counts as masculinity and femininity in any and all cultures. Second, and a kind of mirror image, is the story of *sex polarity*, which starts with the presumption that the sexes are radically divided and that they must and should remain so with the caveat that "women's values" must come to prevail over the debased offerings of the dominant, collective male subject.[1]

What is fascinating about both the sex-neutrality and sex-polarity arguments is the dynamic in and through which they reinforce ways of thinking and constructing cultural *representations* of the male and female, the masculine and feminine, that feed rather than challenge a cluster of normalizing features of American popular culture, academic theorizing, and political life. That, at least, is the case I intend to make by culling exemplars and interrogating phenomena from a variety of sources. There is a moral in all this — that, too, is very American — and I may as well offer intimations of it here at the outset. The conundrums to follow highlight the difficulties of getting outside the imperatives that construct male and female identity in order to criticize them in a way that doesn't simply reinscribe them at another, perhaps deeper level. As well, I hope what emerges will be sufficiently troubling to suggest that much that we now assume as the "truth" of gender and turn into hardened ideology is in fact far murkier and more mysterious than our abstractions allow, including those of the feminist variety. What is at stake is contesting the ground of tradition — our present past — cast as clusters of powerful representations.

It's still the same old story . . .

Well, it is and it isn't quite the *same* old story. Some of the verses change but the tune doesn't alter very much. Here is one example, taking us back to the struggle over suffrage in the nineteenth century. Two pieces of political rhetoric illustrate a mutually reinforcing dynamic, a reading of gender in ways that shore up structures that at least one of the parties to the dispute claims to displace. The first quote is drawn from a speech by a male anti-suffragist; the second, from one of Elizabeth Cady Stanton's rhetorical masterworks. At odds over suffrage, Stanton and her less eloquent counterpart nonetheless *share* a deep symbolic structure that each taps to different ends.[2] The nineteenth century male anti-suffragist urges:

> Man assumed the direction of government and war, woman of the domestic and family affairs and the care and training of the child. . . . It has been so from the beginning . . . and it will continue to be so to the end, because it is in conformity to nature and its laws, and is sustained and confirmed by the experience and reason of six thousand years. . . . The domestic altar is a sacred flame where woman is the high and officiating priestess. . . . To keep her in that condition of purity, it is necessary that she should be separated from the exercise of suffrage and from all those stern and contaminating and demoralizing duties that devolves upon the hardier sex — man.[3]

Countering the "antis" opposition to suffrage, many suffragists went on to embrace the symbolism they shared *with* opponents of women's suffrage. They did so, in part, because they believed it, or some version of it; in part, because the imagery *did* capture features of what women really were or had become; in part, because they hoped they could turn it to their political advantage by predicting that the world men had made, untamed by womanly virtues, would lead humanity to certain ruin. Women's nurturing qualities, now muted, must come out into the public light to purify politics and to tip the balance to peace and decency. Thus Cady Stanton in 1868:

> The male element is a destructive force, stern, selfish, aggrandizing, loving war, violence, conquest, acquisition, breeding in the material and moral world alike discord, disorder, disease and death. See what a record of blood and cruelty the pages of history reveal! . . . The male element has held high carnival thus far, it has fairly run riot from the beginning, overpowering the feminine element everywhere, crushing out the diviner qualities in human nature. . . . The need of this hour is not territory, gold mines, railroads, or specie payments, but a new evangel of womanhood, to exalt purity, virtue, morality, true religion, to lift man up into higher realms of thought and action.[4]

Such assumptions coincide neatly with those of the "antis" and reinforce congealed male and female typologies. Although it was abstractly possible for suffragists to seek out and accumulate historic evidence suggesting that, in fact, the divide between life givers and life takers was less total than either they or the anti-suffragists claimed, neither side (with a few exceptions) was prepared to challenge systematically the symbolic structures each shared. For when we speak of the constitutive role of prototypical symbols, we refer not to interests people may have, or to rational calculations of possible costs and benefits they may compute, but to what in fact people have become: it is a question of *identities*, not of easily sloughed off external garments.[5]

It is nearly 120 years since the debate marked above appeared in several typical rhetorical performances. What has changed? Everything, it seems, is currently up for grabs. But let's slow things down a bit and fade in on a 1950s moment — the apogee of "the feminine mystique" in later feminist readings of the decade. A muckraking journalist named Philip Wylie wrote a best-selling polemic called *A Generation of Vipers*. Wylie went after the American Mom with a vengeance. The Mother in Wylie's tome is a monster, killing her sons (sons are Wylie's big concern) with aggressive kindness and thereby spawning the "vipers" of Wylie's title. Mom is taken to task for holding her sons hostage to an orally craving, competitive way of life that turns them into greedy, self-seeking beings who lack social trust in order that they might, in turn, sustain the individual and collective "her" in a state of idleness and "spiritual parasitism." Mom runs the protection racket, on Wylie's reading of the situation, and she's got it pretty good: she can spend male-earned money to ensure a way of life that requires of men that they adore her.

Men and women in Wylie's constructions are in a game of "eternal ricochet," hardened gender categories, that are destructive to each sex. Wylie is most concerned, however, with the effect upon sons. They become, in our current parlance, wimps but vicious wimps, incarnations of collective *ressentiment*. Lamenting the hard and fast social differentiations of men and women as Graspers and Idlers, Self-Seekers and Parasites, respectively, it was none too clear how this world of destructive, sexually and socially constructed sexual polarity could be broken out of, or free from — given Wylie's equally intense disdain for women who "set out to compete with men in their own activities," as well as idle housewives craving candy and emasculating their male offspring.[6] But an older cultural point got reinforced: men and women exhibit an often destructive need for one another; they are defined with reference to one another; and Mom, finally, is the one who wields the big stick of emotional authority. She can give or withhold affection: the collective Hostess with the Mostess.

It would seem surprising to hear echoes of Wylie's assault on Mom in a *feminist* account of male-female and familial relations and their effects upon the later behavior of male and female offspring. Yet — moving ahead to the mid-1970s and an ongoingly popular mode of feminist argumentation — the plaint resounds in somewhat new guise. If you want to locate *the* trouble, you can zero in on what one commentator calls the "normal psychopathology" of the entire human race, exemplified in our "intolerable," "diseased," "malignant," "maiming," "poisoned" gender arrangements, most especially "monstrous, atavistic" motherhood. That's pretty strong stuff and the burden of argument — made here by Dorothy Dinnerstein in her cultural Freudian account, *The Mermaid and the Minotaur* — is that what makes our current arrangements intolerable is that "for virtually every living person it is a woman" who provides the first and most important "contact with humanity and with nature."[7] The hand that rocks the cradle strikes again! Dinnerstein foresees the end of civilization, and soon, if something isn't done to "break the female monopoly over early child care."[8]

Why is this a feminist argument and Wylie's an anti-female plaint? The answer clearly doesn't lie in rhetorical choices — both texts are overwrought — nor even in impugning blame or, to sanitize this somewhat, "assigning responsibility." The answer can only be because Dinnerstein wants to change the situation in a way that yields a utopian outcome — men and women in harmony with each other, nature and culture, both having been brought into the nursery from the very start — and Wylie can't give up on strong sexual differentiation of social identity even though he finds the particular forms it has taken in American culture debased.

In other words, Dinnerstein's text moves from a strong account of sex polarity to a world of nearly perfect gender symmetry (or sex neutrality); a breathtakingly utopian vault as nothing resembling cogent political markers are offered in her text as a way to get from one situation to the other. Wylie, however, remains stuck with two undesirables: bad sex polarity and undesirable sex neutrality. Each, however, locates *all our woes* inside patterns of complementarity between males and females, in "female-dominated early childhood," in Dinnerstein's language.[9] One text woman-loathing, the other explicitly feminist (though the construction of Mother in Dinnerstein's account is unpiteously negative), each to its own ends and purposes shores up our preoccupation with, and inability to escape from, conundrums of gender. Each also exemplifies a strong American tendency to *displace* politics, overpersonalizing public life and substituting a therapeutic world-view for any notion of collective action.

One other example of how we are trapped in our own representations — this from what I have tagged in previous accounts the "new woman as the old man" variant on feminist discourse. In this reading of our gendered realities, the problem for women has been a world of strong sex polarity and differentiation. The solution is one of sex neutrality in which the ideal normative male of liberal political theorizing — a rational, adult chooser — functions metonymically for "the human being." Although she has had second thoughts that must be acknowledged, the clearest example remains Betty Friedan's 1963 classic, *The Feminine Mystique*. According to Friedan, women have been victimized by a mystique so powerful it has shaped and controlled their lives unawares. Those responsible include women's magazines, television, advertising, newspapers, child psychologists, sociological and psychoanalytic popularizers, and Margaret Mead. Women's views of themselves and their world is distorted and inhibited subliminally, tying them to a suburban life style and leading to a "stunting or evasion of growth."[10]

The markers of this stunting were educated, middle-class women fleeing careers in order to marry and have babies: all sorts of miseries trailed in this unhappy wake. My point is that Friedan represented the life of the achieving male, carried on outside the home in the bowels of corporate America, as exciting, fulfilling, and worthwhile. Women were compared negatively to "able, ambitious" men who went off to the city and kept on "growing." In accepting the values of male-dominated, individualistic society — by shoring up these constructions — Friedan was forced in this particular text to advocate what might be called a turnover in personnel — women bureaucrats for male bureaucrats, women corporate executives for male corporate executives, women generals for male generals, and all the rest.[11] Constricting possibilities, gender constructions even of an explicitly feminist sort, seem to win once again.

At least textually. . . . What I mean by this enigmatic fragment is that perhaps, just perhaps, it is possible that on the level of lived life matters were never as congealed as they were in texts; that there was always more ebb and flow of identities, more fluidity of engendered possibilities, than our accounts seem to allow for. To explore this question would require a book, not an essay, and take us down another path. For the moment we are stuck in texts and what one finds, as one looks at that moment which is our present, are texts that include a variety of representations — from cultural commentary, to feminist theorizing, to popular cultural exhibits. I turn next to the politics of the moment as it is laced through and through with gender markings, including (or so I shall claim), not only traces reincoded in pro- and anti-feminist argumentation but inscribed on the female body itself as a kind of cultural text.

The body politic/political bodies

All sorts of female types vie for contemporary consideration and, except for the "return to traditional womanhood" arguments of anti-feminist spokeswomen, each presents itself as a "new woman" made possible, in part, by feminism and a loosening up of gendered identities. *The New York Times Magazine* has extolled the Career Mom, managing a household (with co-equal participation of an understanding spouse or dependable household help, including nannies), spending "quality" time with her children, succeeding on all fronts. This vision puts lots of pressure on women who are not thus *managing* — the importation of language drawn from industrial engineering is interesting here — and valorizes an ideal of female success, at least for the relatively well-educated and well-to-do. What's new about this new woman is that she is *guilt-free*, or so she says and the up-beat journalists who write such features claim. She can and is having it all. "Succeeding makes us feel good," notes a spokeswomen for this group. All traces of earlier constructions of woman that might put pressure on the individualist/success ethic must be quashed to achieve the guilt-free end.

Take a second example, the super-fit specimen. Jane Fonda rushes at us whooping a war-cry in her penultimate exercise video, "Jane Fonda's Work-Out Challenge," and begins a full hour and a half of non-stop, grueling physical effort. For about a half hour she is flanked by two male bodies, one white, one black, framing her efforts in a scenario that is part Affirmative Action, part transgressive sexual fantasizing. You, too, can look like this as you near 50, the sexily sweating, tautly wired image tells us. This *is* the new woman. You just need willpower and a certain number of hours everyday and you can join this body/politic. What gets eliminated is any physical sign of softness, or roundness, or fecundity or the process of aging. The workout woman is sexualized but curiously defeminized, achieving as near as possible a physical symmetry to the equally fit male.

A third sign: the wasted anorexic. Young women, drawn from middle to upper-middle class ranks, white, privileged, starving themselves . . . to death . . . if no one intervenes to forstall the process. Sharing the demographic "indicators" of the Successful Woman who has it all, and the Super Fit of workout challenges, the adolescent anorexic starves herself back into childhood: menopause ceases, secondary sex characteristics fade, she has control, it seems, over a body *politicized* in a particular and destructive way. The rapid growth of anorexia is curiously linked to a *decrease* in actual power differences — in education and social life — between the sexes. A number of studies indicate that there is a causal connection between a *rise* in opportunities for women ("You, too, can be a nuclear physicist!") and increases in anorexia. The pressures of a social and cultural world moving towards one version of gender equality — the liberal, individualist sex-neutrality ideal — appears to be inscribing itself in and through the bodies of young women whose response to these pressures and to a world in which they are *enjoined* to "have it all," is a poignantly self-defeating revolt. This, at least, is the interpretation I will opt for as it demonstrates powerfully the ways in which the body is a politics. In the case of the anorexic, the body is the young woman's final redoubt, the only "thing" she can control in a world in which she is pressured to become a "male" without losing her femininity.

One final example, this from newer and ever creepier forms of reproductive technology. The experiments with "positive eugenics" take place in, through, and even over bodies of women. Women are now enjoined not to harbor faulty genetic products. It becomes an ethical and political responsibility to engage in pre-natal testing of various sorts, expunging less-than-perfect specimens before they are born. This "new" biology is a souped-up version of an old canard — what used to be called an "old wives' tale." In the older versions, a women who indulged in secret vices, including illicit sex, or who participated in guilty pleasures, including drink, might well give birth to a marked infant: the sign of her disgrace was borne on the body of her offspring. Our new version of this is far more insidious because the woman now has the *power*, hence the socially compelled "free choice," courtesy of the medicalized-technologized reproductive establishment, to intervene in the process and to prevent flawed outcomes. Her body has become the playground of technological hubris.

Mary Douglas writes of the human body as a "symbol of society." She says: " . . . the powers and dangers credited to social structures are reproduced in small on the human body."[12] The female body as a symbol of society historically has signified fecundity, rebirth, the regenesis of social life. Increasingly, however, the female body is marked by the terms set by the dominant body-self, the normative, techno-male of the modern West. And the "powers and dangers credited to the social structure are reproduced in small on the human body," in Douglas's words, and, in the examples above, on the female body as a politicized construction. What we see is sex-neutrality with a vengeance and a stripping of the female body of its compelling if problematic potency tied to gender difference. There is no easy way out of this conundrum.

But we do know a few things. Historic and ethnographic evidence suggests that women's economic and political power and authority is most likely to occur where one finds a "magico-religious association between maternity and fertility of the soil," thus associating women "with social continuity and social good."[13] Cultural anthropologists argue that to view male and female authority in societies like the Iroquois, for example, where women wielded great power in some areas as men did in others, as sexually unequal by definition reflects a Western, state bias. Dozens of societies, they insist, were worlds in which neither sex was dominant over the other, but each prevailed in demarcated areas of social life.

What are we to make of all this? We cannot return to pre-secular, pre-modern ways of life. We are all marked by the present moment. We cannot leap-frog over or out of our gendered conundrums. But we can see that secular male dominance is most visible, and creates the harshest sustained pressure on that gallery of "new woman" noted above, in which complementarity of powers (in the plural) has given way to an enhancement and expansion of institutionalized male authority accompanied by a simultaneous diminution of women's domestic, sacral, and social authority.

Women are left with few apparent options: to acquiesce in their historic loss of symbolic-domestic authority; to manipulate their diminished social role inside increasingly powerless families; or to join forces with the men, assuming masculine roles and identities and competing for power on established, institutionalized terms. Each of these options, however, embodies, figuratively and literally, its own deformations. As none seems particularly attractive, we must rethink the terms of our current situation. I am searching for a language — one that breaks us out of our engendered prisons — a language in and through which we could all, men and women, see that dependence and independence, powerlessness and power, are deeply related and that not all forms of human vulnerability, can or should be rationalized out of our theories and our ways of being in the world. This shifts our focus from obsession with images of female victimization as a feminist vocation, towards recognition of the often terrible costs of being the institutionally and politically dominant sex. For is it not ironic that the powerful male has also been the more expendable of the sexes — that, historically, male bodies were sent into battle to kill and to die in order that female bodies be protected? Do we Americans not convey a peculiar double message to our own eighteen year old sons whose social power and social vulnerability is signaled by registration for the draft?

De-textualising, re-embodying: towards a new politics of representation

I began by noting how difficult it is for men and women in American society, or so our dominant texts tells us, to communicate with one another. Continuing in this vein, I exhumed various texts, including several feminist exemplars, that shored up gendered identities even as they claimed to seek their displacement or dispersion. I moved to the inscription of current social pressures on female bodies as literalizations of our tropes. Or, to put it less fancily, what begins as text, or test tube, or polemic may end as a woman's success with the normative structure, her disempowerment in the name of choice as the one who gives birth, or her starvation as a form of control in a chaotic world of constructed choices.

There is no way *out* but there may be several ways *in*: by going back to the texts and offering readings that track the ambiguities and ironies of our gendered identities rather than reincoding them for whatever purpose; or by breaking out of the texts and reading what I earlier called "lived life" as a set of more fluid representations. This latter would require something of an ethnography along the lines of Clifford Geertz's interpretive cultural anthropology, a world of "thick description," determining how men and women in their many social faces and places act and think and react, outside the world of the academic argument. The former calls upon us to break out of the facticities of encoded truths, whether feminist or not, to return with skeptical eyes to powerful texts and open them up to newer modes of interrogation that might loosen up gender markings, whether of the hard-line sex-polarity or sex-neutrality sorts.

My example will be the writing of Ernest Hemingway, our prime cultural ideal of the man's man — killing animals, brawling, fighting in wars (any war, any time, the more the merrier), loving women, doing it his way. On the one hand there is "Hemingway," the man of the constructed myth, an image he and his culture reinforced and finally he could not have escaped from it had he tried: he had become *that* Hemingway. And, having become "Hemingway," he had to blow his brains out. He couldn't lose it and grow old and not be the blustering, indomitable figure of the tabloids and the Nobel Prize and the valorization of a strong reading of the American male.

What is curious about all this is how feminist critics reinforced the "Hemingway" of gendered rigidities, reading his texts as he, caught in his own facticity, insisted they be read: the work of the he-man contesting all softness and fighting women's attempts to emasculate him and his world and, by extension, that of all good men everywhere. Reading Hemingway through the Hemingway myth, and later feminist attacks that ironically shored it up, one loses the nuance, the terror, the ambiguities that lurk just beneath the surface and from time to time break through. I rely here on my own rediscovery of the world of the texts by Hemingway, not the text of "Hemingway's" world, as I re-read *A Farewell to Arms* and *For Whom the Bell Tolls* and other works as part of my "research" for my own text on *Women and War*. More importantly, I discovered the Hemingway of the text going through Kenneth Lynn's fascinating biography and encountering, for the first time, short stories told from the woman's point of view; themes of androgyny and transsexuality that has escaped my own earlier readings, dominated, as they were, by strong gender codings.[14]

If one is committed to the *dance macabre* of America's gendered rigidities, one can see only "Hemingway," male blusterer or hero. If, however, one believes that we do have alternatives to bleating to, or ranting at, one another from our respective cages, rattling the bars of gendered constructions, worlds of ambiguity, and sympathetic identity, and mutual vulnerability open up — and these, surely must be the starting point to a new politics of gender representation.

Read this:

> The boards were hard. Jim had her dress up and was trying to do something to her. She was frightened but she wanted it. She had to have it but it frightened her.
>
> "You musn't do it, Jim. You mustn't."
>
> "I got to. I'm going to. You know we got to."
>
> "No, we haven't, Jim. We ain't got to. Oh, it isn't right. Oh, it's so big and it hurts so. You can't. Oh, Jim. Jim. Oh."
>
> The hemlock planks of the dock were hard and splintery and cold and Jim was heavy on her and he had hurt her. Liz pushed him, she was so uncomfortable and cramped. Jim was asleep.[15]

Now find some way to discuss this scene of seduction, and desire, and fear, and pain that takes you, and an interlocutor, beyond those reified codes that are ready-to-hand into a discursive realm that frees up the possibility of empathic cross-identification, meaning that neither you nor your partner in communication either give up or shore up your already constructed identities, knowing that the dialogue on which you embark may have the effect of shattering received wisdom, putting pressure on ideologies, and dispersing particular features of both "self" and "other." Kafka once observed that a bird goes in search of a cage. In the matter of gender. American culture has devised a number of cages. We can, perhaps, become the sorts of birds that search for ways out, or at least in and out, knowing we can never fly free for that would be not to exist in culture as an embodied being, hence one who will always confront, and be constituted by, constructions of gender.

10.

Working Class Culture in the Electronic Age

Stanley Aronowitz

I

Individual and collective identities are constructed on three articulated sites: the biological, the social, and the cultural. The biologically given characteristics which we bring to every social interaction are often covered over by social relations (such as the family and the school) and the technological sensorium that we call mass or popular culture. In western culture these biological givens assume meaning over which individuals have some control, but are often beyond our powers to reverse. Our race and sex confer boundaries as well as possibilities in various relations, particularly the kind of friends we can make, work we can do, mates that are available to us. Of course, the meanings of race and sex, like those of class, are socially constituted — there is no "inherent" significance to these identities as social signs. However, we are born into these identities, given the social arrangements.

The second crucial site is our interaction with family, school, the workplace, and other conventional institutions such as the Church. These relationships are often conceived as self-determining, that is, free of their biological givens. Obviously, parents and teachers treat boys and girls differently: we might say they enjoy/suffer a different moral development regardless of class membership or race. As many writers have argued, the family remains, perhaps, the crucial site for reproducing sexual differences.

While schools are crucial secondary institutions in reproducing sexual difference, they play a major part in the reproduction of racial

135

difference, the specific forms of which remain to be fully explored. It is enough here to point out that the school is the first place the child experiences as racially segregated, since modernism ended gender segregation. It is in school that the child experiences itself as white or black: needless to say, textbooks make clear to blacks their subordinate status, apart from any overt content. Black images, even when they appear, are tokens of the power of the civil rights movement over the past thirty years, but black history and black culture remain absent, a silence which signifies relations of domination. Of course, there are less subtle signs of difference: the failure of racial integration since the Supreme Court decision outlawing segregation thirty-five years ago is an overwhelming feature of public schooling. White kids learn that they are of a specific race simply by virtue of the absence of blacks in their classrooms. Blacks understand this by parental instruction, but realize that race means subordination by virtue of second-class education, the inferior resources made available to them, and finally come to realize that their individual and collective life chances have been decided long before they enter the workworld (a realization white working-class kids only have by secondary school).

Class representations are largely constructed by mass-mediated culture, especially since the working-class community, like the urban-based mass-production industries that created it, passed into history. I do not want to devalue the importance of school for determining "how working-class kids get working class jobs" (in Paul Willis's account, mostly by rebelling against the middle-class curriculum[1]). This process still occurs in schools, but the working-class kids' culture — at least among whites — is acutely marginalized in an era when, in the older cities of industrial capitalism, the traditional working class is being wiped out.

In this paper I want to concentrate on the third crucial site where identity is constructed, that of mass-mediated culture. I especially want to trace the *displacement* of representations of the working class in this realm. I will show that there are no longer direct representations of the interactions among workers in American television, but that these have been refracted through the police shows that still (in 1988) dominate prime time. These same shows have become important in British and French television also. In this connection it may be argued that television shows that are "made in the USA" have become important exports. As American-made durable goods no longer dominate world markets for these products, the ingression of American culture in world communications markets has grown. This inverse ratio can be seen in new films in Paris. For example, in any given week, of the dozen new films opening in that city, between four and six are American imports.

Miami Vice, Hill Street Blues, and *LA Law* are among the top twenty shows in English and French television. Only advertising appears to remain truly national, but signs of Americanization are appearing in French commercial videos, including ads.

Mass-media representations can no longer be grouped under institutional socializations which include the family, peer interactions, and schools. The media are *unique* sites precisely because of the specific place of technology in the production of culture. To be more precise, mass-mediated visual culture occupies the "objective" space of the dream work, and constitutes its double. Louis Althusser's claim that the school is the chief ideological state apparatus may hold for the production of the *symbolic* system, that constellation of signs and codes through which is construed the field of what counts as reliable knowledge.[2] But the mass media construct the *social imaginary,* the place where kids situate themselves in their emotional life, where the future appears as a narration of possibilities as well as limits.

I also want to argue that what we call "popular culture" has become technologically mediated, even as the acoustic guitar is now an instrument for the production of high or esoteric music. The popular is still produced by the "people," but is no longer appropriated directly (just as the biological givens return in a subsumed form through social construction). That is to say, we can no longer (if we ever could) distinguish what really counts as a popular form from the electronically produced culture that is consumed as records, television programs, or movies.[3] Television is not just a manipulator of popular culture, it constitutes a crucial element in the construction of imaginary life and is appropriated, just like rock music for young people, as popular culture (in the same manner as songs and dances for rural populations in the preindustrial era).

The electronic media can determine, to some degree, *how* social life is represented (that is, their autonomous field of action consists in modes of representation), but not whether a social category *will* be represented. Therefore, it is literally not possible to totally exclude working-class representations, but is it equally improbable that these representations would remain direct under conditions where the cultural traditions of workers are disappearing or occupying smaller social spaces. Moreover, modes of representation are themselves refracted narratives of working-class history. So, if we find representations of working-class life assuming the configuration of police shows or, in the case of Bruce Springsteen, a nostalgia for the absent subject, we can take these forms as social knowledge open to critical deciphering like all fictions.

II

When I worked in the steel mills, the barroom was far more than a place to have a casual beer or to get drunk. It was scene of union politics, the site of convivial relationships that were hard to sustain on the shop floor because of the noise, frequent speedups, and the ever watchful eye of the foreman. Of course we had the john, but only for twenty-minutes at a time; as the metal was heating up in furnaces, we often took a break. Sometimes the john substituted for the barroom. Animated arguments took place about baseball, women, or an incident that had just occurred, usually one in which one of our fellow workers was hurt (I remember Felix who caught a hot wire in his leg). But inevitably, the warning buzzer would interrupt our discussions — metal was nearly ready to come out and be drawn into wire.

So, the "gin mill" was the place where our collective identity as a community was forged and reproduced. Even when we had harsh disagreements about things that really mattered (whether we should stop work over a safety grievance or whether Jackie Robinson was a better second baseman that Billy Martin, a tinderbox of an issue in 1960), we knew that the next day we would have to pull together in the hot mill, that our disputes were in the family. We also knew that we had to fight the boss together, not only for the ordinary reasons of better pay and benefits, but for our survival. The mill was a dangerous place and, for most of us, losing a limb meant losing the best paying job we were ever likely to own, for in the union shops of the 1950s and early 1960s, the job was a property right. As we used to say, the only reason you could get fired was if you punched the foreman while sober.

Steelwork was definitely male culture. As in Freud's essay on femininity, women were the mysterious "other." We did not know much about them and, apart from the incessant desire that occupied our prurient conversations, they did not enter into our working lives. Women were an obscure object of our desire, but desire also reached out for a secure collective identity. For even as early as fifteen years after the war, the neighborhoods of Newark, Elizabeth, and Jersey City (within which working people saw in the faces of others a part of their own selves, a self that was recognized in the local grocery store, at bingo games held in the basements of Catholic Churches which became the place where the women's community was formed) were in the process of dissolving. I remember meeting shopmates at the movies, in the neighborhood Chinese restaurant where we took the kids for dinner some Sunday evenings, in the bar on South Orange Avenue where a diemaker named John hung out (we became friends because we were both interested in music; he played accordian, professionally, at Polish weddings on weekends).

I went to christenings and confirmations in the area around the place which was located in an industrial suburb. Most of the families were of eastern and southern European backgrounds, not only Italians and Poles (although they were in the majority), but also Czechs, Russians, and Greeks. People lived around the northern New Jersey plants in wood frame one-family houses or in "uppers" (the second and third floors of multiple dwellings). Those of us who were not veterans of the Second World War or the Korean War did not qualify for special mortgage deals, so we rented apartments that ate about 25% of our monthly pay. However, a growing minority of my friends were moving to the middle-class suburbs where single-family housing developments were mushrooming, or more graphically, springing up like weeds. These were more modern homes, often built without firm foundations even though they were constructed on landfill. They surely did not fulfill the letter of James Truslow Adam's "American Dream," but they were an acceptable facsimile until something better came along.

Suburban flight was made feasible by low-interest mortgages, but also by the federal highway program initiated by President Harry Truman and fulfilled by the Eisenhower administration. In earlier years, living fifteen or twenty miles from the plant was simply not an option because the roads were invariably local. Such a round trip could take more than two hours. Now, barring traffic jams, evening- and night-shift workers could make it to work in twenty minutes, and those working days simply left home before rush hour and came back late. For many, being away from the wife and kids presented few, if any, problems; male culture excluded women and the notion that men should share child care was simply unthinkable in most families in those days. Certainly, many workers were left behind — blacks and Hispanics, young workers not yet able to raise a down payment or still unmarried and older workers who had literally failed to recover from the depression wipe-out.

White working-class flight was engendered, in part, by the influx of southern and Caribbean blacks into large northern cities, and also by the failure of federal and state lawmakers to expand the federal housing program beyond the poor. In fact, the choice of the home mortgage program was the alternative to new multi-dwelling housing for workers; housing for large families was simply unavailable in the cities at rents that even relatively high-paid steel workers could afford. Racism was not the "cause" of white flight in the sense that individuals who harbored these attitudes decided to move to get away from blacks. Racism is the result of a combination of developments. In addition to the urban housing shortage (where virtually no new one-family moderate income homes were constructed after the war), the era was marked by a precipitous decline in services — schools, hospitals, and amenities such as recreation and child care were in either serious disrepair or overcrowded.

In historical retrospect, the deterioration of the urban regions after the war was federal and corporate policy. By the mid 1960s center-city industrial plants were closing down. In Harrison, the industrial suburb of Newark, General Motors removed its roller bearing plant to the Union county suburb, Kenilworth. General Electric closed its lamp factory in the black section of Newark, and by the end of the decade, no major industrial plant remained in that city. Jersey City and Hoboken suffered similar fates; industrial expansion was still a powerful spur to economic growth, but not in the big cities. Capital and white working-class flight go together with the federal housing and highway programs, and the enthusiasm of local communities to give away the keys to the town to any corporation willing to build a plant, office building, or research facility.

The dispersion of white workers into the suburbs did not immediately destroy working-class communities, although they were considerably weakened by the late 1950s. The gin mill next to the production mill retained its pride of place. Sometimes this function was performed by a bar located in a local union hall or in a fraternal association of, say, Poles or Ukrainians. Typically, a worker would "stop" at the bar after going off shift for an hour or two before going to a home that could be as far as even forty miles away. There, he would play darts, shuffle board, or pool, or sit at the bar and just drink and talk.

Those who worked days arrived home at 7 p.m. (the shift ends at 3 p.m.). After supper, if there were no chores, the family might sit in front of the television set. The television explosion of the 1950s is generally acknowledged to have changed the leisure-time activities of Americans. The simulations that film brought to theater audiences now became daily fare.

III

Until the early 1960s, a small number of films and TV shows offered direct representations of white workers (usually in a comic or pathetic mode) but the mode of this presentation changed in the next decades. Workers became the object of liberal scorn, portrayed as racist and sexist, and equally important, as politically and socially conservative. Archie Bunker (*All in the Family* [1971–83]) was not only a comic character: he was a moral agent suffused with evil, a direct violation of the code according to which the working class (however scarce its media image) was invariably a hero. In contrast to Marlon Brando's 1954 portrayal (*On the Waterfront*) of a benighted but brave longshoreman who, in the last analysis, comes down for truth and justice, Bunker is a troglodyte, a "hard hat" whose wrath is aimed at the young, the poor, and the blacks.

It was hard for working-class kids to identify with Archie, but he was, as late as the mid-1970s a palpable working-class figure, recognizable by his syntax, his body language, his gruff, semi-articulate speech that parodied the results of working-class culture. As I shall demonstrate, Archie proved to be a rearguard character. After his demise (or, rather, his good fortune in having moved up the social ladder), specifically working-class representations disappear with him. Today, working-class kids may still look forward to getting working-class jobs, but forging a class identity is more difficult than ever. They confront a media complex that consistently denies their existence. However, in what amounts to a grudging acknowledgment that it is really impossible to achieve this result, working-class male identity is *displaced* to other, upwardly mobile occupations (e.g. police, football players, and other sites where conventional masculine roles are ubiquitous).

The message is clear: working-class identity, always problematic in American mass culture, is no longer an option. In media representations, we live in a post-industrial service society in which only the traditional *markers* of working-class culture survive. This is especially true for the barroom, where waves of male industrial workers have congregated to share their grievances against the boss, their private troubles, their dreams of collective power and individual escape, their visions of women, their power displacements to the sports arena. But working-class men do not inhabit these television or movie precincts. Instead, they are the watering holes of off-duty cops, of derelicts, of miscellaneous white-collar administrators. The working class is absent among these signifiers, even as the sites and the forms of conviviality correspond to typical working-class cultural scenes.

Electronically mediated cultural forms play an enlarged role in the formation of cultural identities. Of course, the claim that media are so hegemonic that they exclude the influence of family, peers, and schools appears excessive. But, it would be a serious error to conclude that it is an even match. I claim that electronically mediated cultural forms have the upper hand because they carry the authority of the society that, over the last half century, has displaced patriarchial authority. For the discourse of social authority promises what family and friends cannot deliver: a qualitatively better life, consumption on an expanded scale, a chance to move beyond the limits of traditional working-class life.

No institution represents the promise of this type of transcendence more than the school, for its curriculum is widely understood as a ticket to class mobility. However, the *content* of that alternative is offered working-class kids by the situation comedies of television, the celluloid dreams of the movies, and especially the advertisements which evoke lifestyles considered worthy of emulation. I argue that the relationship between schooling and media representations of vocational and cultural aspirations has become symbiotic: to the extent that the curriculum is almost entirely geared to the presumed occupational requirements of modern corporations and the state, the dependence of what counts as education on the collective cultural ideal is almost total. For these occupational requirements, especially in large parts of the service sector, are not so much technical as they are ideological. That is, just as many advertisements sell not products but capitalism, so school learning is organized around behaviors required by types of bureaucratic work, as well as the rewards offered by consumer society for performance according to established corporate norms. The student is no longer (if *he* ever was) enthusiastic about discovering new things to know, much less Truth. Rather, he wants to find out how the real world works, especially what it takes to achieve a certain level of consumption. In this, the high school is the major site where the "real" world of work is discovered. The student remembers little or nothing of the content of knowledge (facts of history, how to perform algebraic equations, the story line of *Silas Marner*) but remembers how to succeed in receiving good grades, gaining admission to a decent college, or university, and how to curry favor with authorities — teachers, counselors, employers.

Working-class kids often fail to get the message right. As Paul Willis tells us, their rebellion against school authority, manifested as the refusal to internalize the two parts of the curriculum (its manifest "knowledge-based" content and its latent demand for discipline and respect for authority) ensures that they will get working-class jobs rather than make it up the ladder. But, while assembly-line, construction, and other heavy industrial labor was available for school leavers until the 1970s in the US and UK, these options are today foreclosed by the restructured world economy. Parents, especially fathers, can no longer serve as substitute representations of viable occupational alternatives to those imposed by school and the media. Peers may discourage an individual from integrating into the prescribed curricula, but the cultural ideal is now increasingly provided by the media. As this ideal erases working-class representations so the class sensorium disappears.

We see this problematic replayed in the film *Dirty Dancing* (1987). A wealthy family in the early 1960s goes to a Borscht Belt Catskill mountain resort for a short vacation. Two daughters are immediately plunged into the social life, mostly with waiters and entertainers. The waiter chosen by one of the daughters is a Yale Law School student and turns out to be a philanderer. The other daughter commits the transgression that provides the dramatic grist for the narrative: she falls in love with the resort's star attraction, a working-class youth who has succeeded in learning Latin, ballet and other "exotic" dances. He gives lessons, performs, and fools around with the women who work as entertainers or in the kitchen, similarly of lower-class background. Unlike other films of this developing genre of class indiscretion (working-class men/upper-class women), this film has a happy ending because the young woman chooses to become a dancer — she exercises her option to downward mobility, to be declassed. The working-class man has become a professional; he may be working in the Catskills but he certainly is talented. And these qualities have already separated him from his roots, so the relationship is acceptable.

I shall amplify on the theme of displacement later in this paper. For now, it is enough to ask how to engage in a pedagogy among working-class students concerning their social identity. Indeed, if identification is a basis for the forging of a personal identity, school and media consort to persuade, cajole, and, by the absence of representations, force working-class kids to accept middle-class identities as the only legitimate option available to them. However, it is obvious that many will choose neither to accept this course or, having bought into the aspirations, will "fail" to make the grade. The result for both groups is cultural homelessness. Clearly, the task of a pedagogy that addresses this dilemma is to address it by a critical examination of its contours, its motivations, and its consequences.

From this discussion, several issues come to the front as being important: the ineluctibility of the merger of masculinity with working-class identity; the question of displacement and its effects on self-images; and the class/gender reversals in contemporary representations in film and television (that is, the degree to which male "conquest" becomes the power equivalent of class difference). The next section will address these issues.

IV

The stimulation of the unconscious by "imaging" (the term is Teresa di Lauretis's[4]) consists in simulating the dream work so that identities are formed through identification with the gendered characters that appear on the screen. Aural media are also powerful desiring machines, but sound is burdened with an enormous load because images must be produced by the listener. Identification can be fomented but with difficulty. The film form invokes the stark real-life character. Di Lauretis argues that women do not insert themselves into film culture, that they are absent in imagining. They cannot identify with the actual representations of women on the screen, for these women are the objects of male desire — they do not occupy subject positions from which emanates a distinctive female voice. Thus, there is no chance for identification unless women accept the object space to which they have been assigned.

Males identify with characters (protagonists, heroes) who are the subjects of narratives; women are objects of desire/exchange/conflict among males and only assume distinctive character when they occupy male-subject positions from which, in both comedies and drama they must inevitably fall (e.g. the Spencer Tracy/Katherine Hepburn comedies such as *Women of the Year* [1942] and *Desk Set* [1957], and the Joan Crawford soap operas such as *Mildred Pierce* [1945], in which women who speak as male characters find that adopting these personae invites self-destruction). Male workers do find representations in film and television in the 1950s. The characters of Ralph Cramden and Ed Norton in *The Honeymooners* (1951–56; revived 1966–70 as part of *The Jackie Gleason Show*) and Chester Riley in *The Life of Riley* (1949–58) are comically absurd, the situations often artificial and juvenile, but family relationships articulate with the prevalent war between the sexes, the distinctiveness of male culture, the absence of a corresponding women's community.

Ralph Cramden is a bus driver who, like many working-class men, dreams of escaping his routine, relatively low-paid job by entering a constant succession of bound-to-fail business schemes. His driving ambition for wealth and social position is lodged entirely in his (male) imaginary. Ralph's wife Alice can barely disguise contempt for his fantasies and foolish projects — most of which serve not to enhance the opportunity for real social mobility, but Ralph's pathetic efforts to establish his dominance in the home. On the other side is Norton, a sewer worker who harbors neither illusion nor the desire to flee his job. The sewer affords him a considerable measure of autonomy, at least in comparison to factory work or even driving a bus. He enjoys the lack of responsibility his job entails but fervently asserts its dignified character against the constant chidings of his quixotic friend.

As with most television situation comedies, the characters have a cartoon quality: there is no room for complexity in the representations. Additionally, the stripped-down sets evoke 1930s depression decorum rather than the post-war era. The honeymooners have been left behind the white urban exodus; they are transhistorical working-class types.

Norton is invariably dressed in a T-shirt and wears his hat indoors. Cramden dons the uniform of a bus driver, signifying the ambiguity of his situation. Clearly he is a wage laborer, but his will is that of a petty official since genuine wealth has been foreclosed to him. Cramden displaces his frustration onto intrafamilial quarrels. His wife's housework never counts as real work — his characteristic posture is that of an inquisitor (what have you been doing all day?). Since she rarely awards him the deference he urgently needs, given his relatively degraded social position, his usual gesture is the verbal threat of violence (against women): "one of these days . . . pow, right in the kisser." Alice seems bored by his remonstrations, and we, the audience, know that Ralph is simply too henpecked (or, in the male vernacular, pussy whipped) to follow through.

The Honeymooners retains its large audience after thirty years because it displays the range of class and gender relations. Its class ideology is represented by the absence of the labor process except discursively. The family relations displace the class relations, as Ralph seeks to dominate Alice, who as the real proletarian remains recalcitrant. Here we see the inner core of male fantasies: lacking the power individually to achieve the freedom wealth presumably affords, domination becomes the object of male desire. As with Hegel's master, Ralph desperately covets Alice's recognition, but is denied such pleasures, except in the last instance when, at his wit's end, Ralph demands the approbation which she must grant.

The Honeymooners succeeds as a tableau of the sadomasochistic family romance. Ralph's infantile behavior generates Alice's maternal role even as there are no children in the household. Ralph plays master, insofar as he trumpets his breadwinner status, but also is the emotionally dependent male for whom sexuality is identical with submission. Alice is not a moral agent, only a mirror to the absurdity of male will.

Caricature notwithstanding, working-class life demanded representations in the 1950s and early 1960s. By the latter half of the decade, the dispersion of working-class culture made direct representation improbable. The film *Joe* (1970) lacked the framework to comprehend the dimensions of the youth revolt. In this film, Ralph has succeeded in owning a one-family house, complete with a finished basement and late model car. Ralph rejected Alice's hints that maybe they could leave the inner city for greener fields, but Joe has achieved the castle without the power of the Lord, except in the family. Yet, the satisfaction of mastery is denied him by his child's refusal to follow the path laid out by society. The child returns to the jungle of the cities and prefers sex, drugs, and (presumably) rock and roll to the sterility of suburban life. Youth culture respects not at all the middle-class aspirations of its elders. Where the previous generation knew economic class as a regulative principle, including the real subordination of women by men, the generation of the 1960s was, by comparison, free-floating. The universalization of post-secondary schooling (misnamed higher education then, as now) brought many working-class kids in contact with ruling- and upper-class peers. The results from the point of view of the established social structure was potentially devastating. Surely class resentments and distinctions do not disappear in youth culture, but are explicitly challenged by the effort to invent new normative principles of social relations. These relations, which hold equality as its highest cultural ideal, challenge generations of difference, not only of economic power but of sexually construed cultures. In the end Joe must commit murder to expiate the transgressions of the children.

But the worker as tragic hero is a transitional figure, for the tragedy is born of the disintegration already prefigured by consumer society, especially suburbanization. Working-class culture is preeminently urban; it belongs to the industrializing era which, by the late 1960s has passed. Post-industrial culture is already post-modern: it is marked by boundary crossing. As David Halle found, while working-class culture still finds renewal on the shop floor, its residential base is dispersed.[5] In the suburbs of major metropolitan centers, industrial workers mow their lawns alongside professionals, managers, and small business neighbors.

In the 1977–78 season, Archie Bunker, the Queens, New York political and social neanderthal, opened a gin mill. Having pushed himself up into the business-owning small middle class, Archie left his working-class roots behind, not only in his newly found proprietorship, but also in his contacts. In this assimilation, he continued the tendencies of the earlier incarnation of the show; recall, the Bunker family lived in that part of New York that most resembled the suburbs. The only Black family he knew owned and operated a dry cleaning business (the Jeffersons, their *own* TV series beginning in 1975). In other words, he rubbed shoulders with those who had more completely achieved one of the crucial elements of the American dream, a business of one's own. So it is entirely reasonable that Archie should aspire to gaining a toehold in the social ladder. With that, the Archie of *Archie Bunker's Place* (the series' new name, as of 1979) disappears into the middle class.

From the mid-1970s, there simply are no direct representations of working-class males (much less women) in television. Representations are dispersed to beer advertisements (thirty-second images of football players hoisting their favorite brands, jostling each other in timid evocations of the ribbing characteristic of working-class bar culture), and cop shows in which characteristic working-class culture is displaced and recontextualized in the stationhouse, on the streets, and the bars in which cops congregate. These are displacements, so we see only the reminders — conviviality and friendship that is overdetermined by the Police buddy system, the obligatory partnership. It is in these interactions, when the partners of say, *Hill Street Blues* (first aired, 1981), discuss their personal problems or their troubles with the Department, that the old class solidarity bonds are permitted to come to the surface, often against the Captain or even the lieutenants who are a step above the line and possess some authority. We know that the patrolmen (and some patrolwomen) may rise to Sergeant, but are not likely to make Lieutenant, much less Captain. These are not educated men and women. Their bravery entitles them to recognition, not rank. They have their own hangouts, their personal troubles (especially with their love lives). In contrast, officials, whatever their origins, do not congregate in barrooms; they have no sharer of their troubles because they must observe the tacit code of hierarchy.

In recent films, displacement of class to the police continues, but is joined by displacement or sex/gender relations to class as well. Hollywood movies (such as *Someone to Watch Over Me* [1987] and *Barfly* [1987]) are marked by a conventional theme in contemporary narrative: the working-class man is powerfully attracted to an upper-class woman, disrupting not only the prohibition of interclass romance, but also the family romance. In these instances, to be working class is identified with masculinity, upper class with femininity. Barbet Schroeder's *Barfly* is the non-story of a derelict writer who meets two women: a derelict, apparently a renegade from upper-class life, who names her profession as "drinking," and a woman publisher of a literary magazine who "discovers" the writer. The triangle is resolved by his choice of the woman barfly who, like him, lives to drink and engages in barroom brawls. Her masculinity allows him to hook up with her, to combine sex and male bonding. In contrast, his benefactor is a beautiful woman who cannot hold her liquor and, because she lives outside male lower-class culture, cannot hold him.

The woman barfly engages the world like a man in other ways also. She goes off with the writer's arch enemy, a bartender in his favorite hangout, because he comes to work one day with a full bottle of bourbon. Like many males, her loyalty to people is always subordinate to loyalty to pleasure. In the end, the writer admires such priorities, for his own life has been conducted according to the precept that conventional mortality is for the nerds.

Someone to Watch Over Me finds a cop of plainly working-class parentage, married to a tough, fiesty working-class woman, who live together with their kids in a modest single-family house in Queens.

Archie Bunker's kid has become a cop. The cop is assigned to protect an upper-class woman, ensconced in a Manhattan townhouse. He is assigned the midnight shift and quickly has an affair with her, an event that disrupts his tension-filled but stable home life. As with the young publisher of *Barfly*, the woman is attracted by the merger of class identity and masculinity, and he by the reverse class/sex combination. The film reenacts a crucial male working-class fantasy: to dominate a beautiful rich woman, to make the "impossible dream" real.

These films address the insufficiency of middle-class comfort for the generation of upwardly mobile working-class kids born after the Second World War. The protagonist of *Barfly* chooses the underlife, a degraded bohemia punctuated by the struggle for male honor even in the lower depths. The cop is socialized into a conventional honorific position — the centurian — but finds it suffused with mediocrity and, most important of all, marked by repetition and continuity with the anterior generation. What is new is adventure, which can only be fulfilled by sexual indiscretion, "penetration" into the forbidden territory of the upper class. But beside the exotic, for the cop, buried in the routine tasks dictated by a bureaucracy that seems entirely beyond his power to control, sex becomes the power that can propel him out of his own real-life subordination.

It may be that today sex discourse refers to class issues; but it is also true class discourse refers to gender domination. The import of the image of the working class cum cop engaging in sexual relations with a women in an entirely improbable class position is not that American society is somehow democratic — these relationships end in disaster. They are themselves sundered, but more importantly they wreck families, personal lives, and so forth. The significance is otherwise. Class is no barrier when upper-class women are involved. In current representations, the reverse is rarely portrayed. Femininity is not a universal signifier. That privilege is reserved for male culture.

There are, of course, no public representations of working-class culture other than the images associated with male bonding. In fact, one may read *Barfly* as a signal that one key site of class solidarity, the bar, has been declassed. Or, more precisely, the lumpies are the legatees of what was once a marginalized but distinct aspect of American subcultures. And, just as women are absent from media representations of social agents, they do not constitute themselves as a part of working-class culture. Working-class culture is almost always white and male, even in its displaced forms. The community of women is generally denied but, as I have argued, women appear as the new proletarians insofar as maleness exercizes itself as dominating power.

At first glance *Flashdance* (1983) is an exception to the rule. A woman welder in a steel fabricating plant falls in love with the boss, himself cast in the tradition of the self-made made man rather than the MBA or accountant mode. Here class difference is mediated by other bonds of solidarity, particularly sexuality (itself a difference) and membership in the same occupational community. The film presents the "new" woman as both male and female. Yet the relationship presupposes both her male and female personae. Like *Barfly* interclass sexual relations are possible only when the women displays masculinity, which remains the privileged class position.

In short, in contrast to the 1950s when a viable working-class culture, connected to powerful large-scale industry, was accorded considerable status in media representations, class has been displaced in two ways: first, to other signifiers of masculinity, and second, to the code violations entailed in sexual relations between working-class or declassed men and upper-class women. In this case, sex/class relations are reversed. Men, despite lower-class roots, achieve class parity with women due to the status conferred upon masculine sexuality and its powers by society.

In *Someone to Watch Over Me* and other examples of this relationship, the absent male is a businessman. His shadowy existence is owed to the obvious fact entailed by the conditions of his own success: his real marriage is to the business, not to his wife. Sexuality of the traditional sort is confined to those without sublimations, which accounts for its relatively ambiguous role in the barfly's life. Writing and booze are serious competitors, but for the working-class man, neither art nor business provide channels for the discharge of erotic energies. At the same time, sex is not really an acceptable form of power, for unlike art or business (real work) its results are horrendous from a moral point of view. The message of this film is that transgression, although possible, is not desirable. Similarly to 19th-century and early 20th-century novels (Thomas Hardy, D. H. Lawrence), love is forbidden by class difference, and when the barrier is transgressed, dire consequences ensue.

Yet, moral proscription aside, the sex/class/power axis in television and movies constitutes a critique of the cultural ideal of consumer society that passes for the 1980s equivalent of the mobility myth. For the entrepreneurial ambition which motored two generations of immigrants in the 20th century has disappeared from view; the remainder is the civil service which has become the far horizon of well-being for a new working class that can no longer count on high-paying factory jobs. The army and the police have replaced industrial labor for working-class men, for whom professional options simply never existed.

Male bonding persists in these contexts, but not the solidarity that is born of mutual recognition among production workers who share a common fate as well as a common existence. For the civil servant, existence is never identical to essence. There is always one place more in the bureaucratic hierarchy for which to strive. On this material foundation, a family could, as late as 1980, enjoy the prospect of owning a single-family home in the cop or non-commissioned enclaves bordering on the suburbs. Such options are increasingly out of the question. So is social solidarity (at least for the younger officers) because the concept of collective fate is constantly disturbed by the latest promotional examination.

The only vital life consists in dreams of power, the most vivid form of which is male sexuality. Contrasted to earlier direct representations in which sex is virtually absent from discourse, but where class persists, today's movies and television programs code sex, class, and power interchangeably. As with the earlier genre, women do not occupy subject positions: they remain the palpable objects of male desire, and by this precise relation experience class reversal.

In sum, the persistence of even these displaced representations of workers and their culture attests to the media's yearning for a source of vitality and renewal which clearly cannot be derived within ruling-class relationships, a genre that survives not in the drawing room comedy but in the old tradition of portrayals of scandal and corruption (such as Oliver Stone's *Wall Street* [1987]). This lack of credible ruling-class subjects occurs at a time when public confidence in business appears to be considerably higher than at anytime since the Gilded Age. Yet, what excited the old public's imagination rather than admiration was the degree, earlier in the century, to which the capitalist merged with the Frontiersman. Despite his ruthlessness, he was a romantic figure, a conquerer, a risk-taker, and above all, sexy. This figure was displaced to the underworld boss in the 1930s and 1940s when the entrepreneurship had already passed to the hijacker, the bank robber, and the gambler — types revived briefly in the 1960s.

The working class is no longer possible as mythic figure, but neither is Ivan Boesky, and while politicians and investment bankers have lost any semblance of sexuality, male or otherwise, class culture survives as masculinity. What working-class culture may signify is the last hope for class equality, provided the object is a woman.

11.

Nature in Industrial Society

Neil Evernden

Nature, to all appearances, remains remarkably "popular" in America. It is part of everyone's vocabulary, something we all have knowledge of and opinions about, and something many are moved to defend. Nature is very much a part of "popular culture." But *which* nature?

The question seems nonsensical, of course. There is nature, and there is culture, separate and distinct from each other. But while we acknowledge that we do not all dwell in the same culture or subculture, it is seldom acknowledged that we might not all share the same nature or "subnature." So firmly embedded is the notion of nature as a unitary entity, entirely separate from or even antithetical to, culture, that it is very difficult to entertain the notion of there being more than one understanding of nature. (Arthur Lovejoy once listed 66 uses of the word "nature" in politics, ethics, and metaphysics, and another 20 as used in aesthetics.)[1] In colloquial usage, nature is often simply "the world as given," the force that determines the way things are as well as the clutter of objects that we see interspersed between the "developments" of civilization. In the latter sense, it is nearly synonymous with "environment," or at least with "natural environment," and the "environmental movement" is widely understood as a defense of nature. However in recent years the very prominence of that movement has been the cause of some reflection on just what this "nature" is that is being defended. As a result, it is becoming increasingly clear that people do not always have the same thing in mind when they speak of nature. This might be most easily illustrated by reviewing one of the success stories of the environmental movement.

1987 marks the anniversary of one of the most remarkable incidents in the history of nature preservation in America, and indeed the world. In 1962, a biologist named Rachel Carson made a brave and inspired decision to try a different means of defending nature. The result was a book called *Silent Spring*, which evoked a reaction that has never entirely subsided. To the surprise of many, the resulting "environmental movement" has endured remarkably well, and most people still rank environmental issues above all others in importance. Yet it is doubtful whether, twenty-five years ago, they would have been concerned at all. Rachel Carson changed all that when she challenged our collective right to manipulate nature at will. "Control of nature," she said, "is a phrase conceived in arrogance, born in the Neanderthal age of biology and philosophy, when it was supposed that nature exists for the convenience of man."[2] But isn't "control of nature" what our civilization is principally concerned with? Did Carson genuinely challenge that assumption? Or did she merely wish to?

Although Rachel Carson had spent her life in the defense of nature, she concentrated in *Silent Spring* on one problem only: the widespread and indiscriminate use of pesticides. Her challenge drew the inevitable response from those whose oxen were being gored, and she suffered considerably as a result. Her own integrity was impugned, her publisher was threatened with loss of textbook sales, and the popular media attempted to dismiss her out of hand. A sympathetic but patronizing review in Time Magazine concluded that while many scientists might sympathize with her intentions, they "fear that her emotional and inaccurate outburst in *Silent Spring* may do harm by alarming the nontechnical public," who should be reassured that while some pesticides may be dangerous, many "are roughly as harmless as DDT,"[3] (which is, of course, now banned in most industrial countries). The Time review now seems dated; Carson's book does not. People reading it for the first time today are struck by the fact that all that seems to have changed are the names of the poisons. Despite Carson's apparent effectiveness as an advocate, the problem she addressed remains a serious one. Was she actually successful, or did the attempt fail? Or did she, perhaps, accomplish something other than what she intended?

The American debate over the best uses of nature has been unique, and the tradition Rachel Carson represents, following the likes of Henry David Thoreau and John Muir, is a noble one. But because the defense mounted was usually very personal, the audience tended to be made up of those who shared, in some measure, the valued experience of nature that motivated these famous advocates. In others words, they spoke to a constituency of nature-lovers, and however many prestigious names might figure among them, it was still a minority interest. In contrast, everyone had a stake in the economic development of the nation, and everyone was therefore a partner in the quest for control of nature. It was Carson's acceptance of this simple, arithmetic fact — that there were more of "them" than of "us" — that led, however indirectly, to the revolution that was *Silent Spring*. Its success led to widespread concern, and from "Earth Day" in 1970 the environmental movement became a force to be reckoned with.

But Carson's book was revolutionary not because it challenged the indiscriminate use of pesticides. Others had sounded the warning long before she did, and it was common knowledge in "wildlife" circles that many species were being harmed by this practice. Carson's originality lay in the manner in which she chose to speak and the audience she chose to address. She did not try to appeal to nature-lovers alone: she addressed the entire adult population. She did not speak to the protection of particular organisms that most people had no experience of or concern for, but instead created an entirely new protagonist. Rachel Carson made "environment" the endangered entity, rather than a wildlife species.[4] And since humans are similarly dependent on environment, on "ecosystems," she immediately got our collective attention. The endangered species of concern was not the peregrine, falcon or the whooping crane: it was us.

This may seem no more than a tactical improvement on her part: by showing each of us "what's in it for me," she made environmental protection a cause with extremely wide support. The introduction of such legislation as the National Environmental Policy Act of 1969 indicates just how widely accepted it has become. But strangely enough, in order to bring about this widespread popularity Carson had effectively to redefine what she meant by "nature." She had to describe a nature that mattered to "the man in the street." *She had to make nature popular*.

Of course, to make something popular is to make it universally understandable and appealing. Accomplishing this usually entails using language that is already in circulation: to be understandable one must say what is already understood. In Carson's case, this meant abandoning the older rhetoric which presumed a kind of valuing of nature that was not widespread, and replacing it with a valuing that was. Rather than rely on the nature-lover's assumption of a personal nature that is intrinsically valuable and must be defended for its own sake, she asserted, albeit only implicitly, that *human beings* are intrinsically valuable and must be defended at all costs — even if that means restraining development so that we can continue to have clean air and water. The nature she defended, then, was the nature that provides a stockpile of essential objects for humans to utilize. Of course, by linking these to the somewhat mysterious concept of an ecosystem, in which all players are assumed to have an essential role, she was also able to extract some measure of protection for her beloved wildlife at the same time: people were afraid to exterminate toads for fear the ecosystem might collapse. But despite whatever short-term protection this might have provided, the effect has been the reinforcing of a particular understanding of nature.

Nature as Object

Nature — that is, nature-as-object — was now perceived to be vulnerable in a way few had imagined before. It was still perceived to be a collection of objects, but now it was a collection of *important* objects. The general understanding of nature was not challenged in any significant way. For that reason, the consequences of the environmental movement have been less dramatic than one might have predicted of such a broadly supported venture. To understand why this might be so, we have to bear in mind something about the understanding we all have of nature. It might help, as a first step, to imagine what would have happened if Rachel Carson had chosen to speak as a nature-lover, rather than as a resource conservationist.

One of the common means of dismissing a writer like Carson was to accuse her of being "emotional" (as the Time reviewer did), or of being "anthropomorphic": of acting as if animals or nature in general had human characteristics and could feel the harm done to them. In the view of many, even to suggest that there are human characteristics (feelings, intelligence, awareness) in other organisms is to be a victim of the "Bambi syndrome," and to be afflicted with emotional delusions about useful natural resources. Since this kind of criticism enjoys the reputation of being hard-nosed and "objective," it is dangerous for an author to expose herself to it. The consequence was that Carson and others like her were totally vulnerable whenever they allowed their feeling for nature to show through. The notion of a world containing "persons" of other species, or even of nature as a kind of extended self, was simply unacceptable. To encourage nature preservation, she had to speak instead of the nature that most of society understands: a small price to pay for credibility, one might think.

This much is quite understandable. But why is it that a person is so vulnerable to criticism when she implies that nature is in any way sensate, anything more than a collection of objects? The history of the understanding of nature would very nearly amount to a history of human society, since every social group has had a conception of nature which it uses in maintaining its own internal stability. Mary Douglas, the eminent anthropologist, once suggested that every "environment," that is, every understanding of the non-human world around us, is "a mask and support for a certain kind of society." Were we able to describe each of these conceptions, we would have a kind of cultural fingerprint with which to identify any society that has ever existed. Like us, they had a notion of the necessity of nature and of their vulnerability if it is damaged or "polluted." The pollution they encountered was not always of the "contaminated drinking water" variety, but of course the dictionary definition of pollution is somewhat wider than our colloquial usage: the destruction of the purity or sanctity of something. Anything that threatens the purity of the world around us, physically or conceptually, is an instance of pollution. And since polluters put the whole of society at risk, they must be made to mend their ways. The understanding of the vulnerability of nature is, therefore, also a means of social control, since it enables the group to argue against a particular action by one of its members. The consequence is that both the physical environment and the social beliefs of the group are maintained intact.

Given our understanding of nature as a collection of physical properties or objects, it is easy for us to understand the dangers of contaminating these. We have more trouble understanding some other kinds of pollution: the eating of "summer food" (caribou) in winter, for instance, which cost an Eskimo girl her life, or the participation of women in "male" ceremonies. Yet these can also threaten the purity of the social conception of nature, because as Mary Douglas argues,

> The deepest emotional investment of all is in the assumption that there is a rule-obeying universe, and that its rules are objective, independent of social validation. Hence the most odious pollutions are those which threaten to attack a system at its intellectual base.[5]

And we too have trouble with this kind of contamination, whether we recognize it or not. In fact, it may have been fear of just such contamination that made it impossible for Rachel Carson to talk about her own understanding of nature, which we might call "nature-as-self."

The Conceptual Pollution of Nature

My suggestion that there was some conflict between Rachel Carson's personal understanding of nature and the one she espoused publicly in *Silent Spring* is, of course, conjecture. But we can say with confidence that she exemplifies the plight of a great many people who have been faced with this dilemma, and she certainly serves as a useful illustration of the way cultural premises dictate the very mode of communication an individual must select if he or she wishes to be taken seriously. It is a very subtle form of censorship which all societies practice, although perhaps not so massively and effectively as is the case in western industrialized countries. Thanks to modern mass communications, all of us are given daily instruction in the acceptable range of belief and expression. If we wish to share our ideas, we must make our message adhere to the required format and presuppositions. Even if this was less dramatically true in Carson's day, it may well have been the circumstance that provoked her to the kind of discourse she finally chose in *Silent Spring* and that that denied her the ability to state the message that she, as a nature-lover of long standing, would have wished to deliver.

I suggested earlier that one of the things that forced her decision was the fact that she would have been thought foolish had she been overtly emotional or anthropomorphic in putting her case. If someone claims to perceive feelings in nature, it is generally assumed to be because that person is "projecting" some of his or her inner feelings into nature. But it is too mild a statement to say that this is regarded as erroneous. At a deeper level, it is also sensed to be a dangerous act of pollution. Just how this could be so might be more apparent if we briefly consider the notion of "projection" before returning to our main issue, the kind of "nature" that exists in popular culture today.

J. H. van den Berg spoke of the phenomenon of projection in his classic book *The Changing Nature of Man*. Van den Berg is a Dutch psychiatrist who initiated a study of "historical psychology" to discover how humans and their understanding of reality have changed over time. One of the beliefs that is widely held today is that of projection, even though no one has ever successfully explained just how this phenomenon might work. It is essentially an explanatory mechanism to account for the fact that some people see something in the world that the rest of us do not believe to be there. Van den Berg illustrates this with a number of examples from his psychiatric practice. When the patient claims to see a world that is different from our own, we assure him that it is "all in his head," that it is "not real" but merely "projected." And if the patient denies being aware of any such projecting activity, as he almost surely will, then we explain that he is doing it "subconsciously." We cannot, of course, prove a word of what we say. It is simply a means of explaining a discrepancy in worldview which is discomforting to both the patient and ourselves, and of dismissing the patient's version of reality. We could instead accept what the patient says at face value, and conclude that he is gifted with a different insight, that he can see aspects of the world that the rest of us cannot. Some societies have been quite willing to do so, and even to admire the ability of the "insane" to reveal these other faces of nature. But we do not. And, according to van den Berg, we dare not.

> . . .it is quite clear that the patient cannot be permitted a brick — or a street, house, city, train *or nature* — of his own. He must be projecting; *what he sees are his own personal impurities* . . . We smile reassuringly and say, "You are projecting, what you are seeing is within yourself." (emphasis added)[6]

The patient has contaminated the world with the impurities of his inner self — he has *polluted*. That is, he has threatened the sanctity of the world and, in doing so, has threatened us all in some degree. The same is true of the nature-lover for whom nature is what we are calling "nature-as-self" rather than the conventional "nature-as-object": he or she contaminates reality by finding the qualities of persons in the world of nature. Since our agreement is that only physical objects can be said to populate nature, then the assertion of personal qualities is a breach of the accord, and must be a consequence of illegal "projection" on the part of the polluter. But so what? Even if we find this silly, what harm does it do? Why must we ridicule such a person and conjure up the stereotype of the "little old lady in tennis shoes," implying mental incompetence, in order to dismiss the perception out of hand? Van den Berg's answer would be that we can't collectively *afford* to have society members constituting their own personal understandings of nature. With the rise of humanism and the notion that the individual human is the only authority and the only source of value and meaning, the belief of each individual is potentially critical. If each of us is an authority, then it is crucial that we *agree* on what is. And the basis of our agreement, our lowest common denominator of perception, is nature-as-object, a bare-bones nature with no subjectivity and no personal variables at all: just stuff. According to van den Berg, we need agreement on nature-as-object because that is virtually the only thing we can agree on, and therefore the only piece of "certainty" we can cling to for social cohesion.

These specifications for nature have been with us a long time now. Hans Jonas has argued that the rejection of projection, and specifically of anthropomorphism, has been a condition of the modern scientific worldview from its inception: a condition, not a conclusion. It was dismissed by Francis Bacon, without any real attempt to justify the exclusion. Jonas comments that Bacon and his successors succeeded

> in putting a severe ban on any transference of features of internal

experience into the interpretation of the external world . . . Anthropomorphism at all events, and even zoomorphism in general, became scientific high treason. It is in this dualistic setting that we meet the "nature of man" as a source of defilement for "philosophy" (natural science), and the objection to "final" explanation is that it is anthropomorphic.[7]

Again, we find the charge that it is a "defilement" — a pollution — to find any human properties in nature. Is it any wonder, then, that authors like Rachel Carson had to take great pains to make nature-as-object the center of their discourse? To do otherwise would be to risk instant dismissal, except among the small sector of society that shares an understanding of the world as nature-as-self.

Nature as Self

However, the consequences of that decision are difficult to assess. To some, it would appear that Carson's decision was an inspired one, and that the popularity that environmental issues have enjoyed was a consequence of that choice. However, one has to question whether anything more than popularity was gained by this subterfuge. Has the natural environment enjoyed a significantly greater degree of protection as a result? We cannot "re-run the experiment," so to speak, and so can never know for sure. But the very fact that Carson's book still seems so relevant raises serious doubts. Nature is still at risk, still being polluted, still being encroached upon, still being driven to extinction piece by piece, species by species. It may be, some now feel, that more was lost than was gained in the rise to prominence, because the price paid for public attention was the ability to speak of what matters. We cannot know whether Carson would agree with this assessment, but some of her successors have certainly found this to be the case. So many, in fact, that alternate schools of environmentalism have arisen to attempt to repair the damage.

With the realization that the translation to technocratic respectability has enucleated the subject of concern, there have been a variety of attempts to speak in defense of nature without resorting to the language of nature-as-object. One such attempt which has enjoyed a certain vogue is known as "deep ecology," referring to the attempt to attend to the root assumptions that lead to environmental destruction rather than simply to the technical symptoms of that malaise.[8] Proponents of this approach differ from each other in some respects, but they tend to concur in their notion of nature as "extended self." That is, they resist the idea of an individual being entirely restricted to what R. D. Laing calls a "skin-encapsulated ego" and suggest instead that people have a field of concern which they experience as self. Consequently, the nature they perceive is, in some measure, a portion of themselves. The loss of nature is therefore also a loss of self, rather like an amputation of a appendange done without the patient's permission.

But the nature-as-self can also imply a slightly different understanding. Instead of being "extended self," it may instead imply an extension of self-hood to nature — an understanding of nature as "like-self" or as a community of selves, of persons, with whom one has relationships similar to those within human society.[9] It therefore makes sense to think of rights and obligations within nature, or even of a morality of nature. The arguments are complex, but obviously they lead in quite a different direction than does the resourcism implicit in the nature-as-object conception. And they quite commonly lead to talk of environmental ethics and rights,[10] although not among all practitioners (some would argue that the idea of ethics and rights presumes discrete, atomistic individuals, the very kind of dualism they are seeking to avoid).[11] For our purposes, however, the significant point is simply that there is an alternative understanding of nature present in contemporary society which is apparently growing in popularity. And while it is certainly far from challenging the hegemony of nature-as-object, its expansion is significant. Obviously the understanding of nature we have will effect the kind of expectations we have, both of nature and of ourselves in relation to nature: what seems proper and appropriate behavior toward an object is not necessarily appropriate toward a "self." The question one asks of nature-as-object is "what's in it *for* me?"; whereas of nature-as-self one might ask "what is it *to* me?" The former implies simple exploitation, whether "well managed" or not, while the latter implies a concern with the relationship of humans and non-humans.

But while these may be the two contending understandings of nature that figure most prominently in popular culture at the moment, they probably do not exhaust the possibilities.

Nature as miracle

We believe in facts, just the facts. We do not, generally speaking, believe in miracles. It is highly unlikely, therefore, than many of us would hold a conception of nature as "miracle." Many nature-lovers no doubt have had experiences that one might consider "miraculous," even though they would probably choose a more prudent adjective such as "aesthetic." But the possibility of regarding nature as uncanny and unpredictable needs to be mentioned here, even though it is not possible to do more than hint at its possible significance.

It is commonly understood that a miracle, were such to exist, would be something that runs contrary to the laws of nature. Given that, it would make little sense to speak of nature-as-miracle. However, whether something is "against nature" would depend on our definition of nature. Given that we believe we have discovered "laws" of nature, then of course anything that seems to break those laws would be, by definition, unnatural — if not absurd. But to treat the possibility of nature-as-miracle seriously, one would have to ask just where these "laws" come from and what they actually apply to, which is not a simple task.

One of the reasons that the miracle has largely disappeared from our lives is that we have come to know the world as homogeneous and continuous. That is to say, since it is composed of matter which is similar in composition and behaves in a consistent manner, we are able to predict the result of actions confidently. Of course, it has been understood for centuries that one cannot actually *prove* a causal relationship — it could change on the next trial — but we can nevertheless act as if that were so, since nature seems seldom to surprise us. It is interesting, however, where the initial assumption came from. Why did we decide that nature is sufficiently homogeneous and continuous for us to assume consistent causal relationships?

We find the assumption firmly entrenched by the late seventeenth century, when Gottfried Leibniz could assert that "nature does not leap" — "Tout va par degrés dans la nature et rien par saut."[12] And of course such "natural laws" made possible all sorts of revised understandings, the most obvious being Charles Lyell's theory of gradual geological change which in turn fed Charles Darwin's belief in continuous biological evolution. But as J. H. van den Berg observed, the real germ of this idea lies in the meditations of René Descartes, for whom it bore intellectual fruit almost immediately. Once he concluded that discontinuity is inconceivable, that nature never "jumps" or makes abrupt, unexpected changes, he felt assured that the "stuff" of nature is everywhere the same: there are no pockets of resistance, no surprises. Nature is homogeneous.

This expectation permitted Descartes to take a new turn in his reflections on reality, one which continues to affect each of our lives today. If nature is homogeneous, if it is all essentially the same, then all we need to be concerned with is what he called "extensiveness": an object occupies space. Furthermore, what has extensiveness can be subdivided and can be understood in terms of mathematical analysis, which was of course one of Descartes's intentions. In fact, the very notion of a law of continuity may have come from his mathematical theorizing in which he realized that "if the first two or three terms of any progression are known, it is not difficult to find the other terms."[13] Whatever differences there may be between objects must be the result of differences in motion. His success in arguing this conception laid the groundwork for what we now know as nature, and for the tools of analysis — science — which we regard as the only valid means of knowing nature.

Nothing above should come as any surprise, for we are all heirs of Descartes and we all know nature to be a continuous and predictable phenomenon. The "laws of nature" could not permit such rebellious-ness. It comes as something of a surprise, therefore, to find a reputable author like van den Berg making such a description and then saying "Yet it is not true." He denies Descartes's assumption, the one we all take for granted.

> The reader who might think that I do not mean this seriously is mistaken. I *am* serious. The way Descartes treats objects is not fair. If science wants to consider objects as they are, in the form they have as objects, then it is not permitted to speak of objects which consist of nothing but extensiveness. There is no such thing — and there was no such thing. But Descartes' ideas have penetrated so deeply into reality that nobody knows where the idea ends and reality (or, if preferred, another idea of reality) begins.[14]

Van den Berg is simply pointing out that what Descartes did was make an assumption about the nature of reality, an assumption that we, henceforth, have taken as indisputable fact. Certainly it has had useful consequences. But it is, nevertheless, an assumption, and one which, like all assumptions, rules out all other possibilities. Van den Berg argues that much of value is lost in this exclusion, including an understanding of nature that is genuinely compatible with our own *experience* of it rather than with an abstract *conception* of it — we know pigeons and sunsets, but only believe in ecosystems. In order to believe in Descartes's nature, we had to expunge all the qualities we thought we knew, all the colors, smells, weights, and textures — "projection" is a crime, remember — and attend only to what the model requires be there. We had to withdraw ourselves and our senses from the understanding of nature altogether.

> Withdrawing from the things means dehumanizing them. Only if we withdraw, can we find the "laws of nature." These exist, however, only in a close unity, one which does not include us. As a rule, this condition of withdrawal is not mentioned, and therefore it seems that the laws of nature are always valid. But they are only valid in an artificial reality, a

reality from which we are excluded. Only tautologies can make them seem valid in our world.[15]

So according to van den Berg (among others),[16] the understanding of nature which we take as obvious is in fact a rather complex and abstract one which we acquire in a lengthy cultural exercise in indoctrination. Without schooling, who could possibly conceive of it? Even in the 1920s, it was apparent that our educational system was firmly committed to its dissemination. Alfred North Whitehead commented that the view of nature as "a dull affair, soundless, scentless, colourless; merely the hurrying of material, endlessly, meaninglessly" was ubiquitous. Every university "organizes itself in accordance with it." And yet, he concluded, it is quite unbelievable. This conception of the universe is surely framed in terms of high abstractions, and the paradox only arises because we have "mistaken our abstraction for concrete realities."[17] We are persuaded by abstractions — "ecosystems" — in a way we seldom are by realities — frogs and mourning doves. We have become victims of the "fallacy of misplaced concreteness" which requires that we regard our abstractions about nature as actual objects of nature, while simultaneously dismissing as trivial or as "projections" our actual experiences of nature. But experience cannot be entirely suffocated by belief, and even extensive schooling cannot remove all vestiges of the direct experience of a nature from which we are *not* withdrawn and in which the "laws of nature" do not always apply. Heterogeneity cannot be entirely exercised, and the occasional miracle just might still occur.

The reason this may be significant is that the idiosyncratic experience of the world may actually transcend the cultural heritage that has given us an understanding of nature that entails the "environmental crisis" as its consequence. That is, if it is so that nature-as-object is the inevitable consequence of a series of cultural interpretations, it may be that the whole of our behavior, including that which leads to the abuse of nature that we now characterize as the environmental crisis, is a consequence of our belief in nature-as-object. The only long term possibility of alleviating that crisis would be to transcend the understanding of nature that gives rise to it. The alternative could be something like what we have been calling nature-as-self, since this at least entails a greater sense of life in nature and some measure of personal responsibility and obligation towards it. But it might also be that something like nature-as-miracle, some experience that transcends the normal understanding and holds it temporarily in abeyance so that the personal awareness of the living world is restored, is a prerequisite to any real change in the awareness of individuals and therefore also to a change in the conception of nature in popular culture.

I suggested earlier that an understanding of nature-as-object implies a stance toward the world that could only prompt one to ask "what's in it for me" — the very question Carson exploited by appearing to answer it. An understanding of nature-as-self involves the premise of persons in the world beyond the human community alone, and therefore entails a search for some understanding of our relationship to the others: the question asked is, "what is it *to* me." But the third nature, nature-as-miracle, does not prompt questions of control or even questions of kinship. The stance towards the world as miraculous, as awesome, or even as beautiful, could only prompt one to ask "what *is* it?" — a metaphysical question rather than an economic or a political one.

The Social Construction of Nature

The sense of nature we have will obviously affect our idea of what constitutes proper behavior toward it. The nature that dominates popular culture today is one that is consistent with our humanistic and technocratic assumptions. Nature-as-object is the only understanding of the three that facilitates exploitation and the resourcist rhetoric that legitimizes and facilitates it. The rise of nature-as-self in popular culture is an interesting phenomenon which may or may not entail a substantial change. It seems more in keeping with Aldo Leopold's expectation that we will expand our range of moral responsibility (his famous "land ethic")[18] to include the non-human, than with Rachel Carson's public stance as the advocate of human well-being through the defense of ecosystemic integrity. As for nature-as-miracle, as long as it is limited to the experience of relatively few individuals, or even to rather minor experiences interpreted as merely "aesthetic" by a larger section of society, it is probably nothing more than a source of pleasure or puzzlement to the individuals involved. But it *may* be more widespread than we realize: perhaps the occasional experiences of wonder which we all enjoy are symptomatic evidence of the continued possibility of the miraculous. And should this possibility ever gain credence in a larger way, it is conceivable that it might challenge our fundamental perception of the way the world is. Nature-as-miracle challenges the "nothing-but-ness" of contemporary technocratic explanation. It challenges the assumptions of homogeneity and continuity that permit us to exclude the possibility of surprise and to assume confidently public acceptance of a "lowest common nature" that can never be challenged without villainy or "projection." It is, perhaps, the refugium in which alternative "natures" still reside.

There will always be "nature" in popular culture: nature is an hypothesis that every society needs. We all like to claim to be doing what is "natural," and like our ancestors we often admonish each other to "follow nature." However there is some hypocrisy in this, because we only want to follow if nature is willing to lead in our chosen direction. If we have a dog named "nature," we can cheerfully claim to be following it by walking a step or two behind. But to be confident the dog will not deny us this pleasure, we keep it on a leash, lest it take a turn not of our choosing. But our desire to have some sort of control over the direction nature leads us, even while proclaiming to be followers only, is not a perversion unique to our society. In fact, it may be the rule of the day where humans are concerned. Marshall Sahlins described this tendency in his remarkably concise study, *The Use and Abuse of Biology*, in which he used the recent debate surrounding "sociobiology" to illustrate this tendency at work in contemporary society. But he also described the general and possibly essential propensity of human societies to invent the nature they desire or need, and then to use it to justify the social pattern they have developed. He concludes that

> We seem unable to escape from this perpetual movement, back and forth between the culturalization of nature and the naturalization of culture. It frustrates our understanding at once of society and of the organic world.[19]

The nature that functions in the lives of the majority, that functions as a vital part of popular culture, is inevitably a consequence of this pendular movement between the world of nature and human culture. Nature is never irrelevant. It is used habitually to justify and legitimate the actions we wish to regard as normal, and the behavior we choose to impose on each other. The fact that we are content to construe nature as an object at the moment is symptomatic of our desire to avoid any constraints and to have a free hand to manipulate the world into the forms suited to the exchanges of modern technocracy. The investment we have in the maintenance of this understanding of nature is enormous. And yet, it is not secure. Nature-as-self is also a contemporary reality. It is certainly not the norm, but it is credible enough to generate widespread discussion. And if we ever find that nature-as-miracle has found its way into the columns of Time Magazine, we may begin to wonder whether nature, whatever it may be, is about to slip its leash.

PART III
Themes in Popular Culture

The essays of this section show how themes in popular culture are manifestations of movements in the dimensions of cultural experience and their relation to the external influences of empire and consumption. There can be many different investigations of this sort. Such investigations are very important for charting the waters of a cultural politics. The essays selected in this section focus on some central themes of the contemporary situation.

Ellen Willis defends a position on sexual politics that accepts a biological dimension to socialization in contrast to the current emphasis on the social construction of gender identity. The action-adventure genre is investigated by Gina Marchetti in order to show that, despite the obvious aggressive masculinity, it is open to a number of different, contradictory responses from audiences. The automobile as a powerful symbol that has undergone significant changes in popular perception is Andrew Wernick's subject. Of course, advertising is a key component of this change, and Sut Jhally's essay develops the theory that marketplace communication, due to advertising, has reinstated magic in everyday life.

Two essays take up the explicitly political aspect of popular culture. James Der Derian suggests that the phenomenon of terrorism, that is presented as self-evident by mass media, is actually a complex thing to decode. Thus, he offers a preface to a reading of terrorism. The political role of television in American society is empirically examined by Michael Morgan, who shows the affinity of television watching and right-wing politics.

Lawrence Grossberg undertakes an analysis of the importance of affect, or sensibility, in popular music and video.

12.

Sexual Politics

Ellen Willis

Preface

In 1981, when I gave the talk that eventually became this essay, feminists were just beginning to engage in a passionate, explosive debate — or rather, a series of overlapping, intertwined debates — about sexuality. The arguments crystallized around specific issues: pornography; the causes of sexual violence and how best to oppose it; the definition of sexual consent; the relation of sexual fantasy to action and sexual behavior to political practice (if there is such a thing as "politically correct" sex?); the nature of women's sexuality and whether it is intrinsically different from men's; the meaning of heterosexuality for women; the political significance of "fringe" sexualities like sadomasochism. Each of these issues, in turn, became a focus of deeply felt disagreement over the place of sexuality and sexual morality in a feminist analysis and program. In one way or another they raise the question of whether sexual freedom, as such, is a feminist value, or whether feminism ought rather to aim at replacing male-defined social controls over sexuality with female-defined controls.

While there has always been tension among feminists with differing sexual attitudes, it is only in the 1980s that the differences have

This article, without the preface, first appeared in *The Scholar and the Feminist, Volume II: Class, Race and Sex: The Dynamics Control*, ed. Amy Swerdlow and Hannah Lessinger (Boston: G.K. Hall and Co., 1982).

come to the surface and defined political factions, creating a serious intramovement split. The reason for this development (or at least its catalyst) was, I believe, the rise of the new right. The women's liberation movement emerged in a liberal political and social climate; like the rest of the left it devoted much of its energy to making a radical critique of liberalism. Since sexual liberalism appeared to be firmly entrenched as the dominant cultural ideology, feminists put a high priority on criticising the hypocrisies and abuses of the male-dominated "sexual revolution." But as liberalism fell apart, so did the apparent feminist consensus on sex. Confronted with right-wing backlash bent on suppressing all non-marital, non-procreative sex, feminists like me, who saw sexual liberalism as deeply flawed by sexism but nonetheless a source of crucial gains for women, found themselves at odds with feminists who dismissed the sexual revolution as monolithically sexist and shared many of the attitudes of conservative moralists.

In the last couple of years the intensity of the sex debates has waned, not because the issues are any closer to being resolved, but because the two sides are so far apart they have nothing more to say to each other. The debates now brewing are within the libertarian camp itself: while we agree that a sexual liberationist perspective is essential to a genuinely radical analysis of women's condition — for that matter, of society in general — we differ on what that proposition means.

From the 1930s through the 1960s, sexual radicalism was anchored in a radical psychoanalytic tradition whose paradigmatic figure was Wilhelm Reich. Its fundamental assumptions derived from Freud's libido theory; it defined the sexual impulse as in some sense a tangible, biologically given energy, a dynamic force that pushes toward gratification, and assumed that sexual desire blocked from expression or awareness takes indirect forms — that evidence of it will remain, both in individuals' feelings, fantasies, and behavior and in social institutions. But the impact on social theory of structuralist and post-structuralist discourse — in particular the influence of Jacques Lacan, Michel Foucault, and structural anthropology — has generated a major shift in the way most sexual radicals understand and talk about sex. At the heart of that shift is a sweeping, social constructivist rejection of any concept of a "natural" sexual drive, and of the idea that the biological dimension of sexuality, if it can be said to exist at all, in any way determines or shapes our actual sexual experience.

I do not share this view. On the contrary, I believe that we can't understand sex as a social issue, let alone formulate a credible politics of sexual liberation, without some recourse to the idea of sexual satisfaction as a biological need. At this point, the greatest threat to the very idea of sexual liberation as a possibility is the AIDS crisis: those of use who still reject the imposition of a repressive sexual morality stand accused of pushing death. But that argument loses its force if sexual repression is, in its own way, deeply inimical to human well-being and even survival.

This article, then, applies a version of the Reichian paradigm to the feminist sex debates. Though I wrote it before I understood the need to confront the social constructivist argument, it represents one pole in what I believe will be an increasingly important discussion.

Toward a Feminist Sexual Revolution

The traditional patriarchal family maintains sexual law and order on two fronts. It regulates the relations between the sexes, enforcing male dominance, female subordination, and the segregation of "masculine" and "feminine" spheres. It also regulates sexuality per se, defining as illicit any sexual activity unrelated to reproduction or outside the bounds of heterosexual, monogamous marriage. Accordingly, the New Right's militant defense of the traditional family and its values has a dual thrust: it is at once a male-supremacist backlash against feminism and a reaction by cultural conservatives of both sexes against the "sexual revolution" of the 1960s and 1970s.

There is, of course, an integral connection between sexism and sexual repression. The suppression of women's sexual desire and pleasure, the denial of our right to control reproduction, and the enforcement of female abstinence outside marriage have been — together with our exclusion from equal participation in economic and political activity – primary underpinnings of male supremacy. Conversely, a restrictive sexual morality inevitably constrains women more than men, even in religious subcultures that profess a single standard. Not only is unwanted pregnancy a built-in punishment for female participation in sex (assuming the prohibition of birth control or abortion on the one hand, and of lesbianism on the other) and therefore a powerful inhibitor; it is visible evidence of sexual "delinquency," which subjects women who break the rules to social sanctions their male partners never have to face. Nonetheless, it is important to recognize that the Right's opposition to sexual permissiveness — as expressed in its attacks on abortion; homosexuality; "pornography" (defined as any sexually explicit material); sex education; and adolescents' right of access to contraception, abortion, or treatment for venereal disease without parental consent — has consequences for both sexes. Gays and teenagers are obvious targets. But the success of the profamily agenda would also impinge on the lives of adult heterosexual men, who would have to contend with the unwanted pregnancies of their wives and lovers, woman's increased sexual fears and inhibitions, restrictions on frank discussion and public legitimation of sex and sexual fantasy, and a general chilling of the sexual atmosphere. Although some men are willing to accept such constraints on their own freedom in order to reassert certain traditional controls over women, many are not.

At present, our opponents have us at an enormous disadvantage. The profamily movement has a coherent ideology and program whose antifeminist and antisexual aspects reinforce each other. In contrast, feminists are ambivalent, confused, and divided in their views on sexual freedom. Although there have been feminist sexual libertarians in both the nineteenth-century and contemporary movements, for the most part women's liberation and sexual liberation have developed as separate, at times even antagonistic, causes. The sexual libertarian movement that began in the 1950s was conspicuously male dominated and male supremacist. Though it advocated a single standard of freedom from sexual guilt and conventional moral restrictions, it displayed no insight into the social reasons for women's greater inhibition and conformity to moral norms. On the contrary, women were blamed — often in virulently misogynist terms – for adhering to the sexual prohibitions men and a patriarchal society had forced on them. At the same time, male libertarians intensified women's sexual anxieties by equating repression with the desire for love and commitment, and exalting sex without emotion or attachment as the ideal. From this perspective, liberation for men meant rebelling against the demands of women, while liberation for women meant the opportunity (read obligation) to shuck their "hang-ups" about casual sex.

The question that remained unasked was whether men had sexual hang-ups of their own. Was the rejection of any link between sexual desire and tenderness really an expression of freedom — or merely another form of repression? To what extent did men's demand for "pure" sex represent a predatory disregard of women as people – an attitude that could only reinforce the conventionally feminine sexual reluctance, passivity, and unresponsiveness that men found so frustrating? There was also the touchy issue of whether sex as conventionally initiated and orchestrated by men was pleasurable for women. In theory, there was much concern with female orgasm and the need for men to satisfy women; in practice, that concern often translated into a demand that women corroborate men's ideas about female sexuality and protect men's egos by acting satisfied, whether they were or not. Nor did the sexual revolution seriously challenge the taboo on lesbianism (or homosexuality in general).

At its inception, the contemporary women's liberation movement was dominated by young women who had grown up during or since the emergence of sexual libertarian ideology; many radical feminists came out of the Left and the counterculture, where that ideology was particularly strong. Unsurprisingly, one of the first issues to surface in the movement was women's pent-up rage at men's one-sided, exploitative view of sexual freedom. From our consciousness-raising sessions, we concluded that women couldn't win, no matter how they behaved. We were still oppressed by a sexual double standard that, while less rigid, was by no means obsolete: women who took too literally their supposed right to sexual freedom, assertiveness, and pleasure were regularly put down as "easy," "aggressive," or "promiscuous." We still lived in fear of unwanted pregnancy; in 1968 abortion was illegal — except in the most dire circumstances — in every state. Yet at the same time, men were demanding that we have sex on their terms, unmindful of the possible consequences and without reference to our own feelings and needs. In addition to suffering sexual frustration from the inhibitions instilled by pre-sexual-revolutionary parents, fear of pregnancy, and men's exploitative behavior, we had to swallow the same men's humiliating complaints about how neurotic, frigid, and unliberated we were. Unfortunately, the movement's efforts to make political sense of this double bind led to confusions in feminist thinking about sexuality that are still unresolved.

At least in theory, organized feminism has been united in endorsing sexual freedom for women, including the right to express our sexual needs freely, to engage in sexual activity for our own pleasure, to have sex and bear children outside marriage, to control our fertility, to refuse sex with any particular man or all men, to be lesbian. Almost as universally, feminists have regarded male sexuality with suspicion if not outright hostility. From the beginning, radical feminists argued that freedom as men defined it was against women's interests; if anything, men already had too much freedom, at women's expense. One faction in the movement strongly defended women's traditional demands for marriage and monogamy against the anti-nuclear-family, sexual-liberationist rhetoric of the counterculture. Proponents of this view held that the sexual revolution simply legitimized the age-old tendency of men in a male-supremacist society to coerce, cajole, or fool women in to giving them sex without getting anything — love, respect, responsibility for the children, or even erotic pleasure — in return. At the other extreme were feminists who argued that under present conditions, any kind of sexual contact with men, in marriage or out, was oppressive, and that the issue for women was how to resist the relentless social pressure to be with a man. Later, lesbian separatists elaborated this argument, claiming that only women were capable of understanding and satisfying women's sexual needs.

Although the idea that to achieve equality women's sexual freedom must be expanded and men's restricted has a surface common-sense logic, in practice it is full of contradictions. For one thing, the same social changes that allow greater freedom for women inevitably mean greater freedom for men. Historically, a woman's main protection from sexual exploitation has been to be a "good girl" and demand marriage as the price of sex — in other words, relinquish the freedom to express her sexuality spontaneously in order to preserve its bargaining power. Furthermore, this traditional strategy will not work for individual women unless most women adhere to it, which implies the need for some form of social or moral pressure to keep women in line. (If the assumption is that women as a group will voluntarily exchange their increased freedom for security, why bother to demand freedom in the first place?) In practice, relaxing social condemnation of female "unchastity" and permitting women access to birth control and abortion allays social concern about men's "ruining" or impregnating respectable women, and so invariably reduces the pressure on men — both from women and from other men — to restrain their demands for casual sex. Thus the feminist critique of male sexuality tends to bolster the familiar conservative argument that a morality restricting sex to marriage is in women's interest — indeed, that its purpose is to protect women from selfish male lust.

Another difficulty is that judgments of men's heterosexual behavior necessarily imply judgments about what women want. Dissenters within feminist groups immediately challenged the prevailing judgments, arguing with monogamists that they wanted to sleep with more than one man or that they didn't want the state messing into their sex lives, and arguing with separatists that they enjoyed sex with men. As a result, assumptions about what women want were soon amended to authoritative pronouncements on what women *really* want/ought to want/would want if they were not intimidated/bought off/brainwashed by men. The ironic consequence has been the development of feminist sexual orthodoxies that curtail women's freedom by setting up the movement as yet another source of guilt-provoking rules about what women should do and feel.

That irony is compounded by another: the orthodoxies in question dovetail all too well with traditional patriarchal ideology. This is most obviously true of polemics in favor of heterosexual monogamy, but it is no less true of lesbian separatism, which in recent years has had far more impact on feminist thinking. Here it is necessary to distinguish (though of course there has been considerable overlap) between two tendencies in lesbian feminist politics: the first has emphasized lesbianism as a forbidden erotic choice and lesbians as an oppressed sexual minority; the other — aligning itself with the separatist faction that surfaced in the radical feminist movement before lesbianism as such became an issue — has defined lesbianism primarily as a political commitment to separate from men and bond with women.[1] The latter tendency has generated a sexual ideology best described as neo-Victorian. It regards heterosexual relations as more or less synonymous with rape, on the grounds that male sexuality is by definition predatory and sadistic: men are exclusively genitally oriented (a phrase that is always used pejoratively) and uninterested in loving relationships. Female sexuality, in contrast, is defined as tender, nonviolent, and not necessarily focused on the genitals: intimacy and physical warmth are more important to us than orgasm; we like to kiss and hug and hold hands a lot. The early prelesbian separatists argued that celibacy was a reasonable alternative to sleeping with men, and some suggested that the whole idea of a compelling sexual drive was a male invention designed to keep women in their place: women didn't need sex, and men's lust was less for pleasure than for power. In short, to the neo-Victorians men are beasts who are only after one thing, while women are nice girls who would just as soon skip it. The inescapable implication is that women who profess to enjoy sex with men, especially penile-vaginal intercourse itself, are liars or masochists; in either case they have chosen (or been forced) to be victims and to uphold an oppressive system. Nor are lesbians automatically exempt from criticism; gay women whose sexual proclivities do not conform to the approved feminine stereotype are assumed to be corrupted by heterosexism.

Though neo-Victorianism has been most militantly promoted by lesbian separatists, in modified form (one that concedes the possibility that men — some men at least — can change their ways and be good lovers) it has also had wide appeal for heterosexual feminists. (Conversely, lesbians have been among the loudest critics of this stance; this is not a gay-straight split.) Its most popular current expression is the antipornography movement, which has seized on pornography as an all-purpose symbol of sex that is genitally oriented, hence male, hence sadistic and violent, while invoking the concept of "erotica" as code for sex that is gentle, romantic, relationship-oriented — in a word, feminine. Clearly, this conventional view of female as opposed to male sexuality is consistent with many women's subjective experience. Indeed, there are probably few women in this culture who don't identify with it to some degree. But to take that experience at face value is to ignore its context: a patriarchal society that has systematically inhibited female sexuality and defined direct, active physical desire as a male prerogative. Feminist neo-Victorians have made the same mistake — only with the sexes reversed — as male libertarians who criticize female sexual behavior while adopting stereotypical male sexuality as the standard of judging sexual health and happiness. In the process, they have actively reinforced the larger society's taboos on women's genital sexuality. From a conservative perspective, a women who has aggressive genital desires and acts on them is "bad" and "unwomanly"; from the neo-Victorian perspective, she is "brainwashed" and "male-identified."

Overtly or implicitly, many feminists have argued that sexual coercion is a more important problem for women than sexual repression. In the last few years, the women's movement has increasingly emphasized violence against women as a primary — if not *the* primary — concern. Although sexual violence, coercion, and harassment have always been feminist issues, earlier feminist analyses tended to regard physical force as one among several ways that men ensure women's compliance to a sexist system, and in particular to their subordinate wife-and-mother role. The main function of sexual coercion, in this view, is to curb women's freedom, including their sexual freedom. Rape, and the tacit social tolerance of it, convey the message that simply by being sexual women are "provocative" and deserve punishment, especially if they step out of their place (the home) or transgress society's definition of the "good" (inhibited) woman. Similarly, sexual harassment on the street, or on the job, and exploitative sexual demands by male "sexual revolutionaries," punish women for asserting themselves, sexually and otherwise, in the world.

The current feminist preoccupation with male violence has a very different focus. Rape and pornography (defined as a form of rape) are regarded not as aspects of a larger sexist system but as the foundation and essence of sexism. Sexual victimization is seen as the central fact of women's oppression. Just as male violence against women is equated with male supremacy, freedom from violence is equated with women's liberation. From this standpoint, the positive aspect of freedom — freedom for women to *act* — is at best a secondary concern, and freedom for women to assert an active genital sexuality is, by the logic of neo-Victorianism, a contradiction in terms.

Whatever its intent, the objective effect of feminists' emphasis on controlling male sexuality — particularly when that emphasis is combined with a neo-Victorian view of women's nature and the conviction that securing women's safety from male aggression should be the chief priority of the women's movement — is to undercut feminist opposition to the profamily backlash. It provides reinforcement for the Right's efforts to manipulate women's fear of untrammeled male sexuality and intimidate women into stifling their own impulses toward freedom in order to cling to what little protection the traditional roles still offer. The convergence of neo-Victorian and profamily ideology is most striking in the recent attempts by so-called feminists for life to argue that abortion is "violence against women" and a way for men to escape responsibility for their sexual behavior. Although this argument did not come from within the feminist movement but from antiabortion pacifists seeking to justify their position to feminists, it is perfectly consistent with neo-Victorian logic. No tendency in organized feminism has yet advocated outlawing abortion, but one does occasionally hear the argument that feminists should spend less energy defending abortion and more on educating women to understand that the real solution to unwanted pregnancy is to stop sleeping with men.

Neo-Victorians have also undermined feminist opposition to the Right by equating feminism with their own sexual attitudes, in effect reading out of the movement any woman who disagrees with them. Since their notion of proper feminist sexuality echoes conventional moral judgments and the antisexual propaganda presently coming from the Right, their guilt-mongering has been quite effective. Many feminists who are aware that their sexual feelings contradict the neo-Victorian ideal have lapsed into confused and apologetic silence. No doubt there are also thousands of women who have quietly concluded that if this ideal is feminism, then feminism has nothing to do with them. The result is widespread apathy, dishonesty, and profound disunity in a movement faced with a determined enemy that is threatening its very existence.

The foregoing suggests that feminists are at a theoretical impasse. If a feminist politics that advocates restrictions on male sexuality leads inexorably to the sexual repression of women and the strengthening of antifeminist forces, such a politics is obviously untenable. But how can we support sexual freedom for both sexes without legitimizing the most oppressive aspects of male sexual behavior? I believe our hope for resolving this dilemma lies in re-examining certain widely shared assumptions about sex, male versus female sexuality, and the meaning of sexual liberation.

The philosophy of the sexual revolution as we know it is an extension of liberalism: it defines sexual freedom as the simple absence of external restrictions — laws and overt social taboos — on sexual information and activity. Since most people accept this definition, there is widespread agreement that we are already a sexually emancipated society. The easy availability of casual sex; the virtual lack of restrictions (at least for adults) on sexual information and sexually explicit materials; the accessibility (for adults again) of contraception; legal abortion; the proliferation of massage parlors and sex clubs; the ubiquity of sexual images and references in the mass media; the relaxation of taboos against "deviant" sexual practice — all are regularly cited as evidence that this culture has largely overcome its antisexual history. At the same time, it is clear that sexual liberalism has not brought nirvana. Noting that "liberated" sexuality is often depressingly shallow, exploitative, and joyless, many men as well as women have concluded that sexual liberation has been tried and found wanting, that it is irrelevant or even inimical to a serious program for social change.

This is a superficial view, in that it focuses on the quantity and variety of sexual activity, rather than on the quality of sexual experience. Political opposition to restrictive sexual mores is ultimately based on the premise that a gratifying sexual life is a legitimate human need, whose denial causes unnecessary and unjust suffering. Certainly, establishing people's right to pursue sexual happiness with a consenting partner is a step toward ending that suffering. Yet as most of us have had occasion to discover, it is entirely possible to participate "freely" in a sexual act and feel frustrated, indifferent, or even repelled. From a radical standpoint, then, sexual liberation involves not only the abolition of restrictions but the positive presence of social and psychological conditions that foster satisfying sexual relations. And from that standpoint, this society can hardly be considered sexually free. Most obviously, sexual inequality and the resulting antagonism between men and women constitute a devastating barrier to sexual happiness. I will argue in addition that sexual liberalism notwithstanding, most children's upbringing produces adults with profoundly negative attitudes toward sex. Under these conditions, the relaxation of sexual restrictions leads people to try desperately to overcome the obstacles to satisfaction through compulsive sexual activity and preoccupation with sex. The emphasis on sex that currently permeates our public life — especially the enormous demand for sexual advice and therapy — attests not to our sexual freedom but to our continuing sexual frustration.

It is in this context that we need to examine the male sexual patterns that feminists have protested — the emphasis on conquest and dominance, the tendency to abstract sex from love and social responsibility. Sexual liberalism has allowed many men to assert these patterns in ways that were once socially taboo. But to conclude from this fact that male sexual freedom is inherently oppressive to women is to make the uncritical assumption that men find predatory, solipsistic sexual relations satisfying and inherently preferable to sex based on love and mutuality. As I have noted, some feminists argue that male sexuality is naturally sadistic. Others grant that men's predatory tendencies are a function of sexism, but assume that they are a simple, direct expression of men's (excessive) freedom and power, the implication being that anyone who has the opportunity to dominate and use other people sexually will of course want to take advantage of it.

This assumption is open to serious question. If one pays attention to what men consciously or unwittingly reveal about their sexual attitudes — in their fiction and confessional writing, in sociological and psychological studies, in everyday interactions with women — the picture that emerges is far more complicated and ambiguous. Most men, in fact, profess to want and need mutual sexual love, and often behave accordingly, though they have plenty of opportunity to do otherwise. Many men experience both tender and predatory feelings, toward the same or different women, and find the contradiction bewildering and disturbing; others express enormous pain over their inability to combine sex with love. Often men's impulses to coerce and degrade women seem to express not a confident assumption of dominance but a desire to retaliate for feelings of rejection, humiliation, and impotence. As many men see it, they need women sexually more than women need them, an intolerable imbalance of power. Furthermore, much male sexual behavior clearly reflects men's irrational fears that loss of dominance means loss of maleness itself, that their choice is to "act like a man" or be castrated, to embrace the role of oppressor or be degraded to the status of victim. None of this is to deny men's objective social power over women, their reluctance to give up that power, or their tendency to blame women for their unhappiness rather than recognizing that their own oppressive behavior is largely responsible for women's sexual diffidence. My point is only that the behavior that causes women so much grief evidently brings men very little joy; on the contrary, men appear to be consumed with sexual frustration, rage, and anxiety. With their compulsive assertions of power, they continually sabotage their efforts to love and be loved. Such self-defeating behavior cannot, in any meaningful sense, be described as free. Rather it suggests that for all the undoubted advantages men derive from "acting like a man" in a male-supremacist society, the price is repression and deformation of spontaneous sexual feeling.

The view that untrammeled male sexuality must inevitably be oppressive is rooted in one of our most universal cultural assumptions: that the sexual drive itself is inherently antisocial, separate from love, and connected with aggressive, destructive impulses. There is, however, another possibility, advanced by a small minority of utopians, romantics, and cultural radicals: that sexual desire, tenderness, and empathy are aspects of a unified erotic impulse, that the split between sex and love and the attendant perversion of sexual desire into exploitative, solipsistic lust are an artificial social product. This thesis has been most systematically and convincingly elaborated in Wilhelm Reich's radical critique of Freud, which has provided the basis for much subsequent cultural radical thought. In Reich's view, parental condemnation of infantile genital desires and sensations forces the child to split (bad) sex from (good) affection. The child reacts to this thwarting of its sexual expression with frustration, rage, and a desire for revenge; thus its sexuality becomes sadistic. If the sadistic feelings are also forbidden they turn inward, producing guilt and masochism. People's guilt at their own overt or repressed sadism, as well as their observation of other people's antisocial behavior, is behind the conviction that sex is inherently destructive. Yet that conviction rests on a piece of circular reasoning: repression creates the destructiveness that is then cited as proof of the eternal need for repression. Reich saw sexual repression as the self-perpetuating basis of a sadomasochistic psychology which was in turn crucial to the maintenance of an authoritarian, hierarchial social order. He argued that people with an antisexual upbringing tend to uphold established authority — even when the practical conditions for rebellion exist — because that authority fulfills several functions. It reinforces people's inner controls over their sadistic impulses and protects them from the uncontrolled sadism of others; it invites people to express sadistic feelings vicariously by identifying with authority; and it permits people to vent those feelings indirectly on those below them in the social hierarchy. Thus the anger that should inspire social rebellion is transformed into a conservative force, impelling people to submit masochistically to their oppressors while bullying their "inferiors." Yet even for ruling classes, Reich maintained, power is at best a substitute for genuine fulfillment.

It is beyond the scope of this essay to attempt to prove that the cultural radical view of sex — or Reich's specific formulation of it — is correct. Rather, I propose this view as the only hypothesis that is wholly consistent with a *feminist* sexual politics. I have tried to show how efforts to control male sexuality undermine women's struggle for freedom and equality, and vice versa. To take the argument a step further, if the sexual impulse is intrinsically selfish and aggressive, there are two possible explanations for why men's sexuality, far more than women's, has displayed these characteristics. One is that sexual desire, per se, is inherently male; the pitfalls of this idea have been discussed at length. The other is that women have simply not been alowed to be as selfish and exploitative as men. To adopt this notion puts feminists in the position of agreeing with conservatives that liberating women from the feminine role would destroy the social cement that keeps civilization going. If, on the other hand, sexual destructivness can be seen as a perversion that both reflects and perpetuates a repressive system, it is possible to envision a coherent feminist politics in which a commitment to sexual freedom plays an integral part.

If we accept the premise that parents, by rejecting their children's genitality, atomize the erotic impulse and direct infantile sexuality into a sadistic mode, the source of the difference between "masculine" and "feminine" sexual patterns seems clear. While boys are permitted, indeed encouraged, to incorporate their sadistic impulses into their sexual identities and to express those impulses in socially approved ways, girls' aggression is no more tolerated than their genitality. Like men, women experience a split between lust and love, but the lustful component of their sexuality is subjected to severe inhibition. Women who do not suppress their lustful feelings altogether — or sublimate them into disembodied romanticism or mother love — usually feel free to express them only in the relatively safe and socially validated context of marriage or a quasi-marital commitment. Thus what looks like women's superior ability to integrate sex and love is only a more hidden form of alienation.

I am suggesting, then, that sexual repression and sexism function symbiotically to transform male and female children into masculine and feminine adults. To understand this process, it is useful, in my view, to take another look at two Freudian concepts that feminists have generally rejected or interpreted in purely symbolic terms — castration anxiety and penis envy. Children in this culture absorb two sets of messages about their genitals: that to desire genital pleasure is bad (indeed, the prohibited desire is soon contaminated with actual "badness," i.e., vengeful aggression); and that there are two classes of people, one superior and dominant, one inferior and subordinate, distinguished from each other by the presence or absence of the penis. From these facts, it would be quite reasonable for children to infer that girls have been castrated and devalued for bad sexual desires, and that boys risk being punished for their badness in similar fashion. There is also reason to assume an enormous emotional difference between fear of mutilation and the conviction that one has already been mutilated. A boy's fear of castration would be mitigated by the knowledge that so far he has been bad and gotten away with it. A girl, in contrast, would imagine that her defiance has already provoked terrible retribution, and that worse might be in store if she persists. The boy's fear could be expected to stimulate his sexual aggression: It is only by "acting like a man" that he can assure himself he is not a woman; besides, he must vigilantly maintain his control over those deprived beings who surely must hate him and covet his precious organ. But the girl's observation of men's power and sexual hostility would only add to her terror and confirm her in the belief that whatever her feelings of hate and envy, she must be *good* at all costs.

If women's childhood experience leads them to associate their sexuality with violation and doom, it is no wonder that many feminists are more preoccupied with their fears of male violence than with their hopes for sexual freedom. The idea that women who are sexually mistreated have "asked for it," while those who behave will be protected, still has an enormous hold over women's minds. It not only discourages women from rebelling but often moves them to defend rigid standards of sexual morality and resist any blurring of the line between good and bad women: the clearer the rules, the more likely that obeying them will ensure safety. Yet of course "goodness" does not ensure safety and never did. In practice, women can never be good enough, for both women and men know that in their secret hearts all women are "bad" — that is, sexual. This knowledge gives men license to consider all women fair game — their goodness is after all just a hypocritical facade — and impels both sexes to blame women for being raped. Finally, the only way women can escape this trap is to repudiate and destroy the association between sex and badness.

Despite the cultural upheavals with which we are familiar — of which we as feminists are a product — the basic ingredients of a patriarchal upbringing remain. For all the erosion of sexual roles and improvements in women's status, there are still two unequal classes of people distinguished by the possession, or lack, of a penis. Despite (and in part because of) the spread of sexual liberalism, most people — including most feminists — are still too deeply afraid of the sexual impulse to accept fully their babies as sexual beings. As a result, the symbiosis of sexism and sexual repression continues to re-create a complex of patriarchal attitudes that exert a strong pull on our emotions even as they increasingly conflict with both our rational ideas and aspirations and the actual conditions of our lives. It is in fact the social instability and psychological tensions this conflict produces that have made people so receptive to profamily ideology. The Right proposes to resolve the conflict by changing social reality to conform to our most conservative emotions. Feminist politics, in contrast, often seem to embody the conflict instead of offering an alternative solution. Nor is this any wonder, if such a solution must include a fundamental transformation in people's sexual psychology. Yet however dangerous and uncharted the territory, it is precisely this task that we must somehow begin to address.

The first step, I believe, is to affirm the validity, in principle, of sexual liberation as a feminist goal. This in itself will clarify many confusions and contradictions in current feminist thinking and indicate practical political directions. For instance, my analysis suggests that crusading against pornography as a symbol of male violence will impede feminism rather than advance it; that focusing primarily on issues of women's safety (like rape) is more problematic and less effective than focusing on issues of women's sexual freedom (like abortion rights); that it is important for feminists to defend people's (including men's) freedom to engage in consensual sexual activity, including acts we may find distasteful. In short, it is a losing proposition for feminists to compete with the Right in trying to soothe women's fears and the legitimate reasons for them, but our interests as feminists is to demonstrate that a law-and-order approach to sex can only result in a drastic curtailment of our freedom. In the long run, we can win only if women (and men) want freedom (and love) more than they fear its consequences.

13.

Action-Adventure as Ideology

Gina Marchetti

The term "ideology" refers to the realm of thoughts and ideas in circulation in any given society. Although ideas and values may appear to be "true," "universal," and "timeless," the study of ideology reveals that, in actuality, the values and assumptions people take for granted really reflect the power dynamics at work within a given culture at a particular moment in history.

Ideology is intimately related to material circumstances. Ideas do not exist in a vacuum nor do they appear out of thin air. Rather, ideology finds expression in concrete symbolic systems — e.g., language, myth, art. Because we live in an industrialized society, ideas often circulate through mass-marketed, commercial texts like advertisements, television programs, and films. These representations, therefore, embody power dynamics which characterize the ideological sphere.

Although ideology does have an uncanny knack for making the partisan interests of the ruling classes appear to be natural and uncontested, the ideological sphere is filled with contradictions. Those outside of power have difficulty accepting the dominant ideology without question. Within any given society, various ideologies may struggle against the dominance of the ruling ideology and call for an alternative organization of the world. Although this resistance may be only whispered, wherever power is exerted a struggle against oppression usually finds expression.

Removed from the real relations of dominance within our society, fantasy can offer a "safe" expression of ideological tensions so keenly felt by those outside of power and so often denied any real validity.

At present, some of the most popular mass-produced fantasies are action-adventure stories. Although often dismissed as simple good guy versus bad guy escapism, these narratives actually hold within themselves some of our society's most deeply disturbing ideological contradictions.

Although they take the dominant ideology for granted, these texts also must appeal to those outside of power, to those marginalized by the dominant ideology. In order to sell and make a profit, they must somehow allow a place for resistance. They do this grudgingly, however, and only a careful analysis of these texts can really reveal the ways in which contradictions are broached and then usually controlled or simply left in the realm of the impossible, in the domain of entertainment and fantasy.

After looking at the various ways in which popular fantasies have been analyzed as ideology, we will take a close look at the action-adventure genre, the ways it has been defined, and its current manifestations in film and on television. By examining the action-adventure genre, we will see how popular fantasies negotiate contradictions and allow places of resistance for those marginalized by the dominant ideology.

Ideology and Popular Culture Studies

Most of us encounter popular culture in one form or another daily. We watch television, go to the cinema, read comics, magazines, or paperback novels. However, most people seldom stop to think about the importance this material has in their everyday lives.

Taking popular culture "seriously" may appear to be a contradiction in terms. Many dismiss it as simplistic entertainment, crass commercialism, or dangerously manipulative trash. Given that popular culture, by definition, is industrialized, commercial, and disseminated by mass media, the idea that it is somehow forced onto the population at large has its logic. In fact, until recently, most scholars who have studied popular culture have approached it from this perspective.

Some of the best known and most thoughtful representatives of this approach were originally associated with the Frankfurt School in Germany. In 1944, while in exile in the United States, Max Horkheimer and Theodor Adorno wrote a seminal essay critiquing mass culture, "The Culture Industry: Enlightenment as Mass Deception."[1] In it, they argued that commercial culture robs the arts of their critical ability to "negate" the status quo and creates a passive viewer or reader who uncritically accepts the ideas and values sold in this cultural marketplace.

Ironically, although the Frankfurt School is well known for its careful examination of the contradictory nature of ideology, Horkheimer and Adorno's accounts of mass culture, both in this essay and elsewhere, take little account of the contradictions within popular entertainment. In other words, their critique ignores the fact that popular culture tends both to support and condemn the status quo, allowing the viewer or reader a fantastical, often almost utopian, vision of a different order while at the same time denying that resistance and containing it within the same fantasy.[2]

It would be very wrong, however, to underestimate the important contribution the Frankfurt School has made to our current understanding of popular culture, since it did form a foundation for the serious study of culture and ideology from a critical perspective.

Building on this foundation, a number of scholars associated with the University of Birmingham Centre for Contemporary Cultural Studies (under the directorship of Stuart Hall), as well as other British scholars like Raymond Williams and some of those associated with the film journal *Screen*, have begun to formulate a new approach to the study of ideology, popular culture, and society. Unlike many other Marxist scholars who see ideology as a simple *reflection* of economic relations, the British cultural studies theorists see the sphere of ideology as *vital to the functioning* of the social, political, and economic system.

The French Marxist theorist Louis Althusser has exerted considerable influence on British cultural studies' formulation of the relationship between culture and ideology. In his essay, "Ideology and Ideological State Apparatuses,"[3] Althusser sees ideology as playing a vital part in the reproduction of relations of production by assuring that the individual becomes a "subject" by fitting into the niche a class stratified society has ordained. Although Althusser places a great deal of importance on ideology's role in maintaining class relations, his theory tends to be deterministic in its insistence of ideology's ability to "interpellate" the individual within the relations constituted by the dominant class. Contradiction, resistance, uneasy accommodation, and struggle tend not to be very important within this formulation.

To bridge this gap in Althusser's theory of ideology, Hall and others have drawn heavily on the work of the Italian Marxist theorist Antonio Gramsci, who developed the theory of "hegemony" to explain the way in which ruling ideas exert their power through coercion. Instead of looking at the ruling classes as a monolithic force, Gramsci looked at the exercise of power by various groups at various points in history as fluid and constantly in flux to accommodate resistance. The hegemony of the ruling factions, therefore, is never absolute, but always has to be fought for and reimposed on a daily basis.

Ideological hegemony finds expression through "common sense," the very mundane ways in which people make sense of the world. Given that (as Marx and Engels said in *The German Ideology*) "the ideas of the ruling class are in every epoch the ruling ideas,"[4] Gramsci went on to show that the exercise of this rule can never be unproblematic, that hegemony is always assaulted by resistance and the recognition of a very real gap between the ideas of those in power put forward as "true," "natural," "common-sensical" and the actual way the majority of the people live on a daily basis.[5]

British cultural studies' conception of ideology has influenced the way these researchers have approached popular texts like films and television programs.[6] They have been particularly sensitive to the relationship between texts and viewers, i.e., the way in which texts may be open to various interpretations as well as the way in which viewers actively make sense of the text. In his essay, "Encoding/Decoding,"[7] Stuart Hall postulates that meaning is not an inherent property of the text. Rather, even though texts may be encoded with a "preferred" reading in keeping with the dominant ideology, these same texts can be decoded in a "negotiated" or "oppositional" fashion. An oppositional reading may use the text simply as a starting point for an "against the grain" redirection of the fantasy to take more clearly into account the class, gender, generational, racial, or ethnic position of the reader/viewer. In fact, a great deal of work in cultural studies has been done on this type of reading and its relationship to marginalized groups within the social formation known as "subcultures." Some of the most fruitful work in this area has focused on post-World War II British and American youth subcultures, e.g., mods, rockers, rudies, hippies, beatniks, and punks.[8]

However, it seems that most readings of popular culture texts are neither simply dominant nor oppositional but are negotiated in one way or another. To understand how these negotiated readings become possible, it seems important to look at the ways in which the texts themselves may be open to various interpretations. In film studies, for example, there has been a move away from looking at texts as monolithic and univocal, representing only one ideological position, and allowing for only one possible means of reception. Instead, it has been argued that texts need to be looked at as contradictory entities, polysemic in nature, which themselves allow for a range of possible readings.

Although Hall and other members of the Birmingham School have recognized this fact, some of the most fruitful developments in this particular area of ideological criticism have come from scholars working in the United States. In particular, the journal *Jump Cut*[9] has published several articles which take into account the complex orchestration of ideological concerns within media texts. In "Women and Film: A Discussion of Feminist Aesthetics," Julia Lesage, an associate editor of *Jump Cut*, notes the way in which gender and racial contradictions are structured into the film *Saturday Night Fever*:

> In current films, there is a deliberate, industrially structured, response to ideological complexities. The industry wants to let everybody have their ideological cake and eat it, too. In other words, you'll see deliberate ambiguities structured into almost every film . . . The movie *Saturday Night Fever* is fascinating. In so many ways the film is misogynous, but it is also attractive because the male lead is feminized: he's a very delicate dancer, wears colorful clothes and is sensitive. Different attitudes toward race are also structured into that film. A racist could use the film to reinforce racist attitudes: it's right to beat up everybody, it's right to get revenge. If you were a Latino, you could say, "Yeah, look, the Latinos won the dance contest. It proves not only that Latinos are better dancers, but that the system won't let them get the reward they deserve." It is cinema's new way of acknowledging that minorities and women are not going to go away. It is a clever ruse on the part of the people who want to keep the dominant ideology going. They build in the possibilities of all these subcultural responses and incorporate them into the whole.[10]

Television criticism has also produced some interesting discussions of the ideologically contradictory nature of mass media texts.[11] John Fiske, in his essay, "Television: Polysemy and Popularity," summarizes this view of television, ideology and viewer reception as follows:

> In order to be popular, television must reach a wide diversity of audiences, and, to be chosen by them, must be an open text . . . that allows the various subcultures to generate meanings from it that meet the needs of their own subcultural identities. It must therefore be polysemic. The structure of meanings in a text is a miniaturization of the structure of subcultures in society — both exist in a network of power relations, and the textual struggle for meaning is the precise equivalent of the social struggle for power.
>
> Central to this theory is the notion that all television texts must, in order to be popular, contain within them unresolved contradictions that the viewer can exploit in order to find within them structural similarities to his or her own social relations and identity.[12]

Two very important areas of study then emerge for the media critic — an analysis of the polysemic nature of the text and an understanding of the ways in which audiences decode those texts.

Defining the Action-Adventure Genre

In order to understand the way audiences decode films, it is important to look at the common language used by media producers and viewers. Both producers and viewers tend to categorize films and television shows in certain ways, so that a film-goer paying to see a Western would not expect to see futuristic cities, robots, and flying saucers. Instead, that viewer would expect the film maker to provide gunfighters, cowboys, six-shooters, and stagecoaches. A set of common codes and assumptions underlie production parameters and viewer expectations. These popularly accepted classifications for films and television shows are known as "genres."

Popular genres are particularly important for industrialized mass media because they allow producers to remain within tried and true formulas — e.g., the horror film, the Western, the melodrama — which have proved profitable in the past. During the Hollywood studio era and in most television production today, this type of production also holds down costs, since sets, costumes, and props can be used over and over again in different films or television shows fitting within the same genre.

There is also a very important link between genre and ideology. Particular genres tend to be popular at certain points in time because they somehow embody and work through those social contradictions the culture needs to come to grips with and may not be able to deal with except in the realm of fantasy. As such, popular genres often function in a way similar to the way myth functions — to work through social contradictions in the form of a narrative so that very real problems can be transposed to the realm of fantasy and apparently solved there.[13]

Right now, the action-adventure genre seems to be particularly popular. Although always a staple of the film and television industries, action-adventure more recently picked up steam with the immense popularity of Steven Spielberg's *Raiders of the Lost Ark* (1981).[14] In many ways, the contemporary action-adventure genre appears to be very closely related to the literary form of "romance." In *Anatomy of Criticism*,[15] Northrop Frye notes that the romance has a plot which revolves round a series of adventures in which a mortal hero goes on a quest, struggles with a foe, kills the foe, and either attains his objective or else dies himself. Generally, the reward following the adventure involves marriage to a beautiful woman, who may also have been the object of the quest (along with buried treasure or some other valuable object).

The same basic structure holds true for action-adventure stories today. A hero goes on a quest, usually in an exotic land, and encounters villains along the way who hope to thwart his efforts. However, beyond the bare bones of these deceptively simple tales, social contradictions find expression, and the ideological operations of the text can be seen to be at work. The nature of the quest, the characteristics of the hero and villain, the parameters of the story environment, the physical objects which come into play have all changed dramatically over time. These generic specifics — plot, characterization, iconography, and theme[16] — all hold clues to the ideological power a genre might have at a particular point in time within a specific cultural context.

Action-adventure plots are episodic, allowing for wide variations in tone, the inclusion of many different locations and incidentally introduced characters, and moments of spectacle, generally involving fights, explosions, or other types of violence. The hero is usually some sort of private adventurer, e.g., a mercenary, a treasure-hunter, etc., and he (only very rarely *she*) is often accompanied by one or more "buddies" who fit the same mold. Action-adventure stories are set in exotic locations, and the stereotypical accoutrements of the locales form the principle features of the genre's iconography — e.g., decaying temples, deserts, mountains, rain forests, and exotic cities. Guns, knives, and para-military khaki usually flesh out the rest of the visual element of the genre. Principal themes include rights of possession and property; the definition of the national, ethnic, racial self as opposed to "other"; the propriety of intervening in other nations' or other cultures' affairs; the moral consequences of violence; and the meaning of masculinity and male prerogatives.

Even this schematic listing of themes brings up some sorely debated and rapidly changing areas within American culture. Through deceptively simple tales of "good" against "evil," action-adventure texts very often also deal with issues involving changing class, gender, racial, and other social relations. Through this narrative working out of very real problems and concerns, the action-adventure tale does its ideological work of exposing contradictions, transposing them into fantasy, and then resolving them. However, as these narratives do this, they also open themselves up to multiple meanings, readings, and uses. If the dominant ideology, in most reception scenarios, finds a way to win over the viewer, it is at the cost of recognizing the very unstable, multifaceted, heterogenous, and contradictory nature of the actual social fabric.

Why Vietnam? The Contemporary
Action-Adventure Tale

Three types of action-adventure plots seem to be particularly popular at present. The first type, perhaps the most traditional, involves a quest for a valuable object hidden away in a Third World country. *Raiders of the Lost Ark, Romancing the Stone* (1984), and *Firewalker* (1986) all follow this formula. Also, this type of narrative generally involves the capture and return of a woman, who sometimes acts as the hero's buddy and sometimes as the villain's captive.

The second type of narrative popular today involves invasion scenarios. In this case, the foreign villain invades the hero's community or country. Normally ostracized by his own society, the hero must come to its aid in order to save it from destruction. *Invasion USA* (1985) is typical of this sort of action-adventure tale. Television action-adventure shows, like *The A-Team* (NBC, 1982–87), also often rely on this sort of plot for their weekly adventures.

The third type of action-adventure plot in wide circulation in the 1980s involves the search for captives. These stories are told within the framework of a hero's search for prisoners listed as "missing in action" — specifically during the war in Vietnam — whom the hero believes to be alive still in Indo-Chinese prisoner-of-war camps. *Missing in Action* I (1984), *Uncommon Valor* (1983), *Rambo: First Blood II* (1985), and episodes of several popular television series have all contributed to making this an extraordinarily successful subgenre.[17]

All three of these plotlines have several important things in common. They all deal with attitudes and values currently experiencing some sort of social crisis. In this fashion, action-adventure has been able to accommodate historical and cultural changes while keeping the main ideological thrust of the genre intact.

For example, the genre often deals with the definition of property rights and the proper distribution of wealth. The treasure hunt plotline offers a clear elaboration of this theme. Not coincidentally, the treasure hunt generally takes place in the Third World. As Ariel Dorfman and Armand Mattelart point out (in *How to Read Donald Duck: Imperialist Ideology in the Disney Comic*,[18]) Third World people, pictured as innocent children who simply do not understand the value of the objects surrounding them, often symbolically stand in for First World workers in popular fantasies. Within a racist ideology that pictures Third World people as intellectually limited savages, the text can allow the hero to step in, as representative of First World reason and logic, and help the natives "exploit" their treasures. Clearly, this fantasy, at a time when American economic "interests" seem to be "threatened" globally, has a particular appeal. After all, the treasure need not be gold or jewels, but could as easily be South African platinum, Arabian gulf oil, or Central American fruit crops. Hence, fantasies of Indiana Jones traipsing around the globe looking for treasure seem also to have a more contemporary significance in supporting capital's power to exploit labor domestically and internationally.

Invasion narratives also deal with the definition of property, identity, and national boundaries in a similar fashion. They provide the flip-side of the treasure hunt narratives by allowing the shoe to be on the other foot. In this case, America, home and hearth, is penetrated by a malevolent foreign power. While the American hero is always justified in his quest to find treasure abroad, the foreigner can never be right in interfering in American affairs. However, these narratives express a certain ambivalent attitude toward that wealth which the foreigner seems to be after and which, bottom-line, defines the American identity. Here, American abundance is often presented as the source of the entire problem.

In *Invasion USA*, for example, the Cuban and East European villains note that America is "soft," "satiated," and easily conquered because of this "bourgeois decadence." They seem to both covet American wealth and wish to destroy it because of its corrupting influences. In this case, Matt Hunt (Chuck Norris), the penultimate working-class hero, a former C.I.A. operative who wrestles alligators in the Florida swamps and lives in a back-water shack, must single-handedly rescue the bastions of middle-classness the "Commies" have under siege. Once again, like the treasure hunt narratives, these invasion tales justify the violent suppression of anyone who may interfere with American property rights, and it is the working classes that, despite the fact they are presented as having the least to lose, rise up to do battle to secure the right of private property.

It is interesting to note that, in both the treasure hunt and invasion plots, official representatives of the American government — i.e., the police, the army — are either not on the scene or are completely ineffectual. In *The Empire's Old Clothes: What the Lone Ranger, Babar, and Other Innocent Heroes Do to Our Minds,*[19] Ariel Dorfman points out that the Lone Ranger, Superman, and several other of American mass culture's most popular heroes were created during the Depression of the 1930s, at a time of severe economic crisis in which the U.S. Government substantially increased its powers. These heroes personalized that new power, by taking on police and other powers generally considered the prerogatives of governments, and also represented an ambivalence toward those new powers by standing outside the government.

Right now, the MIA captivity/rescue fantasies seem to be popular for a similar reason. On the one hand, they seem to call for increased government and military action — e.g., for increased involvement in foreign affairs, perhaps even for a new war in Vietnam. At the same time, however, they also represent a deep suspicion of the State which is seen both as weak and ineffectual and as corrupt and self-serving. As a panacea for the loss of Vietnam, they conjure up the figure of the heroic individual, who both represents the interests of the nation and goes beyond the strictures of the government.

Once again, territoriality becomes important. In these MIA narratives, the right of Americans to intervene violently in Southeast Asia goes unquestioned. These tales place Americans in the role of the underdog, as prisoners of war or misunderstood and under-appreciated veterans at home. Now victims, Americans are given the moral right to go into the Third World and again retrieve property — this time, in the guise of prisoners of war.

All of these action-adventure scenarios also seem to reflect changing and contradictory feelings about gender roles and women's equality. Recognizing that women are an important part of the audience and that the Women's Movement has changed certain attitudes toward gender, contemporary action-adventure tales have allowed women to expand their traditional function in these narratives a bit. Although women still play the passive part of the captive who must be retrieved from the villain by the hero, they also figure more and more often as the hero's "buddy" as well as the object of the tale's love interest. As a result, some of these action-adventure texts have allowed women a certain camaraderie with the hero, sharing the battle and the danger, that had been rarer in the past.

However, although women may be given a bit more license to pursue goals actively, these tales are still very much male-dominated and male-defined. In fact, most feature a very aggressive masculinity, expressed through guns, tanks, armed helicopters, and other instruments of death. Emphasis is placed on the male body, its musculature and strength, and its ability to withstand torture and to kill efficiently. For example, although *Rambo* features a loyal and efficient female comrade-in-arms, she fairly quickly meets with a violent end, leaving Rambo (Sylvester Stallone) to fight against the male villains and rescue the male prisoners of war. Moreover, although the film devotes a great deal of attention to Rambo's body — e.g., close-ups of his bulging muscles both preparing for battle and during scenes in which he heroically withstands torture — her body is really only given similar attention in one scene in which she must dress as a prostitute in order to penetrate the prisoner of war camp. Here, the visual emphasis is on her sexual allure, rather than her physical strength or power, and this seems to be fairly typical of the way in which female adventurers are treated visually within the genre.

Villains, Heroes and Buddies

Perhaps the most straightforward part of any tale is the antagonist, the villain. Few popular culture texts explore in any, even the most cursory, fashion why the villain must be accepted as villainous. He or she simply exists as a force to thwart the efforts of the hero; the reasons behind the villain's actions remain vague.

Because the villain appears as such a taken-for-granted entity, the common-sensical embodiment of everything a society supposedly finds abhorrent, this figure may be a particularly good place to explore the ideological work of the action-adventure text. In his study of popular literature, *Adventure, Mystery, and Romance: Formula Stories as Art and Popular Culture*, John G. Cawelti describes the role of the villain as follows:

> Formulas enable the audience to explore in fantasy the boundary between the permitted and the forbidden and to experience in a carefully controlled way the possibility of stepping across this boundary. This seems to be preeminently the function of villains in formulaic structures: to express, explore, and finally reject those actions which are forbidden, but which, because of certain other cultural patterns, are strongly tempting.[20]

Therefore, villains in popular fantasies occupy a site of contradiction within those texts since they embody a secret desire for the forbidden while at the same time acting as the embodiment of "otherness," as that which must be eradicated from existence and denied.

In most American action-adventure tales, the villain represents the dark side of the American Dream. If the American Dream promises that anyone in the United States can become wealthy and materially successful with hard work and persistence, the villain represents the realization of that ambition through criminal means. Often, action-adventure villains are drug-traffickers, illegal gun-runners, corrupt politicians, or wealthy merchants who got rich on stolen goods. They represent that side of capitalism which promotes ruthless competition, the monopolization of resources, and the exploitation of workers.

If these villains allow for the exploration of the boundary between "success" and "exploitation" in contemporary capitalism, they also often express a suspicion of political as well as economic clout. Very often these villains are elected officials — albeit, usually officials of foreign governments. Even more often, villains are representatives of the legal or military establishment — e.g., policemen, army officers. For those outside of the operations of power, these villains can embody the secret wish to be on the inside, to have the power and knowledge necessary to control one's own life as well as the lives of others.

Villains also allow for the exploration of issues of identity involving racial, ethnic, cultural, national, and gender boundaries. Villains are outside the norm, and thus allow for the negative definition of that norm — i.e., everything the villain is not is normal and positive. Therefore, villains tend to be foreign and very often non-white. They speak a different language, have different values, even eat different, exotic foods — e.g., the South Asian villains in *Indiana Jones and the Temple of Doom* eat live creatures.

In this way, villains allow for the expression of xenophobia, that fear of the foreign which solidifies a national identity and often becomes the main meat of war propaganda. However, villains also, in a contradictory way, represent a desire to be "different," not to follow the norms and strictures which bind our own society together. Often villains are personally appealing because they are different and exotic; e.g., they can be sexually alluring, stylish, accomplished, intelligent, powerful, and rich. Frequently, action-adventure stories involve the tearing off of this alluring mask to uncover the truly heinous nature of the villain.

In *Romancing the Stone*, for example, Joan Wilder (Kathleen Turner), at first, seems attracted to the dark, mysterious stranger, Zolo (Manuel Ojeda), who offers to help her. The film "codes" him as both "attractive" and "dangerous." His clothes display his wealth and taste; his heavy Hispanic accent codes him as "foreign"; his tall, slender frame and Latin features allow him to be considered sexually alluring. However, Joan soon realizes, when trapped in the middle of a gun fight between Zolo and the hero Jack Colten (Michael Douglas), that Zolo is her enemy.

Here, the text draws a line between the appeal of ethnic-racial otherness and its threatening aspects. However, even as this otherness is dismissed as evil and dangerous, the text has already opened up the possibility that the villain — and by implication, his race, culture, or nation — may have a certain power and validity. The villain, therefore, can be admired as well as hated.

Frequently, too, the villain represents utter contempt for all those things American society holds most sacred — e.g., middle-class respectability, the nuclear family, suburban material comfort, law and order, patriotism. It can be argued that, in expressing contempt for these institutions, the villain may be venting the viewer's own frustrations arising from pressure to succeed or fit in.

In *Invasion USA*, when East European and Cuban forces invade the United States, their campaign involves attacking those institutions which seem so stereotypically "American," e.g., the suburban mall, the neighborhood filled with ranch-style houses, the local church, and grocery store. All of these things represent the American "good life." However, for many viewers, particularly those viewers marginalized by racial, class, or other differences, these lily-white, middle-class bastions represent an impossible dream of success and abundance. When the "Commies" demolish entire suburban neighborhoods filled with intact nuclear families, Christmas celebrations with abundant gifts and decorations, and shopping malls brimming with high-priced items, the villains may be venting many viewers' frustrations with their own inability to cash in on that wealth.

Moreover, the characterization of the hero underscores these frustrations with the middle-class norm. In most respects, the hero differs as much from what may be construed as the social norm — the ideal of "middle-classness" — in the text as the villain does. The hero is an outsider, often a lounger, a drifter, who has no real attachment to a home, family, business, or profession. Although the hero may have been a policeman or a soldier, he is now an adventurer who has an uneasy relationship with his past. In fact, as is the case with *The A-Team* and Rambo, the hero may even be a fugitive, actively hunted by those institutions, like the military and the legal system, which are supposed to operate in the best interests of society. Here, the hero, as a hunted outsider, represents a basic distrust of the "establishment" as well as a freedom from the pressure of trying to conform to middle-class norms.

Similarly, if the villain is foreign, exotic, and dangerous, the hero may also be pictured as "alien," but in a safe and clearly domesticated way. In *Rambo*, for example, a point is made of Rambo's Native American-German ethnicity. Although his ancestors represented two enemy nations, Rambo himself represents the American "melting pot" in which his own ethnicity has been domesticated and put at the service of American interests. This ethnicity can also belie the racism and xenophobia at the root of the text. Rambo cannot be accused of racism in his desire to combat the Vietnamese since he himself is not "white." Similarly, he cannot be accused of going to battle with the Soviets out of a desire to eradicate the foreign, since he himself has a German ancestry.

However, although very much like the villain in many ways, the hero also has his roots in the community besieged by his foe. If the villain is wealthy and part of the established power structure, the hero may be identified with the working classes or the poor, and he has no official place in the power hierarchy.

Therefore, the hero enjoys a peculiar ability to mediate between the domain of the villain and the everyday world of the ordinary person. The hero may be outside the power structure; however, unlike the villain, he acts to secure the status quo and keep the world which seems to have exiled him in operation. Occasionally, at the end of the hero's quest, he is accepted back into the world which had shunned him — i.e., through marriage, a pardon from the legal system, etc. — but, just as often, the hero remains an outsider, tainted by those qualities which enabled him to defeat the villain and restore order to society — i.e., his violence, his otherness, his self-reliance.

In fact, the individual action-adventure hero cuts a rather lonely figure, and he embodies that ambivalence which surrounds the myth of the American individual. If a good deal of the American mythos promises to secure the rights of the individual against the dictates of society, then, the individual must also pay the price for that freedom in loneliness, rootlessness, and homelessness. The action-adventure hero can be a rather tragic figure, ostracized from the very community that he risked his life to protect. Within the figure of the hero, there is always a dialectical play between individualism and community acceptance, freedom and social stigma.[21] Current representations of Vietnam veterans in action-adventure texts embody all these qualities and make the contradictions this figure represents historically concrete.

In order to lighten this tragic aspect of the hero, action-adventure stories usually provide the hero with "buddies," who act as his helpers, or else allow the function of the hero to be taken up by a team rather than a single individual. In general, the buddies or the team also allow the text to compensate a bit for the ideological univocality a single white, male hero may dictate. Therefore, if the hero himself is white, male, and mainstream, the buddy generally is non-white, occasionally female, and marginal. The ethnic, racial, or gender difference the buddy represents allows a space to open up in the text for a non-white, female, ethnic viewer to identify with someone other than the villain. Although this buddy role may be minor, it can draw this marginalized viewer in on the ideological side of the status quo, on the side of the hero who fights to maintain the powers that be.

Moreover, since action-adventure tales generally involve a white American hero going to battle with non-white foreign villains, the fact that the hero's buddy may be part of that alien culture assures the viewer of the moral right of the hero to combat the alien nation violently. By his/her personal loyalty to the hero, the buddy identifies with the power and prerogatives of white, male, American culture.

Similarly, the action-adventure team can act as a point of mediation between a text which seems to assure white, male, American interests and the actual viewer, who may have an uneasy relationship with those interests. The A-Team,[22] for instance, features a heterogeneous group which functions as a microcosm of contemporary American society, reproducing the power hierarchies in operation in that society by placing a black, working-class figure at the bottom rung of the ladder. However, this series also allows this figure, B.A. "Bad Attitude" Baracas (Mr. T), to display the marks of his "past" oppression flamboyantly (e.g., by wearing Native American feathers, an African warrior's hairstyle, gold chains to represent past slavery, and the dressed-up battle fatigues of a common soldier) and to express his anger toward a series of white, middle-class villains violently. Although he remains a "pussycat" underneath, childlike and always subject to his white superior's orders, B.A. still allows for some expression of violent anger and resistance that may make him particularly appealing to non-white or working-class viewers.

In their configurations of heroes, villains, and buddies, action-adventure texts express ambivalent feelings toward race, class, gender, and power. However, any moments in these texts which may point toward a more direct type of resistance against the status quo are usually brief and marginalized within the fantasy. Instead, action-adventure stories feature a dual operation to eliminate the threat that the villain represents — i.e., the threat of national, cultural, racial otherness. On the one hand, these narratives assimilate and domesticate this threat through the figure of the buddy, who shores up the white, American status quo through his/her personal loyalty to the hero, or through the conflicted nature of the hero himself. Moreover, the buddy's or the hero's alien elements are always also kept in check by their unquestioned support for the dominant culture. On the other hand, difference is also eliminated through the violent death of the villain. Therefore, these tales, although decidedly ambivalent about the economic, gender, and racial status quo, ultimately only allow differences to exist on the dominant culture's own terms.

Conclusion

Beyond the very complicated ways in which the action-adventure genre deals with social inequality, these texts also feature another very important ideological masking of the power relations they treat. That is, built within these tales is the myth of entertainment, i.e., that these narratives are meant to be innocent fun and not serious discussions of political or social issues.

In a certain sense, this seems to be true. Within the action-adventure genre, narrative takes a backseat to spectacle. The emphasis is not on plot or characterization but on action, on the visual display of violence.

This is certainly one of the reasons that action-adventure films seem to be particularly popular internationally. A complete understanding of dialogue or plot really is not necessary; instead, the main pleasure of the text revolves around spectacular fights, gun play, torture, and battles.

This reliance on spectacle coupled with the contradictory nature of plots and characters allow the action-adventure genre to appeal to a wide range of viewers. Places seem to be structured into the text for a fluid identification with alluring villains, conflicted heroes, and multi-racial, multi-ethnic buddies. Even women have been acknowledged as having a role to play. The heterogeneity of the text allows these tales to turn profits from a heterogenous audience — in both domestic and international markets.

However, although open to many different readings, these texts also manage to privilege the dominant ideology. The heroes, in the last instance, remain predominantly white and male and, although outsiders, they are always at the service of dominant bourgeois interests in their championing of the middle-class norm. Pleasure, for the vast majority outside that American middle-class norm, remains on the edges. It exists, and audiences pay dearly for it, but, ultimately, it stays buried beneath the surface, always subject to qualifications and limitations.

14.

Vehicles for Myth: The Shifting Image of the Modern Car

Andrew Wernick

He doesn't design cars, he designs missiles — Enzo
Ferrari, referring to Ferdinand Porsche

The Progress of "Progress"

IBM, in the early 1980s, ran a remarkable series of ads preparing the way for the coming PC's. In part, no doubt, their aim was simply to reinforce the identity long built up between the name of the company and computers as such. But as a major in the market IBM also had a stake in the pace at which computers could be introduced, hence a concern to allay the anxieties of those whose lives, particularly at work, were about to be disrupted by the stresses and displacement computerization would bring.

Reassurance, at any rate, was the theme of the campaign, a message deftly delivered by suggesting that the new technology would eventually be regarded with the same wistfulness that earlier "inventions of commerce"[1] have now come to evoke. By this device the shock of the new was magically put into reverse, converting computers, like bicycles, cars, and planes, into the romanticized spirits of a simpler, bygone age.

Considering the excitement that has long surrounded technical progress, and the ideological benefits derived from this by the economic power-holders of industrial society, the defensiveness of the pitch is as noteworthy as its sleight of hand. There is, here, no boundless, Nature-conquering enthusiasm for the future. At the same time, the campaign does link computers to earlier icons of technology, principally from the realm of transport, which have been associated with just that kind of science-based Frontier optimism. All of which would suggest that, on

If computers scare you, just imagine how people felt when they first saw the horseless carriage.

The promise of a new era implies change. And change can be unsettling at first.

That's why we at IBM feel that right now is the time to talk about the computerized office and your power over it.

Right now, because we are on the threshold of a new era. Technologically and economically. The benefits Canadians will derive from the new office technology will be tremendous.

Just look. Today you can use a desktop computer, such as the IBM Personal Computer, to help you see several futures for your business. So you can plan for the right future.

And there are IBM systems that let you communicate with other computers, across the office or across the country, to bring you the information you need to get the job done successfully.

Desktop computers that can simplify and improve almost every aspect of your work.

In fact, affordable IBM computers and office systems not only help you stay on top of your job, they help you get ahead of it.

Yesterday, the car pushed transportation into new frontiers and gave us mobility beyond our wildest dreams.

Today, IBM office technology holds the promise of improving productivity and prosperity, even for small companies, by giving us power over time and information.

And there's nothing frightening about that.

IBM

Figure 1

the one hand, computers have indeed inherited the mantle of the myth of technology, while, on the other — and perhaps as a result — the myth itself has changed.

Particularly revealing is the ad in the series that recalls the birth of the car [Figure 1]. Along a glorious country road a vintage automobile speeds towards a horse and carriage. The horse has bolted upright and a woman passenger leans forward and points in a gesture of astonishment. In the lower right hand corner we see the logo (in computer graphic style) *IBM*; and across the whole scene, the caption: "If computers scare you, imagine how people felt when they saw their first horseless carriage."

The surface meaning is plain: new technologies may upset old ways, but there is no need to worry for computers will become as banally ordinary as cars, their benefits just as self-evident — and all this just through the natural passage of time. When we probe a bit more deeply, however, matters become more complex.

The central image of car-meets-buggy is itself a hoary cliche. But even a dead metaphor for progress, the "modern" overtaking "traditional" society, it implies a whole way of seeing things (History, for example, as an open road) that can easily be made to sustain a host of problematic assumptions about the actual interplay of the developments it depicts. And the same goes for the computer analogy into which it is drawn. What is it, one might ask, that the early car and the new computer are supposed to have in common? And what precisely is the relation between the progress from horse to car, and the progress from the latter to the IBM PC? Does the computer, indeed, have a precursor which parallels the horse?

Since transport and information processing are distinct functions we are left, in the end, with only the vaguest abstractions for an answer: that these artifacts, as a series of ever more advanced forms of applied natural power (animal, engine, electronic), are all instances of "technology"; that the historical movement from one to the other represents "progress"; and that in their succession along the highway of history we see modernity itself unfold. What horse-and-carriage, car, and computer all share, in other words, is the capacity of their images to function as signifiers — and, more particularly, as equivalent signifiers for "technology" in a cumulating series that, taken together, also means "progress." It is only the short-hand character of such symbolism (wherein denotation and connotation fuse) that leads us to think that the designated concepts are real at all, and that the images which conjure them up are embodiments and validations of what, to the contrary, they merely mean.[2]

From this angle, as a kind of cultural language game, the ad's real content is not about cars and computers at all, but about the relation of these objects to a cluster of symbolized values. What it tells us is that the car as a symbol (in the misty past) of technology's cutting edge has now been replaced by the computer. And correspondingly, since the idea of technology associated with a motion machine differs distinctly from that associated with a miniaturized electronic brain, that the aura of meaning around that term has been updated too.

Now, a glance at the real history of symbolized technology will show that the movement depicted in the ad is significantly abridged. The car, as a sign of the eclipsed version of that myth, is shown only at its moment of arrival, and then only in relation to the horse. Its predecessor, the railway, and its successors, the airplane and the spaceship, are not even implied. And, most importantly, the subsequent history of the automobile itself — which, despite its technical supercession by mechanized flight, has continued to present itself, through styling and promotion, as the very sign of the progress it no longer materially embodies — is left out of the frame. What we have, then, is myth about myth. And it works by condensing three symbolic events: the supercession of the internal combustion engine, in the shape of the airplane and then space travel, as the expression of mechanization and thrill-endowed speed; the much more recent decline of the car, borrowing imagery from other transport forms, as the ongoing generalized symbol of progress; and, most recent of all, a shift in the meaning of technology and progress linked to the rise of computers, as a differently inflected sign.

With respect to the erased history of the car it is these latter developments that I particularly want to explore. What, then, has happened — especially since its hey-day in the 1950s — to the imaged automobile as the symbol of technological advance? And how has the meaning of that mythicized idea, which continues to be manufactured into cars, shifted under the sign of "high tech"?

But first a word may be in order about how (and why) values like "progress" and "technology" have come to be tangled up with the imagery of cars at all.

Cars as Signs

The production of cars as symbols is a special case of the way in which, since the industrial revolution of the late eighteenth century, all mass commodities have come to intersect with the world of meaning. Of course, human artifacts, down to the most mundane, have always had symbolic as well as functional significance. But the inception

— with pottery, furniture, clothes, and guns — of commercial mass production marked a watershed by introducing and making systematic the producer's need, prior to consumption, to be strictly instrumental and market-oriented in shaping the meaning products are designed to have.

Attention to image was necessary because of the need to promote — an activity that became important both because of the general need to increase the market's absorptive capacity, and because of the competitive need to give such otherwise hard-to-distinguish items as soap, cigarettes, and beer their own brand identity. The result was the rise of advertising (made increasingly prominent through the media growth it stimulated); and an ever more sophisticated concern with how products, via packaging, decoration and design, are made to appear.[3] That these developments have long been linked is illustrated by the case of Wedgwood pottery. The celebrated neo-classical and pseudo-Ming designs which for centuries have been its hallmark, were originally supplied, with a keen eye for late Georgian middle-class taste, by Josiah Wedgwood's partner, Thomas Bentley, whose role in the company was to handle promotion and sales.[4]

Whether in ads or design the promotional point has been the same: to deck products out as signs endowed with maximum cultural appeal. And, for this, not just any codings would do. Values invoked had to be positive, identifiable, consensual; and it was also necessary to take account of the product's existing insertion into the culture, together with the value associations this would automatically bring. When for example Proctor launched Ivory (the name itself evoking the virtues of the white Empire), soap was already linked, through a germ-based medical model and the propertied classes' fear of urban/industrial disorder, to the Protestant obsession with hygiene. But, as Listerine's later invention of "halitosis" suggests, the values stamped onto products can also have an independent effect, here by heightening hygiene anxiety and giving it a new physiological site.

As a mass-promoted product, the peculiarity of cars, in all this regard, has been two-fold: First, besides their function as transport, for users themselves cars have always had a promotional role. Parked at home, like furniture, like the domicile itself, they project a sense of their owner's relative social standing. Out on the road they carry that same sense of class/cultural identification into the wider cultural domain. Cars, in this respect, are similar to clothes, constituting indeed a kind of third skin for ambient industrial man. Like clothes, too, as markers of identity within an anonymously circulating public they readily become subject to the fashion dynamics of competitive display, which manufacturers themselves have naturally encouraged to accelerate obsolescence and sales.

Despite there being fewer and fewer corporate players, the pro-liferation and turnover of styles has thus kept far ahead of strictly engineering innovation. Ford, the first American auto giant, was at first slow to change lines. But declining sales for its Model T brought home the lesson of fashion. Thus the Model A of 1927 was followed by the V8 in 1932 — after which came a complete change of look with the introduction of streamlining, pioneered by the Chrysler "Airflow" in 1934. After the Second World War, with the establishment of GM's Styling Division[5] the fashion mode became institutionalized, complete with traveling Motoramas and the still surviving ritual of "this year's new model." The overall effect has been that car design (especially at the level of feel and look) has become a predominant element of car promotion. Overwhelmingly, from billboards to showrooms, cars have been advertised by being shown, giving pseudo-auratic texture to that endless parade of vehicles on the actual highway, which itself has served as one vast ad.

Secondly, unlike pottery, furniture and clothes, the automobile was a new product, one that never existed outside the framework of industrialized mass production. The history of its received meaning has always been bound up, then, with that of its manufactured meaning as a promotionally designed product; so tightly, indeed, that for consumers as well as producers cars have been taken, from the start, as veritable emblems of the technical and organizational transformation which made them possible. By the mid-1920s, cars meant mass affluence[6] and Ford(ism) had become an international byword for the whole assembly-line system pioneered in its Michigan plant.[7] In that same period, for Futurist poets like Mario de Leone and Auro d'Alba and visual artists like Francis Picabia the combustion engine itself became a stock image for industrialism, a machine that linked the precise interlocking of parts with the reverie of male sexual power.

More than this, however, like other unprecedented products — e.g. refrigerators, typewriters, phonographs, cameras, radios, etc. — cars became construed and constructed as embodiments of that entire new world — a world of the new — that industry and science were sensed as ushering in. They became, in short, a sign of modernity itself. And quintessentially: for the spread of cars began at once to transform the whole ecology of life, both at the individual level (affecting private and occupational mobility, indeed our whole sense of time and space) and socially (creating massive dependent industries, road systems and transformed cities). Promoting cars as symbols of Modernity, Technology, and Progress, then, has never been entirely arbitrary. For cars really became, for better or worse, a powerful element in that civilizational change to which these mythicized terms ultimately refer.

The Evolving Code

Up to this point I have focused on cars-in-general, but their constructed symbolism has been complicated by divisions within their market. Since the earliest Fords and Oldsmobiles, there have, in fact, been three cultural reference points for car imagery, each broadly corresponding to a different market segment for which different kinds of cars have been designed.

First, and closest to the technology complex itself, is the imagistic set associated with the roadsters, sports cars, and Porsches, Trans-Ams, etc. that are now their "muscle-car" equivalent. Inspiring them all, for over eighty years, has been the spectator sport of car racing, a powerful ritual of male competitive prowess that has conveniently enabled companies to promote themselves while testing research and development. From which, not surprisingly, the racing-car (and the road models derived from it) has emerged as an almost perfect symbol for the masculinist technology values racing itself celebrates: a male identified machine, shaped like a bullet, and experienced from within as an exhilarating rush towards orgasm, death, and the future.[8]

In complete contrast has been the styling characteristic of the luxury car: a vehicle which has continued to trail associations of the genteel upper-class carriage that immediately came before. Such archaism, marked even today by the use of wood and the relative "boxiness" of limousines, has functioned not just as a salve against future shock, but as a sign of that abstract Tradition that industrialism itself has converted into a token of status. Hence, too, the wider diffusion of this complex, whether in the persistence of "tonneau" types until the mid-1920s, or in the use of coachwork language ("Bodies by Fisher") in mainstream ads since then.

Finally, and occupying a kind of symbolic mid-point, we have the family sedan. Designed for mixed use by the whole family (at first: one car per household), its imagery has likewise been mixed. As a commuter/leisure vehicle for the chief breadwinner, it has invited sportiness; as an index of social status, indications that the household is up-to-date, tasteful, or rich. But an element of symbolism has also attached to it as a vehicle for the family as such.

Generally, as a kind of moving home, it has been built to appear respectable, functional, and safe. More specifically, it has been given design features which materially represent "the family" as a particular (yet seemingly universal) type of group. Thus, transposing from the Victorian landau, the two row sedan — throughout this century the family car's instantly recognizable form — not only assumes that the family is nuclear. It also sets up a seating grid within which, by custom, the father/husband drives, the wife sits at his side, and the children form a row at the back. More latterly, as this hierarchical, role-divided model has softened and car ownership by youth and women has increased, the mass car has continued to reflect the prevailing family form, though in a way that is correspondingly more unisex, age-neutral, and varied in size.

This, then, is the matrix within which the history of car imagery has had to unfold. Evidently, like the matrix itself, that history has been multi-leveled and does not reduce to any single thread. Its main features, though, can readily be discerned.

To be noted, first, is a dynamic constant: that, while no type has been symbolically pure, the family car (still the industry's backbone) has peculiarly come to serve as a condensation point for all the image clusters cars can attract. As a mass vehicle it was, and is, designed to appeal to all but the wealthiest households, as well as to all in them. For that reason, too, since artisanal traditionalism, techno-futurism and the values surrounding "the family" (not to mention their class/ethnic variants), do not exactly cohere, its imagery has tended towards ambiguity and compromise. Hence, whatever the idiom of the day, its characteristically "average" look, in which potentially clashing elements are softened at the edges or even made to cancel one another out. Within the mix, it should immediately be added, modernist/masculinist technology values have always been prominently expressed. But by the same token their influence has also been checked; and by considerations no less related to the logic of market appeal.

With respect to the coding of status, secondly, there has been a steady tendency, despite its anachronistic persistence, for Quality Street references to horse-and-carriage to recede gradually from view. A major change came when modernized styling (introduced in the early 1930s in such models as the 1933 Ford V8) began to connect engine to cab in one steady line.[9] Therewith, pre-car imagery migrated from the car's actual body to the once removed rhetoric contained in its ads. In the 1940s and 50s, through such devices as depicting cars as paintings, the Victorian "craft" cluster was still further attenuated: blurring into an image of timeless pre-industrialism ("Buick: a classic") wherein, having separated from the car's material form, it lost contact with that form's history as well.

Besides the present-oriented push of fashion, the boom and bust of capitalism have, as a counter-trend, increasingly made "modernity" itself an essential aspect of the car's capacity to convey esteem. For post-1945 working- and middle-class householders, new-looking cars were a visible way to put the Depression and poverty behind. More generally, in the anxious and dispersed culture of twentieth-century consumerism, being up to date and "modern" became a crucial badge of social membership. The import of this for the imaged car's incorporation of technology values has again been ambiguous. With mid-market cars, as with fashion, if it became important to be contemporary it also became risky to seem too far in front.

Thirdly, and against the background of these dynamics, the technological element of car imagery has itself significantly changed. Most importantly, the car as a symbol of driven speed, and thence of "progress," became outmoded by faster forms of transport, especially ones moving through air. In pace with this, the mass-produced car was successively redesigned — from the "airflows" of the 1930s and the fins-and-tails of post-War Detroit to the "aero" models of today — with each new style mimicking the transport form currently closest to the speed/progress ideal.

On one level, of course, the airplane-influenced trend towards streamlining has been a practical move, reducing not only wind resistance but the attendant costs of fuel. But it has also had a purely symbolic aspect.[10] In such baroque, rocket-like machines as the 1955 Cadillac "Eldorado" aerodynamic efficiency was actually sacrificed in the interest of an aerodynamic look. If the symbolic result was that cars became planes, missiles, and spaceships, driving, in fantasy, became flight: a potent metaphor which, as post-War "depth" promoters well understood, alluded at once to a technicist (and space age) notion of progress and to the promptings of sexual desire.

In its guise as a machine, the car has also been made to seem alive. This has by no means been merely a matter of consumer transference, though the ease with which popular speech has absorbed the metaphor ("she handles really well") shows how culturally resonant it is. Through promotion and design, rather, such animism has been given tangible shape. In a first step, the engine radiator, mounted at the front, was given a grille (mouth). Then two separated headlights (eyes) were added, and a pointed hood (nose) — compensating, presumably, for the vanished face of the horse. The high point came with the customizing craze of the 1940s and 50s, together with the (almost equally) flamboyant monster types it inspired in the industry.[11] Figuration in so blatant a form, however, declined after the Ford Edsel — a car whose spectacular marketing failure (in 1958) was perhaps best explained by customer comments that its grille looked like a vagina (replete, we may add, with teeth). Since then, the beast theme has been domesticated and made the stuff of advertising copy and brand names (Mustangs, Colts, Foxes, Rabbits etc.); while cars, physically, have been contoured more as cyborg-like extensions of their own drivers. On the darker side, this robotic trend has triggered horror film images of riderless vehicles (Stephen King's *Christine*, Stephen Spielberg's *Duel*), out to destroy their human creators for giving them no soul.

The car's imaging as alive has also implied its presentation as sexed. In the first instance, and from the side of the male driver, it has been projected as Woman: whether a flashy possession, boy-toy (as in E. E. Cumming's car-as-virgin poem "XIX"),[12] or wife. But in this (variously nuanced) scene of the male-led couple the car has also figured as rocket, bullet, or gun, i.e. as a sexual extension of the male; while for both sexes, as an enclosed place in which to escape, it has at the same time played the part of a womb. This is, in fact, one of the car's most striking symbolic features: its gender ambiguity. If promotion and use have tied it, like Adam's rib, to the cosmos of phallic technology, they have also given it the character of an androgyne.

Until recently, in the car's symbolization of technology, these intertwined tendencies (towards flight and animation) have constituted the main line of development. But over the past decade the story has been complicated by the rise of two additional symbolic clusters: First, advances in transport (with missiles and space the new frontier) have increasingly come to rely on improvements not so much in propulsion as in guidance systems and their finger-tip control. In turn, with the rise of computers and informatics, this has made communications, rather than transport, the exemplar of technological progress as such. While there are parallels between the accelerated movement of things/persons and of information/thought they are not the same. A shift in attention from one to the other has implied as well, then, a shift in the register of "technology" as a cultural idea. Marshall McLuhan, who was beguiled by this, saw an "explosive"/atomistic world of mechanization giving way to an "implosive"/holistic one of electronics.[13] For imaged cars, more narrowly, it has been reflected in the way that looking "modern" has come to mean not just looking fast and airborne, but being linked to computers and all that they connote.

Secondly, and cutting across symbolism of any kind, car design and promotion have been nagged at by a functionalist conscience. Until the late 1960s, the Bauhaus maxim of "form follows function" was, to be sure, more prevalent among European than American manufacturers, both as a creed and as an aesthetic stick with which to beat their transatlantic rivals. But in the wake of the 1960s cultural upheaval and in the shape of energy-crisis "econoboxes," such anti-decorative purism began to exert a strong pull on this continent too. Like streamlining, to which it has been related, the functionalist *revanche* has had a partly economic motive — reflecting, during the post-Vietnam downturn, the renewed importance of efficiency and price. But the preeminence of function is also a value; and as such (despite itself) it is always liable to become a coded element in the rhetoric and styling of the artifacts made over in its name. For progressive designers in the 1920s[14] functionalist principles provided a utopian definition of modernity itself. In the North American car market, more prosaically, they have come to provide a saleable counter-image to set against the self-congratulatory Frontierism which, at least in the United States, has been that idea's predominant form.

With all these various forces and tendencies in mind let us now turn directly to our original question: the meaning of the car's post-1950s imagistic shift.

The Rise and Fall of the Rocket

The 1950s-style American car, today an object of veneration, is an instantly recognizable type. Through all its variants, from the 1948–49 GM models that initiated it to the fins-and-tails cult classics that came to epitomize the whole Eisenhower period, it was marked by a combination of animism and streamlining taken to almost self-parodying heights of excess. In such a form, serving at once as a commuter vehicle for the suburban family and as a freedom-endowing one for the restless young[15] it became an internationally recognizable symbol of the post-war boom, indeed of free enterprising America itself. Soaked in Buck Rogers images of space and the future, it signified, above all, that new romance with technology which gave Cold War ideology its heady, expansive edge.[16]

In popular form, a 1953 ad for Oldsmobile [Figure 2] shows clearly the value-complex such a vehicle was designed to evoke. The ad is a two-pager, with the car itself, inclined slightly upwards, triumphantly occupying the horizontal plane. Its sleek, forward-thrusting design, emphasized by decorative chrome, repeats the same theme, which is echoed again in the miniature spaceship jetting away in the top left. In case the point is missed we also get a caption: the car's "rocket engine" (what else?) gives you "sm-o-o-o-th" driving. Beyond this, the identified ensemble of car, rocket, and phallus is also framed by a social context, indicted by the respectable young couple ranged alongside. In fact they appear twice. In the main picture he, clean-cut, bejacketed, is smoothly at the wheel while the brunette beside him — decorously apart — looks confidently ahead. At the top left, in the Rocket's

Figure 2

literal reprise, the machine actually lifts off. And here they straddle it like bikers, with hubby waving from the front and wifey lovingly hanging on. In this moment, we are led to suppose, the car becomes theirs: a dream-come-true of upward mobility, growing affluence, and technological progress, all fused together in the happily consummated marriage at the center of the scene.

The arrival of computers aside, there is clearly some discontinuity between this ideological universe and our own. And not surprisingly, for between the two lies a cultural shakeup whose origins (in the story of cars) can be traced back at least as far as the Edsel. The failure of that exaggerated vehicle, as we can now see, signaled not just the end of a design era but the onset of a crisis for the whole nexus of values such styling bespoke.

Most fundamentally, techno-worship itself came under attack. A succession of international crises (Suez, Cuba, Berlin, Vietnam) made the nightmare of the nuclear arms race frighteningly alive. And to this problematizing of blind technology ("a riderless vehicle," as Northrop Frye put it) was added dampened economic expectations that set in after the fifteen-year boom plateaued out and, then, in the financial turmoil of 1971–72, came to an end. The result, aided by the anti-urban side of late 1960s counter-culture[17] and carried forward into middle-class lifestyles ever since, was a wholescale resuscitation of Nature as the repressed Other of all-conquering Industry. In keeping with such changed sensibilities, car design became less blatantly wasteful; fins and chrome were shed; and cars in ads were depicted in fields, identified with free-ranging animals (especially horses) and tied to leisure-related reveries of rural escape.

Reinforcing this, the oil crisis of the mid-1970s, growing traffic congestion, and unease with rampant road construction,[18] changed mass attitudes to the car itself. On the one hand, the car's identification with individual freedom was undermined. On the other, this value came into collision with the car's master value as exemplar of techno-industrial advance. With respect to the latter, cars materially became a bad sign of what they had earlier celebrated. Just as cigarette promoters had to exorcise the cancer scare (hence cigarettes as symbols of Life), car promoters found themselves having to deflect the negative associations with which their own product had become endowed. Reversing the sign (making car into Nature) was one common tactic. Occasionally, though, (as with a 1979 Datsun ad that cited George Orwell, or with a recent Toyota campaign about fighting "road monotony") the car's dystopic associations have been taken head on. As a further response, the decline of the "gas guzzler" paved the way for more functional (and functional-looking) designs. And this was mirrored in the greater stress ads began to place on the product's performative side. (An irony of modern business is that American manufacturers, so attached to their own vision of "technology," were slow to make this turn; leaving a market weakness exploited first by the North Europeans and then by the Japanese with the aid of Italian design.)[19]

With the rise of the women's movement, the emergence of a gay subculture, and the sex/gender *frisson* of the 1970s, the sexual values exemplified by the "Rocket" also came unstuck. The dominance of males and the cowboy complex were not wholly eliminated, but they were pushed on the defensive by the rise of a more egalitarian code. Increased participation by women in work and public life coincided, too, with a proportionate increase in the number of women on the road. In market as well as ideological terms, then, the straightforward insertion of the car into the masculinity complex identified with heroic techno-industrial progress simply ceased to work. In the imaging of cars, correspondingly, assumptions about family structure, the gender of the driver, and the sexual valency of the car itself became more blurred; combined with which, the Nature/Technology categories to which the car was also tied became loosened, as well, from their patriarchal frame.[20]

The Imagery of "High Tech"

All these developments created real difficulties for the imaging of cars. Just as the North American market was becoming tougher, the symbolic resources available to manufacturer/promoters became unstable and difficult to use. To some degree the European-inspired return to functionality has plugged this anomic gap. But in the heartlands of consumerism the appeal of such semantic restraint (which made its appearance with the VW, system-designed European cars, and Detroit compacts) has been safe rather than charged — raising the specter, indeed, of entropy and meaning's final collapse. Additional ways have had to be found, then, for infusing the duller looking vehicles the functionalist reaction has led to with new symbolic life.

It is in just that context, from the early 1980s on, that the car's symbolism as "technology" has begun to be revised. In effect, after a long hiatus, the car's linkage to the romance of rockets has been replaced by a newly generated enthusiasm for the "communications revolution" centered on the microchip. But what, we may wonder, is the broader value import of this new sign? Does it connote anything more than just a differently dressed version of the same old myth?

Again, let us take our cues from ads. Two from *Time* in the winter of

1982, published during the initial burst of mass computer excitement, will at least show the kind of values brought into play. The first, for Volkswagen Rabbit [Figure 3], is constructed around the caption "High tech. Who gives a heck?," each phrase heading a differently designed page. Both are text heavy with various performance-related claims; but the graphics and layout of the "high tech" panel on the left recall a computer screen, while the writing on the right is in hard print. The immediate implication is that with the aid of computers this car is ultra-intelligently designed. But the caption in the lower right (by a picture of the car itself) shows that the computer's supposed qualities of benign intelligence are also (and with disarmingly pet-oriented cuteness) transferred on to the car: "If you thought about Rabbit as much as Rabbit thinks about you you'd think about Rabbit."

The second, for Toyota [Figure 4], plays with a similar theme. Again there are two panels, topped by a visually bifurcated phrase: "The Toyota/Edge." Foregrounded in each is a front-on picture of the car: on the left, as it actually appears; on the right, to the same scale, as a skeletal (X-ray like) engineering drawing, drafted on a screen. Again, one notes the computer's deployment as a sign of embodied intelligence, with that meaning similarly relayed on to the car. In both cases, likewise, the wonders of the computer mediated by its god/man operator as medic and bio-engineer, give us magical access to the car's hidden essence. And in both cases, finally, this focus on the car's inside emphasizes the car's fantasy role as a womb, a role that is immediately qualified by its doubling as the center of designer (and driver) control. In the Toyota case, this whole interiorizing movement is given a further twist by the campaign slogan (from the dance movie *Flashdance*) which appears at the foot of the computer-oriented panel on the right: "Oh what a feeling!"[21]

In other respects, too, the car's entry into the world of high tech has been accompanied by a movement of interiorization. On the material side, we have seen growing design attention to seating and driver ergonomics, to dashboard setups (now digitalized, and with voice controls), and to car sound-systems (quadraphonic speakers, tapedecks, cd's, etc.). In promotion more generally (whether computer-referenced or not) the car has been projected as a king of wraparound experience, or even as a mystical inner trip. A current TV ad for Honda shows a woman stealing from her husband/lover's bed at dawn. She descends to the garage and the car, followed by a dreamy drive along a deserted coastal road. Have you ever wondered, goes the voice-over, where your wife is . . . ? Here, then, is a real difference: in moving from the technology complex that came to a head in the 1950s to the one more

Figure 3

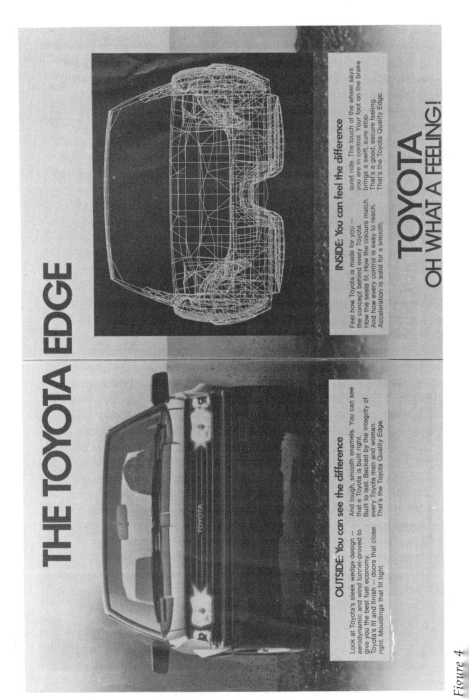

Figure 4

recently linked to computers there has been a change in emphasis from outer to inner space.

It is tempting to treat the linkage between computer images and interiorization as intrinsic, reflecting, for example, a real technological bias.[22] We might further speculate that this bias, reinforced by pressures towards cultural feminization, has also led to a change in Technology's imputed sex. But in a crucial sense the linkage permitting such recoding is also historically contingent. A renewed emphasis on subjectivity, experience, and the personal world extends beyond advertising and has independent roots in the whole socio-cultural crisis of the past twenty years. In ads, as in movies and popular songs, it registers an exhaustion with the growth complex of industrial society and anxieties about its future: a mood which has combined with the ongoing effects of consumerized privatism to deflect attention away from the whole public realm. And here, we may note, the contemporary imaged car is caught in a deep contradiction: it is part of the problem it cannot (for market reasons) name and from which it is posited as an escape.

For that reason, too, paradoxically, the 1950s car and its related insignia (diners, milkbars, ducktails, golden age rock and roll) has made something of a comeback. In films, music, and the general symbology of contemporary youth it has been recycled; so that (just like the vintage model of the IBM ad) what first made its appearance as futurist euphoria has returned, in the context of newer fears, as a symbol of a better past. With respect to cars themselves, the impact of such revivalism has been more evident in ads (through *Grease* and *American Graffiti* type references) than in actual design. Still, in the play of fashion, and throughout our culture, a stylized past is the obverse of novelty as a source for new trends. So we may conjecture that here, too — perhaps building on the recently revived craze for rodding and customizing — nostalgic references to earlier models will make their way into the manufactured appearance of current ones.

Cars, Today

Overall, then, it would be one-sided to suppose that car imagery, in its adoption of computer references, has simply moved to install an updated version of progress-based technological myth. This is certainly one trend, but it has been interwoven with others, including the resurgence of functionalism, the unsettling of patriarchy, a personalist withdrawal from the adventures of industrialism, and indications that cars are beginning to be caught up in what Fredric Jameson calls the "nostalgia mode."[23] All of which, taken together, would suggest that if techno-myth has been partially revamped and restored, it has also, in broader compass, ceased to be symbolically central or even coherent. Indeed, an alternative hypothesis can be advanced: that car imagery, like other sign-bearing material in the cultural vortex of advanced capitalism, is evolving towards a decorative electicism whose signifying gestures refer us only to the universe of symbols from which they are drawn.

In fact, with the public circulation of signs severed from life by commerce, media, and reactive privatism there are grounds for arguing that it is not our technology but our culture that is imploding, parallel with a further disintegration of society in the old organic sense.[24] In its costly, computer-linked, post-modern guise, the contemporary car certainly bears all the marks of such a process. But its witness is blind since, as a promotional construct, its imagery can scarcely acknowledge what has happened, let alone its own — doubly — mystifying role. What the decorative play on the car's functionalized surface ultimately hides, that is, is not just the negativity of the product but the relation between that negativity and the kind of gloss it is given. Simply put: that the car's own disruptive dominance as a transport form is part of the disaffected reality from which our culture, as written into the car's very body, has recoiled.

15.

Advertising as Religion: The Dialectic of Technology and Magic

Sut Jhally

The Magic of the Marketplace

In contemporary America, we are immersed most of our waking hours in a world and a discourse where all normal physical and social arrangements are held in abeyance.

- from deep in the ocean depths, swimming alongside sleek and dangerous sharks, taking on their shape and form, emerges "a new species" of automobile — a Chevrolet Baretta.

- as a woman passes behind him, a man is overcome with desire and immediately starts to pursue her in a blind passion, pausing only to snatch up some flowers that he presents to her when he catches her. We are told the spell is cast because the woman uses Impulse body spray.

- a young male adolescent stares in horror at his pimpled complexion in a bathroom mirror. As he applies a magical lotion, his pimples immediately disappear, even as we watch.

- a young attractive woman boldly enters a pool room where she announces she has had enough of Mr. Wrong and that it is time for Mr. Right. As she sings this she throws a can of Right Guard antiperspirant to individuals with the faces of grotesque monsters. They are immediately transformed into handsome young men who crowd around the woman.

- a young woman walks by groups of men; a "sea breeze" is unleased by her that envelops the young males.

217

In advertising, the commodity world interacts with the human world at the most fundamental of levels: it performs magical feats of transformation and bewitchment, brings instant happiness and gratification, captures the forces of nature, and holds within itself the essence of important social relationships (in fact, it substitutes for those relations).

What is noteworthy about such scenes is not that they are concerned with the role of objects in the social lives of people. Such a relationship is one of the defining features of what it means to be human; the relationship between people and things is a universal one. What is noteworthy in the modern period however is the *extent* to which goods enter into the arrangements of everyday life. Much more so than in previous societies, in the consumer culture it seems that every aspect of life is permeated by the presence of objects. Karl Marx, writing in the middle of the nineteenth century and in the early phases of the development of industrial capitalism, perceptively pointed to what would become the main features of the developing system. In the opening lines of *Capital* he stated that: "The wealth of societies in which the capitalist mode of production prevails appears as an 'immense collection of commodities'."[1] Unlike all previous modes of production, capitalism discovered the "secret" of material production and proceeded to install it as its central and defining activity. While Marx did not witness the emergence of the institution of national advertising, he was able to penetrate to what would become its essential feature:

> It is nothing but the definite social relation between men themselves which assumes here, for them, the fantastic form of a relation between things. In order, therefore, to find an analogy, we must take flight into the misty realm of religion. There the products of the human brain appear as autonomous figures endowed with a life of their own, which enter into relations both with each other and with the human race. So it is in the world of commodities with the products of men's hands. I call this the fetishism which attaches itself to the products of labor as soon as they are produced as commodities, and is therefore inseparable from the production of commodities . . . the labor of the private individual manifests itself as an element of the total labor of society only through the relations which the act of exchange establishes between the product, and, through their mediations, between the producers. To the producers, therefore, the social relations between their private labors appear as what they are, i.e. they do not appear as direct social relations between persons in their work, but rather as material relations between persons and social relations between things.[2]

Marx was able to predict the supernatural world that advertising would create, in which relationships between people are mediated through things and in which things themselves come alive and interact with each other and with human beings. This prediction was based upon his understanding that capitalism as a system of production and consumption entails a very different relationship between people and the world of goods than had existed previously — that the "discourse" about society that takes place through the medium of things has a different content and structure. For him, it came down to the difference between market and non-market exchange.

In older non-market societies there was a much more direct connection between people and the goods that they used in everyday life. Most of the goods they consumed were produced by themselves or were produced by persons and processes whom they knew, so people had a great deal of information about the world of goods. The social relations of production were visible to all and, furthermore, they were in a sense "embedded" in goods as part of their meaning. Indeed in many traditional societies, the exchange of goods was literally an exchange of people, in that people had embedded something of themselves in the goods they produced. In giving a good that you produced you were giving a part of yourself. Inherently, goods are communicators of social relations.

Marx recognized this fundamental feature of goods and installed it as part of his methodological framework for the analysis of capitalism. He starts *Capital* by saying that his investigation will begin with the analysis of the commodity, because he thought that if one could understand how the commodity was produced, exchanged, and consumed, then one would have the basis of an understanding of the entire system of capitalist relations — like goods in any social system, contained within them are the social relations of their production. However in capitalism, and unlike previous societies, there is a problem in terms of trying to "read" goods for the social information they contain. Their origins are hidden from us. There are two dimensions to this.

First, in the world of production the work process is increasingly subdivided and specialized so that workers only work on part of a product. In addition, there is a separation between the planning process for the production of goods and the actual process of production itself — a split between mental and manual labor such that those people who actually physically produce the product (wage-laborers) have no overall sense of the production process or its relationship to other aspects of social life. (Of course, increasingly smaller numbers of people are actually involved in industrial production itself.) Second, most of us use goods that come to us through the marketplace. As such we have little information about them beyond what manufacturers choose to tell us through media advertising or packaging. The social relations of production embedded in goods are systematically hidden from our eyes. The real meaning of goods in fact is *emptied* out of them in capitalist production and consumption. Marx labeled this the "fetishism of commodities," a disguise whereby the appearance of things in the marketplace masks the story of who fashioned them, and under what conditions.

The Development of the Consumer Society

Of course, the implementation of capitalist production methods meant more than merely a new way to produce goods — it entailed a revolution in the cultural arrangements of traditional society. Traditional pre-industrial society was based around agriculture and there was little separation between work and leisure. The extended family and religion were hugely important influences on the conduct of everyday life. The meaning of goods in such a context was intimately tied up with local production and integrated within the structure of ethnic cultural forms. Ethnicity, family, religion, and community structured the discourse surrounding goods.

The coming of capitalist industrial society shattered these bonds. City living, factory labor, and the separation between work and leisure destroyed the vitality of the older traditions that could not be sustained within the new urban context. T. Jackson Lears argues that in the early years of the twentieth century, American society was going through a major crisis of meaning in which an older culture of puritanism, self-denial, and work was dissolving under the strains brought on by modernism. Feelings of unreality, depression, and loss accompanied the experience of anonymity associated with urbanization. Religious beliefs waned in strength as traditional Protestant theology underwent a process of secularization. The feelings of "unreality" that arose in this period could not be dealt with by the traditional institutions that had fulfilled this role previously. Indeed, it was the loosening of their influence that led to the feelings of unreality. These feelings were reflected in a concern for physical and emotional health. Whereas before, the quest for health had been part of a larger communal, ethical and religious framework, by the twentieth century this had become almost entirely a *secular* process. Lears argues that advertisers picked up on these movements and began to exploit the emotional needs of advertisers.

> A dialectic developed between America's new emotional needs and
> advertiser's strategies; each continually reshaped and intensified the

other . . . By the 1920's the symbolic universe of national advertising markedly resembled the therapeutic world described by Philip Rieff — a world in which all overarching structures of meaning had collapsed . . . It is important to underscore the role of advertising in accelerating this collapse of meaning.[3]

Industrial society is a transitional society which can neither draw on the past nor construct its own structures of meaning. It is a cultural void in which old and new ways of living collide.

In addition to this crisis of meaning, industrial capitalism also faced the potential problem of a severe and debilitating economic crisis. The "immense collection of commodities" that capitalism produces also have to be *sold*. Without the consumption of these commodities, capitalism would be in a state of permanent depression and would quickly die. This crisis was especially acute in the early years of this century. Stuart Ewen refers to this complex of relations as the "social crisis of industrialization" and argues that the developing institutions of the consumer society (such as advertising) offered to solve both problems simultaneously. The consumer society resolves the tensions and contradictions of industrial society as the marketplace and consumption take over the functions of traditional culture. Into the void left by the transition from traditional to industrial society comes advertising, the most prominent aspect of the "discourse through and about objects," and the reconstitution of the population not into social classes as the primary mode of identification but into consumption classes.[4]

Advertising: The Theft and Reappropriation of Meaning

How precisely does advertising fit into this scenario? I argued earlier that in non-market societies there is a unity between people and goods, but that in capitalism there is a separation between object and producer. The world of goods in industrial society offers no meaning, its meaning having been "emptied" out of them. The function of advertising is to refill the emptied commodity with meaning. Indeed the meaning of advertising would make no sense if objects already had an established meaning. The power of advertising *depends* upon the initial emptying out. Only then can advertising refill this void with its own meaning. Its power comes from the fact that it works its magic on a blank slate. The fetishism of commodities consists in the first place of emptying them of meaning, of hiding the real social relations objectified in them through human labor, to make it possible for the imaginary/symbolic social relations to be injected into the construction of meaning at a secondary level. Production empties. Advertising fills. The real is hidden by the imaginary. The social significance of the marketplace is only possible after the social significance of production disappears beneath the structure of capitalist property relations. The hollow husk of the commodity-form needs to be filled by some kind of meaning, however superficial. This is why advertising is so powerful. People need meaning for the world of goods. The traditional institutions that provided this have been weakened. Thus, advertising derives its power from providing meaning that is not available elsewhere.

If what I have just described is the broad social role that advertising plays, what specific strategies does it use to accomplish this. Looked at historically, there is no single set of strategies that advertising utilizes. Instead we can identify a number of different strategies that are developed through the course of the twentieth century in response to changing market and social conditions.[5]

In the initial stage of the development of national advertising the consumer society responds to the appearance of the "immense collection of commodities" in a celebratory mode. What is celebrated is the great productive capacities of industrial society as reflected in products. Advertising has a strong theme of veneration of products, almost worshipping the fruits of industrial technology. Commodities are idols in early advertising. "Huge refrigerators towered above tiny towns of consumers; silhouetted against the starry sky, they stood guard over communities like giant sentinels. Immense cars straddled the rivers and towns of miniaturized countrysides below, symbolizing the command over the landscape obtainable through the automobile." Such images "conveyed impressions of the product as dominant or transcendent, if not awesome."[6] The initial development of national advertising can then be labeled as the stage of *Idolatry.*

Such a development is not an accident or a clever creation by the advertising industry alone. Advertisers sought to mediate between the needs of manufacturers to sell products and the changing context of meaning for consumers. Advertising had to reflect some real needs in the consuming public. What advertisers recognized was the nostalgia for the world that was passing, for a stable world of religious, family, and community life. The early stages of national advertising are characterized both by a veneration for the "immense collection of commodities" and a linking back to traditional themes. The transcendental religious realm provided a rich, deep resource from which to draw although its influence was weakening throughout the society. Advertisers recognized that the public yearned to experience moments of enhancement, awe, and rapture.

Advertisers, though, could not be too explicit with this for fear of negative public reaction. Richard Marchand points out that instead they used visual cliches "that employed vague forms of sacred symbolism rather than specific religious figures . . . Such visual strategies sought to transform the product . . . into a 'surrogate trigger' for producing those life-enhancing feelings that consumers avidly pursued. As an ad in *Printers' Ink Monthly* offhandedly noted in 1926, advertisements were 'beginning to occupy the place in inspiration that religion did several hundred years ago' ."[7] Consumers were shown entranced before the power of the object. Refrigerator ads featured women who looked as though they had glimpsed through the open door "a secular revelation as spellbinding as any religious vision." The visual cliche of "radiant beams" that came from outside the picture and highlighted the product was another often used strategy suggesting some divine intervention in the world of commodities. In other versions the beams radiated from the product itself suggesting a kind of "halo" effect round the product. Marchand argues that through such strategies, advertisers were secularizing images without losing their original spiritual overtones. Such imagery "represented a final step in the successful, though largely unconscious adaptation of religious imagery to the advertising tableaux, the modern icons of a faith in mass consumption."[8]

The idolatrous stage of advertising predominates from the 1890s and into the 1920s. The second stage of religious adaptation starts in the 1920s and can be labeled the stage of *Iconology*. Icons are symbols; they mean something. Advertising in this stage moves from the worship of commodities to their *meaning* within a social context. As the traditional customs and behavioral codes became unglued in the cultural void of industrial society, marketplace communication stepped in to provide consumers with the needed advice. Goods became powerful not only through what they could do but through what they could mean. Consumption here becomes explicitly a social activity, and goods are intimately connected with social relations. There is a shift away from the product alone and towards the consumer, but the movement stops halfway. In the stage of iconology both products and persons are embodiments of reigning social values and the world of advertising is neither wholly thing-based or person-based — instead it is meaning-based. Commodities are the icons of the marketplace.

From the 1940s into the 1960s advertising completes the shift towards the consumer. The product is seen as powerful but now its power is put at the disposal of individuals. Further, these individuals are presented in "real" terms rather than the abstract depictions of the second stage. This is the stage of *Narcissism* where the product reflects the desires of the individual. Advertisements show the fantasized completion of the self, of how the product can transform individual existence. The power of the product can be manifested in many ways, but predominantly it is through the strategy of "black magic," where persons undergo sudden physical transformations or where the commodity can be used to entrance and enrapture other people. The world of objects here enters the everyday world of people and performs in magical ways.

From the 1960s to the present the focus shifts yet again into the stage of *Totemism.* Totemism in older societies refers to the correlation between the natural world and the social world where natural differences stand for social differences. In modern advertising, goods take the place of natural species. In this last phase the predominant themes of the previous stages are drawn together and remixed into a unique form: commodities are freed from being merely utilitarian things (idolatry), or abstract representations of social values (iconology), or intimately connected with the world of personal and interpersonal relations (narcissism). In the totemic stage, utility, symbolization, and personalization are mixed and remixed under the sign of the *group.* In lifestyle advertising, products are badges of group membership. Through consumption one has access to and participates in a very specific consumption community which is defined through that very consumption activity. Products give magical access to a previously closed world of group activities.

Although these stages have been presented as an historical progression, they should not be thought of as being exclusive of each other: rather, they should be viewed as cumulative. The labels apply to the dominant tendency within any period. The particular forms that arise in different periods do not disappear, but rather are segregated as a mode of representation for particular products and audiences. In the contemporary marketplace, the person-object relation is articulated psychologically, physically, and socially. Some goods seem to serve primarily for display and social judgment, some for personal enhancement, some for locating us within the nexus of group relations, and some just for simple utility in everyday life.

Further, commodities appear as miraculous products of an invisible process of production. In the marketplace they enter into unique and changing relations with each other, jostling for position to satisfy the needs of the consumer. In some instances, products explicitly take on animate features and come alive. Advertising truly reflects the world that Marx described as being characteristic of capitalism — an enchanted kingdom of magic and fetishism where goods are autonomous, where they enter into relations with each other and where they appear in "fantastic forms" in their relations with humans.

The Fetishism of Commodities

The economic and business literature on advertising is dominated by the concept of "information" — advertising is supposed to provide consumers with marketplace information about goods so that there is some rational basis for choice. Unless one has a very broad definition of what constitutes information this is clearly not a very fruitful way to understand this institution. (The installation of the concept of "information" is, of course, an ideological strategy to deflect debate away from the really important features of advertising.) The real function of advertising is not to give people information but to make them feel good. Ad maker Tony Schwartz explicitly articulates this when he tells advertisers not to make claims that could be proven false but to concentrate instead on creating pleasurable experiences.[9] T. Jackson Lears points out that "feeling" replaced information very early on in the development of advertising. In the most sophisticated version of this "feeling good" theory, Staffan Linder claims that it is unreasonable to expect consumers to gather full information to inform their purchasing decisions — there simply is not enough time to collect all the information that would be needed to make truly rational purchasing decisions. In such a context what consumers require is to have *some* justification for their purchasing decisions, however irrational. Advertising provides this and makes consumers feel that they have made decisions at least on some basis rather than on some totally arbitrary criteria.[10] I argued before that one of the most important functions that advertising performs is to provide meaning for the world of goods in a context where true meaning has been stolen. It helps us to understand the world and our place in it, and it accomplishes this through integrating people and things within a magical and supernatural sphere.

If this function were attributed to an institution in non-capitalist society, we would have no trouble seeing it for what is was — *religion*. Indeed, if the basis of advertising is to make us feel good and it has surrendered any objective basis for this feeling, in what way is it different from religion? Why not also tea leaves, ouija boards, black cats, dice, sounds that go bump in the night? Why not God? All these too can "satisfy" us, can "justify" our choices! Advertising here becomes a secular version of God! When couched in the context of religion, our four-stage developmental model of advertising history takes on new meaning. For instance, is it an accident that advertising messages have moved from focusing on physical functions, to focusing on desires, personal and small-group lifestyles, and the form of being-in-the-world of a whole social formation? Is it an accident that the messages have moved from the verbal to the visual?[11]

Indeed, representatives of established religious faiths have recognized with alarm the manner in which this new "religion" threatens their own existence. Believing that a "gospel is a book of revelation, an ultimate source of reference wherein we find ourselves revealed . . . a response to questions of who we are, what we may hope for, how we may aspire to act, what endures, what is important, what is of true value," the Jesuit scholar John Kavanaugh argues that advertising is part of a gospel based upon the Commodity form — a world where people are identified through the things they consume as well as being dominated by them. Kavanaugh compares this to a life based on more human values, such as justice and spirituality — a gospel based upon the Personal Form. These two kinds of gospels "serve as ultimate and competing 'forms' of perception, through which we filter our experience. Each form, moreover, provides a controlling image for our consciousness in apprehending our selves and our world . . . Each has its own 'church', you might say, its own cults and liturgical rites, its own special language, and its own concept of the heretical."[12]

We should hesitate accepting the notion of "advertising as religion," however, until we have asked one additional question. What *kind* of religion is it? Is it the same as Christianity, Hinduism, Judaism, Islam, etc.? If it is different, how is it different? Clearly, it is different from the established religions in that there is no moral core at its center that is articulated in a ritualized form. We may be able to read the entire set of advertisements for this moral order but that is not the same as having an articulated moral code already existing. In established religions, the icons that are used reflect a central system of beliefs — they are ritualized expressions of it. In advertising the icons of the marketplace themselves are this religion. I will come back to this point below.

The *levels* at which the different religions operate are also important. Advertising operates not at a spiritual level but at a mundane everyday level. In this it resembles systems of belief that have existed in other societies. Early anthropological accounts of nineteenth-century West Africa tribes describe practices whereby objects were believed to be possessed by some kind of supernatural spirit, which if worshipped and appeased could have a beneficial influence on the wordly existence of the owner. The control of the power of the fetish was associated with black magic and was used for personal ends. It could guard against sickness, bring rain, catch fish, make the owner brave, bring the owners good fortune, protect against other evil spirits, cure the ill, sexually attract persons, capture the power of some aspect of the animal kingdom, etc. This system of belief was labeled by anthropologists as "fetishism." Like the world of advertising, fetishism operated at the level of everyday activity; its effects were short-term and immediate and concerned the practical welfare of its possessor. It was not, in and of itself, a *total* spiritual belief system but rather a *part* of a much larger one.[13]

In all societies where the term "fetishism" has been applied, there are different levels of spiritual belief: acceptance of the powers of the fetish should not blind us to the possibility that its user may also have belief in a higher spiritual power, such as a supreme being. There is no denial of God but merely an *indifference* to "Him" as regards the conduct of everyday life. The fetish does not operate at a higher spiritualistic or vague futuristic level, for which other spheres of religion are more appropriate. In fetishism it is to the vast number of spirits in the air that affect physical, social, and psychological human conduct that attention is directed. Advertising, then, can more closely be compared to this fetishistic religion.

> The moral universe . . . is essentially that of a polytheistic religion. It is a world dominated by a sheer numberless pantheon of powerful forces, which literally reside in every article of use or consumption, in every institution of daily life. If the winds and waters, the trees and brooks of ancient Greece were inhabited by a vast host of nymphs, dryads, satyrs, and other local and specific deities, so is the universe of the TV commercial. The polytheism that confronts us here is thus a fairly primitive one, closely akin to animistic and fetishistic beliefs.[14]

Technology and Magic

Raymond Williams notes that advertising is "a highly organized and professional system of magical inducements and satisfactions, functionally very similar to magical systems in simpler societies, but rather strangely coexistent with a highly developed scientific technology."[15] If, functionally speaking, the broad purpose of a religion is to provide a confused population with answers to the problems of existence, why does advertising focus so much attention on the use of magic rather than on some other, more spiritual system of beliefs? To answer this question we need to recontextualize advertising within the broader parameters of seeing it as an institution of a developing capitalist society. Judith Williamson defines magic as "the production of results disproportionate to the effort put in (a transformation of power — or of impotence *into* power)."[16] How does this fit into the cultural framework of advanced capitalist society?

For Raymond Williams the fundamental choice that emerges in a modern industrial society is between seeing people as producers or as consumers. A society that encourages a view of people as producers highlights the political dimensions of industrial activity and recognizes that different ways of organizing material production entails debates about the distribution of power and who benefits within any social system. Such a society recognizes that the important decisions made about the structure of society are made in the realm of production — for it is the economic sphere that structures the distribution of valuable and scarce social resources. To the extent that a society wants democratic discussion about the proper uses of social resources, a view of people as producers is absolutely vital.

On the other hand, to the extent that a society wants to divert attention away from the political consequences of economic structures it encourages people to regard themselves as consumers of industrial products rather than as their producers. Democratic activity in this perspective is equated with the different options that the marketplace is able to offer. Consumption is democracy, in as much as people have "choices" about the products they can buy, but not the productive arrangements under which they live. To the extent that a society is successful in this type of definition of people, we have a deflection of consciousness away from the real areas of social life (production) and towards those that are secondary (consumption). As Raymond Williams writes: "The fundamental choice that emerges, in the problems set to us by modern industrial production, is between man as consumer and man as user. The system of organized magic which is modern advertising is primarily important as a functional obscuring of this choice."[17] It obscures this choice because it both recognizes our reality and then offers a false interpretation of it. It recognizes the reality that modern forms of capitalist production strip away from us any notion of control of our productive activity. At work we are not in control. It gives a false interpretation of this in that it naturalizes the loss of control and instead offers us control in another realm — consumption. Judith Williamson writes:

> In advertising, it is essential to compensate for the inactivity forced on us; hence advertising's Romanticism and its emphasis on adventure and excitement. But the only thing we can *do* in fact is to buy the product, or incant its name — this is all the action possible as *our* part of the excitement offered. Such minimal action inevitably creates a "magical spell" element: from a little action we get "great" results (or are promised them) . . . Magic allows us to feel that we may not be producers of meaning but of *material* effects . . . This creates a never ending exchange between passivity and action, a translation between technological action and magical action with our own *in*activity as the turning point. Technology deprives us of a control which we are given back in the surrogate form of spells and promises.[18]

In modern industrial society the link with nature has been shattered: nature is viewed only as a resource that is there for human consumption. Our defining relationship is with technology. Rather than the spirits of nature invading the body of objects (as in older fetishistic belief systems), in the mythical universe of advertising it is the spirits of technology that invade the body of the commodity and supply the basis for a belief in its power. The "technological fix" is, in modern capitalist society, a deep-rooted way of approaching (and obscuring) *social* problems and it would not surprise us to see this pattern everywhere we look, from SDI to car commercials, cloaked in magical and supernatural modes of representation.

16.

The Importance of Shredding In Earnest: Reading the National Security Culture and Terrorism

James Der Derian

The social intervention of a text (not necessarily
achieved at the time the text appears) is measured not
by the popularity of its audience or by the fidelity of
the socioeconomic reflection it contains or projects to
a few eager sociologists, but rather by the violence that
enables it to *exceed* the laws that a society, an ideology,
a philosophy establish for themselves in a fine surge of
historical intelligibility. This excess is called writing.

Roland Barthes, *Sade/Fourier/Loyola*

Reading the culture of the state requires excessive writing, to offset
silences and to reinscribe the subject, but also to overcome problems
of estrangement. How do we define what defines us, what separates Us
from Them, what draws symbolic boundaries between order and disorder, what distinguishes meaning from meaninglessness in international
relations? There is the temptation to ape traditional diplomatic history,
that is, to sift through the archival accretions which define and constitute a national culture. But if the reader/writer travels to the boundaries
of the national *security* culture, instead of definitions one finds fences of
arcane classifications surrounding the most significant archives; and
when one finally gains entry through freedom of information actions or
by public disclosures, worse news awaits them:

"When did you shred them, sir?"

"My answer, Mr. Nields, is that I started shredding documents in
earnest, after a discussion with Director Casey in early October . . .
Director Casey and I had a lengthy discussion about the fact that this

whole thing was coming unraveled and that things ought to be cleaned up. And I started cleaning things up."[1]

Thus on the first day of his testimony at the Iran-contra hearings Lieutenant Colonel Oliver North informed the American people of the importance of shredding in earnest, of sanitizing the messy margins of the national security culture. Perched on the edge of this culture, Oliver North offers a special perspective on the terrain where its most significant and dramatic activity occurs: terrorism. He first dogged President Reagan's heels when he carried the "football" containing the codes for launching nuclear terror; in 1981 he was brought into the National Security Council "to handle easels and carry the charts" (according to Richard Allen, the first of President Reagan's five national-security advisers); and he eventually worked his way up to the post of Assistant Deputy Director for Political-Military Affairs at the NSC, from which he directed American counterterrorism policy while secretly managing the aid program for the contras and the negotiation with Iran of arms for hostages.

North, then, provides a useful entry-point to traverse the terrorist-etched boundaries of the national security culture. This is not to say that the nature of this culture will be revealed if the "truth" about North's story is uncovered; nor is it to claim that he "represents" or is the incarnation of the national security culture. These were faulty presuppositions of many members of the media and of the House and Senate Select Committee investigating the exploits of North; they also acted as impediments to any lasting, meaningful revelations, because the true North — amplified and globally projected by television — proved *to be* the magnetic North. In this sense, North was the living simulacrum of the national security culture: more real than the reality the Committee sought to uncover, more seductive than anything the polymorphous, acephalous Committee could reconstruct, North's truth was like the CIA outside the CIA that he and William Casey sought to create — an "off-the-shelf, self-sustaining, stand-alone entity" — the perfect agent for constructing and combating a hyperreal terrorism.[2]

What a cultural reading of terrorism must involve, then, is not only an inquiry into the state's archival accretions but also into its most sensitive secretions. The way in which they leak out and then reappear as public narratives, in the news, fiction, and film, provides us with a map of a particular *cultural economy*, by which I mean a flow and exchange of valorized symbols. But how might we reconstruct the "high," or political culture of the national security state, that is, the discursive practices which fence the techno-bureaucrats and para-soldiers of the state in and the general public and critical investigators out? The penumbra of the Iran-contra case provides some immediate material, but our "first" hostage crisis in Iran illuminated — and revealed chinks in — the modern national security culture. Some artful investigative techniques were generated by, among others, the Revolutionary Guard, who used ancient weaving techniques to create politically sensitive tapestries from the shredded documents of our embassy in Teheran and then published them as a fifty-four volume set of the Great Satan's hitherto unknown sayings.[3] Now, however, the most relevant and revealing archives of the NSC are pulverized or crosscut (rather than linguini-shredded) and then burnt. The only recourse for a critical inquiry, it would seem, would be an epiphenomenology of terrorism, a study of the smoke rising from the "burn bags" of the Executive branch.

But let us pretend for the moment that Karl Marx was on epistem-ologically solid ground when he wrote in the Preface to the *Critique of Political Economy* that "mankind always sets itself only such tasks as it can solve, since it will always be found that the task itself arises only when the material conditions for its solution already exist or are at least in the process of formation." Lt. Colonel North shredded in earnest and retyped letters with a doctored IBM golfball; Ms. Fawn Hall surreptitiously removed documents and erased incriminating floppy disks with a vengeance; Director of Central Intelligence William Casey conveniently died with his secrets. Yet an electronic archive was preserved and discovered, for the magnetic tracks of the now infamous PROF notes lived on in the memory of the computers: as all hackers know, you must *overwrite* a file to obliterate it.

The problem confronting all inscriptive readers and semio-critical writers of this story is how, armed with this resurrected data, are we to reinscribe this story of arms, hostages, and terrorism without overwriting the disorder which gave rise to it?[4] This is not just a figurative concern, for the magnification by the media of the terrorist threat, along with their ability to transform an act of violence into a news event, assures, indeed often produces the impossibility of any individual ethico-political response to it. From a safe distance the commentator might condemn terrorism, but the camera zooms in to fascinate us with the fear and spectacle of death which usually attend acts of terrorism.[5] This further complicates the problem of reinscription, and helps to explain the proliferation of terrorist "experts" who appear *ad nauseum* in the media; we hang on the words of national security "consultants" who speak and write to compensate for the fact that we cannot hang (or rather, *deter* through legal homicide) the terrorist, for nations cannot agree to a common definition of terrorism, let alone a common power to enforce sanctions against it. That would require the discipline of a universal law and order, and there can be no law where there is no sovereign, as Thomas Hobbes said but Oliver North embellished: "it is very important for the American people to understand that this is a dangerous world, that we live at risk and that this nation is at risk in a dangerous world."[6]

It would seem, then, that outside the cultural economy of national security, the non-military options for responding to terrorism are severely limited — semantically, epistemologically, ethically, practically. Is it possible to write/read about terrorism without pretending, self-consciously or unself-consciously, to make terrorism "safe" — safe for definition, criminalization, or even legitimation? Or must we remain silent/blind, as we do in the face of "natural" disasters like earthquakes, floods, and famine, when no explanations can possibly encompass the meaninglessness and contingency of catastrophic deaths?[7] Wandering in international relations, between post-modernity in thought and what looks like a neo-medievalism in practice, I can make no claims for an explanatory or analytical reading of terrorism and the national security culture. The best I can offer — and the best I believe the material will provide — is a *description*: in effect, this means a melding of the reconstructive technology of the Iran-contra hearings with the palimpsest technique of the Middle Ages. It is only the first step — I believe a necessary step — to an inquiry into the national security culture beneath the official documents, inside the "erased" electronic files, within the subtext of terrorism which abolishes the distinction between the crime and its repression.[8]

Facts and Factotum of Terrorism

Just as Friedrich Nietzsche has shown us how meaning precedes facts, we see in North how the factotum precedes the facts of terrorism. There are, of course, some commonly accepted facts about international terrorism. A selection of Rand corporation documents on international terrorism reveals the following: over the last ten years terrorists have seized over 50 embassies and consulates; held the oil ministers of 11 states hostage; kidnapped hundreds of diplomats, businessmen, and journalists; made several hundred million dollars in ransom money; assassinated Lord Mountbatten and President Sadat and the former premier of Italy; and attempted to assassinate the President of France, the Pope, and Alexander Haig (a near miss with a rocket launcher when he was supreme allied commander of NATO). Terrorist incidents and their severity *have* increased over the last ten years, but most terrorist actions involve few or no casualties: they are symbolic acts of violence.

Compared to the ruthlessness and destructiveness of states, or even to natural disasters, terrorism is a mere nuisance. Yet it is cause for crises of state, media spasms on a seismic scale, and the hyper-production of institutes, conferences and books on terrorism.

Why is this? International terrorism does represent a crisis, but not in terms of body-counts or a revolutionary threat to the states-system. On a political level, the simulacrum of terrorism, that is, the production of a hyperreal threat of violence, precedes a crisis of *legitimation*.[9] What this means is that international terrorism is not a symptom or a cause of an effect of this systemic crisis: it is a spectacular, microcosmic simulation. International terrorism simulates the legitimation crisis of the international order; conversely, counterterrorism is a counter-simulation, an attempt to engender a new disciplinary order which can save the legitimacy principle of international relations.[10] On a representational level, the spectacle of terrorism simultaneously displaces and distracts us from international *disorder*. As a result, much of what we do know of terrorism displays a superficiality of reasoning and a corruption of language which effects truths about terrorism without any sense of how these truths are produced by and help to sustain official discourses of international relations. Reason of state is afflicted by the crudest expediency posing as principled policy, as repeatedly evidenced by the proceedings and documents of the Iran-contra hearings.

If the reader of terrorism is to break out of the dominant cultural economy, in which each of us is a factotum of given facts, that is, a transmitter of official "truths," then some critical interpretive skills must be deployed. Along with an empirical study of the disorder around us we need a geneaology of our knowledge of international terrorism and legitimacy, and of how we arrive at some shared assumptions about both. One goal, then, of a cultural reading is to reach a better under-standing of whether these assumptions or constructions of terrorism and legitimation serve to preserve principles and practices beneficial to the international order, or whether they forestall the knowledge neces-sary to deal effectively with an increasing fragmentation, a diffusion of power, and a sustained challenge to the sovereign state's once-natural monopoly of force: in short, the neo-medievalism alluded to earlier.

What this entails — and what this essay attempts — is a critical preface to a text that each reader of terrorism must "write." Having asserted the precession of the meaning of terrorism, I recognize the need to address the "facts" of defining terrorism. Some originally useful but now obfuscating distinctions have been made between state terrorism and non-state terrorism; but the forces of the conservative status quo have won out, with Jeanne Kirkpatrick (formerly at the United Nations), and Claire Sterling (of the *New York Times*) leading the definitional battle for the expropriation of the phrase, state terrorism, by the West. The linguistic annexation has been made official through lists published annually by the State Department which inform us which states are or sponsor terrorists. Unsurprisingly, and in spite of our sponsorship of terrorist activities in Central America, the United States does not appear on that list: Libya, North Korea, Iran, and a shifting group of other pariah states do.

But as noted, confusion over definitions arises not just because of terrorism's multiple sponsors and forms, but because of the cultural efforts to tame its arbitrary nature, unpredictability, and chimeric character. Rigorous or rigid, sloppy or broad, definitions are in themselves an important discursive practice of the terrorism industry. Most frequently they appear to be yet another weapon in the vast arsenal of counterterrorism aiming to reestablish order and meaning in international relations practice and discourse at a time when both are undergoing extensive and intensive assaults.

Is it possible, then, to recognize the battlefield of contending definitions without getting bogged down in it, to stand at the edge of the political fray, to launch "truth" — seeking missives which might clear the ground for a new reading of terrorism? Probably not. In the Age of Surveillance and Speed, the ultimate strategic power of terrorism and counterterrorism is not the quantity and secure siting of weapons/targets, that is, geo-politics, but the velocity and timely *sighting* of them, that is, chrono-politics.[11] In other words, a different strategic game requiring a different cultural analysis is being played out: to match the opacity rendered by Stealth technologies, the transparency assured by satellites and ELINT (Electronic Intelligence), the targeting, or "illuminating" power of radar and laser, a new cultural reading is needed. Hence, as a deterrent *description* rather than a preemptive definition, I will offer a view of the boundaries of the national security culture drawn by terrorism from two elevations which might yield a parallax advantage over the conventional one-dimensional definitions: in high orbit and at low resolution, I see terrorism as does Jean Baudrillard, historically "initiated by the taking of hostages and the game of postponed death"; but in a lower orbit and at higher resolution I view it now as a televisual strategic simulation choreographed by fear and violence and staged for an endangered and captive global audience.[12]

A Possible Text for the Preface

So far, we have established the problems of reading/writing about terrorism. First, the question of legitimacy: how we signify statements and discursive practices in international relations as reasonable, justifiable, verifiable, or authorized determines who are the victims and agents of terrorism, the legitimate and pariah state and non-state actors.[13] Second, this signification is difficult enough within the borders and security of the state, but outside the state, with no sovereign authority (in both the juristic and linguistic senses) to rule on legitimacy, we cannot establish facts which will bring an end to terrorism. Third, there is an historiographical problem to contend with. Histories of terrorism are rare: rarer yet is a history of how terrorism has been read, or interpreted.[14] What usually stands in for a history of terrorism is a televized factive, sometimes fictive narration of usually 30 seconds to 3 minutes. Of course, there is always the option of acquiring information from the proliferating Institutes of Terrorist Studies. For the most part, though, what they provide are simply learned repetitions of what can be heard on *ABC Nightline*.[15] Fourth, this is not just a crisis in the legitimation process, but also a crisis of representation in which the once-dominant state's construction of legitimate political violence, now competing with terrorism's fragmentation of power and globalization by the media, is reduced to a pure simulation of terrorism and counterterrorism.[16] Fifth, this evokes a political dilemma: how do we reconstruct a reading of terrorism which criticizes the maintenance of an order favorable to the dominant interests of the superpowers while recognizing the imperative of assuring the internal and external security of citizens who face natural and "artificial" disasters in an international, quasi-anarchical society?

There is the temptation, prompted by the practices of poststructuralist theory, to end with this summation and a critical interrogation, to leave it to the reader to construct an alternative history of terrorism out of the "fragged" remains of the body politic. But this would highlight the worst aspects of poststructuralism, its propensity for the extremes of gaming or despairing when confronted by the seemingly implacable problems of modernity. In international theory we must demonstrate something more than what Nietzsche referred to as "the strength to forget the past," by which he meant the kind of history that neatly adds up past events to rationalize our present condition. Otherwise we leave a void, a vacuum of knowledge and power in which others engaged in a different kind of "positive forgetting" — most notably political leaders who preside over the past through a process of selective senility — can install metaphysical visions of terrorism. For counterterrorism, then, a counter-history: instead of the flash-bang grenades of anti-terrorist rhetoric which have blinded and deafened us to past struggles of international political violence and legitimacy we need a study of the relevant *archives,* in the Foucauldian sense of the "play of rules which determines within a culture the appearance and disappearance of statements."[17]

The Sanitation of Terror: From the Making of Pledges to the Taking of Hostages

The cultural archive of terrorism eternally recurs with the making and breaking of pledges: the loyalty oath of feudal warriors, the first contracts of the traders, the compact for a commonwealth, the *pacta sunt servanda* of the fledgling system of states; all founded on promises — some kept and many broken — to move from an anarchic terror to a ruled order.[18] A skimming of some of the exemplar thinkers of the rationalist episteme discloses the anti-terrorist role of the pledge in reason and history. Although Thomas Hobbes's prescription of a one-sided pledge to the Leviathan for security in the permanent "war of all against all" has dominated modern thinking about international relations, there have been significant challengers to this realist paradigm, like Hugo Grotius and Samuel Pufendorf, the foremost jurists of the seventeenth century who saw in the promise a cultural mechanism through which natural law and a mutual alienation of interests could provide rules for an international society.[19] In the grip of realist and neo-realist paradigms, we have "forgotten" how the pledge/promise acted as an intellectual and discursive vehicle for ordering societies, through social contracts (Rousseau), the confederation of states (Kant), the universalization of Spirit (Hegel), and the solidarity of a class (Marx). But now, in a society fragmented and nuclearized by terrorism and the balance of terror, there are no authors, no subjects, only hostages — actual and potential — for the international pledge. The anonymity of mutual assured destruction and the indiscriminate exchange of hostages by terrorism have constructed an ellipsis in international relations. Held hostage to a pledge which is significant for everyone but signed by no one, inscribed by a death sentence that makes no juristic or grammatical sense, we know there is a terrorist ellipsis but we do not know what it means.

A modern attempt to fill, indeed to flood, the gap in our understanding of the relationship between the pledge and security, terror and freedom is made by Jean-Paul Sartre in his much-maligned but rarely read *Critique of Dialetical Reason.* His theoretical distillation of the pledge offers an interpretive conduit for plotting the historical similarities and transformations of the pledge embedded in the modern national security culture:

But this is precisely what a pledge is: namely the common production, through mediated reciprocity, of a statute of violence, once the pledge has been made, in fact, the group has to guarantee everyone's freedom against necessity, even at the cost of his life and in name of freely sworn faith. Everyone's freedom demands the violence of all against it and against that of any third party as its defence against itself (as a free power of secession and alienation). To swear is to say, as a common individual: you must kill me if I secede. And this demand has no other aim than to install Terror within myself as a free defence against the fear of the enemy (at the same time as reassuring me about the third party who will be confirmed by the same Terror). At this level, the pledge becomes a material operation.[20]

How would a history of the "material operation" of the pledge read? There is no text to turn to, really only fragments, but the best pieces come from the erudite writings of Martin Wight, the "classical" international theorist.[21] Wight's sweeping inquiry into the development of principles of international legitimacy offers a panoramic view of how violence was made safe for the society of states. This story of the sanitation of political violence, what could be called "the hygienics of terror," begins with the establishment of the dynastic principle and ends with the popular principle of legitimacy.[22] It is a long story, which cannot be retold here, of the formation of hierarchies and rituals of power in Latin Christendom (the Holy Roman Empire, papacy, national monarchs, fiefdoms, principalities, and city-states) based on precedence and prescriptive rights. What concerns our inquiry is a counter-plot, how a series of challenges in the seventeenth and eighteenth centuries to the dynastic principle of legitimacy — the republicanism of the Dutch revolt, the theories of political and social contract, and the English, American, and French Revolutions — shifted the pledge from dynastic rules to popular politics; and how from the American revolution to the imperialism of the French revolution the principle of legitimacy underwent a sea change, from all men are created equal and have inalienable rights to the idea of *national* self-determination. "The rights of man," says Wight, "gave way to the rights of nations."[23] With this alienation of obligations, the nation-state takes on the pledge, or contract, of security. But it is the subplot of the counter-plot which concerns our reading of modern terrorism: that is, the emergence of a neo-medieval hostage-taking to enforce, even displace, a newly challenged national security pledge.

In short, will the fragmentation of state-power, the pervasiveness of the nuclear terror, the rise of a new international disorder void international contracts and once again "legitimate" the taking of hostages? We are returning to a practice institutionalized when Europe was evolving from a suzerain system to a states-system, where only a physical pledge was sufficient to maintain order? At best, can we hope for a recurrence of the mutual exchange of hostages as a commitment to keep a pledge, as Spain and France exchanged hostages — one of them William of Orange — to enforce the Treaty of Cateau-Cambresis in 1559? For control of nuclear terror, will we be forced to offer the Soviets a team of State Department lawyers as insurance for maintaining the "narrow" interpretation of the Anti-Ballistic Missile Treaty? If theater nuclear weapons are removed from Europe, will American troops be sufficient hostages for NATO? And will more extreme hostage-takings be institutionalized — such as guaranteed air-time on *ABC Nightline* for the year's most popular terrorists?

I will leave it to more historicist others to prove whether terrorism, the breakdown of the pledge, and the taking of hostages are harbingers of a new medievalism, or morbid symptoms of a Gramscian moment when the old is dying and the new cannot yet be born. Rather, my final speculation returns to the link between international terrorism and the balance of terror, where everyone, combatants and non-combatants alike, are conceivable hostages. At the practical level, the most effective anti-terror tactic would be to end the social and political stasis that presently marks superpower politics, to seek a *rapprochement* with the Soviet Union by a negotiated settlement in the Middle East and a serious rather than opportunistic commitment to disarmament. But at the theoretical level, this requires the expansion of an international cultural economy which might allow us to reinscribe broader, looser borders to the national security culture, to deconstruct fixed entities like the Bomb which we have created but seem beyond our control, and most importantly, to be less earnest when reading/writing/shredding the archive of terrorism.

17.
Television and Democracy
Michael Morgan

All political systems have to struggle with the difficult question of the role and structure of mass communication. In some systems, mass communication is explicitly and consciously used as an official instrument of the state. In a democratic system, however, at least in theory, the media are supposed to be "free."

Yet, political systems and media systems are tightly intertwined in all countries. All media institutions reflect and perpetuate the particular political and economic ideologies and structures of their societies. Just as mainstream mythology proclaims the United States to be a "free country" politically, so too do American citizens believe that their media are free. While these presumed "freedoms" in fact result in intense concentrations of media power, a monopolization of cultural production, and the maintenance of social (and global) inequalities, they are often justified, at least in part, on the basis of some fairly noble goals.

In western democracies, the idea of "freedom of the press" has been seen as the way to keep leaders accountable to the people, and to provide a means for competing interests and conflicting perspectives to be heard. "Free" media are supposed to inform and activate citizens, to offer a wide variety of voices and views, and to help sustain the political plurality necessary for representative government in a complex society. Indeed, in a society where print is the dominant medium, the press *can* cultivate many publics and many interests. Print media tend to foster a diversity of beliefs and perspectives, and many people presume that democracy depends upon this kind of diversity.

Yet, in the United States, the likelihood of attaining this ideal has been seriously derailed and short-circuited by television. Most of our political assumptions about media, nonetheless, continue to stem from a view of mass communication based on print and literacy. We are only beginning to realize that those assumptions no longer hold in the contemporary cultural and political system of the United States, which has television as its mainstream.

This essay explores the implications of television for a democratic system based on some theories and empirical findings from a long-term, ongoing research project called Cultural Indicators.[1] Cultural Indicators is a three-pronged research strategy designed to investigate (1) the institutional processes underlying the production of television content, (2) the most common and stable "facts of life" in the world of television content (called *message system analysis*), and (3) relationships between exposure to television's messages and audience beliefs and behavior (called *cultivation analysis*). In particular, this essay will drawn upon findings from the cultivation analysis aspects of the project.

The basic hypothesis guiding cultivation analysis is that the more time one spends watching television (that is, the more television dominates one's sources of information and consciousness), the more likely one is to hold conceptions of reality that can be traced to television's most stable and recurrent portrayals of life and society. For more than 15 years, cultivation analyses have produced consistent evidence that television viewing makes an independent contribution to people's images and assumptions about violence, sex roles, aging, occupations, education, science, health, religion, and other issues.

This essay highlights some findings from this research that relate to television's impact on political orientations, beliefs, and behavior. To most people in the United States, "politics" is a very narrow term relating to elections, campaigns, and running for office; but "politics" here is also used in the broader sense to encompass the allocation and distribution of social resources and the structures of social power. The data from these studies suggest that television does cultivate underlying values and ideologies about social power in the United States. These outcomes sometimes support but often pose a challenge to democratic principles and practices.

There are several reasons why television in America does not fit well the traditional concept of the role mass communication should play in a democratic society. The press in a democracy is supposed to be a selectively used medium, with readers searching out material which confirms and expands their point of view. Television, however, provides a relatively restricted set of choices for an almost unlimited variety of interests. Unlike print media, television is viewed relatively *non*-selectively; most people watch by the clock, not the program. Television does not require either literacy or mobility, and it provides a steady stream of politically relevant messages to nearly everyone, whether they actively seek them or not.

As with all cultural artifacts and products, television programs reflect and are shaped by cultural assumptions which are often invisible simply because they are so taken for granted. Patterns of casting and demography, conventions of portraying "human nature," and incidental, backdrop images of "reality" carry political and cultural significance.

The stories of a culture reflect and cultivate its most basic and fundamental assumptions, ideologies, and values. From myths and legends to fairy tales and nursery rhymes, from religious parables to fast-food commercials, the function of stories is to enculturate children and provide continual socialization for adults, to remind them what exists and what doesn't, what is important, good and bad, right and wrong.

Television is most of all a centralized system of storytelling. It brings a stable and coherent world of common images and messages into virtually every home in the United States. Television has become the primary, common source of everyday culture, politics, and values of an otherwise heterogeneous population. Tens of millions of people who had been scattered, isolated, provincial, and culturally and politically distant, are now brought into the mainstream by television.

In the average U.S. home, the television is on for more than seven hours a day. As we often hear, by the time children finish high school, they will have spent more time watching television than in school; they will have seen about 18,000 violent deaths and will have spent thousands of *hours* of their lives watching commercials. Adults spend more time watching television than doing anything else except sleeping and working. Storytelling traditionally relies upon repetition; the extent to which we are exposed to repetitive lessons through television is historically unprecedented.

The television system in the United States attracts its massive audiences by offering to all, no matter how young or old, rich or poor, the most broadly acceptable world of stories and action. Each night, 90 million people sit down and spend several hours watching mostly the same programs. Television provides, perhaps for the first time since pre-industrial religion, a strong cultural and political link between the elites and all other publics, in a shared daily ritual. As George Gerbner has put it, television is like religion, except most people watch TV more religiously.

We have inherited many truisms about the power of television in the political realm. One familiar claim is that Richard Nixon's appearance during the 1960 televised debates, replete with five o'clock shadow, cost him that election. Another is that Ronald Reagan's acting background provided him with the media performance skills that assured his victories. That vague entity called "the media" is routinely blamed (or praised) for the ebbs and flows in the popularity of leaders and policies.

Television is credited with having transformed the entire electoral process. We hear about the need to make nominating conventions "entertaining" (and therefore televisable). Pundits moan about (while likely contributing to) the tendency to start the "horse race" earlier and earlier. Losers wail about the alleged ability of newscasters and commentators to make or break their candidacies. Members of Congress (and others) complain about early projections by network news, fearing they lower voter turnout.

The weakening of the traditional power of political parties is often attributed to television. Whether or not television itself has diminished the role of parties, it has certainly stepped into replace them as the chief means of communication between candidates and voters, and it has replaced the party press with a relatively standardized, market-driven, advertiser-sponsored system. With steady declines in party loyalty and party identification, the most important task of political parties today is to raise money to pay for television time and then to produce campaigns that look good on television.

Voting is another example. In a democratic society, voting in free elections is seen as the most basic form of political action. Yet, the longer we live with television, the smaller the percentage of the population that exercises that right — just barely 50% in the last election. Moreover, those who watch more television are less likely to vote.

I have looked at the relationship between amount of television viewing and voting behavior over the last four U.S. presidential elections, by reanalyzing data from large national surveys. Each year, the National Opinion Research Center asks a sample of about 1500 people whether they voted in recent presidential elections, who they voted for, and, for non-voters, who they *would* have voted for if they had voted. The responses can then be compared across light, medium, and heavy television viewers.

The patterns are strong, consistent, and clear: those who watch more television are less likely to say they voted, by an average margin of about 10 percent. The relationship holds up despite statistical controls for age, income, education, sex, race, political orientation, party identification, and other powerful factors.

Over the last 12 years, heavy viewers were also more likely than light viewers to say that they either *did* or *would have* voted for the *loser*. The longer the time from the election, the wider the gap; that is, for each year that passes following an election, the more heavy viewers turn against the incumbent — including Ronald Reagan. Despite the fact that the vast bulk of political campaign money is spent on television, those who watch more television are less likely to vote, and less likely to say they voted for the winner.

This is not to imply that television alone is responsible for the steady declines in voter turnout since the 1940s. But television has turned political campaigns into a kind of spectator sport, where the only thing the viewer has to do is to tune in to see who won — even if the media have already announced it *before* the election.

In another sense, mass communication may produce what Paul Lazarsfeld and Robert Merton 40 years ago called the "narcotizing dysfunction." The quantity of news and information is so vast, so overwhelming, that the citizen comes to mistake simply "keeping informed" about events for doing anything about them. "Keeping up" becomes a solemn duty, making us feel we're concerned and informed, but leaving little time or inclination for any social action. Or, television may promote alienation, complacency, and passivity which in turn reduce political participation; bombarding audiences with images of the "good life" and the benefits of consumption is more conducive to depoliticization than to activism.

But the implications of television in a democratic political system go deeper than voting, candidates, and elections. Over the last 35 years television has transformed political reality in the United States, but the actual nature of that transformation has gone almost unnoticed. In part, this is because we've been asking the wrong questions.

Much research and debate on the impact of mass communication has tended to focus on individual messages, programs, series, or genres, usually in terms of their ability to produce immediate changes in audience attitudes and behavior. Also, it has been assumed that news and information programs are the major sources of people's political orientations, attitudes, and opinions.

In contrast, cultivation analysis is concerned with more general and pervasive consequences of overall immersion in a cumulative exposure to television. It sees television's impact not so much in change among individuals as in *resistance* to change, or in slow but steady shifts across generations. What cuts across most programs, what is largely inescapable regardless of whatever content "types" are "selected," is what counts. Focusing on plots and surface features may distract from what we really absorb.

The underlying political messages of regular entertainment may be among the least visible aspects of television, but they may also be among the most significant. The amount of attention given to such controversial fare as "Rambo," "White Knights," and "Amerika" may deflect attention away from the day-to-day political messages which permeate prime-time drama. From the cultivation perspective, regular, everyday entertainment may be a tremendously powerful means for expressing and sustaining cultural beliefs and values. Most people, most of the time, watch dramatic, fictional entertainment, which teaches them many basic lessons, facts, and values about social and political reality.

Television tells us, over and over, what different social types can and should do, and what fate has in store for them. Its dramatic portrayals of crime, adventure, sex roles, minorities, courtrooms and the conflicts of urban life provide vivid and consistent lessons for viewers. Those basic lessons contribute to broadly shared, common assumptions about risks and opportunities, vulnerabilities and power — the building blocks of political orientations.

For example, males on television represent independence, action, power. Females stand for fun, home, and games to be sought and scared and stalked and saved by heroes and villains. Even more limited representation and life chances goes to young, old, non-white, blue collar, and other relatively less attractive consumer types. Those who protect us from crime and other risks of life — law enforcers, attorneys, judges, doctors and other health professionals — are vastly overrepresented and dangerously overidealized. Life in the world of television is dangerous and risky, but it is also active, affluent, and happy. Stories of hard work, self-sufficiency, or long-delayed gratification do not put audiences at ease and in the mood to buy. These are the political messages of "entertainment."

Furthermore, the power relationships repetitively demonstrated in television drama help maintain the positions of various groups in the real world power structure. Violence, for example, is not evenly distributed in the television world. Women, non-whites, older people, and other less powerful groups are more likely to be shown as victims; white, middle-class males in the prime of life are much more likely to inflict violence than to suffer from it. Those who watch more television are more likely to overestimate their chances of involvement in real-life violence, especially if they belong to one of the more victimized groups. The symbolic power hierarchy thus determines real-world variations in vulnerability to the cultivation of fear.

Institutional and economic pressures mean that these basic underlying features of the television world are remarkably stable and consistent over time, despite surface-level novelties and fads that come and go. In the United States, about $55 million of revenue rides on every rating point. So, program producers *have* to create programs with the broadest possible appeal. That means avoiding political (and most other) "extremes," or making them as bland and non-threatening as possible, glorifying conventional consumer values, and striving for a safe, respectable, "middle-of-the-road" balance in most things.

Avoiding perceived extremes has always been television's strategy, as networks and advertisers expect attacks from special interest groups on the right *and* the left. What the television industry fears most is that people might get upset with what they watch and turn off the TV; so industry takes the obvious way out — navigating between (relative) extremes, safely in the comfortable mainstream that alienates no one and attracts the largest possible audience. "Deviant" or "extreme" groups are rarely shown, or are harshly criticized. All presentations *must* appear "objective," "moderate," "non-ideological," and otherwise suitable for mass marketing.

Some people are to the left of the television mainstream, and others are to the right; in order to maximize its audience, television attempts to steer a middle course — and in the process absorbs and homogenizes people with otherwise divergent orientations. This process of convergence is called "mainstreaming." One result is that those who watch more television are more likely to call themselves moderate (and less likely to say they are liberal or conservative) than light viewers. That is, the more time people spend watching television, the less they claim to be either liberal *or* conservative, and the more they say they are "moderate, middle-of-the-road."

The images of political reality television presents to people in the United States are highly constricted. We are given a basic continuum running from a "liberal left" to a "conservative right." It's a simple continuum, not multidimensional, and has a fairly narrow range. Positions and perspectives *outside* that narrow range of political discourse essentially do not exist.

Every issue is presented as having a "liberal" and a "conservative side — e.g., abortion, homosexuality, school prayer, gun control, racial equality, women's rights, etc. — and the most consistent message is that the "truth" always lies somewhere in between — in the middle, in the mainstream. And the more that people watch television, the more they place themselves in that moderate, middle position.

The mainstreaming effects of television are extremely interesting within groups defined by party affiliation. Figure 1 shows how mainstreaming works when we look at Democrats, Independents and Republicans separately.

The more that members of all three parties watch television, the more they choose the moderate label (dashed line). Heavy viewing Democrats and Independents are less likely to choose either the liberal *or* conservative label. Among Republicans, heavy viewers are less likely to call themselves conservatives, and more likely to say they are either moderate or liberal. Television blurs and distorts the impact of party on where people place themselves on the political spectrum — all groups say they are "moderate" if they watch more TV.

This finding that heavy viewers see themselves as "moderate" holds up in survey after survey, in subgroup after subgroup. And, it's specific to television, not a correlate of general media use; the same results do *not* apply to radio listening or newspaper reading. It is television, and television alone, which cultivates "moderate" self-perceptions in its audiences, in line with the mainstream political lessons of television.

This may be part of a more general phenomenon: the cultivation of homogeneous, "average" self-perceptions. In addition to political moderation, the television world is dominated by characters who fit squarely in the "middle-middle" of a five-point social class category scale; middle-class characters vastly outnumber all others.

Cultivation research has found that when people whose objective

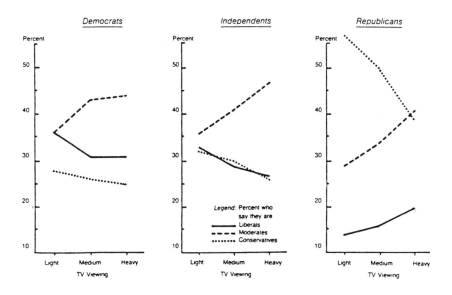

Figure 1. Political Self-Designation by Amount of Television Viewing for Democrats, Independents, and Republicans

social class is low watch more television, they are more likely to call themselves "middle class" as opposed to "working class." Middle-class viewers show the least sense of class distinction at different viewing levels; they are already "in" the mainstream. The upper classes, however, like the lower, show a pattern that is strongly associated with amount of television viewing; the more they watch, the *lower* their self-designated class. Heavy viewers are also more likely to say they have "average" incomes, particularly as real income increases.

Thus, the television experience seems to swamp other circumstances in thinking of one's class. Television viewing tends to blur class distinctions as it does political labels, and to make more affluent heavy viewers think of themselves as just working people of average income. Long-term, cumulative exposure to the consumer-oriented demography and middle-class supremacy of television tends to confound real class distinctions and to cultivate "average" or "middle class" self-perceptions as the norm of the television mainstream.

On the surface, mainstreaming looks like a "centering" or "middling" of political tendencies. But if we look at the actual positions heavy viewers take on specific political issues, we see that the mainstream does not run down the "middle-of-the-road."

Television viewing makes an independent contribution to what people in the United States think about the hard political issues of our times such as women and minorities, fairness and individual rights, defense spending and welfare, taxes and other issues. Its contribution reflects the most common, stable, and repetitive messages of the fictional world of dramatic television.

Much of television's action involves a dangerous world of violence and power, a world that has changed little over the past 20 years. Crime is rampant, and an average of five to six acts of overt physical violence per hour involve almost two-thirds of all major characters each week. People who spend more time "living" in the world of television absorb its lessons and apply them to the real world in ways that have direct political significance. Again, heavy viewers overestimate their chances of being a victim of violence; they are also more mistrustful and suspicious and more likely to demand protection in their neighborhoods. They are hostile to foreigners and more likely to think the United States will fight in another World War within the next ten years.

But the patterns are different for different groups; cultivation depends upon where one is in relation to the mainstream. Figure 2 illustrates this with some typical mainstreaming patterns. Figure 2 shows the associations of television viewing and some political attitudes, separately for those who call themselves liberal, moderate, or conservative. On these and many other issues, the traditional polarization of liberals

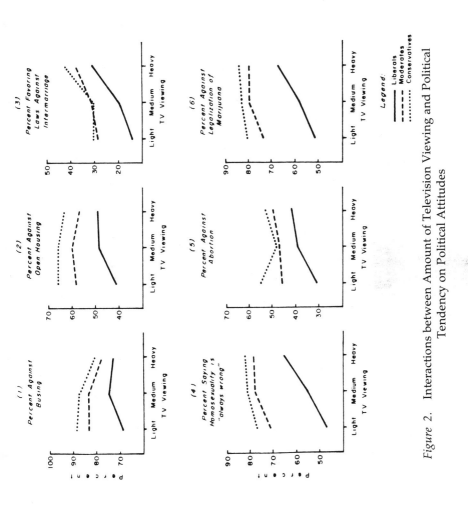

Figure 2. Interactions between Amount of Television Viewing and Political Tendency on Political Attitudes

and conservatives turns into a homogenization of views, in the direction of the television mainstream. These otherwise disparate groups find common ground in, converge, and blend into, the television mainstream.

For example, in terms of attitudes towards racial segregation, the first chart on the figure illustrates the relationship between amount of viewing and respondents' opposition to busing. Heavy viewing conservatives are more "liberal" and heavy viewing liberals more "conservative" than their respective light viewing counterparts. In the second, opposition to open housing laws, we see that heavy viewers of all three groups are more likely to oppose laws about open housing, but that the relationship is strongest among those who call themselves liberal. In the third chart, which shows responses to a question about laws against marriages between blacks and whites, television viewing cultivates a more restrictive attitude among all three political subgroups, but this is significantly more pronounced for liberals, whose heavy viewers join in the anti-integration mainstream. Again and again, light viewers are more diverse and heavy viewers more concentrated, and the three groups converge upon the conservative position.

These charts are just a few examples of the results found for dozens of similar questions. The sample patterns show up in terms of many other issues — sexual tolerance, freedom of speech, approval of legalizing marijuana, and many, many others.

Among heavy viewers, the difference between liberals, moderates, and conservatives are greatly reduced. But the most notable trend is the erosion of the traditionally "liberal" view among heavy viewers. In general, those who call themselves conservatives are "already" in the television mainstream. But liberals express traditionally "liberal" views *only* if they are light viewers. Mainstreaming means not only a narrowing of political differences but also a significant tilt in a conservative direction. Most consistently it reveals a significant loss of support for personal and political freedoms among liberals.

Something entirely different occurs when we look at responses to questions about *economic* issues of government spending and taxes. Instead of heavy viewing liberals taking positions closer to conservatives, the opposite happens: heavy viewing conservatives, as well as moderates, converge toward the traditionally *liberal* position of wanting the government to spend *more* on social programs, such as health, the environment, welfare, the cities, etc. The more people watch, the less they say we spend "too much"; heavy viewers endorse greater government spending, rather than cuts. (Needless to say, heavy viewers are also more likely to think we should be spending more on arms and defense, although here we see the familiar pattern of liberals converging with conservatives.)

At the same time, heavy viewers are more likely to feel their taxes are too high. Those who watch more television are more likely to hold these contradictory positions simultaneously — within every demographic subgroup, heavy viewers are more likely to want more social spending *and* lower taxes.

All this relates to and clarifies television's contribution to many other conceptions of social reality. The more people watch television, the more they are fearful and afraid. They are more willing to accept repressive measures in the name of security, and to approve of more extreme ways to punish those who break the rules of the system. They are alienated, depoliticized, and afraid both of crime in the streets and of world war. They want more protection, more money for fighting crime and drug abuse, more money for defense, but — of course — no more taxes. Heavy viewers of all political persuasions hold these conflicting beliefs more than do light viewers in the same groups.

Television thus contributes to the current political scene in the United States in three ways. First, it blurs the impact of traditional party, class, regional, and other social differences. Among light viewers, factors such as whether you call yourself a liberal, moderate, or conservative, or your social class, or what region of the country you live in, are all powerful determinants of political beliefs. But if you're a heavy viewer, these factors play a much smaller role. Living in the cultural and political mainstream of television thus appears to be diminishing the influence of social forces that traditionally governed political behavior.

Second, television blends otherwise divergent perspectives and ways of labeling one's self into its own mainstream. That is, heavy viewers of all groups are more likely to call themselves moderate, average, middle class.

And third, television bends that mainstream to the purposes of the medium's own marketing and other commercial interests. The result is that heavy viewers are conservative on social issues but liberal on economic issues.

Television cultivates a set of paradoxical currents. In a nutshell, heavy viewers think like conservatives, want like liberals, and yet call themselves moderates. They are less likely to vote but quicker to turn against an incumbent. They think elected officials don't care about what happens to them but are more interested in their personal lives than in their policies. They want to cut taxes but improve education, medical care, social security. They distrust big government but want it to fix things for them, to protect them at home and from foreign threats. They praise freedom but want to restrict anyone who uses it in an unconventional way. They are losing confidence in people who run virtually all institutions, including religion, but they express trust in God, America — and television.

Taken together, these findings suggest that democracy itself may be compromised by these unintended and incidental effects of television. Some may believe that democracy works best when the people don't care much about politics but are deeply concerned about hair spray and deodorants. But the important question, and the critical challenge to democracy, is whether or not citizens are helpless in the tidal wave of the television mainstream.

The answer will depend on the ability of people whose interests are not well served by the television mainstream to mobilize and activate voters to influence both television and public policy. It will depend on our ability to equalize the flow of influence between television and the citizenry, to make television more responsive to rewards besides commercial profit. And it will depend on the extent to which this centralized system of storytelling continues to dominate the symbolic environment and our political consciousness — because these patterns are not *necessary* effects of television *per se*, but the consequences of particular institutional and commercial arrangements which have made television the mainstream of American culture.

The concept of democracy implies that citizens can participate in their political governance on a basis of equality. Numerous studies suggest that even the youngest North Americans value highly the principles of popular government, voting, equality, pluralism. But television — again, not by design, not by conspiracy, but by commercial imperative — tends to work against these principles in practice, while probably strengthening support of the principles.

Any democratic system requires communication for stability, growth, and survival. Democracy in a large and complex society depends upon mass communication to tell us things we "need" to know in a relatively "objective" and comprehensive fashion, since in a large and complex society it is virtually impossible to find out such things for ourselves *without* mass media.

Television is by no means the most powerful influence on people, but it is the most *common*; what it teaches most people, most of the time, is of the highest political, cultural, and moral importance. As mass media become more centralized and homogeneous, the cultural currents become narrower, more standardized, and more sharply defined, and mass communication becomes a more effective mechanism of social control.

In a commercial mass communication system, corporate interests rarely give way to the *public* interest. Concentration of ownership in fewer and fewer hands, and the need to attract larger and larger hetero-geneous audiences, together create blander and less diverse content; when nothing but ratings and commercial profit drive the media, the result can be apathetic and alienated citizens, who nonetheless remain obedient to the authority of the marketplace.

Mass communication is the mass production of the symbolic environment, of the cultural contexts within which we live and define ourselves and others. Earlier media did give us a broader range of sometimes antagonistic perspectives and ideologies. But television has meant that more and more people are exposed to messages created and controlled by fewer and fewer, and in far greater doses, than ever before.

The television mainstream is turning out to be the true twentieth-century melting pot of the United States. Increasingly, it may be having similar consequences around the globe, as dozens and dozens of countries have found that importing U.S. programs is easier and cheaper than producing their own. International and cross-cultural extensions of the research summarized here is now being conducted or planned in numerous other countries, including Argentina, China, India, and others. The results in the United States and elsewhere will be of central significance for the theory as well as for the practice of popular democratic self-government in the television age.

18.

MTV: Swinging on the (Postmodern) Star

Lawrence Grossberg

There is a new "snake" in the cultural garden. Music television is the latest in a series of moral panics organized around particular cultural forms. While different moral constituencies interpret its dangers differently, the attacks have been predictable and boring. Whether coming from the "moral" Right, the "moral" Left, or from rock and roll fans (usually baby boomers), the criticisms echo the fears that have greeted many other popular cultural forms: music television is *another* example (surprise!) of sexist, violent, hedonistic, commodified, and alienating discourse. Reading the various public discussions, one is always aware that the same statements, inflected just a bit differently, could be and have been made in other cultural arenas. The vehemence of the responses to music television seems to be less the result of its actual uniqueness than of its intersections with two powerfully contested domains within our cultural life: the struggle over the meanings and experience of youth, and the resurgence of a moral panic in response to rock and roll more generally (e.g., the Parents' Music Resource Center).

But unlike earlier moral panics, debates about music television have quickly entered the academy; it has already generated its own field of competing interpretations and evaluations. Discussions within the institutions of knowledge production display their own kind

This paper has benefited from conversations with my graduate students. I would particularly like to thank Charles Acland, Jon Crane and Phil Gordon for their comments and suggestions.

of panic-reaction to music television, and while the panic is less emotional, it is no less real. What is perhaps most remarkable is the speed with which this has been accomplished: unlike previous forms of post-World War Two popular culture (especially youth culture), music television has been rapidly incorporated into the canon of legitimated topics.[1] In these debates, music television is rarely offered as just *another* example; it is the *ultimate* example: of the commodification of culture, of the capitalist recuperation of "authentic" forms of resistance, of textual and subjective schizophrenia, of the postmodern disappearance of reality, or orgasmic democracy, etc. If the more public disputes are often carried on unself-consciously, with little empirical research or theoretical reflection, the academic disputes demonstrate how easy it is to find empirical support for many interpretations of the world; isolating one aspect of reality, abstracting it out of its concrete existence and ignoring its specificity, one can readily find "proof" of its absolute power to define and determine the world.

Speaking metaphorically, if you go marching into a jungle looking for snakes, you are bound to find a lot of them; they are, in fact, there. But to assume that the essence of the jungle is revealed in the snake, that the existence of snakes defines the jungle, misses the complexity and richness of the jungle. And it misses what is interesting about the sorts of snakes one finds in the jungle(s). Similarly, understanding music television requires us to identify and locate its specific complexity. We need to look at it contextually and relationally, to ask what is unique in the diverse practices of music television, and what they have in common with other cultural formations. Its current forms were introduced partly in response to significant technological, economic, and musical changes; but it has emerged as well within a particular set of historical conditions, generational struggles, and changes in people's everyday lives. The complexity of music television is defined by the particular links it builds and builds upon, between economic, textual, and communicative practices, historical relations, and subjective identities and experiences. Since these articulations are never necessary, we need to ask how they have been and are being constructed; and, if there are reasons to oppose such ways of defining and producing the forms of music television, we need to ask where alternatives are available?

Further, music television, like our jungle, is full of contradictions and struggles. Recognizing these depends upon our assuming that people are not cultural dopes, nor passively determined by the conditions of their existence. While there are obviously real historical tendencies, lines of force, pushing people in particular directions and into specific relations, nevertheless people are always actively responding to their conditions, taking what they are given, bending it to their own needs, and trying to gain some improvement in their lives, trying to survive and win (as Rambo says). The fact that people are subordinated and often oppressed — and that they sometimes occupy the role of oppressor — does not mean that they have been manipulated, duped, or colonized. It means that people operate in a field of contradictory relations and forces, and within that field, they do what they deem best or, perhaps, what they see as the best they can do.

Rock and Roll on Television

In this paper, I want to briefly talk about three sets of relationships that define the forms and effects of music television in the 1980s: media, economic, and communicative. Let me begin with an obvious but not trivial observation: music television involves *rock and roll* (in its broadest sense) on television, and rock and roll on *television*.[2] It cannot be separated from the forms, histories, audiences, and economies of each of these two cultural formations. Music television refers to the complex set of different but interrelated places and ways in which rock and roll is currently inserted into the discourses of television. It involves us in examining a number of different relationships: the relation between rock and roll and visual images; between different forms of rock and roll and different media (e.g., films, concerts, etc.); between particular songs (genres and groups) and their visual presentations and styles (e.g., the construction of particular video clips); between individual video clips and the particular formats which have come to dominate the presentations of music television (e.g., MTV but also VHF 1, Night Flight, Friday Night Videos, etc.); between the different forms of music television and their overlapping rock and roll audiences; and finally, between the forms of music television and the broader developments within both rock and roll and televisual discourse. Specific phenomena — whether individual video clips or video channels like MTV — cannot be understood apart from this broad range of relationships.

In fact, one does not have to be a video addict to notice that rock and roll is omnipresent on our videoscreens. If it is true to say that television has incorporated rock and roll, it is equally true that rock and roll has conquered television. It not only provides the soundtrack of our lives but increasingly, the visual (video) track as well: in advertisements, sports events, movies, series, themes, it is both visually and sonorially changing the face (the ears and the mouth as much as the eyes) of television. This is neither surprising nor necessarily bad; as the rock and roll generations have grown up and come to define the largest part of the population, it is their music which is taken for granted. And, speaking personally, if one has to hear music in commercials, is it not better to hear the music one likes? Rock and roll has moved into the center of contemporary culture, defining the mainstream of the dominant forms of cultural enjoyment and perhaps even legitimacy. But if rock and roll is increasingly the mainstream of popular culture, it is important to note that it is not only the mainstream of rock and roll that has entered television, nor is music television merely a reflection of the *Billboard* charts. Not only can television make (and in some cases, remake) hits, it has also appropriated rock and roll's wide range of styles and successes. If MTV is television's "AM radio" (with some 1970s FM influences), there are alternative programs and other places to turn for music television. (Consider the diverse playlist of a typical episode of *Miami Vice*: Dire Straits, Bryan Adams, Shriekback, Mark Isham, Fernando Villolona, Grace Jones, and Belkis Concepcion y sus Chicas.)

There are three common but mistaken assumptions about music television. The first is that the televisual image is necessarily less ambiguous than the musical image. On this basis, music videos are often condemned as limiting fans' imaginative freedom by predefining the meaning of the song and thus reducing the fan to a passive recipient. But television is never passively received and its texts are as open to different interpretations as any rock and roll song. If anything, the explicit conjunction of visual images and songs seems to multiply the possibilities of interpretation rather than constrain them.

The second assumption is that music television, by placing rock and roll in the hands of commercial corporations, increases the distance between the fan and the musician, and decreases the ability of both to control the production of the music. But rock and roll has always existed in a variety of marketable and mediated forms: records, tapes, films, radios, etc. There is little reason to privilege the live performance as if it were unmediated or as the only viable source of an "authentic" experience: how small does such a performance have to be, how much electronic equipment is permissible, for an "authentic" rock and roll experience? Rock and roll has always been a part of a capitalist system of production, distribution, and consumption within which both musicians and fans have constantly struggled against the formal, economic, and technological demands of a profit-motivated industry. The so-called "independents" still sell a commodity, although they may operate on a smaller scale and with a smaller profit margin, and with "better" motives.

The third assumption is that there is something radically new about the association of rock and roll with both visual images and television. But, as any fan of rock and roll knows, rock and roll has always been as much about images — images of stars and performers, of fashion and aesthetics, of the body and romance, of dancing and sex, and most importantly, of attitudes — as it has been about sounds. The importance of images, the particular forms they take and the ways they are allowably produced varies, not only across genres but also over time. For example, as Andrew Goodwin has argued,[3] the emergence of MTV cannot be separated from the ways in which punk foregrounded the deconstruction of images and "new pop" legitimated their reconstruction, even through such self-consciously artificial practices as lip-synching. Further, as any historian of rock and roll knows, rock and roll has always been on television and it has used that connection, in different ways and forms, at different times, for different audiences: e.g., live performances (from *Ed Sullivan* to *Saturday Night Live*; from *Kasey Kasem* to *Midnight Special*, from *American Bandstand* to *Putting on the Hits*, from Ricky Nelson to *The Monkees* to *The Partridge Family*); in ads and sports events; as a topic in a series or a particular episode; as a news or feature story; as an image of a character (Kookie), a generation or lifestyle (*Happy Days*) or an attitude (*Miami Vice*, David Letterman).

This list is obviously neither complete nor definitive; among other things, it ignores the important stylistic differences within and between programs. Moreover, an adequate history of rock and roll television would have to take both the audience and history into account, because both program production and viewing are historical activities. Different audiences may watch the same program but interpret it differently, not only because of their own history and relations to rock and roll, but also because of the use to which they put particular images in the larger contexts of their cultural lives and rock and roll fandom. One can, for example, use a particular program for narrative pleasure; for background; for lessons in dance, style, and attitude; for the televisual equivalent of pinups; for dancing or socializing (whether in the home, at parties, or clubs). At certain moments, for particular audiences, television may provide the easiest if not the only access to rock and roll images and performances. Women may not be comfortable attending heavy metal concerts; adolescents may not have the opportunity to enter bars; people living in small towns may not have venues which regularly feature rock and roll; aging baby boomers may not feel comfortable placing themselves in the midst of young rock and roll audiences.

The emergence, the forms, and the effects of music television cannot be entirely separated from changes taking place in television itself. Television is, after all, not a simple, unchanging medium; it has multiple forms, both technologically and textually. Its audiences do not all respond in the same ways, and in fact, no audience has a simple, single response to it. Significant changes in the technology and the economy of hardware have had important effects on the ways in which individuals and groups appropriate the medium. The one family television located in the semi-public, domestically governed space, has given way to the proliferation of televisions, not only in the different spaces of the household but also in public spaces. The small television set, with its poor visual and sonorial quality, has been replaced by technologies with highly sophisticated reproduction capacities (including stereo television). Remote control has changed our ability to control reception (e.g., Zipping, Zapping, muting) at the same time that cable has increased the range of programs available. This has also produced new economic demands: not only to identify particular audiences which can be delivered to advertisers (e.g., narrowcasting), but also to develop more precise guarantees of what is on the screen at the moment. Video tape technology, finally, has opened up new contexts and practices for television viewing, including home editing, video-movies (and their associated rental clubs), videobars (which may play tapes without the sound, or with a different soundtrack), and videotape collecting.

Music Television and the
Commodification of Culture

Music television is not only a response to changing economic, technological, cultural, and sociological conditions, it also enters into and changes these relations.[4] It has changed the ways rock and roll (and perhaps television) works in our culture. I want to describe these effects in two domains: first, as a changing set of economic relations and second, as a changing structure of communication.

The fact that rock and roll and music television operate within a capitalist economy of commodification is hardly remarkable; no doubt, rock videos are not only self-promotions but advertisements for consumption itself. This tells us very little about their concrete relations to the cultural industries and their audiences. The commodification of cultural practices — the formation of the culture industries, including their incorporation into capitalist relations of marketing and production (and most recently distribution) — is neither new nor specific to music television.[5] Music television's economic existence is defined by its complex functions within the contemporary structures of capitalism. In many ways, music television merely continues forms of commodification, packaging, and promotion that have defined postwar popular culture. It also shares many features that are characteristic of the postwar record industry. And, it exhibits certain features which, while not totally unique to it, suggest that it can be seen as the "flagship" or a significant reorganization of the entertainment industry.

Let me begin with some obvious statements: music television produces a number of different commodities: it sells not only advertisers' products but lifestyles and a commitment to consumption; it sells not only records but videos; it sells images and packaged tastes; and it sells audiences. These commercial relations do not all exist harmoniously together. As Will Straw points out, there is an increasing split between the audiences which purchase musical commodities, and those which purchase various consumer goods (especially those designed for the upper and upbeat side of the baby-boom generations). It is also true that the increasing use of videos to promote rock and roll has given the major record companies (with their financial and technological resources) yet another advantage in the struggle to control, if not popular taste, then the availability of particular instances of popular culture. As budgets for video production mount, the commitments to other forms of support (such as tours) decreases, and companies almost inevitably cut their lists as they face ever spiraling costs and risks: musical talent may be weighed against the additional requirement of one's talent as a video performer.

The particular programing formats — such as MTV — that have dominated music television are an appropriation of radio formats defined in the 1950s and refined in the 1970s: its emphasis on the single (as the object of listening if not as the ultimate product to be purchased, since singles are not the dominant market form of popular music in the 1980s), its use of chattering VJ's, its incorporation of "news" and special features, the absence of the audience from the screen (compared with early programs like *American Bandstand*), etc. Yet while the fragmentation of radio formats in the 1970s was an early precursor of MTV's "narrowcasting," MTV offered record companies, musicians, and audiences something which had never been available in the United States: a national rock and roll network. This opens the possibility of new ways of organizing tastes, and of new speeds at which songs and musicians can be disseminated across the country and incorporated into the national consciousness. Music television also brought youth audiences to television which had previously remained largely inaccessible to television's advertising messages, audiences which no doubt increased the pressure on families to be hooked up to cable or satellite systems.

Yet the really interesting — and difficult — questions involve how music videos (whether singularly or in larger formats) work as promotions and as the occasion for advertisements. The two are not identical (although contemporary advertising styles may be erasing the difference); promotions do not make a direct appeal for purchasing a product. Rather, they create a context within which such a purchase is both sensible and desirable. A video clip promotes its own song, the single record, and the album (or tape), much as radio has always done. It may even promote a film or a television show. In this instance, the song is its own image. On the other hand, video clips, like advertisements, do seem to offer more than the musical product; the product is packaged in discourses that are apparently unnecessary to the function of the music itself. Of course, this "packaging" is not extraneous if it is the video itself that is being commodified and promoted (and to some extent, this is certainly true in the marketplace). But more generally, the intricate and important links between rock and roll and images/attitudes make it difficult to separate the commodity from the packaging. One is always buying more than music when buying rock and roll. This leaves open the question of whether, as Simon Frith argues, videos offer the meaning of the song as a commodity.

The economics of music television, and of the video clip as a promotional device, point to a broad transformation of the forms of the commodification of entertainment. Frith has described some of the economic realignments operating here. The music business is increasingly incorporated into multinational corporations with diverse, trans-media interests in entertainment. The production of a hit song is less important than the production of the star as a marketable commodity. While stars have always been produced and promoted, and in some cases (like Elvis Presley) have moved across media and genres, there have always been limits to this mobility. These limits have not only disappeared in the contemporary forms of the production of stardom, but it is their absence which defines the star. The star does not need a history. The old model of a star building an ever wider audience while "paying their dues" seems to have given way to the immediate insertion of a figure into a position of stardom already waiting for him or her. It is less a matter of talent than promotion and visibility; talent is less a necessary prerequisite than a "resource-pool" available for corporate raiding. Stars need no origin or identity outside of their various appearances as stars. Their stardom does not rest on a particular activity which will forever provide the basis for their reputation. In fact, a star's ability to occupy this new dispersed position of stardom may depend on an ironic reference to his or her artistic skills, and it is perfectly reasonable (and common) for an audience to discover such talents only after identifying the star somewhere else. Not only is it increasingly difficult to distinguish between advertisements, videoclips, and episodic sequences from films or television programs, it is increasingly difficult to define where a video-star's popularity is located (e.g., Bruce Willis as a singer, the star of *Moonlighting*, and a spokesperson for Seagram's wine coolers; Phil Collins has probably won as many fans through his commercials as through his actual records).

The star has to remain distant from any particular activity in order to be free to occupy the space of a particular image or attitude. It is the star — as the emblem of a particular mood or attitude — who is the major product promoted by music television; the star is a mobile sign which can be linked to any practice, product, or language, freed from any particular message or set of values. It is the star who is produced and promoted by the discourses of music television, sold to its advertisers and producers, and delivered over to its audiences. Stars are no longer individuals measured by their creativity, their authentic relation to their performance, or even the possibilities of audience's projecting their fantasies onto them. Within this new corporately constituted space of cultural images, the star becomes a commodified (and therefore mobile) sign, moving across the broad terrain of cultural tastes and entertainment.

Music Television, Communication, and Postmodernity

Still the question remains, where do we locate music television's popularity, its cultural power, and its communicative effects?[6] Music television certainly communicates images and lifestyles, interpretations and ideologies. But it does something more; Robert Pittman, one of the "designers" of MTV, described it as a "mood enhancer." We need to take this notion of the communication of mood, affect, and emotion seriously if we are to understand the particular force of music television's message. The meanings and images communicated by the different forms of music television are relevant only insofar as they get us somewhere else: to a particular attitude or mood. Moods are, after all, contentless, although they have both quality and quantity; they construct the "tone," "texture," or "coloration" of the world within which particular experiences and meanings are located. Moods are also infectious; they do not follow linear paths from senders to receivers; nor are they easily controlled by the normal strategies of interaction.

Of course, music itself frequently works precisely by foregrounding affective and emotional responses. But the uniqueness of music television's communication is defined by the fact that the construction and dissemination of moods is increasingly separated from the communication of any particular meanings or values. This affective overindulgence is partly the result of a set of historical changes which cumulatively define a rather unique — postmodern — condition, especially for those generations which grew up after the Second World War: the relationship between affect and ideology has become increasingly tenuous. The postmodern condition can be described as the perception of a growing gap between these two aspects of our experience, between the meanings and values which are available to us to make sense of our lives and actions, and the places where it appears possible to care about something enough, to have enough faith that it matters, so that one can actually make a commitment, that one can invest oneself in it. Whatever the reality of such perceptions, the future has become increasingly uncertain (and its images bear a striking resemblance to contemporary Beirut!); it has become increasingly difficult to differentiate between reality and its images, and most of the traditional values and pleasures (love, family, sex) which may have given our lives some meaning in the past have become treacherous traps which never seem to deliver on their promises. The result is that it is ever more difficult to make sense of our affective experiences ("life's a bitch and then you die") and to put any faith in the taken for granted interpretations of the meanings of our lives and actions. We no longer trust our common sense even as we are compelled to live it. (Even the promise of "sex and drugs and rock 'n' roll" has given way to the three R's: "romance, rejection, and rock 'n' roll.") We are condemned to try to make sense of our lives in structures that clearly contradict our experiences.

The emergence of rock and roll in the 1950s, and its history since then, can be partly understood as a response to this postmodern condition. Rock and roll was never concerned with communicating meanings, but rather, with providing the energies and the attitudes with which you could reshape your own moods against the increasing pessimism, boredom, and terror of contemporary life. This "empowerment" depended upon rock and roll's elitism, and its construction of "affective alliances." The definition of rock and roll, the boundaries which define, not what is good or bad, but what deserves to be included within the category itself, is never simply available. Different fans construct the boundaries in different places and different ways: to be a fan of rock and roll is precisely to claim that one has a privileged access to those affective states which allow one to understand what truly constitutes the power of rock and roll. By circumscribing the limits of rock and roll, the fan also draws a field, a mobile bubble, around themselves; although their relation to rock and roll need not define a particular identity for them, it marks them as different. It encapsulates them within the affective possibilities of their particular version of the rock and roll culture. There are always others (including many who think they are rock and roll fans) who are not within this space, who do not understand rock and roll, and who do not share in the "secret" knowledge. The knowledge is not hidden but it is only available by entering into the particular conjunction of music, style, attitude, images, etc. that defines such a rock and roll culture. The knowledge is there, in the affective experiences that are constructed by the particular set of relations. Rock and roll empowers its fans by placing them into a particular "affective alliance" which marks their difference, not in terms of their beliefs and values as much as their ability to struggle against the dominant moods of contemporary life without being able to rely on its languages. Obviously, there is nothing about this strategy which necessarily implies any sort of political resistance, personal authenticity, or cultural marginality. On the contrary, rock and roll is always located within the mainstream of everyday life; knowing that anything you believe in or desire is likely to end up being another trap, rock and roll offers strategies to continue believing in something, if only the need to believe and the sense of difference (elitism) that being a fan defines.

What happens when rock and roll's elitism, and its fascination with mood and attitude as a viable response to one's historical situation, is transferred onto the television screen, into televisual modes of communication? Affective alliances are democratized in a new cultural logic of "authentic inauthenticity." Television negates rock and roll's elitism by locating it within its own democratizing impulses. Of course, television's democratic tendencies are always limited by the real economic and political interests involved in the selection, framing, and distribution of its images. But once any image, in whatever form, makes it onto the screen, it becomes equal to any other image. On the video screen, every image is equally available, equally real, equally artificial, and equally worthy of emulation. There is no secret knowledge on television, or rather, the secret knowledge is instantly available and constantly repeated for any viewer. While this doesn't guarantee that everyone will "get it," television's power does not depend upon its encapsulating an audience in order to define it as different from those who do not "get it." Television's "attitude" does not depend upon its limited availability but rather upon its knowing self-consciousness. Its "hip-ness" can never be taken too seriously. Its secret knowledge is precisely that there are no secrets because there is nothing behind the screen. This "hip" attitude is a kind of ironic nihilism in which ironic distance is offered as the only reasonable relation to a reality which is no longer reasonable. Television, however unreasonable (and it certainly is strange these days), is as reasonable as reality. In fact, reality is already stranger than any fantasy we could construct. Consequently, the strange is already disturbingly familiar. This estrangement from the familiar and the familiarization of the estranged means that the lines separating the comic and the terrifying, the mundane and the exotic, the boring and the exciting, the ordinary and the extraordinary, disappear. If reality is already cliched, cliches can be taken as reality. If we are in fact totally alienated, then alienation is the taken for granted ground upon which we build our lives.

Within the logic of authentic inauthenticity (quite different from inauthentic authenticity), one celebrates a difference knowing that its status depends on nothing but its being celebrated. In the end, only one's affective commitment, however temporary or superficial, matters. Authentic inauthenticity refuses to locate identity and difference outside the fact of temporary affective commitments. If every identity is equally fake, a pose that one takes on, then authentic inauthenticity celebrates the possibilities of poses without denying that that is all they are. It is a logic which allows one to seek satisfactions knowing that one can never be satisfied, and that any particular pleasure is likely, in the end, to be disappointing. For even if all images are equally artificial, and all satisfactions equally unsatisfying, one still needs some image, one still seeks satisfactions. Although no particular pose can make a claim to some intrinsic status, any pose can gain a status by virtue of one's commitment to it; it can become an important landmark on one's affective map of what matters.

This logic or attitude dominates MTV. I am always surprised that critics take MTV, and particular videos, so seriously. MTV is neither a contemplative text which is constantly demanding interpretation and attention, nor is it some wonderfully orgasmic pleasure. MTV's format and playlist is AM/AOR, but what makes it so powerful is not the particular videos but its hip attitude, its refusal to take anything — itself, its fans, and the world — seriously, even as it appears to do just that. This attitude is captured most explicitly in its self-promos (e.g., in an apparent commercial for MTV beer, the beer is dismissed as tasting terrible, but, the actor concludes, at least the videos are *pretty good*). MTV, and music television more broadly, debunks every image, presenting it as precisely what it is — an image, but acknowledging that there is nothing else to choose from. Thus, paradoxically, music television has freed music from the image. For example, whether one likes Madonna — whose music always sounds the same but whose images are constantly changing — often depends upon whether one think she takes her images too seriously. Music television makes the specific content, the specific style, the specific tastes irrelevant; in their place, it foregrounds one's willingness to take on a pose and one's ability to invest in it precisely knowing that it is a pose, that the only reason it has any value or that it can make any claim on you is that one takes it on, one makes it matter.

a whole new form of music relevation

music & stars are commodities

This logic, and the aesthetic-textual forms which are often used to code it, are not only characteristic of music television. The use of fragmentation, of images without referents, of subjects without substance, of history without reality, and of narratives without coherence, is increasingly visible across the forms of popular culture. Texts no longer appear to seek their own originality or significance; they gleefully celebrate the sense of repetition and of the lack of difference, not only between messages, but between different genres. This is not merely an aesthetics of advertising (although it is often most effective in advertising). These techniques have a long history in both "high art" and popular culture. What is unique is how widespread and common they have become, and the particular shapes these techniques take on in forms such as music television.

The fact that the basic attitude of music television is defined by this logic of authentic inauthenticity does not deny that there are real differences within its various practices. By embracing this broad communicative strategy, music television creates a series of images of stars who embody, not authentic instances of subjectivity and political resistance, but temporary attitudes and moods which can be appropriated by fans as impossible identities, strategies by which they can continue to struggle to make a "difference" — if not in the world, at least in their lives — even though "difference" has become for them impossible and irrelevant. Pee Wee Herman, Madonna, and Max Headroom are examples of an "ironic authenticity" which foregrounds and self-consciously celebrates the artificial and fragmented nature of any identity. Many of the ads associated with music television and youth audiences define a second strategy of "hyperreal inauthenticity" in which "reality" itself — represented as bleak, dismal, gritty, and meaningless — becomes its own image (e.g., the Jordache commercial in which a young man is emotionally distraught over his parents' divorce; or the Converse commercial in which a couple is breaking up and the sentimental plea that they remain friends is greeted with an icecream cone in the face and the command, "take a walk").

But perhaps the most compelling, and certainly the most successful strategy is the position occupied and offered by Bruce Springsteen. Springsteen's phenomenal success not only crosses age, gender, class, and national boundaries, it does not seem to depend upon how one interprets his songs or even whether one is able to identify with the particular narratives he constructs. His fans' passionate commitment to him enabled him to perform before 100,000 people and to incorporate video screens into the concert without apparently losing the sense of immediacy. Moreover, the stylistic diversity of his videos defies any generic identification of musical and visual style. Four observations may help to locate the source of his popularity. First, especially since *The River*, Springsteen has explicitly created pop images of the postmodern condition (e.g., "Is a dream a lie if it don't come true, or is it something worse?"). Second, Springsteen's own image is that he is just like us, an ordinary person with the same emotional experiences. Third, his image of authenticity is artificial, and his fans know it (although they may constantly avoid admitting it). His performances are extraordinarily well-rehearsed and planned, his gestures and stories repeated over and over again. But this does not interfere with his image of authenticity (although it obviously should); in fact, his fans go to see him repeatedly, in order to see him repeat his "spontaneous" performances. Finally, what makes Springsteen different is that anyone can see that he cares more about rock and roll, and his fans, than any other contemporary performer. In the perfectionism with which he produces records, in his concerts, and in his lifestyle (he refuses the pleasures of the rock and roll life so that he can make better rock and roll), Springsteen's "sentimental inauthenticity" (which he shares with other stars like Sylvester Stallone) celebrates the magical possibility of making a "difference" against "impossible" odds simply on the basis of the intensity of his commitment to ordinary activities. One need not agree with his particular commitment; one need only recognize that something matters so much to someone that one is transformed from an ordinary individual into someone "heroic" — if not superhuman.

Conclusion

Music television can only be understood if we understand its relations to economic, technological, historical, and cultural changes. Moreover, its real effects are not guaranteed in advance, by either its existence within capitalist circuits of commodification and ideologies, nor by the particular formal techniques used to construct its texts. In fact, one can argue that the construction of commodified stars as emblems of moods which can be attached to anything (e.g., Bill Cosby, David Bowie, or the current use of the cast of *Mash* in character to endorse IBM computers) has to be partly understood as the cultural industry's response to changing cultural as well as economic conditions. Whatever the economic and ideological intentions of such corporate relations, these mobile stars open up affective possibilities for responding to, surviving within, and perhaps even occasionally "winning" against a world that seems increasingly hostile and disabling. In fact, the relations between these two domains

— capitalism and affective communication — remain an open question. It is precisely here that fans, critics, and scholars continue to struggle over the politics of music television, each attempting to produce the reality they read onto its surfaces.[7]

Part IV

The Logic of Contemporary Culture

The first three sections have progressed from the general to the specific in order to enable specific investigations to exhibit the tensions inherent in popular culture, especially the way these tensions are worked out over time. This section shifts direction to identify the underlying logic of contemporary culture. Each of the essays addresses one aspect of this dynamic.

Russell Jacoby describes the decline of public intellectuals as a consequence of social and economic transformations in American society. These transformations are further investigated by William Leiss who argues that the much touted notion of the information society is a myth, while recognizing that a much broader media revolution toward imagistic modes of communication has occurred which also produces widespread illiteracy. Stephen Kline continues this line of thought by documenting the impact of the integration of the commercial media system with the total marketing strategies for children's toys. This results in limiting the imaginative capabilities of children. In fact, this may preview a more wide-ranging change in adult consciousness. As Herbert Schiller shows there is an increasing privatization of all realms of culture.

Ian Angus accounts for this increasing significance of media by suggesting that media have moved from merely representing social reality to constituting social relations. Todd Gitlin supplements this account of postmodern culture and discusses the issue of what is an appropriate politics in this situation.

19.

The Decline of American Intellectuals[1]

Russell Jacoby

At the end of World War II, C. Wright Mills, the sociologist, surveyed the state of American intellectuals. He was not impressed. He found them worried and helpless, suffering from a "political failure of nerve." These were not simply personal failings; rather they reflected a situation in which intellectuals had become minor employees of major enterprises, a fate common to Hollywood writers and university professors. They succumbed to market and academic imperatives, exchanging caution and calculation for truth and forthrightedness. According to Mills, intellectuals had become powerless and resigned individuals.[2]

Mills was hardly the first to raise an alarm about intellectuals; controversy has long dogged them — almost from the beginning of the term itself. At the turn of the century, some French artists, writers, and teachers, including the novelist Emile Zola, challenged the state's prosecution of Alfred Dreyfus, the Jewish captain falsely accused of spying for Germany; they became known as the "intellectuals." To those rallying to the French state and army the intellectuals were a new and dangerous group.

"The interference of this novelist [Zola] in a matter of miliary justice," wrote a government supporter, "seems to me no less impertinent than, let us say, the intervention of a police captain in a problem of syntax or versification . . . As for this petition that is being circulated among the *Intellectuals!* the mere fact that one has recently created this word *Intellectuals* to designate, as though they were an aristocracy, individuals who live in laboratories and libraries, proclaims one of the most ridiculous eccentricities of our time . . ."[3] Moreover, the Russian term "intelligentsia," referring to the students and children of nobility who constituted the prehistory of the Russian Revolution, gradually passed into English, or at least rubbed off on "intellectuals," darkening its oppositional hues.

This history colored subsequent arguments in the United States and Europe. Some wanted to bury this past, overcoming the legacy of intellectuals as perpetual critics and subversives; others, like Mills, wanted to reclaim it. For the Americans the 1950s marked a critical juncture in these discussions by and on intellectuals, a period when the contending positions attained a rare lucidity. Why? In that decade the situation of intellectuals was changing. The years following World War II marked a swing period between two breeds of intellectuals; independents and bohemians receded before academics and professionals. Intellectuals, previously ignored if not maligned, entered established American institutions. Many in the 1950s pondered the meaning of the transition. If there is a decline of American intellectuals, the 1950s mark not its beginning, but its public notice. Earlier it was not sufficiently obvious to elicit comment; later it becomes too obvious.

"Is the intellectual obsolete?" asked H. Stuart Hughes in 1956 in a typical piece. Troubled by McCarthyism and popular sentiment that denigrated intellectuals as egg heads, Hughes concluded that America allowed little room for the "freely-speculating mind." The range of debatable issues had narrowed. Expanding universities and government bureaus hired experts and technicians, not critical writers and thinkers. "We are living in a society and in an era where there is scope for comparatively few intellectuals." Overwhelmed by the "almost irresistible pressures" of conformity, America's intellectuals faced a "dubious future."[4]

Numerous commentators in articles with titles such as "The Intellectual: Will He Wither Away?" or "The Twilight of the Intellectuals" joined in.[5] "The intellectual in 1953," concluded Arthur Schlesinger, Jr., "faces an incalculable but depressing combination of factors."[6] For some observers, not persecution or indifference, but affluence threatened intellectuals. In John W. Aldridge's view, American intellectuals, disenchanted with communism and European culture, succumb to "money, status, security and power."[7] "Economically," remarked Merle King in *The New Republic*, "the intellectual is better fed, better housed and more elegantly pampered than ever before."[8] Another critic argued that college teachers who lived conventional lives and thought conventional thoughts were supplanting free-lance, bohemian, and avant-garde intellectuals. "The academic hierarcy . . . enforces caution on the imaginative or adventurous thinkers." Even in personal life, professors cannot afford to be "conspicuously out of line."[9]

Perhaps the most famous discussion of the changing situation of intellectuals appeared in an influential left literary magazine, *Partisan Review*. In the *Partisan Review* symposium, "Our Country and Our Culture," (1952) numerous intellectuals assessed, and generally celebrated, their new roles as honored experts and professors. The editors of the symposium remarked that only 10 years earlier intellectuals savaged America for its philistinism and emptiness. "Since, then, however, the tide has begun to turn, and many writers and intellectuals now feel closer to their country and its culture." They put it sharply, "for better or worse, most writers no longer accept alienation as the artist's fate in America; on the contrary, they want very much to be a part of American life. More and more writers have ceased to think of themselves as rebels and exiles."[10]

Several respondents, including Philip Rahv, the critic, Norman Mailer, the novelist, and C. Wright Mills, disagreed. Rahv reflected on the passing of "the intellectual bohemian or proletarian," a byproduct of postwar prosperity which "at long last effected the absorption of the intellectuals into the institutional life of the country." For Rahv intellectuals now viewed America from the inside. "We are witnessing a process that might well be described as that of the *embourgeoisement* of the American intelligentsia."[11]

The dissenters, however, were a distinct minority. Intellectuals "have arrived, they count," commented David Riesman, noting with pleasure that the wealthy now prize culture. "Many of the former enemies of the intellectuals from the upper social strata" — lawyers, doctors, executives — are now "taking up" culture. Too many intellectuals, however, remain fixated on European models, believing that their status depends more on a "widening circle of dislikes than on a widening circle of sympathies."[12] Max Lerner offered his own autobiography as an "exhibit." He is now working on a study of American civilization that ten years earlier he himself would have judged "sentimental, conformist, even chauvinist." But times have changed, and his "long suppressed" love for America is finally being "released."[13]

Lionel Trilling, the literary critic, expressed similar sentiments. "In many civilizations there comes a point at which wealth shows a tendency to submit itself, in some degree, to the rule of mind and imagination . . . [to] taste and sensitivity." Trilling announced the good news. "In America the signs of this submission have for some time been visible." Prosperity undermined the proverbial alienation of American intellectuals, who are now "close to the top of the social hierarchy." Even professors, traditionally ridiculed and underpaid, obtain new status and good salaries, making academic careers attractive to those who once spurned them. "One cannot but be struck by the number of well-to-do students," crowed Professor Trilling, who "now elect the academic life."[14]

Do these reflections and celebrations signify a decline of intellectuals? Not exactly. They may mean, however, that the lives and experiences of intellectuals were changing. Joining institutions, they ceased to be marginal, bohemian, or independent. Eventually — not immediately — their thinking and concerns reflected their new situations, usually academic communities. As professors, intellectuals no longer wrote for a larger public, but devoted themselves to colleagues and professionals. Not their knowledge or diligence, but their public presence and impact altered. Professionalized, they also became privatized. To put it more exactly, the 1950s marked an eclipse of *public* intellectuals. Mills alluded to this; the new intellectuals have renounced "the public relevance of knowledge."[15] To be sure, the term public intellectual is not easy to define. It roughly means an intellectual who uses everyday language to discuss issues of general relevance, someone writing not simply for professional journals but general periodicals.

Even "decline" may be misleading. What happened in the postwar years was the professionalization, mainly the academization of intellectuals. As American intellectuals decamped from garrets and seedy apartments to offices and campuses, their lives and perspectives changed. Specifically their audience shifted, from a lay general audience to professional colleagues; the language of intellectual work also shifted. It was no longer necessary to write in lucid or accessible English; colleagues cared for findings, not form. The decline of American intellectuals is their virtual disappearance from a public world, their collapse into or embrace of professional roles.

Of course, intellectuals did not suddenly abandon their apartments for suburban homes and office complexes, but the accelerating trend in the 1950s left few untouched. By the end of that decade intellectuals and university professors became almost synonymous; academics even filled the pages of small magazines, once outposts beyond the campus. *Partisan Review* itself, the symbol of irreverent New York intellectuals, finally passed into university hands, its editors largely English professors.

The writers of the 1950s palpably sensed what the next generation could not, the restructuring of their lives. "I was my own staff researcher," recalled Alfred Kazin of his years in the reading room of the New York Public Library, "a totally unaffiliated free lance and occasional evening college instructor who was educating himself . . . in the middle of the Great Depression."[16] For intellectuals coming of age in the 1960s and after, life outside universities was not even a memory. However, intellectuals like Philip Rahv, Alfred Kazin, and Irving Howe became professors after years as free-lance writers and editors.

Others such as Lewis Mumford, Edmund Wilson, Gore Vidal, or Dwight Macdonald never made the transition. All, however, were aware of the migration and its consequences. In the early part of the century, recalled Malcolm Cowley, teaching and writing had been "separate worlds"; but today, no longer "independent craftsmen," writers assume roles as professors or as well-paid employees in government or magazine bureaus.[17]

The evidence of change seemed everywhere; universities and national magazines eagerly hired intellectuals; either Luce publications or *The New Yorker* sent checks to Dwight Macdonald, Alfred Kazin, Edmund Wilson, Kenneth Galbraith, Norman Podhoretz, Daniel Bell, and many others. Major publishing houses launched "little" magazines for young and avant-garde writers. Pocket Books founded *discovery*; Avon offered *New Voices*, Doubleday put out *New Writers*; and New American Library, the paperback publisher of Mickey Spillane established the most successful series, *New World Writing*. One issue ran "Jazz of the Beat Generation" by a "Jean-Louis," an excerpt from Jack Kerouac's unpublished *On the Road*.[18]

To Isaac Rosenfeld (1918–1956), a Chicago essayist, these developments demonstrated that an intellectual life of poverty and protest belonged to the past. "The writer very seldom stands over against the world as he used to, and when he does, the danger is that he may be attitudinizing." Even the bohemia that sheltered poor writers and artists showed signs of renovation. "The garret still exists, but the rent has gone up."[19]

Of course, intellectuals did not simply choose these new roles; they were responding to economic and social developments. When Mills surveyed the plight of intellectuals, he also highlighted the major economic facts that structured professionalization: the shift from independent workers and craftsmen to salaried and corporate employees. Moreover, the midcentury witnessed an explosion of the specific employment situation for intellectuals: universities. Between 1920 and 1970 the American population doubled, but college teachers multiplied tenfold. College faculty numbered about 50,000 in 1920; 500,000 in 1970.

The newly opened and enlarged colleges allowed, if not compelled, intellectuals to desert a precarious existence for stable careers. They exchanged the pressures of deadlines and writing for their daily bread for the security of salaried teaching, pensions, and writing — with summers off. When Daniel Bell left *Fortune* magazine in 1958 for the university life, he told Luce he had four good reasons: "June, July, August, and September."

These gains of academic life — salaries, security, summers — seemed hardly offset by the drawbacks: the occasional lectures at 8 in the morning, the committee drudgery, and, sometimes, a new location distant from old friends. Yet the balance sheet does not include the real losses, less visible, but finally decisive. In recasting the lives of intellectuals, intellectual life was recast.

Intellectuals as academics no longer relied on either the small magazine of opinion and literature or the bigger periodicals, such as *The New Yorker* or *Fortune* as their outlets. Professional journals and monographs became their lifeblood. Scholarly editors and "referees," professional colleagues of the same speciality, now judged their manuscripts, supplanting the general editors of *The New Republic* or *Partisan Review*. The ante was much smaller, at least initially. A manuscript rejected by an academic journal did not lead to personal bankruptcy or catastrophe. A salary was still paid, the contract still honored. Nevertheless, to obtain promotions and, finally, to retain a position, academics needed to present themselves as neutral and competent technicians; they had to fit into disciplines.

The constraints and corruptions of academic life are hardly news. Savage criticism of American universities date back to Upton Sinclair's *The Goose-Step* (1923) and Thorstein Veblen's *Higher Learning in America* (1918), which Veblen intended to subtitle "A Study in Total Depravity." The critical issue, however, is not the novelty of the situation, but its extent. When universities occupied a quadrant of cultural life, their ills (and virtues) meant one thing. When they staked out the whole turf, their rules became *the* rules.

These rules did not encourage a leathery independence. Yet the "total depravity" that Veblen denounced — "a conspicuous conformity to popular taste" and the kowtowing to business — lags behind the reality. These imperatives never disappear, but they do not address the new situation, the vast university system of the 1940s and 50s that hungered for palpable scholarship. Political timidity of new academics was, in the long run, less decisive than the compulsion to feed the system, and themselves, with scholarly product. More was better — publish or perish. New academics wrote and read books and articles with an eye to the bottom line — the findings, the arguments, the facts, the conclusions.

In their haste, they did not linger over the text. Academic intellectuals did not cherish direct or elegant writing; they did not disdain it, but it hardly mattered. Most scholarly literature included summaries of the argument or findings; the fact of publication far outweighed any quibbling over style. These imperatives increasingly informed how intellectuals both read and wrote; professionals cared for substance, not form. Academic writing eventually developed into unreadable communiques sweetened by thanks to colleagues and superiors.

Crabbed academic writing is hardly new; again, the extent, not the novelty, is the issue. An earlier intellectual life and its prose were dying out. Independent intellectuals wrote for marginal journals, usually smaller than the academic periodicals. Yet these journals participated, if only through hope, in the wider educated community. Intellectuals wrote in *Seven Arts* or *Partisan Review* not for coteries, but for a wide community, perhaps the world. They viewed themselves as men and women of letters, who sought and prized a spare prose. For this reason they could be read by the educated public, and later they were. Schooled in the small magazines, the Max Eastmans or Dwight Macdonalds or Irving Howes easily shifted to more popular periodicals and publics.

Today non-academic intellectuals are an endangered species; industrial and urban developments threaten their habitats. They continue to loom large in the educated world because they mastered a public idiom. Younger intellectuals are almost exclusively professors; they far outnumber the older independent intellectuals, but insofar as the professors do not command a public prose, they remain virtually invisible to outsiders; their endless articles and books are for each other, not the more scattered educated community.

In other words: behind the erosion of public intellectuals a generational flux seems at work. An older generation of public intellectuals is passing on, and a new one is not showing up. This "missing" generation is more or less those intellectuals who came to maturity during the upheavals of the 1960s. Once they were a decided force for change and revolution; today they are scarcely present as a coherent intellectual generation.

For instance, to provide some benchmarks, it is possible to chart an American public philosophy from William James through John Dewey, but afterwards it seems to vaporize. Successors to Dewey, younger philosophers addressing public issues in a public language, seem almost nonexistent. "The older sort of philosophy professor," writes Richard Rorty, "is dying out." The newer type is technically trained, devoted to "cases," and argumentation — not history, morals, or public issues.[20] The same might be said of psychoanalysis; it is possible to describe an older public psychoanalysis (mainly represented by refugees) from Erich Fromm to Erik Erikson and Bruno Bettelheim all of whom wrote on public issues from a psychoanalytic perspective for an educated audience. While psychoanalysis has prospered in the United States, it is difficult to name younger successors to these figures.

Of course, there is no hard and fast evidence on the decline of public intellectuals; in evaluating cultural life, surveys and quantatitive analysis hardly capture the essence. However, in comparing intellectual life of the 1950s and 1980s some fundamental changes emerge. It seems striking, for instance, that today it is difficult to name the important younger intellectuals, perhaps because they have professional, not public reputations. In the 1950s, however, it was quite easy to name and discuss the new young intellectuals. Moreoever the intellectuals active in the 1950s remain the important intellectuals today; their books after thirty years have hardly been surpassed. All this suggests that a young intellectual generation is succumbing to professionalization.

Some impressionistic evidence might be offered: The 1950s could claim numerous talented critics, young and old: Mary McCarthy, Philip Rahv, C. Wright Mills, Dwight Macdonald, Lionel Trilling, David Reisman, Irving Howe, Arthur Schlesinger Jr., Edmund Wilson, Lewis Mumford, Malcom Cowley, Sidney Hook, and others. Or consider the many vital works bunched around the end of the decade: Kenneth Galbraith's *The Affluent Society*, Betty Friedan's *The Feminine Mystique*, Paul Goodman's *Growing Up Absurd*, Jane Jacob's *Death and Life of Great American Cities*, C. Wright Mills's *The Power Elite*, William Whyte's *The Organization Man* and Michael Harrington's *The Other America*. The successors to these works to not seem obvious.

To turn to slightly more "scientific" evidence. Over ten years ago a sociologist studying influential intellectuals observed that a new generation seemed absent. Charles Kadushin presented the findings of an extensive empirical study of American thinkers; he wanted to characterize — name and describe — America's "intellectual elite." To do this he interviewed 110 influential intellectuals, who were identified by regularly appearing in "influential" periodicals such as *The New York Review of Books*, *Commentary*, *Harper's*, *Atlantic*, *The New Yorker* and *The New York Times Book Review*.

From his study Kadushin obtained cartons of interesting and not-so-interesting information, including a list of the most prestigious intellectuals. In 1970 the ten leading intellectuals were: Daniel Bell, Noam Chomsky, John Kenneth Galbraith, Irving Howe, Dwight Macdonald, Mary McCarthy, Norman Mailer, Robert Silvers, Susan Sontag, and tying at 10th place, Lionel Trilling and Edmund Wilson. None could be considered young, with the possible exception of Susan Sontag (37 in 1970). That the extended list of "top" seventy intellectuals also included very few younger faces troubled Kadushin. He did not fault his research methods. "The fact there are few young intellectuals [on the list] is not an 'error'; it reflects the structure of intellectual life in the United States at this time." Young intellectuals are simply not present in cultural life, nor have they been for some time. Moreover, the aging "elite" did not recently fall into place; it assumed prominence twenty years earlier. "The elite American intellectuals as we saw them in 1970 were basically the same ones who came to power in the late 1940s and early 1950s."

Kadushin asked his "elite" to identify younger intellectuals on the horizon; they were unable to do so. Doubting this indicated a permanent vacancy, Kadushin surmised that "the heirs have not yet made themselves known."[21] He confidently suggested that this situation would soon change. Fifteen years later this confidence looks ill-founded; the heirs have still not made themselves known. A list of significant intellectuals today would look very much like Kadushin's (minus the deaths) — and they were greying fifteen years ago.

Current anthologies of leading opinion display the same aging literati; for instance, the 50th anniversary issue of *Partisan Review* (1984) — almost 400 pages — reveals few younger faces. Even more popular efforts to parade young talent comes up short. *Esquire* magazine regularly runs a fat annual issue on "the best of the new generation: men and women under forty who are changing America." They cast a wide net, filling the issue with sketches of bright young people. Leaving aside computer entrepreneurs, architects, designers, however, they come up with precious little in the traditional humanities; their 1984 issue offers a novelist Jim Dodge (1945-), author of *Fup* or an historian Walter McDougal (1946-) author of *France's Rhineland Diplomacy 1914–1924*. If they represent an "under forty" generation changing America, there is no generation — nor is America changing.

A recent study of one field, "area studies," confirms the impact of professionalization. Area studies essentially belongs to post World War II America, when Congress and universities pressured the government to study the rest of the world. And the United States government did what it often did in the 1950s, it threw money at the problem, lavishly funding scholars, new programs, and buildings in area studies.

Robert McCaughey in a new book entitled *International Studies and Academic Enterprise: A Chapter in the Enclosure of American Learning* argues that the monies and new slots, which of course coincided with the expansion of the universities, yielded not so much new knowledge as a new fiefdom. The old foreign policy experts, including the old China hands, were quite knowledgable and played important public roles — or course, they were frequently ignored; they are supplanted by scores of younger scholars, busily writing unreadable monographs and applying for grants; they do not really contribute to public discussions. In this one discipline a generational progression is visible; older free-floating intellectuals who spoke out about the world are replaced by university professionals more interested in government careers and technical issues.

McCaughey himself suggests some interesting, perhaps predictable political consequences. He examined a number of the important "stop the bombing" petitions during the height of the Vietnam War. At the time academics were signing these on the way to work. One might imagine that some of the experts, the area studies people researching the China and the Far East might have added their names. The reverse is true. McCaughey found that wherever there were well-funded international studies programs, such as at Harvard or Stanford, its professors were conspicuously absent from any protest activity.[22] Insofar as the area studies professors depended on government funds and supports, they ceased to function as critics.

Another field, Marxism, confirms the same trajectory of professionalization. Again taking the 1950s as a benchmark, it would be extremely difficult to name many public Marxists in the universities; the few that could be found would include Paul Baran, C. Wright Mills, and perhaps a half dozen others. To jump ahead 30 years the situation is very different. A complete discussion of leftists in the universities might take 10 pages in the 1950s; for comparison, Bertel Ollman has recently edited a three volume survey of *The Left Academy*, each about 300 pages, which lists and evaluates Marxists in all disciplines from geography to philosophy. Moreover, there are now a dozen or more radical or left professional journals, from *Canadian Journal of Political and Social Theory* to periodicals such as *Radical History Review, Insurgent Sociologist, New Political Science, Dialectical Anthropology, Antipode, New German Critique, Review of Radical Political Economy, Feminist Studies, Social Text.*

The change is startling. In both periodicals and books there has been an incredible increase. However, and this is the rub, the quantity does not seem to convert easily to quality. Obviously in surveying a vast amount of intellectual work, it would be foolhardy, indeed false, to write it off as inferior; this is not the point. The issue is different; on the one hand it is possible to identify individuals like Paul Baran, and his friend Paul Sweezy who wrote Marxist works of a public nature, books which rightly enjoy, or enjoyed, a certain amount of influence because of their lucidity; on the other hand, they have been supplanted by scores of well-trained Marxists. Yet decades after Baran's *Political Economy of Growth* or Baran and Sweezy's *Monopoly Capital* it is difficult to find any texts that come close to them. There are many monographs and specialized studies, but few public contributions.

Perhaps this point can be driven home by the following: When Paul Baran died in 1964, *Monthly Review* published a special issue which included some 40 statements about Baran from old friends, associates, and students. It was a large international cast, which ran from Issac Deutscher, Che Guevera, Eric Hobsbawm, Herbert Marcuse, Joan Robinson, Ralph Miliband, and many others. It also included statements by four younger intellectuals from the United States and Canada: Peter Clecak, John O'Neill, Maurice Zeitlin, and Freddy Perlman.[23]

At the time the first three of the younger group were assistant professors; they have all gone up to become full professors at major universities, and have made important contributions to radical scholarship. Yet none have established themselves in the same way as Baran or Sweezy; they are known primarily to people in their fields. In short they are specialists. (The fourth, Fredy Perlman, is a name familiar only to cognoscenti of left literature; he founded and for many years ran an anarchist press in Detroit, Black and Red, which has published little known classics in Marxist and Situationist literature). This transition from Baran and Sweezy to younger perhaps more scholarly, but also less public intellectuals typifies the entire intellectual shift. Is this the cunning of reason or at least the cunning of bourgeois society? Marxism, the critique of bloodless scholastic knowledge, has become bloodless scholastic knowledge.

Other disciplines reveal the same trajectory. It is possible to take C. Wright Mills as a test figure. Few would doubt that there has been a flowering of radical sociologists since Mills's death. Yet from Erik Olin Wright's efforts to mathematize class relations to Immanuel Wallerstein's world systems theories, only technical issues and methodologies have apparently progressed. Mills wrote and lived as a moralist, polemicist, and public citizen; his successors write and live as radical sociologists. Literary studies seems also to fit the pattern. Classic literary criticism was kept alive by vital figures such as Edmund Wilson and Lewis Mumford; yet literary criticism finally passes into the hands of deconstructionists and postmodernists oriented towards each other.

If these are major trends in American cultural life, there are certainly counter instances, people and journals that buck the tide. Yet it seems clear that a certain kind of independent intellectual is on the eve of disappearing; there are no successors to the New York intellectuals once centered on *Partisan Review*; there seem to be no successors to Baran and Sweezy; to Edmund Wilson, Lewis Mumford, Jane Jacobs, C. Wright Mills, and many others. A deathly professionalization and academization permeate society, draining public culture of vitality. Professional life and thought thrive, but the larger culture turns grey.

20.

The Myth of the Information Society

William Leiss

The notion that technological innovation can bring about qualitative changes in social relations is a hallmark of modern thought or, to use the current jargon, of "modernity." Its great early propagator was Francis Bacon, who regarded conventional politics as a zero-sum game where benefits could be extracted by one party only at another's expense; the conquest of nature through science and technology, however, promised to overcome this limitation and to deliver an ever-increasing supply of unqualified benefits.

For Bacon the essential promise of technology was not that it could address directly the traditional sources of human unhappiness, but that it could gradually render them irrelevant.[1] In his view a significant proportion of the traditional failure to realize the importance of scientific and technological innovation was rooted simply in intellectual confusion, what today we are wont to call "ideology"; those who remained mired in such confusion, he believed, would appear more and more ludicrous in relation to the tangible increases in human welfare won by the new technology. Two and one-half centuries later, the very title of a 1966 journal article by an eminent political scientist, Robert E. Lane — "The Decline of Politics and Ideology in a Knowledgeable Society" — shows how much vitality this mode of thinking still possesses.[2]

In the second phase of its development, beginning in the nineteenth century, a new variation emerged which emphasized the inevitability or necessity of social changes induced by technological innovation. Employing a crude version of the evolutionary metaphor, this variation insisted that societies must "adapt" to their new "environments" or suffer the consequences. This reinforced the fundamental thrust of technocratic thinking, which favors the displacement of questions about value choices, regarded as ultimately ideological, by a simple overriding determinant for decision-making that is "objective" and quantitative in nature: efficiency in the allocation of resources. Since what is happening is allegedly inevitable, whether or not we like it is irrelevant. A 1981 report for the Government of Canada, entitled *The Information Revolution and its Implications for Canada*, maintains that "like the industrial revolution, the information revolution is unavoidable. Consequently, the objectives of public policy should be not to prevent the revolution from occurring, but rather to turn it to our advantage."[3]

The mention of public policy in this context signals the advent of a decisive new phase in technocratic thinking. In earlier phases the inevitability or necessity allegedly inherent in technological innovation was presumed to have a direct, unmediated impact on social relations. Of course the economy, where the determination of the efficient allocation of resources occurred, was the actual transmitter for these impacts. In the current phase public policy is supposed to serve historical inevitability by facilitating a favorable social response to it.

Two quite different sets of circumstances have produced the new phase. First, the rate of innovation and turnover apparently has accelerated; this, together with the intensity of international competition, means that societies must respond much more quickly than they did in the past, and public policy must provide some "grease" to insure a faster response time. Second, at least some interest groups are now much better able than they used to be to defend themselves by protecting their income, status, and influence against innovations that threaten to erode their relative advantages.

The enhanced ability of social groups to articulate their interests, and to require governments to protect those interests to some extent, places an important intervening variable between technological innovation operating through the economy and social relations. Public policy must seek in part to persuade us to acquiesce in what we can no longer be forced to accept, at least not without a protracted struggle. And that is just the point: Because, even if, as is believed, the innovating forces must triumph in the end, they will have achieved only a Phyrric victory, for if serious delays occur the economic advantages of early entry will have been lost, and our society will drift further and further away from the "action" as each successive wave of innovation rolls in.

The concepts of "information revolution," "information economy," and "information society" constitute an important new stage in the tradition of technocratic thinking in modern society. In large part their importance lies precisely in how perfectly they represent this tradition. They enable us to see clearly what role public policy is thought to have in the interaction between technology and society: namely, to "soften up" public opinion so that a compliant response to a new technology may be delivered. It seems to matter little to its propagators that their show includes some quite outrageous sleight-of-hand routines, for what is important is not the act's constitution but its effect: in this case, as in technocratic thinking generally, to attempt to persuade us that we are free to choose only the timing of our submission.

The effort at persuasion introduces a nice circularity into the process. If we can be cajoled into believing that some future state is inevitable, and further to alter our behavior in order to conform to its anticipated requirements, the end result will be a retrospective proof of the prediction's accuracy. These are its principal steps:

1. *Analysis* develops a conceptual model, namely, the concept of the "information society" whose objective is to influence

2. *Policy* initiatives that will create favorable conditions for shaping a

3. *Social Response* that over time results in changed social behavior and new

4. *Behavior Patterns* that resemble those originally predicted as desirable in the

5. *Analysis* itself, thus confirming the model's predictions about what was "inevitable."

At the time in the past when many thought that it was salutary for society to be utterly at the mercy of the marketplace's allocative mechanisms, and that "interference" by public authority was to be avoided, the apparent "necessity" in the process required no further justification. Public policy today, however, as the explicit voice of public authority, abdicates its responsibility and loses it *raison d'être* when it limits itself to the "recognition of necessity." For there is no necessity, strictly speaking, in social events; rather, they represent the outcomes of individual and collective choices (including both conscious and unconscious motivations) that rest ultimately on fundamental values. From this standpoint it is the duty of public policy discussions to clarify the full range of choices to be made, and their possible impacts on values, so that enlightened decisions may be made about the future directions of social change.

The "information society" and its associated notions evolved in a three-stage process during the past twenty years or so: from the "technological society" to the "knowledge society" and/or "service society" to the "information society." These notions will be examined in this paper as representative examples of the long tradition of technocratic thinking, the essential premise of which is that technical innovations produce social effects in and of themselves. A good example is provided in another recent Canadian government report, which states with a flourish that the "advent of microelectronics is rapidly and irreversibly leading to a major and fundamental transformation of western society."[4]

This statement incorporates the two most common faults of a certain type of social forecasting, namely technological hyperbole and technological fetishism. The hyperbole is characterized by the systematic and unwarranted exaggeration of the general social effects of introducing new technologies — usually, as we shall see, by providing a grandiose phrase ("fundamental transformation of western society") and precious little detail. And the fetishism consists in making far too much out of the specific characteristics of the new techniques themselves, and by suggesting that we have "no choice" but to adapt our behavior to the requirements of our instruments.

This examination of the information society will be made in the context of my own evaluative standpoint, summarized briefly here, to which I will return in the concluding section. It has three major features:

1. Increases in the stock of information are counterbalanced by an equally large growth in misinformation, and in many cases by deliberately constructed batches of disinformation.

2. In some cases there is a serious erosion in the capacity to utilize information, on the part of many citizens, in making informed judgments on social and political issues. This is chiefly due to inadequacies in basic literacy.

3. Even if it is true, to some extent, that powerful pressures are exerted on industrial societies to adopt new technologies, given their integration into an international economic structure, these societies can and should resist the notion that they must adapt to the new environment in any predetermined way. The mode of adaptation for societies is not fixed in advance but can be made responsive to reflective processes, through which societies retain a measure of freedom from necessity and of freedom of choice based on the autonomy of value systems.

Background

In the 1960s there emerged an extensive set of publications and organized research projects on the theme "technology and society." The most prominent project and its associated publications was the Harvard University Program on Technology and Society (about 1964–71), funded by a large IBM grant and headed by E. G. Mesthene, who summarized its overall outlook in his book *Technological Change* (1970); the best known single work is John Kenneth Galbraith's *The New Industrial State* (1967). Much of the literature was a response, in one form or another, to the exasperating and formidable tract by Jacques Ellul, *The Technological Society* (1964), originally *La Technique* (1954); in general the writing brought to fruition a theme that had been articulated shortly after the end of the Second World War, as represented best in a UNESCO symposium (still worth reading today) published in *The International Social Science Bulletin* in 1953.[5]

The key concept in this literature is that of "technological society" itself. It was intended to suggest that a new "type" of society had emerged: A type of society distinguished by the centrality of continued technical innovation in its midst, one that was qualitatively different from all earlier societies by virtue of the centrality of technology, and thus one that required of its social relations that they be capable of responding continuously and, of course, favorably to technology's relentless upwelling. Mesthene gave these propositions their most extreme formulation: "Technology, in short, has come of age, not merely as a technical capability, but as a social phenomenon . . . . We are recognizing that our technical prowess literally bursts with the promise of new freedom, enhanced human dignity, and unfettered aspiration."[6]

Many writers emphasized the key social role of "organized knowledge" in the technological society, and this quickly became an important theme in the literature. Daniel Bell developed this angle most fully, and his *The Coming of Post-Industrial Society* is the major transitional work in the tradition under examination here. Bell's notion of post-industrial society laid the foundations for the later concept of the information society: "Broadly speaking, if industrial society is based on machine technology, post-industrial society is shaped by an intellectual technology. And if capital and labor are the major structural features of industrial society, information and knowledge are those of the post-industrial society."[7] Bell's chief emphasis, however, was on the transition from a stage of modern society dominated by goods production to one in which "services" were fast becoming the dominant economic sector. A few years later others reconceptualized the process, and the "service society" was transformed into the information society with but a minimum of further tinkering.

The broad background theme in this literature is composed of the so-called imperatives of technology. Industrial society developed by reorganizing the matrix of social relations so that there could be a receptiveness to continued technological innovations; it did so by largely increasing the flexibility and responsiveness to market conditions of the factors of production. Originally, therefore, modern technology was the means for enhancing productivity, which in turn was the means for bettering the general welfare. In ironic reversal, however, the means became autonomous and thus increasingly an end-in-itself: Technology imposed the hegemony of its own supreme value (that is, efficiency) on society generally.

Ellul's famous book tracks this process throughout all the crevices of social life and bitterly laments the outcome. Most other commentators are more phlegmatic. Galbraith, for example, argues simply that, once a commitment to a high level of industrialization is made, the "imperatives of organization, technology and planning" overawe ideologically grounded differences (such as capitalism versus socialism) and give rise to a basically identical outcome dictated by the nature of the technically oriented infrastructure itself.

For most writers this outcome is not the unmitigated disaster lamented by Ellul. Precisely the opposite: technology opens vast new "possibilities" for mankind, and we are free to turn these opportunities to our advantage in any ways we choose. What we must do is simply adapt ourselves to the new technologically formed environment, to develop a "readiness" to exploit the myriad new opportunities for action. Donald Schon stated this point well: "But, as we are learning, technological innovation belongs to us less than we belong to it. It has demands and effects of its own on the nature and structure of corporations, industry, government-industry relations and the values and norms that make up our idea of ourselves and of progress."[8]

Since the notion of the information society is a legitimate offspring of this tradition, its distinguishing features are those it inherited:

- *Qualitative changes*: There is a major shift in socioeconomic structure, defined by broad changes in occupations and in the social significance of productive factors. Stated most provocatively, the idea is that knowledge replaces capital as the governing factor. This precipitates equally significant changes in decision-making processes, including control over the political process and how political power is exercised.

- *Social Responses*: Society is encouraged to respond positively to "new opportunities" that can and should have wide-ranging impacts on lifestyles and the quality of life.

Post-Industrial Society

In 1979 a report prepared for the Government of Canada offered the following definition: "An Information Society is a set of social relationships based on an Information Economy. In turn, the Information Economy exists whenever over 50% of the Gross National product belongs within the broad information sector."[9] In a very short time the concept of an information society has received considerable attention. How did it arise?

Daniel Bell's *The Coming of Post-Industrial Society* is the major project in social analysis that paved the way for the concept of an information society. Bell had relied heavily on some statistical evidence (from Organization for Economic Cooperation and Development studies and other sources) to argue the growing preponderance of scientific and technical knowledge in economy and society. Subsequently there appeared an elaborate study, *The Information Economy*, prepared by Marc Uri Porat for the United States government, on which many later works have rested their case for the existence of the information economy.[10] "The information economy" is the mainstay for the ensemble of social impacts that are said to make up the information society.

Bell described five distinguishing characteristics for post-industrial society:[11]

1. Economic Sector: The change from a goods-producing to a service economy;

2. Occupational Distribution: the pre-eminence of the professional and technical class;

3. Axial Principle: the centrality of theoretical knowledge as the source of innovation and of policy formation for the society;

4. Future Orientation: the control of technology and technological assessment;

5. Decision-making: the creation of a new "intellectual technology."

Let us examine these claims, especially the first two.[12]

The traditional classification in the U.S. Department of Labor statistics used by Bell and the percentage of the work force in each category are as follows (rounded):

	1900	1960	1974
White collar workers	17.5	42.0	48.5
Manual workers	36.0	37.5	35.0
Service workers	9.0	12.5	13.0
Farm workers	37.5	8.0	2.0

When these categories are reanalyzed into just two sectors, goods-producing and services-producing, the figures for 1968 in the United States are: Goods, 36%; Services 64%. In this far more simplified stratification, the actual composition of the two, especially the services-producing, is crucial. The services sector includes the following: transportation and utilities, 5.5%; trade (wholesale and retail), 20.5%; finance, insurance, and real estate, 4.5%; services, 18.5%; government, 14.5%. Services are composed of personal (laundries, garages, hair-dressing, and the like), professional (lawyers, doctors, and account-ants), and business (office equipment, cleaning, and so on). The goods-producing sector includes only those directly employed in mining, construction, manufacturing, agriculture, forestry, and fisheries.

The heterogeneous character of the services sector should give one pause at the outset. First, replacing the white collar-manual labor distinction with the services-goods one can be misleading if one does not remember that the two are not symmetrical (that is, white collar and services are not identical). Second, and more importantly, a large proportion of the services sector is a necessary and integrated part of goods-producing activities; this is especially true of transportation and utilities, but it applies to part of wholesale and retail trade, government, and business services as well. To some extent the inflated services sector reflects only the greater internal complexity of the goods-producing sector itself, which requires a higher level of infrastructural support now than it did earlier. In short, the goods-services distinction is a conceptual dichotomy, not a simple reflection of economic activity itself; one must be careful not to make too much of it.

The second point has to do with the alleged "pre-eminence" of the professional and technical occupations in the economy as a whole. Included in the white collar category, their percentage figures increased from 4.3% in 1900 to 10.8% in 1960 to 14.4% in 1974. Who are they? For the United States in 1975, the breakdown for this category was as follows: scientific and engineering (including social scientists), 15%, of whom three-quarters were engineers; technicians (excluding medical and dental), 11%; medical and health professionals, 17%; teachers, 23%, of whom three-quarters were elementary and secondary teachers; and general, 34% (accountants, lawyers, media, architects, librarians, clergymen, social workers, and so on).

What conclusions can be drawn from the data? The more traditional categorization (white collar, manual, and so forth) shows in fact the remarkable stability of the "manual" sector as a percentage of the total labor force throughout the twentieth century. The principal redistributional shift has been the precipitous decline in farm workers, and these have been absorbed almost entirely into the white collar sector. Although the white collar sector is now numerically predominant, nothing in the numbers *per se* implies any kind of qualitative change in social influence. As Bell himself notes, traditional agrarian societies also have large services sectors, for example, household servants, made up of low-status occupations. The services sector today includes, as well as the high-status professions, a large proportion of low-status jobs in retail sales, clerical-typist positions, minor bureaucratic functions, and the like.

Bell says very little about this matter because it is point 2 that is the real heart of his analysis, namely, the idea that the professional and technical "elite" of the service sector is "pre-eminent" in our "new kind of society." He says: "The central occupational category in the society today is the professional and technical."[13] Even if we limit ourselves to his own framework for analysis, however, it is difficult to see why this is supposed to be so. In the first place, the breakdown presented above shows clearly that this collection of professions is by no means a homogeneous social entity which has, or potentially could have, a sense of self-consciousness as a group and thus a distinctive social interest. The category itself is composed of sharply divided strata in terms of self-identity and perceived status differentiation; it lumps together the high-status professional "elites" (doctors, lawyers, accountants, engineers, architects) along with teachers, technicians, nurses, social workers, and so forth.

Second, each of these two basic divisions seems to have much more in common, in terms of income and social status, with those in other categories than they do with each other. For example, the professional elites have much in common with the stratum of corporate and government-sector managers and the more successful small proprietors, who are included in a separate occupational category. There is very little, if any, evidence (Bell presents none) to suggest, as his scheme does in moving from point 2 to points 3–5, that the professional-technical group as a whole is increasingly in charge of directions for social change through policy formation, or even seeks to be in charge, based on what Bell calls their ability to use "intellectual technology" (a fancy name for systems analysis, organizational theory, and the like).

The analysis is a classic case of special pleading. Bell highlights the pre-eminence of the professional-technical group by pointing to the dramatic rate of increase in this "sector" relative to others. For the 1958–74 period there was a 77.5 percent increase, as opposed to a 55 percent increase for white collar workers as a whole. Nonetheless, the clerical sector grew by 65 percent in the same period! There are also enough possible anomalies in this particular period, including the deliberate channeling of resources into education, space research, and military expansion, to induce a need for caution. In any case, the highlighting is achieved by segregating in separate boxes occupational groups, such as professional and managerial ones, which in reality have strong affinities in contemporary society.

The ultimate conclusion is as shaky as the analytical premises on which it is founded. For Bell the distinguishing characteristics of post-industrial society signal "the emergence of a new kind of society," and as in all such occurrences, this one "brings into question the distributions of wealth, power, and status that are central to any society."[14] The reason is that in post-industrial society knowledge has emerged alongside property to constitute the two "axes of stratification" for social relations. One does not denigrate the important social function of knowledge today if one concludes, that on the evidence submitted, this contention appears to be most implausible. Occupational categories are useful for keeping statistical records but otherwise are rather arbitrary in nature; one cannot concoct a social theory out of such ingredients alone, which is what Daniel Bell sought to do.

The Information Economy

All major commentaries on the information economy rely on the pathbreaking work by Porat, published by the United States Government's Office of Telecommunications in 1977. This work concluded that 46 percent of the gross national product (GNP) could be classified as information activity, and 53 percent of all income as income earned by information workers. (The data go back mostly to 1967.) Porat employed the following basic definition, stated at the outset of his study: "Information is data that have been organized and communicated. The information activity includes all resources consumed in producing, processing and distributing information goods and services." It is composed of six subsidiary types of activity: (1) information generation or creation; (2) information capture, or the channeling of information; (3) information transformation; (4) information processing (at the receiving end); (5) information storage; and, (6) information retrieval.

The principal working hypothesis is that information activity is not an independent sector in the traditional sense, such as manufacturing is, but rather is something that cuts across all sectors. Thus, the information component of all types of economic activity must be segregated, and the results combined to provide an overall picture. Parenthetically, Porat concedes that a similar operation could be performed with regard to educational activity, for example, since most types of economic activity have an educational or learning component. This type of approach does not exclude others that employ similarly broad of "synthetic" concepts. This is an important qualification; not surprisingly, it does not reappear in the policy literature that is otherwise dependent on Porat's scheme, which would like to convert Porat's purely conceptual exercise into a statement about a "new kind of society" that supposedly now actually exists.

When this reshuffling is done, there are six sectors: a primary information sector, two secondary information sectors, and three non-information sectors:

1. Primary Information Sector: a private market sector, including all of the computer and telecommunications industry, finance and insurance, media, and private education, as well as varying percentages of other industries.

2. The Secondary Information Sector: (a) public bureaucracy; (b) private bureaucracy, including all "information support" activities in large organizations.

3. Non-Information Sectors: (a) households; (b) private productive sector; and (c) public productive sector (for example, government-owned corporations).

The primary information sector accounts for 25 percent of the GNP, and the secondary, for 21 percent, giving a total of 46 percent.

The proportion of information workers in the total labor population is classified by means of a three-part typology. The first part consists of knowledge producers (engineers, lawyers, most specialist occupations) and knowledge distributors, primary teachers; the second, of knowledge users, including in one sub-category managers, administrators, and bureaucrats, and in another, clerical and office staff; and the third, of the direct operators of information-processing machines. By an elaborate segregation of activities in industries, Porat arrived at the figure of 53 percent as the share of total income earned by information workers.

An Appendix to the Government of Canada report referred to earlier offers an overview of the major classifications and occupational types in what is called information work, taken from an OECD study entitled "Report on Economic Analysis of Information Activities":

I. Information Producers
   A. Scientific and Technical: natural scientists, engineers, social scientists.

        B.   Market Specialists: brokers, buyers, insurance agents.

        C.   Information Gatherers: surveyors, inspectors.

        D.   Consultative Services: architects, planners, dieticians, accountants, lawyers, designers.

        E.   Other: authors, composers.

II. Information Processors

        A.   Administrative/Managerial: judges, office managers, administrators.

        B.   Process Control: supervisors, foremen.

        C.   Clerical: typists, clerks, bookkeepers, receptionists.

III. Information Distributors

        A.   Educators: teachers (at all levels).

        B.   Communications Workers: journalists, announcers, directors, producers.

IV. Information Infrastructure

        A.   Information machines: office machine operators, printers and associated trades, A/V equipment operators.

        B.   Postal and telecommunications Workers.

Two general considerations arise immediately. First, there is a lack of correlation between the size of the information sectors in national economies, on the one hand, and overall economic performance on the other. The United States leads the way, in terms of size, followed by Canada and the United Kingdom; but West Germany is significantly lower, and Japan lowest of all. This is almost certainly related to productivity figures. During the past decade industrial productivity in the United States grew 90 percent, whereas office productivity grew only 4 percent; since so much of the information sector is office work, the Government of Canada report concedes that "low growth in productivity may well have contributed to an expansion in information employment."[15] If this is a part of an "information revolution," something seems amiss, for it sounds a good deal more like a counter-revolution.

Second, much of what was said above in a critical vein about the service sector applies here as well. The information economy is a mixed bag of occupations; whether we see any unifying ingredient in the mixture depends very much on our level of tolerance for terminological laxity. In any event they are the same cat, with only slightly different stripes: The Government of Canada report tells us that in Canada in 1971, 76% of information workers belonged to the service sector.

I hasten to add that this relabeling exercise is a perfectly legitimate undertaking for social analysts; very little under the sun is actually new, and fresh understanding often is derived from nothing more dramatic than rearranging familiar facts to fit another paradigm. Exercises such as Porat's, and speculative treatises such as Bell's, challenge other ways of thinking about the contemporary phase of industrial societies; even if one cannot accept them, one can appreciate the testing of accepted approaches that they cause to happen.

What is an Information Society?

It is a different matter altogether when others attempt to compose marching music out of these scattered notes. A report on the information society commissioned by the Government of Canada in 1979 states boldly that "it is reasonable to assume that the Information Society is now as inevitable for the OECD countries as puberty is for an adolescent." It further warns us to eschew reliance on either market forces or uncoordinated public policy, and urges the Canadian federal government to adopt a "concerted and comprehensive information policy." The later Canadian report on the "information revolution" concurs:

> The social and economic impact of the information revolution could be as profound as that of the industrial revolution. Many industrialized countries recognize this fact, as well as the need for comprehensive approaches to policy in order to deal effectively with the widespread changes expected to result from pervasive application of these new technologies.[16]

But before we leap on this bandwagon, let us pose a few unpleasant questions. We can easily grant the point that our economy and society is now dependent on a rapidly increasing and quickly circulating stock of data (that is, specialized knowledge) for *specific* purposes — building machinery, growing crops, producing entertainment, perpetrating crimes, conducting covert operations, and above all launching total war. But when we sum it all up, and consider the general relation between knowledge and the uses to which it is put, and by whom, what is the result?

The answer given below is: The "information society" itself is a mythic creature. There is no such beast that now actually exists or is about to emerge, not at least under present conditions. Quite the contrary: In seeking to answer the question posed above, we are driven to the conclusion that, in some respects and in some places (particularly the United States), we are witnessing the emergence of its polar opposite, the Misinformation Society.

To avoid misunderstandings I wish to state explicitly that I accept the contention that our advanced industrial economy rests on an increasingly rich information base; that the "information component" of the economy, and thus the proportion of what is called "information workers" (both based on the Porat definition), is steadily growing and now accounts for over half of all economic activity, in the United States at least. And yet I contend that, in the absence of other essential conditions, this does not constitute anything that sensibly may be called an "information society," no matter how great is the information component in the economy. In other words, I take issue with what I regard as the illicit jump from the information economy (a rational and defensible concept) to the information society (in its present form, an illogical notion).

The reason is that the concept of an information society is a "rational" notion only under certain conditions. There are two chief conditions: The first is that the great majority of the population should be in process of becoming increasingly "knowledgeable" through its access to, and utilization of, the overall information treasure house. The second is that this general utilization of enhanced information sources should result in an measurable improvement over time in the *quality* of the democratic citizen's capacity for informed judgment, and moreover that this improved capacity of informed judgment should be brought to bear on the fundamental political issues of the day. In the absence of these conditions, I maintain, the mere existence and availability of vast new information stores is irrelevant, so far as the quality of social and political life is concerned, and the emphasis on their technical qualities alone (for example, the size, interrelations, and speed of access to massive electronic databases) is only a curious fetish.

These propositions will appear less outrageous than they do at first glance in a moment. No one can doubt that specialists can and do utilize new information to do new things of all sorts; when the process of systematically searching for new knowledge and applying it to practical ends is incorporated throughout an economy, we can speak of an information economy. But, as we have already seen, the tradition of technocratic thinking wishes to go well beyond this straightforward observation: the argument is that *qualitative* change (change for the better, of course) in social relations generally will be another outcome of this process. And this tradition suggests that, when this regular utilization of steadily growing knowledge is institutionalized, an "information society" results.

What is especially overlooked here is this: At the very same time when an information economy is coming into being, other changes in society (or at least in some societies) may be eroding the ordinary citizens' abilities to employ richer knowledge sources to make improvements in their capacities for informed judgment on social and political issues. I have three kinds of abilities in mind — basic literacy, ordinary knowledge about the social and political world, and information processing. Since these are complex matters, and since situations in Western nations differ sharply, I shall confine what I have to say on these points to circumstances in the United States.

The technological fetishists among us rejoice in the daily innovations in information delivery through electronic means. Much less attention is paid to a simple question: How many and what kinds of "ordinary citizens" are capable of utilizing this information? It is my contention that the elementary basis for using knowledge in informed judgment in everyday life is *basic literacy*. By this I mean just the capacity to understand and use ordinary, nontechnical language as well as basic mathematical operations: the old-fashioned "three Rs." Many elaborate studies have documented the abysmally poor state of basic literacy in broad sections of the population in the United States. At least one-third of the adult population cannot read at a level adequate to comprehend survival information, such as warning labels on products, or to ascertain whether their paychecks have been properly computed.[17]

Other surveys have sought to measure the average citizen's knowledge of current events both at home and abroad, such as the identity of prominent political figures and the nature of major events reported in the mass media. Results here are equally dismal, showing among other things that much of the vast information stream flows past many individuals unobserved and untapped.

Finally, there is the increasing use of visually oriented media of communication, especially television, as well as the growing predominance of visual imagery for communicating messages, such as in advertising and signposts, in contrast to the relative decline in reading and in the use of print-based information. It is certainly true that information, including highly technical information, can be communicated well by graphical means — and in many cases this may be a superior form of communication. However, a great part of our knowledge base will always involve the manipulation of words and language; and even among those persons who would be counted as having basic literacy, therefore, there is a decreasing amount of exercise for this facility, which over time will result in a diminished capacity. Moreover, in the most important aspects of social and political life we are required to reach an amicable state of mutual understanding with our fellow citizens, in the absence of which the tools of violence are often employed. It seems to me that, for the foreseeable future, we must rely primarily on the medium of words, not the play of visual images, for our attempt to reach such an understanding both at home and abroad.

The Perils of Data Flak

It is no accident that in many economically advanced democratic nations politics is tending to become more of an elaborate exercise in staged image management and less of a meaningful conceptual dialogue.[18] Current technology can offer politicians a second-by-second continuous readout, in graphs, bar charts, and numbers, of the responses by selected audiences to their speeches (the audience members hold electronic response mechanisms in their laps). The politicians' "handlers" then can gauge exactly which words, facial expressions, body gestures, and language tone are correlated with positive and negative reactions, and make the necessary adjustments.[19] The carefully staged appearances of Oliver North before the Congressional committee themselves caused huge swings in public opinion on United States aid to the anti-Sandinista forces.

Examples abound; and what is at stake is by no means a lack of information for the electorate. On the contrary, information is abundant, particularly via the print media, so long as one has the literacy skills and the willingness necessary for finding and digesting it. However, image management and other techniques give rise to an equally impressive quantity of misinformation, disinformation, and what might be called — borrowing from the strategy of anti-aircraft defense — "data flak." As the sum total of accumulated information/misinformation grows, so also there arises the need for skilled piloting to shepherd the precious cargo of genuine knowledge and wisdom through the intense barrages of data flak. To change the metaphor, the abundant data flow carries a great deal of mischievous flotsam and jetsam; elaborate filtering is called for, but the requisite technologies are relatively underdeveloped.

The paradox of the so-called information society is this: On the great issues of society and politics, the role of knowledge in the composition of informed judgment very well may decline in proportion to the increase in available information.

In conclusion: The notions of information society and information technology, at least in their present form, show the impoverished state of technocratic thinking. Erected on flimsy conceptual foundations, composed of hastily recycled terminology, and motivated solely by the conviction that the show must go on, they offer us the old routine: A new technology demands a response from us that is appropriate to *its* essence and modes of action. Since little can be specified at the moment as to what is the larger significance of the so-called information society, the actual message can be stated in stark simplicity: Whatever is happening is inevitable, and therefore we should prepare for it (whatever it is).

Few will deny that the marriage of the computer and communications technologies will have a noticeable impact on occupational structures, industrial and office productivity, employment opportunities, and everyday life. Equally few should be so incautious as to assert that we are in the throes of an "information revolution" that will rival the Industrial Revolution's impact, or that major qualitative changes in social relations will occur as a result. For what is still in the balance is whether the stock of information will exceed that of misinformation, or vice versa.

This skeptical perspective is grounded in a more general outlook concerning the nature of major public policy issues in contemporary society. This outlook in turn is based on the conviction that it is not new technologies, or the "new possibilities" for action embodied therein, which are or will govern the definition of those issues or our responses to them. Rather, they are principally what may be called "allocative" issues, and the solutions to them, such as they are, have zero-sum characteristics.[20] Examples are income policy, national versus regional interests, the relation between employment and social status, environmental protection, and redistribution of inequalities. The great task for public policy is to assist us in finding reasonably civilized ways of dealing with such issues. If we can do so, we will discover that managing the social impact of new technologies is by comparison mere child's play.

21.

Limits to the Imagination: Marketing and Children's Culture

Stephen Kline

The dynamic principle of fantasy is play, and as such it seems inconsistent with serious work. But, without play with fantasy, no creative work has ever come to birth. The debt that we owe to the play of the imagination is incalculable.

Carl Jung

Psychic structure must always be passed from generation to generation through the narrow funnel of childhood; society's child-rearing practices are not just one item in a list of cultural traits. They are the very condition for the transmission and development of all other cultural elements, and place definite limts on what can be achieved in all other spheres of history.

Lloyd deMause

The Patterns of Child-Rearing

This essay[1] argues that a transition is taking place in the "funnel" of contemporary American socialization. Children's obsessions with toys and their apparent "capture" by television fictions are the surface indications of a deeper process. Children's imaginative play has become the target of marketing strategy, allowing marketing to define the limits of children's imaginations.

In *The Evolution of Childhood*, Lloyd deMause has argued that the notion of "socialization" is historical. Socialization, he writes, is a fairly recent way of thinking about and rearing children which arises in the late Victorian period and persists as a dominant feature of American society. "Childhood is a nightmare from which we have only recently begun to awaken."[2]

Earlier approaches to child-rearing, deMause notes, ranged from the "infanticidal" attitudes in Rome to the purposefully harsh and intrusive approaches of eighteenth century England which reflected a propertarian orientation to children. The contemporary "socialization" phase is characterized by new attitudes which are less concerned with conquering the child and dominating its will than with "guiding it into proper paths, teaching it to conform." In industrial society, learning, especially the acquisition of skills (including social skills) and moral codes of conduct, become the most important modality of childhood.

DeMause writes optimistically of an emerging postwar American child-rearing practice he terms "helping," in which the parent believes the "child knows better than the parent what it needs at each stage of its life" and parents struggle to "empathize with and expand its particular needs." The aim of such a practice is the liberation of the child, producing a generation which, parents hope, will be "gentle, sincere, never depressed, never imitative or group orientated, strong willed and unintimidated by authority." While helping children play their way into adulthood is not the predominant mode in contemporary child-rearing, it is one deMause identifies as likely to increase.

Child-rearing in the Culture of Consumption

Writing as he did in the early 1970s, deMause may be forgiven for his mistaken optimism about emerging approaches to childhood. David Reisman and W. Rosenborough, in their outlook at postwar child-rearing, observe a similar growing emphasis on meeting autonomous needs through play and imagination; but they interpret this pattern as pertaining to the problems of socialization in a consumerist "other-oriented" society. As they note, the new consumption ethic is embracing the new child-rearing practice.[3] American socialization processes are being transformed as the exigencies of life in fluid and socially complex consumer culture are destabilizing many of the moral and social dispositions of an earlier work-oriented society.

As William Leiss, Sut Jhally, and I have also argued, market society is a distinctive phase of industrialization which privileges the discourse "through and about goods."[4] In market society, the desire for, and relationships between, persons and products is transformed — as are the social relations and identities which people establish in their everyday life. In contemporary America, the perception of needs and the ability to achieve satisfaction are subsumed by a "magical rationality" of self-transformation through possession and use. This privileged discourse helps to locate satisfaction within the regions of immediate gratification — particularly leisure and entertainment — and accentuates social interactions which engage social judgment and identity. It is not surprising therefore that new patterns of child-rearing reflect these changes, positioning entertainment and play as the crucial activities of childhood. For modern childhood learning about identities and roles has become more important than acquiring skills and moral codes of conduct.

More recent trends only extend these observations. By the time of high school graduation, the average American child spends 17,000 hours being entertained by television while only 11,000 in schooled learning. Before age 12, children average over four hours of television viewing per day (up from about 1.2 hours spent with media in 1955). This implies that they have seen about 20,000 advertisements in a given year or 350,000 before they leave high school. Television advertising for children rose from a very limited $25 million in 1956 (mostly cereal) to over half a billion by 1986. About 55% of this current advertising budget, or $350 million, is for toys.

Parents report rarely watching television with their kids, and have limited ability to play with them on a regular, daily basis.[5] When not in front of the TV or at the movies, the modern child is generally encouraged to play — by which is meant to interact with toys and games either alone or among peers. The toy and games market which is now a $12.3 billion business has grown enormously since 1955. Statistics like this might lead one to wonder whether modern "child-oriented" practices constitute "liberation" — or the abdication of child-rearing itself.

The Cultural Industries and Child Rearing

Historically, as children's involvement with television and toys grew, the "socialization" principle demanded guidance and restriction of children's learning in these venues — especially television advertising. In the 1970s, goaded by advocacy groups like Action for Children's Television (ACT), the Federal Communications Commission (FCC) and Federal Trade Commission (FTC) supervised the development of an elaborate and complex set of guidelines (self-regulation via the Broadcasting Code was an important component of this policy structure) for children's programing and advertising. The guidelines were based on the idea that "children are viewed as a 'special' audience, one that is particularly vulnerable to television messages."[6]

Regulation of children's advertising and programing was built upon the premise that children were not cognitively skilled, sufficiently knowledgeable, or emotionally sophisticated enough to make appropriate decisions in the marketplace; moreover children were more subject to undue influences of peer pressure and advertising. Children could not be expected to know what they want or need, and thus were unable to act as rational, informed decision-makers in the market.

In 1983 this perspective on the special status of children's cultural products was struck a devastating blow by the FCC's *de facto* deregulation of children's television. Deregulation in effect brought into force a new order of child-rearing where kids are implicitly regarded as aware of their needs and capable of expressing them through choice. Indeed many supporters of this view (mainly broadcasters, advertisers, and producers of products for children) portray consumer learning as a necessary feature of childhood in a market society.[7] America's current policy supports the notion that children's consumer interests will be best served by the unrestrained activities of the cultural industries. Consumer education itself is to be conducted in and by the marketplace.

Even while they argued no special status for child audiences, marketing executives recognized kids as a unique market segment. Ironically, they embodied and applied the same "helping" philosophy of childhood that deMause urged for contemporary parenting: Find out what the child says it needs and then help him or her get it. As an executive at Milton Bradley stated:

> Our management philosophy maintains that contact with children through the product development cycle is the best way to assure that we make toys that children will enjoy . . . Research is the vital link between management and the most important people in our business: the children.[8]

Thus the apparent abdication of parenting does not take place in a vacuum. Where the average parent has come to believe that the child "knows its own needs," they take a less directive role in the child's development. But where parents retract their interest, marketing forces increasingly attempt to know and address the needs of children in their drive to profit through satisfying those needs.

One consequence has been increased market research on children. Practical knowledge has accumulated through testing and retesting kids' responses to programs, toys, and play as well as through a careful examination of the child in the family context. This broad research enterprise is eloquently and simply summarized in a recent industry advertisement by a major advertising agent intended to help prospective clients to get to know the children's market. The ad reproduced here [Figure 1] can be read in two ways. First, as a summary of research into children's responses to advertisements. The second reading is as a strategic document which articulates the parameters which have guided children's marketing.

Children as Consumers

The modern parent seeks to achieve satisfactory relations with their children through providing them with the appropriate things, and leaving their children to discover themselves within the environs of the marketplace. This reflects, in part, the change in parents' attitudes described above towards the skills the child needs to survive in modern society. As researchers observed, parents believe that having the right things is essential to a child's social development. Moreover, whereas parents used to give money to children to teach them how to save (and delay gratification) the current practice is now to provide money in order to teach children how to spend.[9] Children are gaining a larger share of discretionary spending because parents want them to learn to buy for themselves.

By way of consequence, the children's market has grown considerably. The discretionary income of the under age 17 set has expanded to approximately $40 billion. For the 44.3 million age 12 and under, allowances ($5 for the average 12 year old) and presents bring their spending power to $4.2 billion. Most of it gets spent very quickly on food treats and toys. Demographics announce greater promise as sheer numbers of children are expected to expand until 1993 and then contract slowly.[10]

Moreover, as students of children's consumption point out, consumerist patterns have become deeply rooted in children's attitudes. For example a recent "Topline" report by McCollum/Spielman Associates reported on thousands of interviews with kids between 6–12 age range.

> Kids today are very brand-conscious, particularly so when it comes to names, labels and brand symbols on the clothing they wear. Clothing has become more important to kids at an earlier age, and stature is conferred when the right brand name is on display . . . . Children who are unsure of themselves will postpone clothing purchases until after they've seen how the class trend-setters are dressing. While they want to be individualistic, they'll stay within the boundaries of what is popular and acceptable.[11]

The above commentary highlights one of the most important things

DMB&B POCKETPIECE #53

How to advertise to the changing child

There are 4½ million children in Canada 12 years old and under. Today they enjoy greater independence, have more money to spend and take a more active role in family purchasing decisions than ever before. Children accompany their parent(s) to the supermarket 1 in 4 times, and choose where the family will eat out 40% of the time. They're very brand-conscious, particularly when it comes to names, labels and brand symbols on the clothing they wear.

It is vital for marketers to understand the complexity of the children's market, which is not one market but three, with children's preferences and values showing major differences according to their age: (1) Pre-schoolers (relying on parental decisions); (2) the 5-8 year olds (the magic years, but also the "age of why"); (3) The 9-12 year olds (with strong peer orientation). Key characteristics common to the 5-12 year olds are: Egocentricity; fun orientation; a need for continuity; the desire to be a little older and the desire to be like other boys or girls. And 7-8 years is the important breakpoint in children's reactions to advertising.

How best to reach this young, aware and growing consumer? Studies by communications experts and psychologists offer some directional guidelines.

1. **Consider the effects of the media themselves on children.** Print fosters reflection and imagination. Radio stimulates imagination. Television leads to an impulsive rather than a reflective style of thought. Typically today's child eats, drinks, plays games, and does homework while the TV set is on and is thus exposed to over 4 hours a day.

2. **Children need a reward/reason to watch.** Children have a low threshold for frustration and boredom. They need an immediate reward either from entertainment provided by the commercial execution or from the product shown as giving pleasure through consumption or use. Show the product big and advertise the brand to children, not the category. Identify and individualize some characteristic of the brand or endow it with 'magic power' which may not be believed at the rational level but can create an aura about the brand. Brand names should receive special emphasis and repetition. Fun is the critical element in appealing to children.

3. **Children enjoy plot or story.** They identify with action and characters in a story, which should be simple, clear, concrete, moving quickly to completion or resolution. The pace, however, should not be too fast, particularly for the under 6's. Story line should not be dependent on audio. Create a personality for your product, it helps promote loyalty. Children respond well to a variety of strategic and tactical elements:

   A. **Fantasy/Role Playing:** Children enjoy a make-believe world they can enter into; and are also drawn to characters with extraordinary capabilities (super heros, folk heros, sports heros or entertainment stars and celebrities). Boys prefer invincible action figures (younger boys animatic or fantasy figures; older boys living male role models and athletes). Girls prefer cuddly creatures, fashion figures or incline to romanticism.

   B. **Conflict:** Children find the use of a conflict situation emotionally arousing and its resolution brings happy feelings.

   C. **Mystery:** The unknown intrigues children, generating curiosity and interest.

4. **Children respond strongly to emotional, non-verbal stimuli.** The following are extremely effective with children:
   Sound Effects/Music/Rhythm—Children are captured by catchy sounds, tunes and tricky combinations of words, which they frequently repeat. They are more attention-getting than dialogue.
   Humor/Comedy—Physical humor (slapstick, surprise and shock effect, etc.) communicates to children of all ages. Adults looking foolish (unsuitable for the very young). Verbal humor (puns, satire, jokes, riddles, dialects, mannerisms) is more effective with the over 8's.
   Action/Movement—Graphic motion is most important in attracting and holding children's attention—people doing things or the product in use.

5. **Children like things that are uniquely their own.** They enjoy non-adult situations and a non-restrictive environment.

6. **Children like to see themselves.** They enjoy watching children like themselves having fun with a product or mastering a problem. The children should be cast a little older than the target group since children desire to be older/stronger/masterful. If there is only one main character, make it a boy since boys will be accepted by both genders, but girls will be accepted only by girls.

For an agency that's not just "kidding around" but knows how to handle this volatile market, please call or write Rupert Brendon, President and C.E.O., D'Arcy Masius Benton & Bowles Canada Inc., 2 Bloor St. West, Toronto, Ontario M4W 3R3, (416) 922-2211.

DMB&B

The D'Arcy Masius Benton & Bowles and
Léveillé Group of Companies

Figure 1

about children as consumers. The social judgment of peers plays a crucial role in children's relationship to products. In the consumer society, as in all societies, people communicate to others through the things they own and use; for children this modality of communication through things is becoming relatively more important.

Marketing people know and accommodate this by designing within television campaigns a saturation factor. Because of limited memories, children must be repeatedly exposed to the toy or brand name. They must also see other children play with them (in ads and real life) and become aware of the popularity of the item through peer as well as television pressure. Reach figures from 80–90% of market and five repeated exposures are considered the minimum to get recognition in the children's market and establish effective peer pressure. The importance of the idea of saturation is that it provides the means of engaging children's social perceptions.

The Limits of Childhood

That children exhibit the consumerist concerns and lifestyle preoccupations of their parents should not surprise us. Other consumer research however, has identified some of the unique features of children's response to the marketplace which reveals a less sophisticated understanding of the social context in which their needs are to be met.[12] Children under age 6 are not really able cognitively to differentiate a program from a commercial. Moreover, kids do not understand much about the commercial television system or the persuasive intent or purpose of advertising. By 8 or 9 years of age they exhibit a growing skepticism about advertising and clearer identification of its persuasive intent and purpose, but this skepticism is not in and of itself an effective defense against the peer pressures advertising engenders.

Kids under age 8 have a different understanding of and relationship to brands. They understand very little about the competitive structure of business and respond to a brand image. The brand image must be easily recognizable to them, unique and memorable if they are to remember it. They show loyalty to products they decide they like and experiment very little with new products. Experience and peer judgment play the largest role in their appreciation of a brand.

Kids' cognitive systems and memory work differently from adults and therefore they cannot retain complex messages about products and need a fair bit of repetition. Therefore advertising for children must use devices which make the idea of the product easily accessible and repeat that idea enthusiastically and often.

Children's Influence on Parents

Spending by children is only a fraction of the spending going on in the children's market. In 1988, parental spending on children under age 12 could total up to $50 billion in the United States. S. Ward and D. Wackman long ago remarked that children's personal consumption is only one of their points of contact in the market and only one of the reasons for marketing through children.[13] A marketing director recently echoed their observation: "The trend is for children to get more decision making authority and exercise that authority at a younger and younger age."[14]

Children influence their parents', friends', and relatives — especially grandparents' — choices in spending money on them. Children do this in several ways, including direct requests in stores and at home, and through "passive dictation" of daily dialogue with parents wanting to avoid conflict and who know what "children want." Much of the purchasing of kids' things is done by others, although giving presents of money to children is, in the late 1980s, increasingly popular. Christmas has always played an important part in children's lives. In 1955, 80% of the toy sales used to be in the three months leading up to this holiday. This is now closer to 60%, in part reflecting kids' own purchase of play things but also the relative expansion of toy gifts for birthdays or even their importance as everyday expressions of parental "caring."

Children shop with parents frequently and many make requests for specific products like cereal and candy. And family life entails a heavy dose of children informing parents, and being consulted about their preferences. A marketing executive from Kenner states "Kids are the determining factor for toy purchases 90% of the time."[15] The changing patterns in the relation between kids and parents and the role of the dialogue about consumption is a crucial element in marketing toys. It means advertising must get kids to want a particular toy and to be able to communicate that want to a parent, friend, or relative. Although children are clearly influencing more of the spending decisions there are also clear limitations as to what marketing to children can achieve. As one executive observes, the ability to motivate pressure on others has limits: "This has to stop some place. There's a point where children simply do not communicate well enough to select favorite brands."[16]

The above limitations help to put changes in the attitudes of parents and kids, and the interactions between them, properly in the context of changes in marketing, because this relationship is a crucial problem for the expansion of the children's market. If special marketing methods are to be developed for the children's market they have first to attract children, provide them with the means of forming and retaining branded preferences, and then enable them to communicate these preferences clearly and directly to those who are purchasing for them.

Marketing to Children

Children are back in style. With their increasing numbers, their own purchasing power, the billions spent on them by their families and their influence on family purchasing decisions, the children's market is strong and will be getting stronger in the years ahead.[17]

As this document for marketers trumpets, kids marketing has arrived in the 1980s. The current changes in the children's market do not merely reflect a shift in parental attitudes, but arise from the concentrated attention of manufacturers and marketers.

More importantly, the 1980s have seen the development of a new strategy for marketing to children. Tom Englehart has termed this the "Strawberry Shortcake" strategy in recognition of the fact that everything that marketers had learned about children's marketing was crystalized as an intentional plan in the marketing of this new line.[18] Brought out in 1980, Strawberry Shortcake wasn't just another doll promoted by mass market advertising. She was a sellable image conceived of by Those Characters from Cleveland, the licensing branch of American Greetings Cards Ltd., to provide instant strong public identification. The image was worth several hundred million dollars in sales of a wide variety of licensed goods ranging from the Kenner produced doll and accessories to stickers, cut-out books, clothing, cups, jewelery, shoes, and food. Moreover, Strawberry Shortcake was not only a decorative motif, but an identifiable character carefully crafted and conveyed through advertising and her very own series of TV specials — the 30 minute animated commercial provided as cheap programing to syndicated private TV stations. These combined licenses provided the total exposure and momentum the new comprehensive strategy demanded.

This combination of television and playthings in a comprehensive and integrated market gambit reversed the time-honored marketing approaches of spin-offs and changed the way kids' cultural products are developed. As Cy Schneider put it these "programming properties are now being designed more for their merchandising potential than for their pure entertainment value."[19] The new barrier to entry into this market is the $20 million or so development costs to be raised by the licensing agent or toy manufacturer for the product-featuring animation program.

Mattel had tried to launch a program featuring its Hot Wheels toys in 1969, but the FTC had frowned on this approach. But in the new climate of the 1980s the FTC and FCC did not seem to object. Licensed character tie-ins have become the new standard. He-Man, Thundercats, Transformers, and Care Bears all quickly followed this new pattern, extending the television special to a full 65 episode, animated serial, providing even higher definition to what had now become the hordes of character toys. The toy market boomed as licenses proliferated and new animation programs flooded the screens. There are currently over 45 different product-tied animation programs showcased on kids-time TV or about 65% of children's programing. Character toys have become the biggest sellers not only in the traditional girls' doll markets but also with boys who used to play predominantly with vehicles. Whereas in 1976, licensed toys represented 20% of the toy market, they now account for almost 70% of toy sales.[20]

The License

Although this strategy is new, in the sense that it has now become the predominant approach for marketing to kids, its roots are deep. Many of the elements of the strategy have been developed in kids marketing over the last 80 years. Product licensing, a crucial aspect of this approach, dates from Teddy Roosevelt's licensing of his name for the "Teddy" Bear (he gave the money to nature conservation). The success of Walt Disney's 1920s Mickey Mouse cartoons soon proved that fictional characters could provide the basis for effective licenses. Disney called his animation "imagineering" — the engineering of imagination; Herman Kamen, an advertising executive, quickly showed him that kids imagining happened while playing, eating, and dressing too. By 1933, over 10 million dollars of Disney licensed merchandise was sold. The subsequent licensing of Disney cartoon characters and later the Disney fantasy world — Disneyland and Disneyworld — is reputed to be making 2 billion dollars a year worldwide for Disney enterprises.

Licensing has become a 54.3 billion dollar a year business with a 15.5% share located in the toy market.[21] Both well known stars (i.e., Mr. T and Michael Jackson) as well as fictional characters (Care Bears, Transformers, etc.) provide the models for these toys while many other lines (clothes, food) reveal a children's character imprint. One of the biggest boosts to licensing in the toy industry were the *Star Wars*/Lucas Films sequels, which have spawned over 2 billion dollars in licensed goods and created an avalanche of character licenses. Licensed toys grossed 8.2 billion dollars in 1986, proving that popular characters could spawn profitable playthings.

Spin-offs

A second element in the strategy was the spin-off. Popular media events could also replicate themselves in other venues. Wrestlemania characters, Farrah Fawcett, A-Team, and Superman have all parlayed their exposure in one venue and market into spin-offs for kids, each with a toy tie-in. The crucial feature of the spin-off is that it cashes in on the already established character and media exposure which helps to increase the personality's definition and recognizability inexpensively.

The most important spin-off in the development of the kids market was probably the Mickey Mouse Club television program created in 1955. Before that time, total children's market advertising only amounted to about one million dollars and the product array for children was rather narrow. Toy manufacturers were on record as believing that they would thrive without mass market advertising on television. Television advertising on kids' TV (especially before the development of video tape) was very limited, consisting of sponsorship announcements and product demonstrations. The problem of funding children's production reflected the lack of interest of advertisers in this market. Kids, they believed, didn't have much money to spend and kids' programing was not sufficiently enticing to draw big audiences.

By transposing Mickey's established film reputation into another venue, the Mickey Mouse Club almost single-handedly established the mass market for kids' cultural products by proving these assumptions midguided. Kids it turned out, even with their limited disposable incomes could still influence consumption. And programing could be devised that provided a full 90% exposure in the marketplace and a sizeable and loyal market share. The unheard of sum of $10 million in advertising revenues was necessary to launch it, but daring marketers, like Mattel with its burp gun promotion quickly learned of the benefits of mass advertising to kids.

The Character

The third and most important element in tie-in marketing is the personality toy. Although Mickey Mouse showed that animal cartoons could be popular with the very young, it was Barbie — the bestselling character of all time — who during the late 1950s and 1960s provided the object lesson in character marketing. "The people at Mattel and the agency . . . began thinking of toys in an entirely new way. We began to see toys as concepts that could be depicted or demonstrated in television commercials" argued one the originators of this approach.[22] Barbie was carefully and consciously designed and marketed not just as another doll, but as a personality. "We didn't depict Barbie as a doll, we treated her as a real-life teenage fashion model." And so Barbie was provided with a Barbie story — a narrative that established Barbie's personality profile within an imaginary but familiar universe.

Barbie's attraction as a doll lay in the way children identified with her character rather than her role. Hence the way they played with her changed. "Somehow Barbie filled a very special need for little girls' imaginations. She was the fulfillment of every little girl's dream of glamour, fame, wealth and stardom." Young girls identified with Barbie and became deeply involved with her. They didn't rehearse motherhood as they did with other dolls but spent hours dressing and undressing her, or just staring and admiring her in her various outfits. The Barbie-story worked and Barbie sold in the millions.

Although character toys came to dominate the girls' market of the 1970s, action toys, especially vehicles for boys, were still dominant attractions. Darth Vadar, the first technomorphic character toy tie-in showed that the action character doll could sell brilliantly to boys as well. Pretty soon, science fiction became the parable of the toy and character toys were freed from the identity constraints of the familiar and the personal. Transformers — half vehicle and half being — parlayed this into a multi-million dollar inconography. The invention of character toys for the boys' market is probably one of the most significant breakthroughs resulting from the tie-in strategy.

Comprehensive Strategy

The final element in the total approach to tie-ins is concept marketing, which uses a comprehensive strategic communication plan. It is comprehensive in that it orchestrates all available channels of communication, achieving a kind of synergy amongst them. This synergy is contained by the unified thematic framework (including the imagery, narratives, characters, and music) which establishes the concept. This concept gives shape to all executions in the strategy, including in-store display, interpersonal communication, advertising, and television programing. Total marketing positions the character toy and its fantasy world as the overarching concept for a whole range of licensed products to be marketed through saturation of all media. The animated series featuring the character toy as its hero is the flagship of this flotilla because of the importance of TV exposure.

Herein we see the deeper problem as children's cultural product design becomes completely subsumed within the tie-in strategy. He-Man, like so many other children's heros, is not just scripted for a child's amusement and moral education. Children must want him, to own and to play with him, to recreate the He-Man Universe within their bedroom. To quote even an outspoken supporter of marketing to children, "What was once the sole province of children's authors, comic strip artists and film artists . . . has now become a creative outlet for toy and greeting card manufacturers."[23] In contemporary television, marketing, rather than entertainment, considerations dominate the design of children's characters, the fictions in which they appear, and hence the way children play. Play, the most important modality of childhood learning is thus colonized by marketing objectives making the imagination the organ of corporate desire. The consumption ethos has become the vortex of children's culture.

Barbie's Problem — The Limits of Imagination

All products have a limited lifetime, toys more so than most. Kids lose interest in particular toys, quickly moving on to other things. After all, emotional and cognitive maturation implies that new psychological needs and states are being expressed and worked out in the child's imaginative play. And besides, kids are extremely peer-oriented. They are subject to the collective whims of their immediate cultural environment which is constantly changing shape and focus. Barbie's miraculous longevity is testimony to the perspicacity of her creators. In part this can be explained by the constant updating of her image achieved through advertising and accessory design. But Barbie represented an old strategy. She was not a tie-in with a show of her own. She was a stand-alone character toy. Barbie relied on children's active imaginations.

Barbie's current rival in the market — Gem — was launched by Hasbro in 1984 with her own Japanese produced animation series and is outselling Barbie. Gem is the embodiment of a comprehensive market strategy — she is a total package. Gem's character is clearly defined and punkishly modern. But most importantly Gem's personality, friends, and exploits are vividly portrayed in a animated television series with a narrative that kids can identify with and follow regularly. Gem achieves this weekly exposure in most young girls' households.

Barbie has a problem. The solution is for Barbie to go modern. She needs a TV show and a rock band and she will be getting both before the 1987 season is out. Barbie's problem is that of the whole toy industry which is changing in the face of the new tie-in strategy. Animate or perish. Barbie's creators believed that Barbie's personality should not be too specific because this might limit the imaginations of the girls who play with dolls. "Each little girl has her own dreams about who Barbie is . . . If you give her a specific personality it could mean that little girls will lose their ability to project whatever personalities they want onto Barbie."[24] Gem proves that the fiction and fantasy provided by programing serve the purposes of marketing more effectively than little girls' imaginations.

The Fiction of Imagination

Bruno Bettleheim has pointed out what every parent knows: children's fiction serves an important part in socializing children, in forming their imaginations, and in creating the framework for learning about their social world.[25] What is at stake is the shape and structure of children's popular culture — children's mythology, heros, and view of the world. As marketing criteria begin to dominate the conjunction of television and toys, so too they underwrite children's imaginative activities through narrative and play.

The 30-minute commercial disguised as a program starts with the distinct advantage that young children don't really conceptually differentiate the toy, the commercial, and the program. Older ones who are more cynical about advertising's persuasiveness than the under 7 year olds also do not see the same intent-to-sell hidden in these "programs." In both cases what matters to the child is the fictional universe which envelops product, program, and advertisement. Children are disarmed by their absorption in the story.

More to the point, the marketing orientation fundamentally changes the nature of the television programs themselves, and hence their broader impact as children's myth and folklore. Programing designed to move products has features unique to those purposes. The fiction in the tie-in strategy must also be cheaply produced while still holding the audience's attention. Moreover it must involve the child with the toy's personality and provide the child with a simple means of communicating with parents their preference for this product. This must be done within the child's limitations of understanding, retention, and communication. These programs reflect everything that marketers have learned about selling to children.

First and foremost, in the 1980s children's fictions are more specifically targeted for children's audiences than previous kids' programing.

This represents clear market segmentation. Unlike Bill Cosby or Disney's nature programs these animations are not intended as family viewing, or even for mixed age groups of children. These programs are designed for afternoon or Saturday morning "ghetto" viewing, with only young children watching. By implication the stories they present preoccupy the child's imagination and fantasy life, but remain almost unknown to the parent. This is a radical departure from folklore traditions where the shared narrative provides a means for parents to convey complex and subtle moral and ethical ideas to their children.

The new programing is animated not only because of the ease and swiftness of production but because, as Disney long ago showed, animation is the superior form of imaginative fiction. Disney discovered that animation brings to life in the visual media themes and characters long extant in old folk and fairy tales. The vividness and attractiveness of anthropomorphic beings represents an acute balance between the familiarity necessary for recognition and the distance necessary for allegory. (Bugs Bunny, for instance, is a classic trickster.) Animation has the added feature that it is never constrained to real objects and their physical properties of movement, transformability, and potential. Animation codifies the break with reality. It is the genre of fantasy par excellence.

Action, especially battle sequences are easily executed in animation. The sequences appear little more than a continuity of poses reminiscent of actors' movements in Kabuki drama. The cartoon creature who acts, thinks, and feels just as humans, but is simplified in form and personality provides a perfect vehicle for children's characterization. The drawings appear infantalized. Characters' features and expressions are reduced to the simplest and most easily recognised by the young. Animators emphasize those features and expressions that children most quickly and easily identify with. Indeed, the characters rarely learn anything in these programs — their nature is inherent and fixed by their species-specific and immutable characteristics. Children can remember these characters well enough to ask their parents for Liono or Starburst She-ra without ever knowing the Mattel name or label. Character serves this function better than brand names.

The narratives are similarly simplified along with the characters. Repetition and predictability are important because younger kids can only remember sequences as isolated bits; only older kids get a sense of program as a whole.[26] Older cartoon shows, such as ones featuring Bugs Bunny or Donald Duck, have folk tale characteristics combined with common quotidian domestic conflicts. Newer cartoon programs are more mytho-heroic in nature. The moral struggles are basic bouts between good and evil, the social contexts less quotidian and realistic, and the resolutions more predictable. Good and evil are clearly differentiated and rarely ambiguous. The forces of Evil are always anti-democratic in their social organization.[27]

Newer cartoon stories have a strange quality of simplified abstraction. For example, in the Care Bears there are no integrated personalities. Each bear represents a single emotional dimension. Similarly, the forces of good and evil are often deployed in teams. This not only arrays the action around specifically skilled personalities (i.e. in the Thundercats each character has a special ability like speed, technical intelligence, strength) but also means that children have to buy multiple characters to reproduce the whole concept in their play.

These narratives are highly gendered. Market research taught the designers that boys and girls respond to different things and become engaged in TV through different forms of imaginative engagement. Action is necessary for boys and caring and social relations for girls. Boys like to engage in conflict and solve problems in play; girls like to touch, cuddle, stroke, dress, and care for their toys. Whereas Bugs Bunny and the Flintstones have been appreciated by both audiences, the current programing reflects a stronger gender bias — with action-oriented science fiction and cute animal fantasies defining the divide.

In fact, the overall momentum of these new animated narratives is towards the fantastic. Each story creates an alternative fictional world in which imagination is (presumably) given free reign. This is the seemingly creative and exciting feature of these programs which have made fantastic fiction and sci-fi the idiom of childhood. Were these fictions unconstrained by the marketing concept one might be in a better position to celebrate this new dimension of children's culture. It is clear, however, this shift to the fantastic is dictated by the marketing problem. As one toy marketer aptly puts this point, "we also realized something more important that persists to this day. The play situation in which you place a toy becomes a fantasy for the child. The fantasy presented becomes as important as the Product."[28] The problem is to engage children's imagination so that the whole of their creative impulse is directed to absorbing the desired orientation to the toy product.

Playing with Imagination

By fusing television and toys within a singular fantasy world, the tie-in strategy must have its most serious consequences on children's play. It is no longer the case that children's television programing functions as a spectacle, drawing children to the medium like the modern pied piper. The programing is there to provide a fictional world in which the attraction to and characteristics of the toy are defined and situated. When the television is off, the fantasy world lives on in the child's imagination, and is recreated regularly in their play. The child therefore, is still "working for" the toy manufacturer long after the program has ended for as long as the fictional world generated in programing still defines the play of the child.[29]

The consequence then is the overdetermination of the structure of play — and the social interaction which surrounds it — by marketing considerations. Observations of children playing with these toys or conversations with them about what they are doing quickly indicates that the emphasis on multiple characters and accessories and on conflict, the bifurcation of good and evil, the simplification of character and narrative, the episodic fragmentation, and the mythological social framework are all internalized and reenacted in play.[30] Play in fact has become highly ritualized — less an exploration and solidification of personal experiences and developing conceptual schema than a rearticulation of the fantasy world provided by market designers. Imaginative play has shifted one degree closer to mere imitation and assimilation.

The consequences however go beyond these limitations on creative exploration. In the first place, because play entails the recreation of a "total fantasy world," multiple character toys, their accessories, and special bases, etc., are necessary for appropriate play. The expense of toys and the numbers of them one must buy to engage in appropriate fantasy play has increased. In addition the child-orientation itself and the segmentation of audiences by gender implicit within the marketing strategy has a most noticeable effect. First, parents are further excluded from play with their children simply because parents do not know the fantasy world well enough to engage their children in imaginative play with these toys. Most parents report hating playing with these character toys (they find it boring and pointless), and most children report that their parents don't know what to do with them. What neither understands is that playing together assumes a shared fantasy — a condition which no longer exists.

The same exclusion by imagination is at the root of a growing divide between boys and girls at play. Since the marketing targets and features different emotional and narrative elements (action/conflict vs. emotional attachment and maintenance) boys and girls also experience difficulty in playing together with these toys. The advertisements, which most precisely represent marketing's conception of how children play with toys, reveal single sex groupings in 95% of ads.

No parent can deny that toys and television are attractive, some would say obsessive, mainstays of contemporary child-rearing. Yet watching children play absorbed in their packaged fantasy life, many have begun to wonder whether ritualized imaginative production isn't limiting children's creativity while isolating the child from parents and children of the other sex. Yet these are the direct consequences of letting the increasingly sophisticated marketing orientation dominate the most important modalities of socialization — children's imaginations. More worrisome still, is the possibility that the marketing approach developed in the children's market will become the adult marketing of the future: Coming soon — the Miami Vice Strategy.

22.

The Privatization and Transnationalization of Culture

Herbert I. Schiller

The commercialization of culture is no new phenomenon in the United States. It extends back to the earliest days of the Republic. In contrast with Western Europe capitalist economies, where for historical reasons at least some elements of culture were promoted and sustained by national and local governmental treasuries, with few exceptions, in the United States, the arena of culture has been largely in the hands of business.

A brief period of governmental support for the cultural arts occurred during the Great Depression in the early 1930s. At that time, cultural workers, no less than industrial workers, received some Federal assistance. An unexpected consequence was a burst of creativity that lasted beyond the few years that the assistance was available.

After the Second World War federal subventions to the arts — those that were forthcoming — can be attributed mainly to the ornamentation and "humanizing" of the newly emerged Imperial Society.

The Post World War II Period

In the last forty years, and especially in the last twenty, new social forces, with their own special needs, have come into prominence. The central actors in this era, increasingly influential, are the giant private companies (transnational corporations, TNCs), that operate on a global scale, busy in dozens and sometimes scores of countries. *IBM*, for example has a presence in 130 countries.

Developed also in this interval, have been the new information technologies: the computer, the communication satellites, cable and fiber optics. These technologies, powerful and unprecedented in their capabilities by overcoming spatial and temporal constraints, have been acquired by the global companies, enormously facilitating their daily operations, creating a world market for their goods and services, drastically changing the balance of power between capital and labor to the advantage of the former, and eroding rapidly the authority of national decision-making.

In the present era of transnational corporations and electronic information technologies, the national market, the national public sphere — where it exists — and national sovereignty increasingly are either bypassed, weakened, or eliminated. The imperatives of the global market set the agenda that the actors in that market, the TNCs, *must* follow. It is hardly a matter of corporate malevolence, managerial deviousness, or commercial insensitivity. One, or all, or none of these factors may be involved. But they are not decisive, and most often, not even relevant.

Given the scale of the drama and the size and power of the participants, the pressures released by the forces at work are tremendous. It is to be expected that individuals, values, institutions, even governments, that find themselves dissatisfied with these forces, will be compelled, all the same, to make accommodations, agreeable or not, if they hope to survive.

One important additional circumstance affects global relationships at this time. This is the conjunction of vast American *national* power, alongside the transnational authority of its corporate sector. It is embodied in the awesome nuclear arsenal, and the means to deliver it anywhere in the world. This power affords the leaders in the United States a large — though by no means complete — measure of exceptionality from the general condition of weakened national sovereignty throughout the capitalist world sector. For the time being, the United States must still be regarded as the center of the transnational system, more capable of influencing others than being influenced itself. But this has to be understood as a qualified and temporary condition, undergoing continuing erosion.

These circumstances produce what seems to be a contradiction in the developments in the United States. The rise to paramountcy of the transnational corporation has been achieved earlier and has gone further than elsewhere. These super, private economic entities exert enormous politico-cultural influence. At the same time, the role of the United States as the center of the TNC world system has meant a correspondingly more active command assignment for the American State. The paradox then, is this: the TNCs insist on and achieve "deregulation" — exemption from social accountability. Moreover, the wave of deregulation that began in the United States, in recent years, has washed over Western Europe and elsewhere. More about this later.

While giant American-owned companies cavort domestically and internationally, increasingly outside the rule of national law and governance abroad, United States state power, in its most coercive forms — military, police, intelligence — also grows rapidly. The Imperial State, and the deregulated giant corporation, are the centers of gravity in the world market economy in the waning years of the twentieth century.

The impact of these developments is experienced deeply and daily in the lives of working people across the nation — and increasingly, across the globe. No less affected are the cultural institutions as they are enveloped by corporate efforts to control individual consciousness in all spheres of its formation. Accordingly, the structural bases of education, science, and the arts are being reshaped to the specifications of the corporate order and its guardian, the "law and order" State.

Education

To secure a labor force with the training and outlook a "modern" corporation active in the world market requires, a company finds it can no longer depend exclusively on State-supported educational facilities and systems. To be sure, the business community continues to employ those who have been trained in the general educational, private enterprise framework provided in the public schools and state and private universities.

Yet even more frequently, longterm relationships are being established between major companies — sometimes consortia — and leading universities. These arrangements usually involve high technology subject areas of profit potential to the firm. For the universities and the engaged academics, it is a source of additional funds and equipment. The full impact of these still-evolving relationships is yet to be known. Already there is evidence and concern that the "science business" may be imposing structural, market priorities, though never absent in the past, in a much more systematic way on university activity.

Beyond the growing ties between corporate business and the academy, there is a still more direct link between education and the corporation. A Carnegie Foundation special report, suggestively titled, *Corporate Classrooms: The Learning Business*,[1] informs that American corporations now are spending each year upwards of $40 billion, "approaching the total annual expenditure of all America's four-year and graduate colleges and universities, to train and educate their employees" (p. ix). In 1978, it is reported that "business firms gave in-house training to about 6.8 million trainees" (p. 7). The dimensions of direct corporate education are astonishing. *A.T. & T.*, according to one account, "performs more education and training functions than any university in the world" (p. 8). *IBM* in 1982 invested half a billion dollars in employee education. Not surprisingly, "corporate learning centers are more modern, sleek and up-to-date (than traditional colleges with classrooms)." "They surpass many universities in their sophistication both in range of offerings and in the delivery of systems and methods as well. They are not factory-bound, *they are global*, and a single corporation may be educating in New York, Rio de Janeiro, Tokyo, and Rome" (pp. 47–48, emphasis added). Since the bulk of direct corporate education is provided by the transnational companies, the *Fortune 500*, "their education and training programs are exported to large numbers of employees and customers; they create global classrooms. *And corporation trainers are teaching the citizens of other countries in a new kind of universal education*" (p. 9, emphasis added). This internationalization of corporate instruction is regarded as unequivocally beneficial to foreign recipients — who are considered to be fortunate to share in what U.S. trainees also are receiving. The Carnegie Report sees this education meeting "the real needs of an interdependent global community" (p. 1).

Is it not remarkable how the language of cooperation and community is utilized to describe a process that might more truthfully be viewed as a blatant means of cultural indoctrination, of service primarily to the national companies?

In any case, education in America, and in numerous locales abroad, is being saturated with corporate values, as well as selective job skills, either directly transmitted in "corporate classrooms," or through the intermediation of universities, increasingly interlocked with, and dependent on, corporate finance.[2] The Carnegie Report finds this a necessary development. "If America is to be an effective international competitor, their innovation, vitality and effective training of the work force are key ingredients. Corporate education and university-business ties will need to be strengthened" (p. 4). And they *are* being strengthened, year by year.

The Informal Educational System:
The Broadcast Media

Television, despite academia, where it is still generally regarded as unworthy of scholarly attention, is now the main, though largely unac-knowledged, educator in the country. The omnipresence of television, and the amount of time consumed in its viewing, far surpass total formal instruction. Today, for a large part of the population, TV is the teacher, though the lessons transmitted rarely are recognized as such. Perhaps most important of all, the programing that is sandwiched between the commercials invariably is produced with the sponsor's interest in mind. Serious (to say nothing of socially critical) programs are rarely broadcast as they are likely to unsettle the major advertisers — the TNCs. Because home-situated television is so central to family routines, it is watched for many hours daily in the "free time" of the viewer. It makes no claim to; in fact, it denies, instructional value. It is simply providing "entertainment." It is the combination of this home-based medium and its illusory value-free imagery that makes television the preferred, indeed, the indispensable instrument of commerce and ideological mastery.

Since its arrival in the late 1940s in the United States, television has served essentially as a marketing force, flooding viewers with thousands of electronic advertisements, dozens of them inserted in each transmitted hour. In 1985 on network television alone, excluding local station advertising, there were 5,131 commercials broadcast.[3] Yet even this deluge of commercialism presents an incomplete picture. Increasingly, efforts are being made to introduce marketing where it is not immediately recognized as overt sponsorship. As *Business Week* describes it: "If you've got thousands of dollars to spend and the right intermediary, you don't have to buy a TV commercial for exposure. You can buy your way on to the guest lineup of a talk show or even star in a feature segment focusing on your life." The magazine notes that these developments "are blurring the distinction between advertising and programming content."[4]

The near-total monopolization of television for corporate marketing, represents at the same time, the daily ideological instruction of the viewing audience. This occurs, first of all, in the incessant identification of consumerism with democracy. Additionally, more recently, the advertisements (commercials), carry special social messages that emphasize anti-communism, jingoism and entrepreneur worship.

Non-Commercial Broadcasting

One development in American broadcasting that has special saliency for the rest of the world, is the fate of public (non-commercial) television and radio. Never a strong institution, as it has been in Western Europe and other locales, public broadcasting has lost most of the little autonomous space it once briefly held. Always short of resources, and generally occupying the less preferred part of the radio spectrum — the

UHF band — public broadcasting did succeed, on the basis of some program importation and some thoughtful domestic cultural material, to gain a small, though affluent and influential slice of the national viewing audience.

These high income viewers who were attracted to the non-commercial channels, though relatively few, constituted an important opinion-making grouping and a high disposable income class. It was inevitable that they would become a target of the big advertisers. And so it has gone. At first, discreet announcements at the beginning and the end of programs indicated that the shows were being made available by courtesy of the public-spirited super companies.

Once the corporate foot was in the door, the erosion of the principle of non-commercial broadcasting accelerated. Under "enhanced guidelines" — language that soothes, while it conceals the destruction underway — the deregulation-prone Federal Communications Commission in 1984, allowed greater scope for sponsors' messages. Still discreetly framed, they were accepted "as part of a Federal effort to decrease public broadcasting's reliance on government support." A year later, the *New York Times* was asking rhetorically, not desiring to confront the reality, "Is Public TV Becoming Overly Commercial?"[5]

Since public TV never was a flourishing enterprise in the United States, its further enfeeblement is mostly symptomatic of the general malaise — the *seizure of all cultural space by corporate business*. Yet it provides a model of what lies ahead for other national systems of public broadcasting and public cultural sphere activity if they follow in the American wake. In sum, what was never permitted to develop extensively in the United States, and what is being attacked and undermined elsewhere, are the principle and practice of public service broadcasting, and, more broadly, the public sphere of culture.

What the public sphere of culture in the broadcast realm means, and what its loss entails, are explained by the British Broadcasting Research Unit:

> Public service broadcasting is an attempt to embody, in the era of electronic communication, the notion of a public sphere as central to the democratic polity. The public sphere is that arena of social interaction within which public opinion is formed and mobilized by a reasoning public . . .
>
> In the public sphere human beings act as citizens possessing duties as well as rights. It is here that public service broadcasting as an embodiment of the public sphere comes most fundamentally into conflict with any market-based system of broadcasting; for the two systems mobilize fundamentally different concepts of their audience and of the set of social relations which bind them to their audience and

each member of that audience to other members. The market addresses humans as individual consumers driven by the pursuit of self-interest . . . Public service broadcasting is obliged to address its audience as rational citizens and to provide them with the information upon which a long national debate can be based.[6]

Rational citizens are the last thing on earth that corporate advertisers seek. It is no accident that structures of public service broadcasting and culture are their primary targets, scheduled for demolition.

Libraries and the Public Sphere of Information

Along with the general education of non-commercial broadcasting, the public library system constitutes a basic component in the public sphere of culture. The library has been a community project from its earliest origins in America. Its longterm contribution has been to provide information, *as a social service*, to all who seek it. Yet here too, the pressure of commercialism is transforming what has been a major democratic bulwark of information access into a system that offers information as a commodity for sale to those with the ability to pay for it. The increasing commercialization of information and the destruction of the public library principle of universal access to information provided by the community is a process still underway but already well-advanced.

The combination of huge stocks of information derived from enormous governmental expenditures, mostly military, on research and development over the last half century; the development of the computer and sophisticated information handling and processing techniques; and the informational needs of transnational business (banks, transport, service, and industrial), the Pentagon, and huge governmental bureaucracies, have created in the last few decades a powerful private information industry. It is this for-profit information sector that is appropriating information stock, capturing the collection and organization of data, insisting on its right to process and sell information, and, most audaciously, claiming that social criteria for informational access and use are detrimental to (its) growth and viability.

The private for-profit information industry in the United States is creating networks, establishing data bases, gaining access to governmental supplies of information originally collected at public expense, and denying the library system its historic function of supplying the general public with information paid for by social subvention.

The growing strength of the private information sector, it may also be noted, is regarded by some influential American decision-makers as a new means of worldwide control, one which may replace the crumbling pillars of manufacturing power. The dynamics of the private information industry and its corporate clientele continue to widen the sphere of commercialized information, weaken the public's access, and try to prepare for a new international division of labor in which the information component confers privilege and authority.

Free Speech and the Corporate Voice

Public expression of the business perspective also is not a new phenomenon in the United States. The existence of private, commercial media since the beginning of the Republic guaranteed that the outlooks and interests of property would be well, if not overrepresented, in the land.

What characterizes the present moment is the availability of a new technological capability of communication — television, cable, satellites, computers — that is available, very largely though not exclusively, to corporate messages and imagery. A tremendous production of "corporate speech" at this time is the outcome of enormously expanded corporate resources, the availability of new means of communication that penetrate the home, and the increasing number of social conflicts, domestic and international, that affect company balance sheets. The modern company defends and extends its interests with every conceivable technological, economic, political, and ideological instrument. Corporate activity in the ideological sphere is now commonly called corporate speech.

At the same time, corporations have been pressing, with considerable success, to have their messages and imagery regarded as individual speech. This may seem unexceptionable, but if this interpretation prevails, as it seems likely to, it will recast completely the cultural climate at home and abroad. Seizing on a fiction that was first created more than a century ago, when judicial rulings accorded corporations the status of legal "persons," the current extension of the fiction insists that the corporate legal "person" is no less entitled to the protection of the free speech provisions of the United States Constitution's First Amendment than is the ordinary "human" citizen. With this interpretation, still disputed but receiving increasing acceptance in judicial rulings, multi-billion dollar enterprises are enabled to move boldly into the arena of public expression. Their voices, amplified with the dense mass media circuits that their huge resources can command, are making it difficult to hear the faint voices of individuals and the general public.

Applying the free speech principle to advertising, the results are grotesque. Still, corporations realize that market control depends on unrestricted advertising, domestically and internationally. Interference with the corporate marketing message threatens market penetration and share and, more critically still, the viability of the system itself.

The highly publicized Nestle infant formula case in the mid-1970s — featuring worldwide protest against Nestle's promotional campaigns in poor countries — alarmed the global marketeers.[7] More upsetting still was the passage of an International Code by the World Health Organization in 1981. (The United States' delegate voted *alone* not to accept the code, while more than 100 national delegates supported it.) The code upheld the principle of national supervision of messages that affected the health of the population.

More recently, efforts by respectable organizations such as The American Cancer Society and the American Medical Association to limit or ban entirely tobacco ads have made the advertising industry and its corporate clientele more insistent than ever to secure free speech rights for their promotions.[8] The president of the American Association of Advertising Agencies argues that a ban on cigarette advertising, for example, is unconstitutional. "We have studied the situation in great depth," he said, "Our position has always been that a product that is legal to sell should be legal to advertise because advertising is the most efficient form of selling."[9] More shrill is the claim of the senior vice president and general counsel of *Ted Bates Worldwide*, one of the ten largest United States owned international advertising agencies before it was bought up by the new super ad firm, Satchi and Satchi, in May 1986:

> The suggestion that commercial speech be denied First Amendment protection is chilling to those who believe both in civil liberties and in a free market system . . . Luckily for all of us, the Supreme Court has recognized that the First Amendment protects speech whether used for the purpose of selling goods or selling ideas . . .[10]

In light of the most recent Court rulings, this may be an overly sanguine view. The threat to the domestic and global market system that an assault on advertising poses, is not imaginary. The daily reinforcement and promotion of the consumer society and its corporate foundations constitutes the primary role of advertising. Not unimportantly also, in 1985, $95 billion were spent on advertising in the United States.

The defense of corporate speech receives the support of Western European, corporate-dominated bodies as well. As reported by two English researchers: "Currently the EEC and the Council of Europe are interpreting Article 10 of the European Human Rights Convention to suggest that 'commercial speech . . . and freedom of expression are so intimately connected as being incapable of being dissociated.' " They conclude: "Law is mobilized to constitute freedom — the freedom of consumer capitalism — as the right to transmit advertisements across national frontiers, and as the right to consume such multinational messages and images.[11]

More will be said in the next section about the internationalization of corporate culture through advertising and other means. Here, it cannot be overemphasized that the far-ranging campaign to confer free speech privileges on corporate messages is, and will remain, a crucial ideological and economic battleground. The chief contending forces are the corporate titans in the economy, including but extending far beyond the advertising industry. It embraces all those groups comprising the general public concerned with the physical, cultural, and human environment.

In the current climate, that finds bigness in business good, and any governmental effort that protects the citizen, bad, it is not unlikely that corporate speech will continue to increase and that it will receive greater protection under different national laws. At the same time, the channels that are open to genuine individual expression, are closing down, partly as a consequence of inadequate economic support — who can afford to communicate? — and partly as a result of judicial rulings that tilt the balance more decisively toward corporate, and away from, individual expression.

Indicative was a recent decision of the New York State Supreme Court which ruled that private shopping malls "are not public places where citizens are free to distribute politically related pamphlets as they please."[12] According to the Court, the shopping mall is not the modern equivalent of yesteryear's Main Street, though the mall is where most Americans now do their shopping. Further, the guarantees of freedom of speech and assembly in the New York State Constitution are, according to the Court, applicable only to protect people against government action, not against the restrictions that may be imposed by the private property owners of the mall.

This is a frequently encountered argument in corporate-dominated America. Attention invariably is directed to the threat of governmental abuses (of excess power, restrictions on individual freedom, etc.), of which there have been an abundance in the historical record, to be sure. Yet little or no concern is evident about the *actual* situation of almost limitless corporate capability to do what it pleases in the economy and with the culture.

In any case, the mall ruling, if extended to other states — California, for example, permits public expression in malls — is a significant abridgement of the public's right and possibility to communicate. Coming as it does, at a time when corporate speech waxes, the effect is to make still more marginal and feeble, non-commercial expression. The public sphere of expression and creativity is being narrowed to the point of inaudibility and invisibility. The corporate sector's speech has become the indisputable national voice. We are, to borrow an expression from Stafford Beer, in "a reduced ecology of thought, sensation and environment."[13]

Transnational Media Culture

While corporate speech has become a central component of domestic cultural and economic life, it is also, increasingly an urgent issue in international relationships. Actually, corporate speech is closely connected to the concern evident in many nations — largely, but by no means entirely, in Asia, Africa, and Latin America — expressed in the demand for a new, international information order. Clearly, this concern collides with the "free flow of information" principle, the non-negotiable standard of corporate America. "Free flow" is the ultimate embodiment of corporate speech. Included are familiar media products such as film, TV programs, magazines, records, cassettes, books, and advertising, as well as the huge volume of financial, economic, and organizational data that allows the transnational corporate order to function. In fact, the free flow of information principle serves as the protective umbrella for the totality of the corporate product in the informational-ideological-economic sphere. It is the expression of the non-material activity of the global corporate system, crucial to its operation in all fields.

Corporate speech, in this sense, is indistinguishable from corporate global activity. Accordingly, challenges to this "speech" are regarded as violations of freedom. Specifically, it is the corporation's freedom to receive and transmit messages anywhere, anytime.

The media products of the American cultural industries began to flow into the international area after World War I, with the growth of Hollywood and the movie industry. By the mid-1920s, American films were shown on screens around the world and the industry had developed a global distribution apparatus that rivaled the size of the United States foreign service. At the end of World War II, a new surge of American media-cultural outputs flooded the world market. This time the flow expanded to include television programs, news agency transmissions, books, magazines, and musical recordings. The late 1940s and the 1950s constituted the brief era in which the free flow principle was elaborated and promoted at the governmental level and which offered full state support to the export of American media goods and services.

By the end of the 1960s, the principle began to be questioned, especially by the newly independent nations, in UNESCO, the United Nations, and many meetings of the non-aligned states. This was the time of the genesis of the demand for a new international information order (NIIO). The order was never fully formulated, but essentially it emphasized less unidirectionality of the cultural-information flows from a few centers to the rest of the world, less concentration in the production of the imagery and messages, and less commercialization, or, at least, an expanded value of non-commercial cultural materials.

The movement for a NIIO crested in the mid-1970s, and was the source of some spirited discussions but few substantive changes, In fact, before any reduction in the inequities in the international information flow could be effected, the NIIO movement encountered the telecommunications "revolution."

The introduction and utilization of the new information technologies, the computer and communication satellite in particular, in the United States economy, increased strikingly the power and flexibility of the big transnational companies. Served by the satellite and computer, the information infrastructure has become the nervous system of the world business economy. Companies are enabled with the new instrumentation to shift capital and production to wherever returns can be maximized. The same capability permits transnational capital to batter down, or sometimes merely elude, whatever national and public protection and accountability exist and which stands in the way of unalloyed market decision-making.

The *Business Roundtable*, an organization that includes the chief executives of the few hundred most powerful United States companies, explains the new role of information in the worldwide operations of its members:

> In the past fifteen years, the flow of information across national borders has increased dramatically. This international information flow (IIF) includes everything from internal corporate information transfers to trade in information-based products and services. IIF has expanded international markets and made possible the provision of new products and services to those markets. IIF has allowed multi-national enterprises to improve their services to their customers, consolidate their resources, control their costs, and reduce their financial risks. IIF has transformed the way in which all companies, manufacturing or service, do business internationally.[14]

For these reasons, the *Roundtable* puts at the top of its Information

Policy Issues Agenda, the free flow of information. It states: "The free flow of information internationally advances the human condition and enhances both national economies and the world economy." Accordingly "The U.S. approaches (all information questions) from the premise that the 'free flow of information' should be foremost, and that any exceptions to this principle for other overriding public policy interests should be limited and narrowly drawn" (p. 17). It is now blindingly apparent that the 'free flow' principle serves the totality of transnational capital's objectives and fuses economic, political and cultural ends.

The clearcut economic contribution of the new information technologies resides in their capability to allow companies engaged in worldwide operations to make important resource allocation decisions rapidly — labor, raw materials, investment, technology transfer — on the basis of global intelligence reports, and to implement their decisions quickly. Less obvious is the greatly strengthened capability the new communications affords to penetrate old and new territories and realms with the marketing/ideological message. It is in this latter sphere that the activities of the transnational advertising agencies assume significance — first, in overcoming national barriers to the commercial messages they create and transmit and, second, in saturating the information and cultural space of the newly penetrated regions. How this works and how it is assessed by the ideological combines that carry out these missions, is succinctly put in a publication of the International Advertising Association's Global Media Commission: The objective is "World class products being sold by uniform advertising campaigns on commercial television around the world."[15]

In 1986, the already huge international advertising agencies are preparing for still greater global activity. The motivation for a recent merger of three major U.S. firms into the second largest advertising company in the world, is explained by its new chief executive officer: "We want to be nothing less than advertising's creative superpower."[16]

Up until recently, several obstacles limited the international advertisers and their transnational corporate clientele.

> Broadcasters have long had the technical resources to reach the whole world with commercial signals, notes the IIA's study, but many political, economic and social barriers made such services impractical. Now those barriers are being splintered and scattered by irresistible technological innovations and the social, political and economic repositioning that follow.[17]

In a word, the national institutions and organizations that protected or insulated the cultural space of a nation, i.e., the state-owned posts, telegraph and telecommunications services (PTTs), and national broadcasting systems, are being weakened and circumvented by the efforts of the transnational corporation to gain access to previous strictly supervised national information circuits.

As the International Advertising Association sees it:

> The magical marketing tool of television has been bound with chains of laws and regulations, in much of the world, and it has not been free to exercise more than a tiny fraction of its potential as a conduit of the consumer information and economic stimulation provided by advertising. Those chains are at last being chiseled off. Irreversible forces are at work to vastly increase commercial television in Europe and around the world. There will be new commercial channels and far fewer restrictions on existing advertising media. (p. 18)

The International Advertising Association also is aware that the great expansion of advertising that it foresees will require programing around which commercials will be sandwiched. Where will this material come from? One source, surely, is the vaults that contain thousands of old Hollywood films and more recent U.S. commercial TV programs. Another source, if the IAA's recommendation is followed, is for: "Advertisers" (to) underwrite programing of general appeal, providing that programing free of charge to the financially struggling broadcasters of the world. The programing will include advertising for the world-class products of the advertisers (p. 40). In either case, the ultimate sponsor of the world's TV programing — the daily culture of the late twentieth century — will be transnational corporate enterprise. The IAA recognizes that this may create some dissatisfaction. It notes therefore:

> There always will be those who find the very idea of advertising repulsive, and would prefer that programs be paid for by public taxation . . . There is no real answer to that kind of economic isolationism; its proponents have a view of the world that regards capitalistic bustle with distaste. Perhaps U.S. broadcasters should sponsor seminars for European broadcasters so they can pass on their techniques for coping with such criticism. (pp. 49–50)

Seminars do not seem to be necessary. The continuing expansion of electronic networks, cable, and satellite, and their utilization for commercial broadcasting proceeds uninterruptedly in Western Europe and is underway elsewhere.

The 1986 International Television Annual, published by *Variety*, announced triumphantly on its first page: "Europe Is Facing Commercial TV" and that "Media Barons (are) Gathering Local Support." Dozens of laudatory pages are devoted to Silvio Berlusconi, the Italian entrepreneur who has transformed Italian TV into a commercial system and who is now devoting his energies to doing the same for France and other European countries. "Under the free-flow rules of the European Common Market," *Variety* observes, "there's nothing to stop him, or any other European, setting up shop in each of the 12 EEC nations." No less blunt, is *Variety's* appraisal of what the commercialization of European TV represents: ". . . the historical concept that a nation can control the shape and content of broadcast media is out the window . . ."[18]

But it is not only the capability of the nation to shape its broadcast media to its own specifications — important as that is — that is being destroyed. It is the entire informational-cultural sphere that is being withdrawn from national jurisdiction by the transnational corporate system, availing itself of the new communication technologies. The *Business Roundtable* is emphatic on this:

> The sovereign right of nations to determine their own telecommunications policies is not the issue; rather, it is the international consequences of these national policies that may be subject to legitimate challenge by other countries whose interests are adversely affected.[19]

Otherwise put, it is not the transgressor of national sovereignty who is at fault. It is the defense against the transgressor that the corporate order proscribes.

No less enthusiastic in cheering on the perceived demise of national sovereignty, is the former chairman of *Citicorp*, a longtime influential advocate of deregulation in all spheres of the economy. "The electronic revolution [sic]," he writes, "affects economics as well as politics, radically weakening the power of governments to dictate politics that run counter to the preferences of individuals in the market place without paying a price in the value of their currencies."[20] The "individuals in the marketplace," who are given so much weight by the former *Citicorp* executive, are the transnational companies who, it is true, to not hesitate to transfer their funds from place to place, at a moment's notice, depending on rates of return and their perception of "stability."

The weakening of national sovereignty is the international equivalent of the erosion of the public cultural sector domestically. In both instances, the burdens are borne by the individual and the community. The benefit is appropriated by capital. When the non-commercial media — broadcasting, the public library, public space itself — are victimized by the onrush of privatization and deregulation and rampant profitmaking, the very roots of democratic governance are cut.

When asked why there should be a subsidized national theater, funded from the State Treasury, Peter Hall, the British director, observed that a national theater had to be considered the last defense against United States commercial television programing.[21]

Conclusion

Though the drive of the world business system into national cultural-information space is powerful and cannot be minimized, it also should not be exaggerated and made to seem irresistible. The fragilities and rivalries in the international market economy each day grow more intense. The possibility of ruptures, breakdown and collapse in the system is never absent and is, in fact, not a distant likelihood.

Alongside the deep fissures in the economic-financial crust of the system, there are cultural resistances, manifested in innumerable ways, in regions and countries in the world community. Not least, the experiences of colonialism in scores of societies are deep and still fresh. They are hardly conducive to new, however modernized and cosmetized, forms of external control and tutelage. How these forms of resistance will develop in one site or another, must be the subject of detailed analysis and scrutiny. Inside the United States, a revitalization of the public sphere is imperative, but how and when this will occur is still obscure.

23.

Media Beyond Representation

Ian H. Angus

But as for myself, that unfailing pastime, I must say it
was far now from my thoughts.

Samuel Beckett, *Molloy*

The Media in Competitive Capitalism

Modern society begins with the separation of the economic sphere of
action from the control of the state. Economic self-interest, which is
defined by the individual alone, is the sole consideration of value in this
private sphere. Politics, by contrast, is taken to be the sphere of public
deliberation about the good society, where what is good for all is the
sole consideration. Thus, we may speak of "conflict of interest" when
private, economic self-interest invades the public, political domain.
We take the separation of these two institutional spheres for granted
and criticize any other society in which this separation has either
not taken place or is not regarded as legitimate for its suppression of
individual rights. By "individual rights," we mean the economic right
of the pursuit of individual wealth, and also of rights of individuality in
general — such as the defense of a private sphere of action free from
state control, participation in democratic self-government, "personal"
religious beliefs, and so on. This separation of economics from politics
is the liberal core of modern society. Its institutional basis is generally
regarded as legitimate by those called "conservatives" and "socialists,"
as well as those known as "liberals" in a conventional sense.

   The American, French, and (more historically drawn out) English
revolutions set the stage for this institutional separation. The sphere of
economic self-interest, or "capitalism," was taken to be legitimate but
not sufficient for the self-governance of society. For, clearly, a society
that is *only* ruled by individual self-interest will constantly tend to be

torn apart or taken over by the strongest.

Adam Smith's doctrine of the "hidden hand" in economic exchange both reflected this principle, and played a role in social policy. He argued in *The Wealth of Nations* (1776) that a society in which each individual pursues only individual self-interest produces, behind the back of the individuals, without anyone's direct attention, the general good for society as a whole. Variants of this doctrine still abound as defenses of a "minimum" of state intervention in the economy. However, even this position requires a minimum state to provide the *preconditions for* a capitalist economy. It must guard against monopoly control of the market and regulate the printing and circulation of money, for example. Moreover, there are several essential functions for capitalism which cannot be made cost-effective for individual enterprise — such as transportation, and, more recently, education. There are still more functions that are required to stabilize society beyond simply providing the preconditions for a capitalist economy (though of course they do serve to stabilize society in its capitalist form) such as combating crime and national defense. These functions have grown much larger as capitalist society has developed. Thus, a minimum wage, regulation of production processes such as the use of chemicals, a certain level of health and welfare for the population at large, as well as subsidies for "culture," have been increasingly guaranteed and developed by the political function of the state. There are considerable differences between countries in the extent to which these functions are taken over by the state, and the United States probably has less commitment in this area than any other advanced capitalist country. Nevertheless, in all such societies some concern with the general good is regarded as the legitimate concern of the state.

In all societies characterized by an institutional separation between economic and political spheres there is a question of how self-interest can be "mediated" such that political life is concerned with the general good and is not just a tool of the most powerful economic interests. How can individual self-interest "pass over" into the public good? In general, it is the function of media of communication to perform such a "mediating" role. During the American revolution, public meetings, pamphlets such as Tom Paine's *Common Sense* (1776), and newspapers played a key role in articulating individual discontent in such a way that it became a common political issue. This role was ratified in Article 1 of the 10 original amendments to the Constitution which came into force in December 15, 1791.

> Congress shall make no law respecting an establishment of religion, or prohibiting the free exercise thereof; or abridging the freedom of speech

or of the press; or the right of people peaceably to assemble and to petition the Government for a redress of grievances.

It is this article, and its subsequent interpretations by the courts, that provides the basis for the role of media of communication in mediating private economic self-interest and a public, political conception of the general good. (The Canadian Constitution Act of 1982 sought to update the reference to freedom of the press by adding "and other media of communication" to the standard guarantee.)

This article places alongside each other the three central aspects of the question of mediation — belief, discussion, and action — and implicitly, by its very structure, sets up a relationship between them. First, everyone is free to believe as he or she likes. To say this one must regard "belief" as not having direct social consequences, as an individual rather than a social production. Next, free speech and the press: Public discussion sorts and reformulates the various beliefs that the people hold. In discussion some fall out because they do not stand the test of being "universalizable," that is they remain only private, self-interested, and cannot command general assent. Others are given a universal form and become part of the society's conception of the good life. Finally, the assembly of the people, its private beliefs generalized by free discussion, can act together. Action cannot be directly based on belief, which would lead to a chaos of individual self-interests. But, through the mediation of free communication, action can further the general good.

In a feudal or authoritarian society, where politics is merely the interest of the most powerful, the question of mediation does not arise. But a society that allows individual self-interest must provide a mechanism of mediation in order that it not fall into a chaos of competing beliefs and interests. Once the key role in democracy of free discussion in the essential media of communication is understood in this way, an important contemporary question looms: If there are only three television networks, a few newspaper chains and wireservices, in short, if access to the media of communication is sharply restricted, can the discussion in the media be regarded as really "free"? What are the consequences for democracy if only a few voices, all corporate ones, are heard? It seems that the role assigned to mediation of beliefs by the media is only tenable where there is widespread *access to* the media as well as free expression within them.

The model of mediation of beliefs and action by media of communication in liberalism presupposes that economic processes are "prior" to the mediation and that political processes are "subsequent" to it. In other words, it presupposes that the spheres of economy and politics are separate from the process of mediation in communication. Their institutional separation thus entails the presupposition that the necessary mediation is external to them. In consequence, media of communication are understood as domains of objects of a certain type — such as newspapers, televisions, and so forth — rather than a process inherent in all social life.

Contemporary Myths of the Media

However, the institutional separation of economy and politics has been undermined by twentieth-century developments in capitalist society. The concentration of ownership into large monopolies has involved an increasing control of the market and a stimulation of demand. Moreover, the responsibility for assuring that the profit-driven prerequisites of these monopolies are made acceptable to the public by mitigating their worst dysfunctions has become the major function of the political realm. The economy has become a political matter. Not in the sense of direct political power by single economic groups, but in the sense that managing or steering the economy as a whole has become the task of government. Concomitantly, the political sphere has come increasingly to serve the interests of monopoly capital as a whole. Friedrich Pollock, in "State Capitalism: Its Possibilities and Limitations" (1941), phrased this transformation in the following way:

> [T]he hour of state capitalism approaches when the market economy becomes an utterly inadequate instrument for utilizing the available resources. The medium-sized private enterprise and free trade, the basis for the gigantic development of men's productive forces in the 19th century, are being gradually destroyed by the offspring of liberalism, private monopolies and government interference.[1]

This new reintegration of economy and politics has wide consequences. It tends to produce a closed social system in which the economic cycle of production and consumption is validated and steered by the political order, a system in which the needs, desires, and participation of individuals are internalized from the system as a whole. In short, a system in which every individual part confirms the whole structure and in which the whole structure dominates and forms the part. The capitalist social order becomes not merely an economy with extensive implications, but a "form of life," a unitary cultural form which manifests itself in the economy, in politics, and indeed throughout all dimensions of social life. The predominance and continuation of this cultural form is inherent in the mechanism by which cultural meaning is produced and exchanged — the code of signs. As Jean Baudrillard puts it:

> This mutation concerns the passage from the form-commodity to the form-sign, from the abstraction of the exchange of material products under the law of general equivalence to the operationalization of all exchanges under the law of the code. . . . The monopolistic stage signifies less the monopoly of the means of production (which is never total) than the monopoly of the code.[2]

The system of production, exchange, and consumption of signs is the cultural cement of the monopoly capitalist form of life. In this system the role of media of communication is expanded from its "mediational" function in liberal society to become the major determinant in this cultural cement.

The cultural code of monopoly capitalism becomes a unified, closed system in a historical development that consists of two closely related parts. Signs are unhinged from their origin in the life-practice of social subjects. Signs "float" through their circulation in social life without reference to the meaningful practices that produce them. As a consequence of this, signs do not refer to a realm of social practice outside the sphere of signs, but become a "code"; that is to say, a sign is related to a *system of signs*. It is through this double movement — loss of external reference and systematization into a code — that the cultural logic of monopoly capitalism emerges. In this situation the specific character of the sign is arbitrary or conventional, and its meaning derives from its difference from other signs within the code. Thus, each sign calls forth the code as a whole. Henri Lefebvre has characterized this historical development in the following way:

> A hundred years ago words and sentences in a social context were based on reliable referentials that were linked together, being cohesive if not logically coherent, without however constituting a single system formulated as such. . . . However, around the years 1905–10 the referentials broke down under the influence of various pressures (science, technology, and social changes). . . . In these circumstances it seems that the only basis for social relations is speech, deprived of criteria, veracity and authenticity and even of objectivity. In other words such relations have no foundations, and speech, the form of communication, is now instrument and content as well . . .[3]

It is in this situation that we encounter the ideology of objectivity in media. As we have seen, early liberal capitalism assigned a key role to media of communication, especially the press, to public discussion. In so doing, media were expected to *form* public opinion, to play the active role of expressing and molding beliefs into statements concerning the general good. This active role of "universalization" cannot be publicly avowed in monopoly capitalist society precisely because it is so central to the social process. Lack of widespread access to media would be seen to constitute a formidable restriction of democracy if the formative function of such media were avowed. Moreover, if the system of signs were recognized as a political formation, the social role of media images would become a source of political contention. The ideology of objectivity serves to keep this destabilizing possibility at bay by asserting that the media simply "represent" what is going on. Only by denying the productive role of media in the legitimizing sign-systems of the logic of monopoly capital can the media play their role. They can only work when veiled. The signs that we circulate through the predominant media of communication are our images of the "good life," which once was the domain of politics.

Thus, a systematic misunderstanding of the role of media of communication is inherent in the contemporary cultural system of meaning. This ideology is pervasive throughout both popular and academic accounts of media. Its most basic form is the "transportation" model of communication, that is, a model in which the process of communication is simply a transfer of information from one location to another. Consider the following sketch, which is a common presentation of the process of communication.

source → transmitter → signal → receiver → destination

These five aspects of the communication process were distinguished by Claude Shannon and Warren Weaver in *The Mathematical Theory of Communication* (1949). There have, of course, been other influential ways of schematizing the various aspects of communication. Harold Lasswell's formula "who says what to whom in what channel to what effect," for example. Also, Roman Jakobson's six factors of addresser, context, message, contact, code, addressee; and David Berlo's source, message, channel, receiver.[4] While these schemes differ from each other in some respects, primarily about where to draw the lines in subdividing the process, they nevertheless contain some basic common assumptions. It is these common assumptions that are significant in characterizing the ideological features of most inquiry into communication. Indeed, it is often the case that an explicit rejection of the transportation model does not serve adequately to displace these assumptions.

The basic structure of the transportation model involves a message which is put into acceptable form (encoded) for transmission through a medium of communication, transmitted and received, and retrieved from its altered form (decoded). Communication is understood in this model as simply a transfer of a content from one location to another. The origin and destination of the transfer pre-exist the transference itself and are not altered by it. We can isolate three main assumptions in this model that have become problematic in a contemporary context. First, there is a separation of channel and content. The message precedes the transfer and exists apart from it at the destination. The contribution of the channel is restricted to "noise," that is, a distortion of the original message. Second, the subjects who communicate are preconstituted and not really affected by the process of communication. They simply send and receive messages; what they "are" is another question entirely. Thus, in this model there arises the intractable question of whether "society affects media" or "media reflect society." It is characteristic of ideology to direct inquiry into such insoluble dead-ends rather than clarifying real social relationships. Third, the effect of communication is understood only as the effect of isolated messages. There is no question of a general social effect and, especially, of a social effect deriving from the medium of communication itself rather than from the messages which it carries.

Representation versus Constitution

These assumptions are rooted in the current character of liberal democratic capitalist society. The erosion of the institutional separation of economics and politics during the twentieth century requires a conception of cultural logic at the center of the whole process of social reproduction. Instead, communication is generally understood as a certain set of objects — TV, newspapers, and the like. The ideology of objectivity attributed to the functioning of this set of objects denies the productive role of media in the prevailing cultural logic and thereby serves to keep it disguised and depoliticized. The most basic claim in such an ideology of objectivity is that media are purely "representational," in other words, *media simply represent* events previously existing in the world. At present, we need to go beyond representation to the recognition that *media constitute reality*, that media are constituents of the social world. Whereas the representational function of media derives from its position in modern society, the constitutive function of media can be called "postmodern."

From this perspective, Marshall McLuhan's media theory is an important point of departure. He views media of communication as technologies that extend and develop the capacities of the human body. Thus, the bodily capacity for movement by walking is externalized in technologies of transportation such as bicycles, automobiles, airplanes, and so forth. As we externalize our capacities, we remove them from the exercise of our own bodies; McLuhan calls this an "autoamputation." The development of media technologies is a continuous process of altering the environment by amputating our human capacities and delegating them to media. The characteristics of these media are the significant elements in cultural change. Whatever their content, the media are potent constituents of culture. For example, McLuhan is not interested in what is on television (why these programs rather than those programs?), but in the significance of television as a medium of communication in defining the cultural environment and thereby the perception of individuals. This is the meaning of the slogan "the medium is the message"; media do not have a definite content for McLuhan, rather they define and convey the perceptual patterns crystallized in previous media. The "content" of TV is the play, the public announcement, and the con artist. What is new about TV is its form, the technological alteration of perceptual experience, and its influence on the whole media environment — which includes also other media such as film, speech, computers, and so on. This starting point recognizes the significance of media in constituting social reality (not merely representing it), a recognition that is particularly important in our media-saturated era, though it is not confined to it.

McLuhan claims that a medium of communication has two cultural effects, a first effect and a later one that is a "reversal" of the first. The first effect is due to the fact that a technology is introduced by specific social groups in order to fulfill goals and purposes that they already have. The new medium is thus filled up with a previously defined content which it presents in a new fashion. This function of a medium may be called "representation" insofar as its function is limited to a new manner of presenting a prior cultural content. However, as a medium is developed the technology improves, and the perceptual and sensual autoamputation that it achieves is progressively more successful, requiring less and less active participation from the viewer. In McLuhan's terminology a medium "heats up" over time and accelerates the externalization of human capacities. Moreover, the technology becomes more widespread and affects more pervasively the whole cultural environment. It no longer simply represents a previous content, but becomes a significant new form of experience itself. In short, it becomes a constituent of a changed cultural order. This constituent role is not simply different from the first, more limited, effect but *reverses* it. Thus, the road was initially a means of transport between cities, but has now come to define the inner organization of cities themselves. War was initially a conflict on the edge of communities, but has come to define the inner structure of societies themselves through a constant military preparedness in the name of national security.[5]

Thus, as a technology improves and increasingly comes to pervade the environment, it reaches a "break boundary" in which the initial effect is reversed and the medium plays a constituent role in defining a new mode of perception and social relationship. Not only does this occur with each medium of communication, it also occurs to the whole process of communication itself when this process reaches a break boundary. The externalization of human capacities in media technologies comes to a break boundary when the most basic capacity of the body is externalized. The nervous system, the means of coordination of capacities in the human body, is externalized in the electric age. Not only capacities, but what coordinates them into a functioning whole, is externalized. The patterning and coordinating function of the nervous system is autoamputated and externalized into the global system of automation. At this point the extension of human capacities through technologies comes to a break boundary. Having expanded, or "exploded," to its farthest limit, the process reverses. Media technologies now "implode" to define the innermost capacities of the human individual, uniting each one in a coordinated "global village."

> The stepping up of speed from the mechanical to the instant electric form reverses explosion into implosion. In our present electric age the imploding or contracting energies of our world now clash with the old expansionist and traditional patterns of organization. . . . Obsession with the older patterns of mechanical, one-way expansion from centers to margins is no longer relevant to our electric world. Electricity does not centralize, but decentralizes.[6]

McLuhan's global village of unimpeded, multi-directional information flow is his utopian projection of the tendency of media of communication in the electric age. It has often, quite correctly, been criticized for ignoring the political and economic constraints under which this global system develops.[7] Nevertheless, he quite clearly saw that this state was not yet achieved and that the present era is as much defined by anxiety, unconsciousness, and apathy as by integral connection. Where global connection rules, the opposite tendency is toward total drop-out, a depth anxiety from which there is no escape. "Such amplification is bearable by the nervous system only through numbness or blocking of perception."[8] It is this tension between a total, free-flowing integration through information and a numbing anxiety of disconnection that is McLuhan's diagnosis of our present state as we enter the information age.

The media environment is comprised of a plurality of media which together constitute the contemporary cultural order. Media are not isolated from each other but refer to each other continuously. For example, there is a sense in which an event seen on TV, read about in a newspaper, and told about by an eyewitness, is the same event. If we consider media representationally, this is simply because all the media *refer to the same event*. But when we consider media as constitutive of cultural order, this comparison of media representations to "real" events is not possible. The identity of the event in this case is not based on its "reality" prior to representations, but on the mutual "translation" of various media versions. Media continuously translate each other; thus, they constitute an *environment*, rather than a simple plurality. Postmodern society is constituted by a media environment characterized by the continuous circulation of signs and messages. The distinctions between reality and a model, or a map and the territory, which are representational distinctions, become insufficient to grasp the "simulation" of signs by the media. They are not copies of "real" events, but the simulation of media events that produce real social relationships. Even material objects such as commodities are drawn into simulation through the mediascape. They function through their sign-value, which is the translation of every medium of communication into information.

Information is the universal translation of communication and thereby proposes a new stage of human culture. McLuhan says:

> By putting our physical bodies inside our extended nervous system, by means of electric media, we set up a dynamic by which all previous technologies that are mere extensions of hands and feet and bodily heat-controls. . . . will be translated into information systems. . . . [P]revious technologies were partial and fragmentary, and the electric is total and inclusive.[9]

Information is the reprocessing of all the previous content of culture and situating it within a mediascape of simulation. Whereas McLuhan sees a new utopian possibility for communication here because of its unprecedented universal scope, on closer examination a far more ominous situation is emerging. Indeed, everyone is potentially included in the new coding of culture, but the form of this inclusion is determined by the specific character of its universal translation. Far from allowing "participation," the response demanded by contemporary media systems are provoked by previously defined questions. In Jean Baudrillard's words:

> No contemplation is possible. The images fragment perception into success-ive sequences, into stimuli toward which there can be only instantaneous response, yes or no — the limit of an abbreviated reaction. Film no longer allows you to question. It questions you, and directly. Montage and codification demand, in effect, that the receiver construe and decode by observing the same procedure whereby the work was assembled. The reading of the message is then only a perpetual examination of the code.[10]

In short, the production, reprocessing, and exchange of the coded messages serve to introject the code into the receiver. The code has been severed from life-practices which produce meaning and closed into a self-referring system. In order to close the system it requires the turning of switches that complete the circuit. The code interrogates the receiver and returns the minimal yes/no messages, recorded as inputs, into the simulation system.

The role of this interrogation-function in information as constitutive of social relationships is to form all social groupings increasingly on the model of "masses." Masses have no direct relationship to each other; they are connected only by their role in being interrogated. Yes/no inputs are their lifeline to social life. Their compulsory participation completes and closes the code. For Baudrillard, the "implosion" of the media destroys all distance between social subjects, the "one" and the "other," which is necessary for them to initiate communication and thereby constitute culture. The mass is the indistinct plurality of points of input, who have no relation between themselves, whose relation is only simulated as a side-effect of the media system.

> There is no longer any polarity between the one and the other in the mass. This is what causes that vacuum and inwardly collapsing effect in all those systems which survive on the separation and distinction of poles (two, or many in more complex systems). This is what makes the circulation of meaning within the mass impossible: it is instantaneously dispersed, like atoms in a void.[11]

The implosion of universal translation and simulation destroys locations from which there could be social relationships and the give and take that produces meaning. Implosion shatters relationship and thereby mean-ing. The most basic feature of culture is eradicated when sign-systems circulate divorced from any meaning for those within the system. We no longer use media of communication to say what we mean, we are simply simulated effects of a system that produces our inputs.

Postmodern culture simulates society by shattering meaning in the reprocessing of cultural remnants. It is like a genetic code, in which there is no distinction between the code and the "real" effect of the code. The map simulates the territory. We are in the hyper-real geography of effects that produce their causes. What comes first is the code, which spurts forth its effects; content is irrelevant; in every case it is the code that is its own message, produces its own audiences, and simulates social relationships that howl for another fix of the code.

Information is the interrogation of the masses by the code which simulates hyper-reality. The transportation model of communication, including information theory, becomes ideological by treating communication merely in its representative dimension and disregarding its simultaneous (and at present more important) constitutive dimension. While media can be analyzed as *referring* to social life, as mirroring it well or badly, they also *produce* social relationships. Any communication has both of these dimensions — representation and constitution. Moreover, these are not merely separate dimensions that could be properly understood in isolation from each other. Every representation is simultaneously a constitution. Media as constitutive of the cultural code posit a representation that refers outside itself to an original that supposedly precedes simulation.[12] Understanding media beyond representation requires acknowledging the constitutive role of media, but also that the representative role is produced in constitution. It is the interpenetration of these two dimensions that is first on the agenda for a contemporary media theory.

Strategies of Resistance

The politics of media as representative center on the question of "access." Traditional political power undermined resistance by repression, by denying the power of expression. Power attempted to silence the opposition. But how is this silence now obtained? Not directly by repression in the Western capitalist democracies, at least most of the time. Opposition is not so much repressed as drowned out by the noise of mainstream media. Monopolization of the media has undermined the crucial role delegated to media of communication by liberalism. The question of access to media representations is by no means unimportant, but it remains insufficient unless it is based on a politics of media as constitutive. What would such a politics be like? We can broach this question by focusing on a central element in the transportation model of communication by which its general ideological nature becomes concretely political. In regarding the production of "noise" as extrinsic to the content of a medium, the transportation model conceals its politics. Noise is introduced into the channel during transmission; since noise increases available information, it increases the freedom of choice in decoding a message. Thus, there is a contradiction in which extrinsic noise seems equivalent to the production of information. In a manner characteristic of ideological thought, this contradiction is neither addressed or resolved, but is simply arbitrarily and stipulatively removed. Warren Weaver comments that "It is clear where the joker is in saying that the received signal has more information. Some of this information is spurious and undesirable and has been introduced via the noise. To get the useful information in the received signal we must subtract out this spurious portion."[13] But who decides what is spurious? Even more important, what is the function of noise? Ideology operates by treating a necessary aspect of a system as merely a contingent, extrinsic factor. A critical theory of contemporary media must reverse this ideological view and focus on the political dimension of noise. The production of noise is a central and necessary function of contemporary media, especially insofar as a general translatability is constitutive of social relations. The production of noise conceals the strategies of resistance within postmodern society.

One strategy has been recently uncovered by Jean Baudrillard. Insofar as the media interrogate the masses to complete the circuit of the cultural code, the masses respond with silence; they refuse to throw the switch of their yes/no inputs.

> Thus, in the case of the media, traditional resistance consists of reinterpreting messages according to the group's own code and for its own ends. The masses, on the contrary, accept everything *en bloc* into the spectacular, without requiring any other code, without requiring any meaning, ultimately without resistance, but making everything slide into an indeterminate sphere which is not even that of nonsense, but that of overall manipulation/satisfaction.[14]

In short, the masses reject the manipulation of meaning by rejecting meaning. The proliferation of simulations which hopes to confine the masses to switches in the circuit may be undermined by the withdrawal from simulations of their necessary input, with an acceptance in silence that is a strategy of objectivity, of the recalcitrant child.

While this strategy does follow from a telling analysis of the contemporary role of the media, it is somewhat unsatisfying as it seems to undermine any sense of political direction in the name of a generalized obstinacy. However, there is a second strategy which is not merely traditional. Since information is a universal reprocessing of culture, it undermines the core of activity that produces meaning. There is a loss of the fundament of culture in the embodied and local enactments of speaking subjects. A recovery of this fundament of the production of meaning is not merely a traditional strategy in the sense of a "reinterpretation according to the group's own code" since it refers to the conditions for producing any sort of cultural meaning not merely to the assertion of a given meaning. It is a radicalization of the traditional strategy in the conditions of universal reprocessing and translatability of the information culture.[15]

A third strategy can also be discerned which focuses on the widespread production of simulations. This is not a strategy of refusing inputs as suggested by Baudrillard, not a strategy directed to the fundamental conditions of cultural production. It is concerned with the proliferation of simulations, an overburdening of the cultural code of excess, that may undermine the self-confirming character of the code that is required by monopoly capital. Armed with video cameras, cultural guerrillas may multiply simulations beyond any possibility of control by a code.

These three strategies all resist the noise produced by contemporary media — either by silence, by recovery of the conditions for speech, or by the increase of noise beyond control. None are simply traditional strategies directed primarily to the representative dimension of media insofar as all three address the universal aspect of political strategy raised by the constitutive dimension of media. All are concerned not so much with the success of particular messages as with the conditions of communication as such. When we start to see noise as the main ideological function of contemporary media, we can begin to discern new strategies of resistance, strategies which extend to the omnipresent constitution of society through media, which embrace the festival of meaning beyond the closure of the cultural code.

24.

Postmodernism: Roots and Politics

Todd Gitlin

Something must be at stake in the edgy debates circulating around and about something called postmodernism. What, then? Commentators pro, con, serious, fey, academic, and accessible seem agreed that something postmodern has happened, even if we are all (or virtually all) Mr. Jones who doesn't know what it is. (At times the critical world seems to divide between those who speak with assurance about what it is and those who are struggling to keep up.) The volume and pitch of the commentary and controversy seem to imply that something about this postmodern something *matters*. In the pages of art journals, popular and obscure, abundant passion flows on about passionlessness. It would be cute but glib and shortsighted to dismiss the talk as so much time-serving, space-filling, the shoring up of positions for the sake of amassing theoretical property, or propriety, or priority. There is *anxiety* at work, and at play, here. I think it is reasonable, or at least interesting, to assume that the anxiety that surfaces in the course of the discussion — and I confess I share in it — is called for. A certain anxiety is entirely commensurate with what is at stake.

"Postmodernism" usually refers to a certain constellation of styles and tones in cultural works: pastiche; blankness; a sense of exhaustion; a mixture of levels, forms, styles; a relish for copies and repetition; a knowingness that dissolves commitment into irony; acute self-consciousness about the formal, constructed nature of the work; pleasure in the play of surfaces; a rejection of history. It is Michael Graves's Portland Building and Philip Johnson's AT&T, Rauschenberg's silkscreens and Warhol's Brillo boxes; it is shopping malls, mirror glass facades, William

Burroughs, Donald Barthelme, Monty Python, Don DeLillo, *Star Wars*, Spaulding Grey, David Byrne, Twyla Tharp, the Flying Karamazov Brothers, George Coates, Frederick Barthelme, Laurie Anderson, the Hyatt Regency, the Centre Pompidou, *The White Hotel, Less Than Zero*, Foucault, and Derrida; it is bricolage fashion, and remote-control-equipped viewers "zapping" around the television dial.

To join the conversation I am also going to use the term to refer to art located somewhere in this constellation. But I am also going to argue that what is at stake in the debate — and thus the root of the general anxiety — goes beyond art: it extends to the question of what sort of disposition toward the contemporary world is going to prevail throughout Western culture. The entire elusive phenomenon which has been categorized as postmodernism is best understood not just as a style but as a general orientation, as what Raymond Williams calls a "structure of feeling,"[1] as a way of apprehending and experiencing the world and our place, or placelessness, in it. (Just whose place or placelessness is at issue is an entirely legitimate question I shall return to.) Likewise, controversies about postmodernism — the whole of what inevitably has to be called "the postmodernism discourse" — are in no small part discussions about how to live, feel, think in a specific world, our own: a world in nuclear jeopardy; a world economically both alluring and nerve-racking for the fitful middle classes; a world two decades from the hopes and desperate innocence of the 1960s; a world unimpressed by the affirmative futurology of Marxism. Not for the first time, debates over cultural politics intersect with larger intellectual and political currents, prefiguring or tracing conflicts that have emerged, or ought to emerge, in the sphere of politics strictly understood. When the *Partisan Review* embraced modernism in the 1930s, for example, they were taking a position on more than style: they were taking a position on reason, the State, the (ir)rationality of history; finally they were driving a revisionary wedge into left-wing politics in the large. Postwar American versions of modernism, as artistic practice and critical exegesis, can also be understood as a way to inhabit a drastically changed political space.[2]

I am going to take the position that the discussion of postmodernism is, *among other things*, a deflected and displaced discussion of the contours of political thought — in the largest sense — during the 1970s and 1980s. The aesthetics of postermodernism are situated, historical. The question is, what is postmodernism's relation to this historical moment, to its political possibilities and torments?

I want to broach some intersecting questions: What do we mean by postmodernism, both as a style and a "structure of feeling"? Why has it come to pass? What is troubling about it? Finally, postmodern is pre-what? What is the relation between postmodern aesthetics and a possible politics?

1. *What is postmodernism?* A sortie at definition is necessary. Things must be made to look crystalline for a moment, before complications set in. Here, then, is one person's grid — hopelessly crude, in the manner of first approximations — for distinguishing among premodernism (realism), modernism, and postmodernism. These are ideal types, mind you, not adequate descriptions. And they are not necessarily ideal types of the work "itself"; rather, of the work as it is understood and judged by some consensus (albeit shifting) of artists, critics, and audiences.

The premodernist work aspires to a unity of vision. It cherishes continuity, speaking with a single narrative voice or addressing a single visual center. It honors sequence and causality in time or space. Through the consecutive, the linear, it claims to represent a reality which is something else, though to render it more acutely than happens in ordinary experience. It may contain a critique of the established order, in the name of the obstructed ambitions of individuals; or it may uphold indivdiuals as the embodiments of society at its best. In either event, individuals matter. The work observes, highlights, renders judgments and exudes passions in their names. Standing apart from reality, the work aspires to an order of beauty which, in a sense, judges reality; lyrical forms, heightened speech, rhythm and rhyme, Renaissance perspective and compositional "laws" are deployed in the interest of beauty. Finally, the work may borrow stories or tunes from popular materials, but it holds itself (and is held, by its audience) above its origins; high culture holds the line against the popular.

The modernist work still aspires to unity, but this unity, if that is what it is, has been (is still being?) constructed, assembled from fragments, or shocks, or juxtapositions of difference. It shifts abruptly among a multiplicity of voices, perspectives, materials. Continuity is disrupted, and with enthusiasm: it is as if the work is punctuated with exclamation marks. The orders of conventional reality — inside versus outside, subject versus object, self versus other — are called into question. So are the hitherto self-enclosed orders of art: poetry vs. prose, painting vs. sculpture, representation vs. reality. There is often a critique of the established order; the work is apocalyptic, fused with a longing for some long-gone organic whole sometimes identified with a fascist present or future. The subject is not so much wholeheartedly opposed as estranged. Instead of passion, or alongside it, there is ambivalence toward the prevailing authorities. The work composes beauty out of discord. Aiming to bring into sharp relief the line between art and life, modernism appropriates selected shards of popular culture, quotes from them.[3]

In the postmodernist sensibility, the search for unity has apparently been abandoned altogether.[4] Instead we have textuality, a cultivation of surfaces endlessly referring to, ricocheting from, reverberating onto other surfaces. The work calls attention to its arbitrariness, constructedness; it interrupts itself. Instead of a single center, there is pastiche, cultural recombination. Anything can be juxtaposed to anything else. Everything takes place in the present, "here," that is, nowhere in particular. Not only has the master voice dissolved, but any sense of loss is rendered deadpan. The work labors under no illusions: we are all deliberately playing, pretending here — get the point? There is a premium on copies; everything has been done. Shock, now routine, is greeted with the glazed stare of the total ironist. The implied subject is fragmented, unstable, even decomposed; it is finally nothing more than a crosshatch of discourses. Where there was passion, or ambivalence, there is now a collapse of feeling, a blankness. Beauty, deprived of its power of criticism in an age of packaging, has been reduced to the decoration of reality, and so is crossed off the postmodernist agenda. Genres are spliced; so are cultural gradations. Dance can be built on Beach Boys songs (Twyla Tharp, "Deuce Coup"); as circus can include cabaret jokes (Circus Oz); avant-garde music can include radio gospel (David Byrne and Brian Eno, *My Life in the Bush of Ghosts*). "High culture" doesn't so much quote from popular culture as blur into it.

All master styles aim to remake the history that precedes them, just as T. S. Eliot said individual talents reorder tradition. In one sense, then, postmodernism remakes the relation between premodernism and modernism: in the light of postmodern disdain for representational conventions, the continuity between the preceding stages comes to seem more striking than the chasm dividing them. Yet it is worth noticing that "postmodernist" — in the spirit of its recombinant enterprise — is a compound term. It is as if the very term had trouble establishing the originality of the concept. If the phenomenon were more clearly demarcated from its predecessor, it might have been able to stand, semantically, on its own feet. Instead, *post*modernism defines the present cultural space as a sequel — as what it is not. Postmodernism is known by the company it succeeds. It differs from modernism by nothing more than a prefix. It shadows modernism. Modernism lurks in its sequel, haunts it. The very fact that a phenomenon is called "postmodernism" — that it differs from modernism by nothing more than a prefix — pays tribute to the power of modernism's cultural force-field, and suggests that postmodernism might be no more (or less) than an aftermath or a hiatus.

So what's new? It has been argued, with considerable force, that the lineaments of postmodernism are already present in one or another version of modernism; that postmodernism is simply the current incarnation, or phase, in a still unfolding modernism.[5] Roger Shattuck, for example, has recently made the point that Cubism, Futurism, and artistic spiritualists like Kandinsky "shared one compositional principle: the juxtaposition of states of mind, of different times and places, of different points of view."[6] Collage, montage, these are of the essence of modernism high and low. Then what is so special about (1) Philip Johnson's AT&T building, with its Chippendale pediment on high and quasi-classical columns below; (2) the Australian Circus Oz, which combines jugglers commenting on their juggling and cracking political jokes with (their list) "Aboriginal influences, vaudeville, Chinese acrobatics, Japanese martial arts, fireman's balances, Indonesian instruments and rhythms, video, Middle Eastern tunes, B-grade detective movies, modern dance, Irish jigs, and the ubiquitous present of corporate marketing";[7] (3) the student who walks into my office dressed in green jersey, orange skirt, and black tights?

Put it this way: Modernism tore up unity and postmodernism has been enjoying the shreds. Surely nothing is without precedent; surely modernism had to set asunder what postmodernism is mixing in and about. Modernism's multiplication of perspective led to postmodernism's utter dispersion of voices; modernist collage made possible postmodernist genre-splicing. The point is not only juxtaposition but its attitude. The quality of postmodern juxtaposition is distinct: there is a deliberate self-consciousness, a skating of the edge dividing irony from dismay or endorsement, which make up a distinct cultural mood. Picasso, Boccioni, Tatlin, Pound, Joyce, Woolf in their various ways thundered and hungered. Their work was radiant with passion for a new world/work. Today's postmodernists are blasé; they've seen it all. They are bemused (though not necessarily by bemusement). The quality of deliberateness and the sense of exhaustion in the postmodern are what set it apart.

It might be objected that we are talking about nothing more than a fad. We read in a "Design Notebook" column in *The New York Times* of March 12, 1987, that "Post-Modernism Appears to Retreat." Apparently *Progressive Architecture* is no longer giving its awards to pastiches of columns, capitals, and cornices; the writer suggests that the popularization of the premium architectural style of the last ten years signals its uniformity, mediocrity, and impending end. Actually, postmodernism as a stylistic avant-garde movement in achitecture had probably already reached a plateau (but does this mean it ended?) at the moment when photographs of Michael Graves's buildings were featured in *The New York Times Magazine*. But what is interesting about postmodernism goes beyond the fashion in architecture —

for the recombinatory thrust, the blankness, the self-regarding irony, the play of surfaces, the self-referentiality and self-bemusement which characterize postmodernism are still very much with us. What is interesting is not a single set of architectural tropes but postmodernism as what Raymond Williams calls a "structure of feeling" — an interlocking cultural complex, or what he calls "a pattern of impulses, restraints, tones" — that forecasts the common future as it colors the common experience of a society just at or beneath the threshold of awareness. In this flickering half-light, postmodernism is significant because its amalgam of spirits have penetrated architecture, fiction, painting, poetry, urban planning, performance, music, television, and many other domains. It is one wing, at least, of the zeitgeist.

2. *Why this postmodernism?* If this is so, the interesting question is, Why? We can distinguish more or less five approaches to an answer. These are not at all necessarily incompatible. To the contrary: Several forces are converging to produce the postmodernist moment.

The first is the bleak Marxist account sketched with flair in a series of essays by Fredric Jameson.[8] The postmodernist spirit, with its superceding of the problem of authenticity belongs to, is coupled to, corresponds to, expresses — the relation is not altogether clear — the culture of multinational capitalism, in which capital, that infinitely transferrable abstraction, has abolished particularity as such along with the coherent self in whom history, depth, and subjectivity unite. Authentic use value has been overcome by the universality of exchange value. The characteristic machine of this period is the computer, which enthrones (or fetishizes) the fragment, the "bit," and in the process places a premium on process and reproduction which is aped in postmodernist art. Surfaces meet surfaces in these postmodern forms because a new human nature — a human second nature — has formed to feel at home in a homeless world political economy. Postmodernists ransack history for shards because there is no "here" here; because historical continuity is shattered by the permanent revolution that is capitalism (which, by the way, I find clumsy and inconsistent to call "late capitalism," a formulation haunted by a peculiar nostalgia for sequential time — as if we could know whether it is late early, middle, or early late). Uprooted juxtaposition is how people live: not only displaced peasants cast into the megalopolis, where decontextualized images proliferate, but also TV viewers confronted with the interruptus of American television as well as financial honchos shifting bits of information and blips of capital around the world at will and high speed. Art expresses this abstract unity and vast, weightless indifference through its blank repetitions (think of Warhol or Philip Glass), its exhausted anti-romance, its I've-seen-it-all, striving at best, for a kind of all-embracing surface which radiates from the world temple of the postmodern, the glorious Centre Pompidou in Paris.

A second stab at explanation calls attention to our political rather than our strictly economic moment.[9] In this light, the crucial location of the postmodern is *after the '60s*. The postmodern is an aftermath, or a waiting game, because that is what we are living in: a prolonged cultural moment that is oddly weightless, shadowed by incomplete revolts, haunted by absences — a Counterreformation beating against an unfinished, indeed barely begun, Reformation. From this point of view, postmodernism rejects historical continuity and takes up residence somewhere beyond it because history *was* ruptured: by the Bomb-fueled vision of a possible material end of history; by Vietnam, by drugs, by youth revolts, by women's and gay movements — in general, by the erosion of that false and devastating universality embodied in the rule of the pyramidal trinity of Father, Science, and State. It was faith in a rule of progress under the sway of that trinity that had underlain our assumptions that the world displays linear order, historical sequence, and moral clarities. But cultural contradiction burst open the premises of the old cultural complex. The cultural upwellings and wildness of the '60s kicked out the props of a teetering moral structure, but the new house has not been built. The culture has not found a language for articulating the new understandings we are trying, haltingly, to live with. Postmodernism dispenses with moorings, then, because old certitudes have actually crumbled. It is straining to make the most of seriality, endless recirculation and repetition in the collective image warehouse, because so much of reality *is* serial. As Donald Barthelme's fiction knows, we live in a forest of images mass-produced and endlessly, alluringly empty. Individuality has become a parody of itself: another world for a fashion choice, a lifestyle compound, a talk-show self-advertisement logo. It might even be argued that postmodernism plays in and with surfaces because that is what it must do to carry on with its evasions: because there are large cultural terrors that broke into common consciousness in the 1960s and there is no clear way to live out their implications in a conservative, contracting period.

From this point of view, postmodernism is blank because it wants to have its commodification and eat it. That is, it knows that the cultural industry will tailor virtually any cultural goods for the sake of sales; it also wants to display its knowingness, thereby demonstrating how superior it is to the trash market. Choose one: the resulting ironic spiral either mocks the game by playing it or plays it by mocking it. A knowing blankness results; how to decode it is a difficult matter. Take, for instance, the "Joe Isuzu" commercials of 1987, in which the spokesman, a transparently slick version of the archetypal TV huckster, grossly lies about what the car will do, how much it costs, and so on, while the subtitles tell us he's lying, and by how much. The company takes for granted a culture of lies, then aims to ingratiate itself by mocking the conventions of the hard sell. Or consider the early episodes of *Max Headroom* during the spring of 1987, which in nine weeks sped from a blunt critique of television itself to a mishmash of adorability. "20 Minutes into the Future" — so the pilot film shows us — the computer-generated Max fights the tyranny of the ratings-crazed Network 23, whose decidedly sinister (shot from below with wide-angle lens) boardroom tycoons will stop at no crime in their pursuit of profits. (Cherchez la japanoise: the venal Zik-Zak corporation which brings on the ratings panic is conveniently Japanese.) Is Max a revolutionary guerrilla or a sales gimmick? In the British prototype, he throws in with a revolution against Network 23; in the American version, the self-proclaimed revolutionaries are thuggish terrorists, as despicable as the Network bosses. In any event, Max in his early American weeks reaches out of the fictional frame to yawn in the face of ABC's impending commercials. As the weeks pass, however, Max loses his computerized bite and becomes regressively cuter. The same Max is deployed to promote Coca-Cola over Pepsi, as if Coke were both subversive and mandatory (the "wave" to be "caught") — to an audience encouraged to laugh at the distinction and still, as consumers, act on it. Commerce incorporates popular cynicism and political unease while flattering the audience that it has now, at least, seen through all the sham: Cynicism, Inc.[10] Andy Warhol would have grasped the point in a second, or fifteen.

A third approach to explaining postmodernism is a refinement of the second: an argument not about history in general but about a specific generation and class. Postmodernism appears as an outlook for (though not necessarily *by*) Yuppies — urban, professional products of the late baby boom, born in the late 1950s and early 1960s. Theirs is an experience of aftermath, privatization, weightlessness: they can remember political commitment but were not animated by it — more, they suspect it; it leads to trouble. They cannot remember a time before television, suburbs, shopping malls.* They are accustomed, therefore, to rapid cuts, discontinuities, breaches of attention, culture to be indulged and disdained at the same time. They grew up taking drugs, taking them for granted, but do not associate them with spirituality or the hunger for transcendence. Knowing indifference is their "structure of feeling"

---

* Cecelia Tichi[11] argues that the blank-toned fiction of Ann Beatie, Bret Easton Ellis, Bobbie Ann Mason, and Tama Janowitz, among others, is the anesthetized expression of a TV-saturated generation.

— thus a taste for cultural bricolage. They are, though, disabused of authority. The association of passion and politics rubs them the wrong way. Their idea of government is shadowed by Vietnam and Watergate. *Their* television runs through *Saturday Night Live* and MTV. Their mores lean toward the libertarian and, at least until the AIDS terror, the libertine. They like the idea of the free market as long as it promises them an endless accumulation of crafted goods, as in the (half-joking?) bumper sticker. "THE ONE WITH THE MOST TOYS WINS." The idea of public life — whether party participation or military intervention — fills them with weariness; the adventures that matter to them are the adventures of private life. The characters of *The Big Chill* spoke to them: "the Sixties" stand for a cornucopia of sex and drugs; they can easily gather for a weekend in "the Eighties" without bringing up the subject of Ronald Reagan and Reaganism. But they are not in any conventional sense "right-wing": They float beyond belief. The important thing is that their assemblage of "values" corresponds to their class biographies.

A fourth approach starts from the fact that postmodernism is specifically, though not exclusively, *American*. Again, Andreas Huyssen makes an interesting argument which carries us partway but needs to be extended.[12] Postmodernism couldn't have developed in Germany, because postwar Germans were too busy trying to reappropriate a suppressed modernism. Where it developed in France at all, it did so without antagonism to or rupture from modernism. But in America, the artistic avant-garde, in order to break from Cold War orthodoxy and corporate-sponsored smugness, had to revolt against the officially enshrined modernism of the postwar period; had to smash the Modern Art idol. I would add the obvious: that postmodernism is born in the U.S.A. because juxtaposition is one of the things we do best. It is one of the defining currents of American culture, especially with Emancipation and the rise of immigration in the latter part of the nineteenth century. (The other principal current is the opposite: assimilation into standard American styles and myths.) Juxtaposition is the Strip, the shopping mall, the Galleria, Las Vegas; it is the marketplace jamboree, the divinely grotesque disorder, amazing diversity striving for reconciliation, the ethereal and ungrounded radiance of signs, the shimmer of the evanescent, the good times beat of the tall tale meant to be simultaneously disbelieved and appreciated; it is vulgarized pluralism; it is the cultural logic of laissez-faire but perhaps, the suspicion arises, even more — of an elbows-out, noisy, jostling, bottom-up version of something that can pass as democracy. We are, central myths and homogenizations and oligopolies notwithstanding, an immigrant culture, less melting pot than grab bag, perennially replenished by aliens and their singular points of view. As long ago as 1916, Randolph Bourne wrote that "there is no distinctively American culture. It is apparently our lot rather to be a federation of cultures."[13] Hollywood and the radio and TV networks flattened the culture, but there is still life in Bourne's vision. The postmodernist, from this point of view, is hitching high art to the raucous, disrespectful quality that accompanies American popular culture from its beginnings. And indeed, the essential contribution of postmodernist art is that it obliterates the line — or the brow — separating the high from the low. What could be more American?

3. *Postmodernism and poststructuralist theory: The problem of unstable bedrock.* I want to lurch, in properly postmodern style, to the domain of theory. For the forms of representation displayed in postmodernist art rhyme or dovetail with — extend? extenuate? correspond to? — a crisis of thought that runs throughout poststructuralist theory, what we could call a crisis of bottomlessness. The territory of theory and the territory of art share an intimacy greater than ordinary. Among the practitioners of postmodernism are peculiarly a generation schooled in poststructuralist theory: variously Michel Foucault, Jean Baudrillard, Jacques Lacan. Style illustrates text. Characteristically, it is critics who have named the phenomenon which the practitioners practice as they wriggle away from it, insisting in virtual chorus on their individual artistry.

All theoretical maps have empty spaces; there are things they cannot disclose, even acknowledge. I think of a graduate student I met in 1987. She presented herself as a committed feminist working the deconstructionist beat. She was partial to the notion that the world "is" — in quotation marks — everything that is agreed to be the case. Or as Lily Tomlin puts it, that reality is a widely shared hunch. The category of "lived experience" was, from this point of view, an atavistic concealment; what one "lives" is expressed as, constituted by, a layer of discourse which has no more — or less — standing than any other system of discourse. I asked her if she wasn't troubled by the fact that her politics was rooted in a decision to pursue the cues supplied by her experience as a woman, yet from the poststructuralist point of view her emotions were to be forbidden any primacy. Yes, she said, it bothered her, chagrined her, embarrassed her. As a feminist she was unwilling to make her commitments dissolve into ungrounded discourse, "just discourse," discourse comparable to any other discourse. Yet as a theorist she was compelled to explode the very ground on which she stood as a political person — the very ground which had brought her to discourse theories in the first place.

The self-exploding quality of the poststructuralist theories is the fundamental Kuhnian anomaly for discourse theories. One is drawn to a politics out of a complex of understandings and feelings — *moral* feelings. They crystallize into the Archimedean point, the unmoved and essential standing place, for one's intellectual project. Proceeding from that point, one tries to locate oneself in history. In the course of working out one's politics, one employs a language of unmasking. Ideology, one comes to understand, freezes privilege and encases it in a spurious idea of the natural. Now one sets out to thaw the world, to show how the "natural" is situated, arbitrary, partial. Discourse, one discovers, is a means through which domination takes place. The dominated collaborate with the dominators when they take for granted their discourse and their definition of the situation.

We can only sympathize with the project. Yet discourse theories cannot account for the impulse from which the politics proceeded in the first place. Indeed, they hold, quite clearly, that such impulses should not be taken at face value. There *is* no human experience — at least none that deserves special treatment. It is discourse all the way down — analogous to postmodernism's endless play of surfaces. Poststructuralist critics generally agree that the concept of "literature," say, "assumes that something recognizable as human experience or human nature exists, aside from any form of words and from any form of society, and that this experience is put into words by an author" — thus Diane Macdonell,[14] as if the idea that there is "human experience" were as dismissable as the idea that there is "human nature." But then the ideal of a way of thinking which liberates has been thrown — thrown *fundamentally* — into question. What constitutes liberation, and who says? Who is entitled to say?

The impulse toward this sort of unmasking is certainly political: it stemmed from a desire to undo the hold of one system of knowledge/language/power over another. It followed from the 1960s revelation that various systems of knowledge were fundamentally implicated in injustice and violence — whether racist or sexist exclusions from literary canons, or the language and science of militarism and imperial justification. But the poststructuralist move in theory has flushed the Archimedean point away with the sewage of discourse.

If there is one theorist whose work seems, at first, to be animated by the promise of the postmodern, it is Michel Foucault. Foucault's popularity today stems in good measure from the flair with which he engaged "the politics of the personal" in a succession of *tour de force* studies documenting the ways in which institutions (psychiatry, medicine, prisons, sexuality) are encrustations of power and epistemology. His insistence on the unavoidability and irreducibility of power relations — a revival of anarchist traditions long eclipsed by Marxism — was refreshing: it shattered any lingering idea that all oppression amounts, "ultimately," to that of capital over labor. It thereby appealed to academics desirous of a radical stance beyond Marxism. But perhaps there is also something in his popularity which suggests a radicalism of gesture and not of action, suggests the paralysis of radical politics rather than the fruition of it. Alas, Foucault's work was interrupted. But the last phase to reverberate throughout the Anglo-American world, the phase that culminated in Volume 1 of *The History of Sexuality*, outlined a world of power that not only instigated resistance but required it, channeled it, and turned its energy back upon it. Power was everywhere, micropower, strategies constantly "deploying" (to use the military language to which Foucault was partial) against other strategies — apparently without a basis for solidarity or a reason to support resistance against power. Against Enlightenment ideas of universal rationality, serving to justify the suppression of those found wanting in rationality, Foucault constituted a considerable advance: an anticolonial respect for the principle of human diversity. But as universalist structures were swept away, something essential was left wanting. As Foucault said to a group of us in Berkeley in November 1983, "There is no universal criteri[on] which permits [us] to say, 'This category of power relations are bad and those are good' " — although Foucault the person had no trouble taking political positions. Why support some resistances and not others? He could or would not say. As we pressed him to articulate the ground of his positions, he took refuge in exasperated modesty — there was no general principle at stake, and no substantial problem for his system (which was not, after all, intended to be "a system"). Altogether too easy. A theoretical nihilism, then, is a fair charge to level against the discourse move; it is the equivalent of the blank stare of the postmodern. What, in short, is the ethical basis for politics?

As the ontological bedrock shakes, nostalgia will return for the old unmoved movers — the unbudgeable signified, the true, the essential, the godly. How tempting it will be, for example, to regress to a labor theory of value, a notion of labor-power as human essence, with alienation reduced to the theft of the fruits of labor. How tempting to trumpet forth, one more time, the incantation to class struggle — as if it were long since ordained what constituted a class, what impelled a class to make history, and what was defensible (and not) in its "struggle." I call this regression for two reasons: first, because it screens out the dreadful history of state socialism — neglects, on the theoretical plane, the problem of state power; and second, because it fails to honor the contribution of the discourse-theory move, namely to have pointed out how discourse not only reflects but helps *constitute* the domain of production in which class relations are rooted.[15]

This is not the place to try to develop a political point of view that would transcend Foucauldian relativism without taking refuge in an unworkable universalism. But I do want to outline where I think we ought to be looking. The overarching concept we need is *a politics of limits*. Simply, there must be limits to what human beings can be permitted to do with their powers. Most of the atrocities to which our species is prone can be understood as violations of limits. The essence of a politics must be rooted in three protections: (1) The ecological: the earth and human life must be protected against the Bomb and other man-made depredations. (2) The pluralist: the social group must be protected against domination by other social groups. (3) The libertarian: the individual must be protected against domination by collectives. A politics of limits respects horizontal social relations — multiplicity over hierarchy, juxtaposition over usurpation, difference over deference: finally, disorderly life in its flux against orderly death in its finality. The democratic, vital edge of the postmodern, the love of difference and flux and the exuberantly unfinished, deserves to infuse the spirit of a politics adequate to our time. Needless to say, this way of putting the matter leaves many questions unsettled: most grievously, what happens when there are conflicts and internal fissures among these objectives: What kind of authority, what kind of difference, is legitimate? Respect for uncertainties is of the essence. . . . This is the properly postmodern note on which I suspend the discussion for now.

4. *What after postmodernism, then?* Alongside blasé postmodernism, I am trying to maintain, there is an intelligent variant in which pluralist exuberance and critical intelligence reinforce each other. Here we find jubilant disrespect for the boundaries that are supposed to segregate culture castes, but disrespect of this sort does not imply a leveling down, profaning the holy precincts of high culture. The exuberant and parodic side of postmodernism tunnels under the gossamer structures of belief. Where fey, blasé postmodernism skates along the edge of belief, cheerfully or cheerlessly leaving doubt whether it is to be taken as critical or affirmative, the exuberant kind tries to undermine the apparently solid ground of belief with dynamite. Absorbing every scrap of leftover culture, it gets involved with nothing. It is suspicious of crusades and commitments outside the self; it does not galvanize citizenship in a larger community — or imperial enthusiasms, for that matter. The music of the "Vietnam syndrome" is strangely akin to the music, if that is the word, of commodities trading.

The postmodernist arts, then, express a spirit that comports well with American culture in the 1980s. Alongside ostensible belief, actual disengagement. The standard ideological configurations of "liberal" and "conservative" belief are decomposing, although the decomposition is masked by the fact that the old political language is still in force.[16] The patriotic words are mouthed while the performers signal, in the manner of *Moonlighting* (and Reagan at his self-deprecating best), that they don't really mean them (quite). There is laissez-faire in economics as long as you can find an apartment you can afford and as long as you have not thought too long about near-collisions between passenger planes. In *Stranger Than Paradise* and David Letterman[17] as well as in the Republican Party, there is a love for the common people and their kitsch tastes that is indistinguishable from contempt. In politics as in the arts distrust runs rampant while, beneath the surface, as David Byrne and Brian Eno have put it, "America is waiting for a message of some sort or another."

Postmodernism is an art of erosion. Make the most of stagnation, it says, and give up gracefully. That is perhaps its defining break from modernism, which was, whatever its subversive practices, a series of declarations of faith — Suprematism's future, Joyce's present, Eliot's unsurpassable past. What is not clear is whether postmodernism, living off borrowed materials, has the resources for continuing self-renewal. A car with a dead battery can run off its generator only so long. Postmodernism seems doomed to be intermission. But historical time is treacherous to assess. Intermissions can last a very long time, and who is counting?

Notes

Introduction

1. Alexander Cockburn, Public Lecture, "Media, Empire and the New Cold War," Hampshire College, March 4, 1986.

2. Part of this is of course created out of the necessity of budgets (or lack of) but it is also a stated preference of the producers of these shows.

3. Jesse Lemisch, "I Dreamed I Saw MTV Last Night," *The Nation* (Oct. 18, 1986), p. 374.

4. Lemisch, "I Dreamed I Saw MTV," p. 376.

5. Marshall Berman, "Blowin' Away the Lies," *Village Voice* (Dec. 3–9, 1986), p. 114.

6. Daniel Hallin, "Network News: We Keep America on Top of the World," in Todd Gitlin, ed., *Watching Television* (New York: Pantheon, 1986).

2. The Imperial Cannibal

1. Jonathan Swift, *A Modest Proposal for Preventing the Children of the Poor People in Ireland from Being a Burden to Their Parents or Country, and for Making Them Beneficial to the Public* (1728). This little bombshell can be found in any number of collections of great essays in English. All my quotations from Swift are taken from this short essay.

2. Judith Williamson, *Consuming Passions: The Dynamics of Popular Culture* (New York: Marion Boyars/Scribners, 1986).

3. Pierre Bourdieu, *Distinction: A Social Critique of the Judgement of Taste*, trans: Richard Nice, (Cambridge, Mass: Harvard U. Press, 1984), p. 491. Hereafter cited in the text. From the difference between those social formations which are bound to material necessity, above all to labor, and those who are free from necessity, Bourdieu develops an astonishingly rich analysis of all the great issues in aesthetics.

The tastes of freedom can only assert themselves as such in relation to tastes of necessity, which are thereby brought to the level of the aesthetic and so defined as vulgar. This claim to aristocracy is less likely to be contested than any other, because the relation of the "pure, disinterested" disposition to the conditions of existence which are rarest because most freed from economic necessity, have every chance of passing unnoticed. The most "classifying" privilege thus has the privilege of appearing to be the most natural one. (p. 56)

The only fault in this fine work is that Bourdieu sees that the *tastes* of freedom are *internally related* to the *tastes* of necessity, but he does not consider how the actual material freedom of some and material necessity of others are also internally related. This relation leads us to exploitation; Bourdieu does not examine the tastes and passions which develop on the basis of *that*. Jonathan Swift did not forget this point, as we shall see.

4. I heard recently on the CBC radio that a TV ad on AIDS used a banana to demonstrate the proper use of a condom. The network received a letter of complaint from the banana industry that, "the banana is a food and should be treated with consideration and respect." I think Freud would have answered: "Yes. Precisely."

5. Teodato Hugwana, Minister of Information, Mozambique; quoted in *Briarpatch* (April 1987), p. 7.

6. G.E.M. de Ste. Croix, *The Class Struggle in the Ancient Greek World* (Ithaca: Cornell U. Press, 1981), pp. 502–03. This great work not only applies Marxist analysis to antiquity, it deepens the conceptual tools of Marxism. As a result, one can read this morning's paper with the eyes of this book. For a brief account of these tools, and of the personal development of his thinking, see Ste. Croix, "Class in Marx's Conception of History, Ancient and Modern" (*Monthly Review*, 36:10 [March 1984], pp. 21–46). For a critical appreciation, see Perry Anderson, "Class Struggle in the Ancient World" (*History Workshop Journal*, no. 16, [1983], pp. 57–73). When *Class Struggle* was published, Ste. Croix was seventy-one. For once, I feel uplifted by the term, "Senior Citizen."

7. Today, the top 10% of the United States population owns 90% of the stocks, bonds, and business assets in the country. The top *one-half of one percent* owns 50 percent. The inequality of ownership of wealth has increased over the past two decades. See Jerry Kioby, "The Growing Divide: Class Polarization in the 1980's," *Monthly Review* 39:4 (September 1987), pp. 1–8.

8. Todd Gitlin, *Inside Prime Time* (New York: Pantheon, 1983).

9. William Leiss, Stephen Kline, and Sut Jhally, *Social Communication in Advertising: Persons, Products, and Images of Well-Being* (London: Methuen, 1986), pp. 55–61; ch. 11, pp. 259–98); also, Sut Jhally, *The Codes of Advertising: Fetishism and the Political Economy of Meaning in Consumer Society* (London: St. Martin's Press, 1987), pp. 12–19.

10. In one of his American historical novels, Gore Vidal has Aaron Burr evaluating Thomas Jefferson as an empire builder. Jefferson,

> set for the west and the south an imperial course as coldly and resourcefully as any Bonaparte. Had Jefferson not been a hypocrite I might have admired him. After all, he was the most successful empire-builder of our century, succeeding where Bonaparte failed. But then Bonaparte was always candid

when it came to motive and Jefferson was always dishonest. In the end, candour failed; dishonesty prevailed. I dare not preach a sermon on *that* text. See *Burr* (New York: Random House, 1973), p. 209.

11. William A. Williams, *Empire as a Way of Life: an Essay on the Causes and Character of America's Present Predicament, Along with a Few Thoughts about an Alternative* (London: Oxford U. Press, 1980), pp. 58–59. The next quotation is from p. 149.

3. American Empire and Global Communication

1. Harlan Cleveland, "Rethinking International Governance," IFDA Dossier #59, (May/June 1987), p. 51.

2. For a discussion of the crucial component of expanding American influence in the postwar period, see Herbert Schiller, *Mass Communication and American Empire* (Boston: Beacon Press, 1971).

3. See M. Wilkins, *The Maturing of Multinational Enterprise: American Business Abroad from 1914–1970* (Cambridge: Harvard University Press, 1974); and R. Gilpin, *The Political Economy of International Relations* (Princeton: Princeton University Press, 1987).

4. See K. Nordenstreng, *The Mass Media Declaration of UNESCO* (Norwood: Ablex, 1984).

5. See Herbert Schiller, *Who Knows: Information in the Age of the Fortune 500* (Norwood: Ablex, 1981).

6. Quoted in Herbert Schiller, *Mass Communication and American Empire*.

7. L. Joinet, *Les Aspects Juridiques, Economiques et Sociaux des Flux Transfrontiers des Donnes Personnelles* (Paris: Organization for Economic Cooperation and Development, 1977).

8. See S. Nora and A. Minc, *The Computerization of Society* (Boston: MIT Press, 1979); and Consultive Committee on the Implications of Telecommunications for Canadian Sovereignty, *Telecommunications and Canada* (Toronto: Federal Department of Communications, 1979).

9. See D. Schiller, *Telematics and Government* (Norwood: Ablex, 1982); J. Tunstall, *Communications Deregulation* (New York: Basil Blackwell, 1986); and Herbert Schiller, *Information and the Crisis Economy* (Norwood, Ablex, 1984).

10. Herbert Schiller, "Expanding the Club: New Vistas for TDF," (Springfield, VA: Transnational Data Reporting Services, Inc., 1985).

11. "OECD Data Declaration Stalled," *Transnational Data Report*, Vol. 5, No. 2, 1982, p. 58.

12. R. Pipe, "Searching for Appropriate TDF Regulation," *Transnational Data Report*, Vol. 7, No. 1 1984.

13. C. Raghavan, "A Rollback of the Third World IFDA Dossier #52 (Rome: *International Foundation for Development Alternatives*, 1986).

14. Jan Pronk, "The Case for a World Public Sector," IFDA Dossier #54 (Rome: *International Foundation for Development Alternatives*, 1986).

4. Power, Hegemony, and Communication Theory

1. *TV Guide*, 34, No. 11 (March 14, 1987).

2. Martin Carnoy, *The State and Political Theory* (Princeton: Princeton University Press, 1984), p. 10.

3. Steven Lukes, *Power: A Radical View* (London: Macmillan, 1974).

4. Carnoy, *State and Political Theory*, p. 34.

5. Daniel J. Czitrom, *Media and the American Mind: From Morse to McLuhan* (Chapel Hill: University of North Carolina Press, 1982), p. 91.

6. Everett M. Rogers, "Communication and Development: The Passing of the Dominant Paradigm," in *Communication and Development: Critical Perspectives*, ed. Everett M. Rogers (Beverley Hills: Sage, 1976), pp. 121–148.

7. John Westergaard, "Power, Class and the Media," in *Mass Communication and Society*, ed. James Curran, Michael Gurevitch, and Janet Woollacott (Beverly Hills: Sage, 1977), pp. 95–115.

8. Philip Elliott, "Uses and Gratifications Research: A Critique and a Sociological Alternative," in *The Uses of Mass Communications*, ed. Jay G. Blumler and Elihu Katz (Beverly Hills: Sage, 1974), pp. 249–268.

9. Peter Bachrach and Morton S. Baratz, *Power and Poverty: Theory and Practice* (New York: Oxford University Press, 1970).

10. Michael J. Shapiro, "Literary Production as a Politicizing Activity," *Political Theory*, 12, No. 3 (1984), 387–422.

11. See Rogers "Communication and Development."

12. George A. Donohue, Philllip J. Tichenor, and Clarice N. Olien, "Gatekeeping: Mass Media Systems and Information Control," in *Current Perspectives in Mass Communication Research*, ed. F. Gerald Kline and Phillip J. Tichenor (Beverley Hills: Sage, 1972), pp. 41–69.

13. Theodore R. Sarbin and Karl E. Scheibe, *Studies in Social Identity* (New York: Praeger, 1983).

14. Peter L. Berger and Thomas Luckmann, *The Social Construction of Reality* (New York: Anchor, 1966).

15. George Gerbner, Larry Gross, Michael Morgan, and Nancy Signorielli, "The 'Mainstreaming' of America: Violence Profile No. 11, *Journal of Communication*, 30, No. 3 (1980), 10–29.

16. Nicholas Garnham, "Contribution to a Political Economy of Mass-Communication," *Media, Culture and Society* I (1979), 123–146.

17. Louis Althusser, "Ideology and Ideological State Apparatuses: Notes Toward an Investigation," in his *Lenin and Philosophy and Other Essays*, trans. Ben Brewster (New York: Monthly Review Press, 1971), pp. 127–186.

18. Michel Foucault, *Power/Knowledge: Selected Interviews and Other Writings 1972–1977*, trans. Colin Gordon, Leo Marshall, John Mepham, and Kate Soper, ed. Colin Gordon (New York: Pantheon, 1980).

19. Lukes, *Power: A Radical View*, p. 21.

20. Lukes, *Power: A Radical View*, p. 22.

21. Stuart Hall, "The Rediscovery of 'Ideology': Return of the Repressed in Media Studies," in *Culture Society and the Media*, ed. Michael Gurevitch, Tony Bennett, James Curran, and Janet Woollacott (London: Methuen, 1982), pp. 56–90.

22. Carnoy, *State and Political Theory*, p. 65.

23. Hall, "Rediscovery of 'Ideology'," p. 85.

24. Todd Gitlin, *The Whole World is Watching: Mass Media in the Making and Unmaking of the New Left* (Berkeley: University of California Press, 1980).

25. Gitlin, *Whole World is Watching*, p. 292.

26. Carnoy, *State and Political Theory*, pp. 87–88.

27. Christine Buci-Glucksmann, "Hegemony and Consent," in *Approaches To Gramsci*, ed. Anne Showstack Sassoon (London: Writers and Readers, 1982), pp. 116–126.

28. Steven Lukes, "Introduction," in *Power*, ed. Steven Lukes (New York: New York University Press, 1986), pp. 1–18.

29. Larry Grossberg, ed., "On Postmodernism and Articulation: An Interview with Stuart Hall," *Journal of Communication Inquiry*, 10, No. 2 (1986), 45–60.

30. Ernesto Laclau and Chantel Mouffe, *Hegemony and Socialist Strategy: Towards a Radical Democratic Politics*, trans. Winston Moore and Paul Cammack (London: Verso, 1985).

5. The Political Economy of Culture

1. Ben Bagdikian "The U.S. Media: Supermarket or Assembly Line," *Journal of Communication* Vol. 35, No. 3 (Summer 1985), p. 97.

2. Quoted in B. Owen, *Economics and Freedom of Expression* (Cambridge, MA: Ballinger, 1975), p. 1.

3. Hans Enzensberger, *The Consciousness Industry* (New York: Seabury Press, 1974).

4. Ben Bagdikian, *The Media Monopoly* (Boston: Beacon Press, 1983), p. 4.

5. P. Drier and S. Weinberg "Interlocking Directorates," *Columbia Journalism Review* (November/December 1979), p. 51.

6. Dallas Smythe, *Dependency Road: Communications, Capitalism, Consciousness, and Canada* (Norwood, NJ: Ablex, 1981), p. 8.

7. Smythe, *Dependency Road*, p. 9.

8. See my "Advertising as Religion" in this volume for further discussion of this.

9. A. Swingewood, *The Myth of Mass Culture* (London: Macmillan, 1977).

10. Theodor Adorno and Max Horkheimer "The Culture Industry: Enlightenment as Mass Deception," in J. Curran, M. Gurevitch and J. Woolacott, eds., *Mass Communication and Society* (London: Edward Arnold, 1977).

11. D. Held, *Introduction to Critical Theory* (Berkeley and Los Angeles: University of California Press, 1980), p. 90.

12. Adorno and Horkheimer, "Culture Industry," p. 351.

13. See the Appendix "Results of the Immediate Process or Production" in Karl Marx, *Capital*, Volume 1 (London: Penguin, 1976), trans. by Ben Fowkes. Also see Sut Jhally, *The Codes of Advertising*, (New York: St. Martin's Press, 1987), for a fuller discussion of these issues with regard to the commercial media.

14. Nicholas Garnham, "Contribution to a Political Economy of Mass Communication," *Media, Culture and Society* No. 1 (1979), p. 126.

15. Garnham, "Political Economy," p. 142.

16. Garnham, "Political Economy," p. 133.

17. Bagdikian, *Media Monopoly*, chap. 7.

18. There is a second newspaper in Washington today — The Washington Times. This is owned and operated (at a substantial loss) by the right-wing "Moonies" organization.

19. Bagdikian, *Media Monopoly*, p. 4.

20. R. Samarajiwa, "The Canadian Newspaper Industry and the Kent Commission: Rationalization and Response," *Studies in Political Economy* No. 12 (Fall 1983), p. 132.

21. Todd Gitlin, *Inside Prime-Time*, (New York: Pantheon, 1983), pp. 77 and 85.

22. See Jhally, *Codes of Advertising*, pp. 80–83 for further discussion.

23. See William Leiss, Stephen Kline, and Sut Jhally, *Social Communication in Advertising* (London: Methuen, 1986) for further discussion.

24. See Jhally, *Codes of Advertising*, pp. 93–102 for further discussion.

25. See Sut Jhally "The Spectacle of Accumulation: Material and Cultural Factors in the Evolution of the Sports/Media Complex," *The Insurgent Sociologist* Vol. 12, No. 3 (Summer 1984).

26. Karl Marx and Friedrich Engels, *The German Ideology* (New York: International Publishers, 1956), p. 64.

27. Garnham, "Political Economy," p. 144.

6. Advertising and the Development of Consumer Society

1. Georg Simmel, "The Metropolis and Mental Life," trans. Hans H. Gerth. In Richard Sennett, ed., *Classic Essays on the Culture of Cities* (New York: Appleton-Century-Crofts, 1969), p. 48.

2. Robert Park, "Human Migration and the Marginal Man" *The American Journal of Sociology*, Vol. XXXIII (1928). The Sennett, *Classic Essays*, p. 131.

3. Louis Sass, "The Borderline Personality," *The New York Times Magazine* (August 22, 1982), p. 12.

4. Peter Marzio, *Chromolithography 1840–1900: The Democratic Art* (Boston: D. R. Godine, 1979), p. 104.

5. Edward A. Filene, *Successful Living in the Machine Age* (New York: Simon & Schuster, 1931), pp. 144–146, 157.

6. Quoted in Robert Park, *The Immigrant Press and Its Control*, (New York: Harper & Brothers, 1922), p. 448.

7. Christine Frederick, *Selling Mrs. Consumer*, (New York: The Business Bourse, 1929).

8. Helen Woodward, *Through Many Windows* (New York: Harper & Brothers, 1926), p. 298.

9. Edward A. Filene, *Successful Living*, p. 96.

10. Edgar Jones, *Those Were the Good Old Days*, (New York: Simon and Schuster, 1959), p. 439. This 1920s ad is reprinted in the above anthology of American advertising.

7. Circumscribing Postmodern Culture

1. Walter Benjamin, "The Work of Art in the Age of Mechanical Reproduction" in *Illuminations*, ed. Hannah Arendt (New York: Schocken Books, 1969), pp 222, 239–41. Benjamin's account of the audience is taken from Brecht. See, for example, Bertolt Brecht, *Brecht on Theatre*, trans. John Willett (New York: Hill & Wang, 1964), pp. 44, 50, 56.

2. Max Horkheimer and Theodor W. Adorno, *Dialectic of Enlightenment*, trans. John Cumming (New York: Herder and Herder, 1972), p. 129f.

3. Walter Benjamin, "Work of Art," pp. 232ff, 235ff. Theodor Adorno, "Letters to Walter Benjamin" in *Aesthetics and Politics* (London: Verso, 1980), p. 122. Adorno wrote his essay "On the Fetish Character of Music and Regression of Listening" precisely to document audience regression as against the expectations of Benjamin. In *The Essential Frankfurt School Reader*, ed. Andrew Arato and Eike Gebhardt (Oxford: Basil Blackwell, 1978).

4. Benjamin, "Work of Art," p. 224, cf. p. 230.

5. Benjamin, "Work of Art," p. 218. Dean MacCannell in *The Tourist* (New York: Schocken Books, 1976), p. 47f, developed a similar critique of Benjamin. The present account, however, is closer to an immanent development of Benjamin, rather than the substitution of a semiotic account, and is distinct in some crucial places from MacCannell. The position developed here as a characterization of postmodern experience is consistent with Jacques Derrida's critique of metaphysics, in which a centered structure is only possible through the effacement of a play of differences. Only the "second" promotes the anxiety to *establish* an origin, a "first." See, for example, "Structure, Sign and Play in the Discourse of the Human Sciences," in *Writing and Difference* trans. Allan Bass (Chicago: University of Chicago Press, 1978), p. 278ff. With regard to the notion of authenticity, see Lionel Trilling, *Sincerity and Authenticity* (Cambridge: Harvard University Press, 1972).

6. Horkheimer and Adorno, *Dialectic of Enlightenment*, p. 145f.

7. See my essay "Media Beyond Representation" in this volume.

8. Many contemporary cultural critics lay emphasis, in polemical relation to traditional Marxism, on the contingency of the association of these images into sets. This seems overstated. Once can imagine the difficulty of articulating together sports with cooking or ballet. The "solidity" of the historical accretions of culture that constrain associations needs a better account at this point. This presentation, through the account of postulation of originals, provides the basis for understanding this solidity — though it is not developed here.

9. This account differs from that of Jean Baudrillard insofar as the hermeneutic component of authenticating originals is not regarded as exploded or eliminated, but as constructed by the media system as a merely apparent outside. Therefore, the ideology of media "merely reflecting (a prior) reality" is seen as essential to its present functioning and, most importantly, as imbedded in the concrete practices of the media system. See Jean Baudrillard, *Simulations* (New York: Semiotext(e) 1983) and *In the Shadow of the Silent Majorities* (New York: Semiotext(e), 1983).

10. The present discussion is oriented primarily to advanced capitalist societies legitimated by privatized consumption. Nevertheless, it is claimed that the tendency toward "industrially produced identities in the face of the enemy through staged difference" is characteristic of industrialism *per se*. Industrial consumption admits of two major modes of incorporation into identity-formation. First, identity through uncoerced and unrelated consumer choices. Second, through a coerced control over consumption, or a "forced acceptance" of identity. The latter characterizes societies of the Soviet type. Both modes of identity-formation revolve around the social organization of consumption. For the analysis of Soviet-type societies as "dictatorship over needs" see Ferenc Feher, Agnes Heller, and Gyorgy Marcus, *Dictatorship Over Needs* (Oxford: Basil Blackwell, 1983). See the review symposium on this book in *Thesis Eleven*, No. 12 (1985), pp. 145–68, with Antonio Carlo, Mihaly Vajda, and Gianfranco Poggi.

11. See Ian H. Angus and Peter G. Cook, "Nuclear Technology as Ideology," *Canadian Journal of Political and Social Theory*, Vol. XI, No. 1–2 (1987).

12. Jan Patochka, "Wars of the Twentieth Century and the Twentieth Century as War," *Telos*, No. 30 (Winter 1976–77), p. 124.

13. Gwyn Dyer, *War*. Series aired on CBC television and on various public television stations. Especially part one, "The Road to Total War."

14. Patochka, "Wars of the Twentieth Century," p. 125.

15. I have attempted to sketch the ground for an ethics responding to this situation in "Displacement and Otherness: Toward a Postmodern Ethics" in *Ethnicity in a Technological Age* ed. Ian H. Angus (Edmonton: University of Alberta Press, 1988).

8. In Living Color: Race and American Culture

1. Reynolds's remarks were made at a conference on equal opportunity held by the bar association in Orlando, Florida. *The San Francisco Chronicle* (7 February 1987).

2. Economic Development Department of the NAACP, "The Discordant Sound of Music (A Report on the Record Industry)," (Baltimore, Maryland: The NAACP, 1987), pp. 16–17.

3. Campanis's remarks on "Nightline" were reprinted in *The San Francisco Chronicle* (April 9, 1987).

4. Ellen Wulfhorst, "TV Stereotyping: It's the 'Pits'," *The San Francisco Chronicle* (August 24, 1987).

5. Stuart Hall, "The Whites of Their Eyes: Racist Ideologies and the Media," in George Bridges and Rosalind Brunt, eds. *Silver Linings* (London: Lawrence and Wishart, 1981), pp. 36–37.

6. For an excellent survey of racial beliefs see Thomas F. Gossett, *Race: The History of an Idea in America* (New York: Shocken Books, 1965).

7. W. L. Rose, *Race and Region in American Historical Fiction: Four Episodes in Popular Culture* (Oxford: Clarendon Press, 1979).

8. Melanie Martindale-Sikes, "Nationalizing 'Nigger' Imagery Through 'Birth of a Nation'," paper prepared for the 73rd Annual Meeting of the American Sociological Association (September 4–8, 1978) in San Francisco.

9. For a discussion of Italian, Irish, Jewish, Slavic, and German stereotypes in film, see Randall M. Miller, ed., *The Kaleidoscopic Lens: How Hollywood Views Ethnic Groups* (Englewood, N.J.: Jerome S. Ozer, 1980).

10. Michael R. Winston, "Racial Consciousness and the Evolution of Mass Communications in the United States," *Daedalus*, vol. III, No. 4 (Fall 1982).

11. Tom Engelhardt, "Ambush at Kamikaze Pass," in Emma Gee, ed., *Counterpoint: Perspectives on Asian America* (Los Angeles: Asian American Studies Center, UCLA, 1976), p. 270.

12. Hall, "Whites of Their Eyes," p. 38.

13. Gretchen Bataille and Charles Silet, "The Entertaining Anachronism: Indians in American Film," in Randall M. Miller, ed., *Kaleidoscopic Lens*, p. 40.

14. Elaine Kim, "Asian Americans and American Popular Culture" in Hyung-Chan Kim, ed., *Dictionary of Asian American History* (New York: Greenwood Press, 1986), p. 107.

15. Donald Bogle, "A Familiar Plot (A Look at the History of Blacks in American Movies)," *The Crisis*, Vol. 90, No. 1 (January 1983), p. 15.

16. Frank Chin, "Confessions of the Chinatown Cowboy," *Bulletin of Concerned Asian Scholars*, Vol. 4, No. 3 (Fall 1972).

17. Winston, "Racial Consciousness," p. 176.

18. *San Francisco Chronicle*, September 21, 1984.

19. Quoted in Allen L. Woll, "Bandits and Lovers: Hispanic Images in American Film," in Miller, ed., *Kaleidoscopic Lens*, p. 60.

20. Bogle, "Familiar Plot," p. 17.

21. Dave Marsh and Kevin Stein, *The Book of Rock Lists* (New York: Dell Publishing Co., 1981), p. 8.

22. *Rock & Roll Confidential*, No. 44 (February 1987), p. 2.

23. Steven C. Dublin, "Symbolic Slavery: Black Representations in Popular Culture," *Social Problems*, Vol. 34, No. 2 (April 1987).

24. *The San Francisco Chronicle* (June 13, 1987).

9. Cultural Conundrums and Gender: America's Present Past

1. The full version of this story of engendered narratives is recounted in my essay, "The New Feminist Scholarship," *Salmagundi* (Spring/Summer, 1986), 3–43.

2. I've used this example before, not because it stands alone but because it *stands in for* so many others from the nineteenth century to the present — and because it's always good to cite Cady Stanton, to get some sense of the verve of her style.

3. Quoted in Elizabeth Cady Stanton, Susan B. Anthony, and Matilda Joslyn Gage, eds., *History of Woman Suffrage*, Vol. I (Rochester, N.Y.: Charles Mann, 1889), p. 145.

4. Stanton, Anthony, and Gage, *History of Woman Suffrage*, Vol. 2, pp. 351–352.

5. This is a point I make throughout *Women and War* (New York: Basic Books, 1987), using male and female embodiments of war and peace and imbeddedness in or distancing from individual and collective violence as my critical launching point.

6. If you want to read the whole story, in its hyperbolic effloresence, the reference is: Phylip Wylie, *Generation of Vipers* (New York: Rinehart and Co., 1955).

7. See Dorothy Dinnerstein, *The Mermaid and the Minotaur* (New York: Harpers, 1977). Dinnerstein's appropriation of Freud is highly selective. Only two works are cited. Freud's descriptions are allowed to stand but his evaluations and mordant sense of limits are trashed.

8. Dinnerstein, *Mermaid and Minotaur*, p. 33.

9. Dinnerstein, *Mermaid and Minotaur*, p. 210.

10. Betty Friedan, *The Feminine Mystique* (New York: W.W. Norton, 1963), p. 77.

11. Her revisions of this position are really *reversions* to earlier notions of women's special qualities of mind and spirit which will somehow immunize her from the worst male characteristics even as she takes on their roles. See *The Second Stage*.

12. Mary Douglas, *Purity and Danger* (London: Routledge and Kegan Paul, 1966), p. 115.

13. Peggy Reeves Sanday, *Male Dominance and Female Power* (Cambridge: Cambridge University Press, 1981), p. 155.

14. Kenneth S. Lynn, *Hemingway* (New York: Simon and Schuster, 1987).

15. From Hemingway's "Up in Michigan," cited in Lynn, *Hemingway*, p. 110.

10. Working Class Culture in the Electronic Age

1. Paul Willis, *Learning to Labor* (New York: Columbia University Press, 1977).

2. Louis Althusser, "Ideology and Ideological State Apparatuses," in *Lenin and Philosophy* (London: New Left Books, 1971).

3. I exclude "film" from this list because of the market distinction made between the art film and movies in the last two decades, eg. the cinema of Eric Rohmer, Louis Malle, Yvonne Rainer, Agnes Varda, and the late John Huston, compared with Stephen Spielberg, Sidney Lumet (whose position is a bit ambiguous), and Oliver Stone (whose location is not).

4. Teresa Di Lauretis, *Alice Doesn't: Feminism, Semiotics, Cinema* (Bloomington: Indiana University press, 1984) pp. 37–69.

5. David Halle, *America's Working Men: Work, Home and Politics Among the Blue-collar Property Owners* (Chicago: University of Chicago Press, 1984).

11. Nature in Industrial Society

1. Cited by Marjorie Hope Nicolson, *Mountain Gloom and Mountain Glory* (New York: W. W. Norton & Co., 1959), pp. 22–23. See also "Nature as aesthetic norm" in Arthur O. Lovejoy, *Essays in the History of Ideas* (New York: G. P. Putnam's Sons, 1960), pp. 69–77.

2. Rachel Carson, *Silent Spring* (Boston: Houghton Mifflin Co., 1962), p. 297.

3. "Pesticides: The Price of Progress," *Time* (September 28, 1962), p. 297.

4. For further elaboration of this see Neil Evernden, *The Natural Alien* (Toronto: University of Toronto Press, 1985).

5. Mary Douglas, "Environments at Risk," in Jonathon Benthall, ed., *Ecology: The Shaping Enquiry* (London, Longman, 1972), p. 144.

6. J. H. van den Berg, *The Changing Nature of Man: Introduction to a Historical Psychology* (New York: Delta, 1975), pp. 225–226.

7. Hans Jonas, *The Phenomenon of life* (Chicago: University of Chicago Press, 1966), pp. 35–36.

8. See Bill Devall and George Sessions, *Deep Ecology: Living as if Nature Mattered* (Salt Lake City: Peregrine Smith Books, 1985).

9. See Erazim Kohak, *The Embers and the Stars* (Chicago: University of Chicago Press, 1984).

10. See, for example, Peter Singer's *Animal Liberation* (New York: Avon Books, 1975).

11. Warwick Fox, *Deep Ecology: A Response to Richard Sylvan's Critique of Deep Ecology* (Hobart, Tasmania: University of Tasmania, Environmental Studies Occasional Paper #20, 1986).

12. Van den Berg, *Changing Nature*, p. 52.

13. Van den Berg, *Changing Nature*, p. 53.

14. Van den Berg, *Changing Nature*, p. 56.

15. Van den Berg, *Changing Nature*, p. 125.

16. Similar arguments have been put by many writers. See for instance John Livingston,

One Cosmic Instant (Toronto: McClelland, 1973); Morris Berman, *The Re-Enchantment of the World* (Ithaca: Cornell University Press, 1981); Theodore Roszak, *Where the Wasteland Ends* (New York, Doubleday, 1972); Neil Evernden, *The Natural Alien*; David Ehrenfeld, *The Arrogance of Humanism* (New York, Oxford University Press, 1978).

17. Alfred North Whitehead, *Science and the Modern World* (New York: The Free Press, 1925), pp. 54–55.

18. Aldo Leopold, *A Sand County Almanac* (New York, Oxford University Press, 1949), pp. 201–226.

19. Marshall Sahlins, *The Use and Abuse of Biology* (London: Tavistock Publishers, 1977), p. 105.

12. Sexual Politics

1. For a lucid exposition of this distinction, I am indebted to Alice Echols's paper, "Cultural Feminism: Feminist Capitalism and the Anti-Pornography Movement," a shorter version of which appears as "The New Feminism of Yin and Yang," in *Powers of Desire: The Politics of Sexuality*, ed., Ann Snitow, Christine Stansell, and Sharon Thompson (New York: Monthly Review Press, 1983).

13. Action-Adventure as Ideology

1. Max Horkheimer and Theodor W. Adorno, "The Culture Industry: Enlightenment as Mass Deception," in *Dialectic of Enlightenment*, trans. John Cumming (NY: Continuum, 1972), pp. 120–167.

2. For a more detailed discussion of the Frankfurt School's views on commercial culture, see Martin Jay, *The Dialectical Imagination: A History of the Frankfurt School and the Institute of Social Research, 1923–1950* (Boston: Little, Brown, 1973). For an excellent discussion of the relationship between the Frankfurt School and other types of mass media criticism, see Tony Bennett, "Theories of the Media, Theories of Society," in Michael Gurevitch, Tony Bennett, James Curran, and Janet Woollacott, *Culture, Society and the Media* (London: Methuen, 1982), pp. 30–55.

     For an overview of several Marxist approaches to media studies, see Lawrence Grossberg, "Strategies of Marxist Cultural Interpretation," *Critical Studies in Mass Communication* 1:4 (Dec. 1984), pp. 392-421.

     For a general introduction to popular culture debates, see Herbert Gans, *Popular Culture and High Culture* (NY: Basic Books, 1974).

3. Louis Althusser, "Ideology and Ideological State Apparatuses," in *Lenin and Philosophy and Other Essays*, trans. Ben Brewster (NY: Monthly Review, 1971), pp. 127–186.

4. Karl Marx and Frederick Engels, *The German Ideology*, ed. C. J. Arthur (NY: International Publishers, 1970), p. 64.

5. For more on the theory of hegemony, see Antonio Gramsci, *Selections from the Prison Notebooks*, ed. and trans. Quintin Hoare and Geoffrey Nowell-Smith (NY: International Publishers, 1971).

6. For more detailed information on British cultural studies' approach to ideology, see Bill Schwarz, ed., *On Ideology* (London: Hutchinson, 1978). Stuart Hall, "Culture, the Media and the 'Ideological Effect'," in James Curran, Michael Gurevitch, Janet Woollacott, eds., *Mass Communication and Society* (Beverly Hills, Ca.: Sage, 1977), pp. 315–348. Stuart Hall, "Signification, Representation, Ideology: Althusser and the Post-Structuralist Debates," *Critical Studies in Mass Communication* 2:2 (June

1985), pp. 91–114. Special issue on Stuart Hall, *Journal of Communication Inquiry* 10:2 (Summer 1986). Thomas Streeter, "An Alternative Approach to Television Research: Developments in British Cultural Studies at Birmingham," in Willard D. Rowland, Jr. and Bruce Watkins, eds., *Interpreting Television: Current Research Perspectives* (Beverly Hills, Ca.: Sage, 1984), pp. 74–97. Samuel L. Becker, "Marxist Approaches to Media Studies: The British Experience," *Critical Studies in Mass Communication* 1: 1 (1984), pp. 66–80. John Fiske, "British Cultural Studies and Television," in Robert Allen, ed., *Channels of Discourse: Television and Contemporary Criticism* (Chapel Hill, NC: U of North Carolina, 1987), pp. 254–289.

7. Stuart Hall, "Encoding/Decoding," in Stuart Hall, Dorothy Hobson, Andrew Lowe, and Paul Willis, eds., *Culture, Media, Language* (London: Hutchinson, 1980), pp. 128–138.

8. For more information on subcultures, ideology and the media, see Simon Frith, *Sound Effects: Youth, Leisure, and the Politics of Rock'n'Roll* (NY: Pantheon, 1981). Stuart Hall and Tony Jefferson, eds., *Resistance Through Rituals: Youth Subcultures in Post-War Britain* (London: Hutchinson, 1976). Dick Hebdige, *Subculture: The Meaning of Style* (London: Methuen, 1979). Gina Marchetti, "Subcultural Studies and the Film Audience: Rethinking the Film Viewing Context," in Bruce Austin, ed., *Current Research in Film: Audiences, Economics, and Law* Vol. 2 (Norwood, NJ: Ablex, 1986), pp. 62–79.

9. For an excellent introduction to the journal, see Peter Steven, ed., *Jump Cut: Hollywood, Politics and Counter-Cinema* (NY: Praeger, 1985).

10. The Editors, "Women and Film: A Discussion of Feminist Aesthetics," *New German Critique* #13 (Winter 1978), p. 89.

11. For some examples of work done from this perspective, see Douglas Kellner, "TV, Ideology, and Emancipatory Popular Culture," in Horace Newcomb, ed., *Television: The Critical View* 3rd Ed. (NY: Oxford), pp. 386–421. Todd Gitlin, "Prime Time Ideology: The Hegemonic Process in Television Entertainment," in Newcomb, (Television), pp. 426–454. Horace Newcomb, "On the Dialogic Aspects of Mass Communication," *Critical Studies in Mass Communication* 1:1 (1984), pp. 34–50. Mini White, "Ideological Analysis and Television," in Robert Allen, *Channels of Discourse*, 134–171.

12. John Fiske, "Television: Polysemy and Popularity," *Critical Studies in Mass Communication* 3: 4 (Dec. 1986), p. 392.

13. For a more extensive discussion of the relationship between genre and myth, see Thomas Schatz, "The Structural Influence: New Directions in Film Genre Study," in Barry Keith Grant, ed., *Film Genre Reader* (Austin: U of Texas, 1986), pp. 91–101.
   For a discussion of the relationship between ideology and myth, see Roland Barthes, *Mythologies*, trans. Annette Lavers (NY: Hill and Wang, 1972). Fredric Jameson, *The Political Unconscious: Narrative as a Socially Symbolic Act* (Ithaca, NY: Cornell U, 1981).

14. For more on RAIDERS, see Patricia Zimmerman, "Soldiers of Fortune: Lucas, Spielberg, Indiana Jones and RAIDERS OF THE LOST ARK," *Wide Angle* 6:2 (1984), pp. 34–39. For an interesting analysis of the sequel, see Moishe Postone and Elizabeth Traube, "The Return of the Repressed: INDIANA JONES AND THE TEMPLE OF DOOM," *Jump Cut* #30 (March 1984), pp. 12–14.

15. Northrop Frye, *Anatomy of Criticism* (Princeton, NJ: Princeton U, 1957).

16. These attributes of genre are outlined in Douglas Pye, "The Western (Genre and Movies)," in Grant, *Film Genre Reader*.

17. For interesting analyses of these MIA films, see Susan Jeffords, "The New Vietnam Films: Is the Movie Over?" *Journal of Popular Film and Television* 13:3 (Winter 1986), pp. 186–194. Elizabeth G. Traube, "Redeeming Images: The Wildman Comes Home," *Persistence of Vision* Nos. 3/4 (Summer 1986), pp. 71–94. On the new image of the Vietnam veteran, see Lisa M. Heilbronn, "Coming Home a Hero: The Changing Image of the Vietnam Vet on Prime Time Television," *Journal of Popular Film and Video* 13:1 (Spring 1985), pp. 25–30.

18. Ariel Dorfman and Armand Mattelart, *How to Read Donald Duck: Imperialist Ideology in the Disney Comic*, trans. David Kunzle (NY: International General, 1975).

19. Ariel Dorfman, *The Empire's Old Clothes: What the Lone Ranger, Babar, and Other Innocent Heroes Do to Our Minds* (NY: Pantheon, 1983).

20. John G. Cawelti, *Adventure, Mystery, and Romance: Formula Stories as Art and Popular Culture* (Chicago: U of Chicago, 1976), pp. 35–36.

21. In this regard, the action-adventure hero is quite similar to the Western hero; see Robert Warshow, "Movie Chronicle: The Westerner," in *The Immediate Experience: Movies, Comics, Theatre and Other Aspects of Popular Culture* (NY: Atheneum, 1975), pp. 135–154.

22. For a more detailed analysis, see Gina Marchetti, "Class, Ideology and Commercial Television: An Analysis of THE A-TEAM," *Journal of Film and Video* 39:2 (Spring 1987), pp. 19–28.

14. Vehicles for Myth. The Shifting Image of the Modern Car

1. See Harold Innis, *The Bias of Communication* (Toronto: U. of Toronto Press, 1953), pp. 132–141.

2. For an account of myth "as a kind of speech" and the mystifying character of second-order signification see "Myth Today" in Roland Barthes's *Mythologies* (translated by Annette Lavers) (London: Paladin 1973).

3. For a critical account of this historical process see, for example, Stuart Ewen, *Captains of Consciousness*, (New York: McGraw-Hill, 1976); and Dallas Smythe, *Dependency Road* (Norwood, N.J.: Ablex, 1980).

4. Q.v. Adrian Forty, *Objects of Desire: Design and Society from Wedgwood to IBM* (New York: Pantheon, 1986), pp. 22–24.

5. Under the direction of Harley Earl, it was first called "Art and Color," then renamed in 1955. For a vivid description of Earl and his pivotal place in the history of post-War car design see Stephen Bayley's *Sex, Drink and Fast Cars: the Creation and Consumption of Images* (London: Faber and Faber, 1986), pp. 9–20 and ff.

6. In President Hoover's memorable 1924 election phrase: "a chicken in every pot; two cars in every garage."

7. The American painter Charles Sheeler, who developed a whole purist aesthetic on the basis of such industrial landscapes, transformed the Ford plant at Dearborn into a quintessential incon of the new era. Patronized by Ford himself, several of his paintings, including Criss-Crossed Conveyors (the name says it all) hung in the Henry Ford Museum. See Gerald Silk, "The automobile in Art." Gerald Silk, Angelo Anselmi, Henry Robert Jr., and Strother MacMinn, *Automobile and Culture* (New York: Abrams, 1984).

8. This sense of the car has perhaps never been more passionately expressed than in Marinetti's 1905 encomium (also called "To Pegasus") "To the Automobile":

    > I finally unleash your metallic bridle . . . You launch yourself,/intoxicatingly into the liberating Infinite! . . . Hurrah! No longer contact with the impure earth! . . ./Finally , I am unleashed and I supplely fly/on the intoxicating plenitude/of the streaming stars in the great bed of the sky!

    Cited in Silk et al, *Automobile and Culture*, p. 67.

9. Q.v. John Heskett, *Industrial Design* (New York and Toronto: Oxford University Press, 1980), pp. 72–74.

10. The streamlining idea, replete with futurist enthusiasm, was popularized by the publication of Norman Bel Geddes's *Horizons* in 1932.

11. A wonderful extension of such imagery is to be seen in the classic Australian underground film. *The Cars That Ate Paris.*

12. The poem begins

    > she being Brand
    > —new; and you
    > know consequently a
    > little stiff i was
    > careful of her and (having
    > thoroughly oiled the universal
    > joint tested my gas felt of
    > her radiator made sure her springs were O.
    > K . . .

13. Q.v. Marshall McLuhan, *Understanding Media* (New York: Signet, 1963).

14. And also architects, of whom the most influential in this regard was Le Corbusier, both through his actual buildings and through his own manifesto, *Vers Une Architecture.*

15. It was no accident that several of Chuck Berry's rock and roll songs were about or set in cars, and that Jack Kerouac's beat classic was called *On the Road.*

16. This did not pass critical commentators by, and there were masterful dissections of the car's stylistic embodiment of the technology complex on both sides of the Atlantic. See, for example, Marshall McLuhan's *The Mechanical Bride: Folklore of Industrial Man* (Boston: Beacon, 1951), pp. 82–84; and Roland Barthes's essay in *Mythologies* on the 1955 Citroen DS.

17. A good account of this is provided in Theodor Rosak's *The Making of a Counter-culture* (Garden City, NY: Doubleday, 1969).

18. For the relation between expressway construction and the modernity crisis see Marshall Berman's account of Robert Moses and the South Bronx expressway in *All that is Solid Melts into Air* (New York: Simon and Schuster, 1982), pp. 290–312.

19. See Bayley, *Sex, Drink and Fast Cars*, pp. 63–67, 101–110.

20. I have explored this point with respect to the overall development of recent advertising in "From voyeur to narcissist: the changing imagery of men, 1950–80," in Michael Kaufmann, ed., *Beyond Patriarchy: Essays by Men on Pleasure and Power* (Toronto: Oxford University Press, 1987).

21. On another level, Toyota's reference to *Flashdance* was a tactic for Americanizing its product in the face of protectionist (and, to a degree, xenophobic) resistance to

"foreign competition." In the present phase of its assimilationist campaign Toyota has reached back to Gershwin: "Who could ask for anything more?"

22. See McLuhan, *Understanding Media*, pp. 346–369.

23. See Fredric Jameson's essay "Post-modernism: the Cultural Logic of Capitalism," *New Left Review*, No. 146 (July–August 1984).

24. For this now familiar neo-Marxist inversion of McLuhan see Jean Baudrillard's *In the Shadow of the Silent Majority* (New York: Semiotext(e), 1983).

15. Advertising as Religion: The Dialectic of Technology and Magic

1. Karl Marx, *Capital*, Vol. 1, trans. Ben Fowkes (London: Penguin, 1976), p. 125.

2. Marx, *Capital*, pp. 125–126.

3. T. Jackson Lears, "From Salvation to Self-Realization: Advertising and the Therapeutic Roots of Consumer Culture," in T. Jackson Lears and R. Fox, *The Culture of Consumption* (New York: Pantheon, 1983), pp. 4,21.

4. See William Leiss, Stephen Kline, and Sut Jhally, *Social Communication in Advertising* (Toronto: Methuen, 1986); and Sut Jhally, *The Codes of Advertising* (New York: St. Martin's Press, 1987), for further discussion of these issues.

5. See Leiss et al, *Social Communication*, for the development of the four stages of advertising and culture frames for goods.

6. Roland Marchand, *Advertising the American Dream* (Berkeley and Los Angeles: University of California Press, 1985), pp. 264, 267.

7. Marchand, *Advertising*, p. 265.

8. Marchand, *Advertising*, p. 282.

9. Tony Schwartz, *The Responsive Chord* (New York: Anchor, 1974).

10. Staffan Linder, *The Harried Leisure Class* (New York: Columbia University Press, 1975).

11. This paragraph is based upon Bill Livant "On the Religion of Use-Value," Unpublished paper, University of Regina, 1983.

12. John Kavanaugh, *Following Christ in a Consumer Society* (New York: Orbis, 1981), p. 15–16.

13. See Jhally, *Codes of Advertising*, p. 53–58.

14. Martin Esslin, "Aristotle and the Advertisers: The Television Commercial Considered as a Form of Drama," in H. Newcombe, ed., *Television: The Critical View* (New York: Oxford University Press, 1976), p. 271.

15. Raymond Williams, "Advertising: The Magic System" in *Problems in Materialism and Culture* (London: New Left Books, 1980), p. 185.

16. Judith Williamson *Decoding Advertisements* (London: Marion Boyars, 1978), p. 141.

17. Williams, "Advertising: Magic," p. 186.

18. Williamson, *Decoding Advertisements*, pp. 140, 142.

16. The Importance of Shredding in Earnest: Reading the National Security Culture and Terrorism

1. *Taking the Stand: The Testimony of Lieutenant Colonel Oliver North* (New York: Pocket Books, 1987), pp. 26–27.

2. "Abstraction today is no longer that of the map, the double, the mirror or the concept. Simulation is no longer that of a territory, a referential being or a substance. It is the generation by models of a real without origin or reality: a hyperreal," From Jean Baudrillard, *Simulations* (New York: Semiotext(e), 1983), p. 2.

3. Entitled *Documents From the U.S. Espionage Den* (not readily available at $248), the collected work contains intelligence reports on Iran, Parkistan, Kuwait, Turkey, the Soviet Union, and other Near- and Middle-Eastern countries. Of special interest is a 170-page study of international terrorism which shows that Syria "sponsored" many of the incidents of Middle-Eastern terrorism in the 1970s.

4. "Hence, there exists today a new perspective of reflection — common, I insist, to literature and to linguistics, to the creator and the critic, whose tasks, hitherto absolutely self-contained, are beginning to communicate, perhaps even to converge, at least on the level of the writer, whose action can increasingly be defined as a critique of language . . . This new conjunction of literature and linguistics, which I have just mentioned, might provisionally be called, for lack of a better name, *semiocriticism*, since it implies that writing is a system of signs." From Roland Barthes, "To Write: An Intransitive Verb?," in *The Rustle of Language*, trans. by Richard Howard (New York: Hill and Wang, 1986), pp. 11–12.

5. " 'Is it the media which induce fascination in the masses, or is it the masses which divert the media into spectacle?' Mogadishu Stammheim: 'the media are made the vehicle of the moral condemnation of terrorism and of the exploitation of fear for political ends, but, simultaneously, in the most total ambiguity, they propagate the brutal fascination of the terrorist act.' " Jean Baudrillard, "The Implosion of Meaning in the Media," in *In the Shadow of the Silent Majority* (New York: Semiotext(e), 1983), pp. 105–106.

6. *Taking the Stand*, p. 12.

7. Two provocative studies of how cultures of terror subvert order and meaning, and how disasters compel silence or dissimulation, are Michael Taussig's *Shamanism, Colonialism, and the Wild Man: A Study in Terror and Healing* (Chicago and London: The University of Chicago Press, 1987); and Maurice Blanchot's *The Writing of the Disaster* (Lincoln and London: University of Nebraska Press, 1986).

8. "There is no distinction possible between the spectacular and the symbolic, no distinction possible between the 'crime' and the 'repression.' It is this uncontrollable eruption of reversibility that is the true victory of terrorism." From Jean Baudrillard, "Our Theater of Cruelty," in *In the Shadow of the Silent Majorities*, pp. 115–116.

9. See Jean-François Lyotard's *The Postmodern Condition: A Report on Knowledge* (Minneapolis: University of Minnesota Press, 1984), particularly the foreword by Fredric Jameson, pp. vii–xxi.

10. Two seminal writings which anticipate Baudrillard's study of simulation and hyperrealism as legitimating forces for political order — one of the "culture of distraction" and the other on the "society of the spectacle" — are Siegfried Kracauer's *Das Ornament der Masse* (Frankfurt a.M.: Suhrkamp Verlag, 1963), forthcoming as *The Mass Ornament*, translated and edited by Thomas Y. Levin (Cambridge: Harvard University Press, 1988); and Guy Debord's *Society of the Spectacle* (Detroit: Black and Red, 1983).

11. See P. Virilio, *Pure War* (New York: Semiotext(e), 1983), and *Speed and Politics* (New York: Semiotext(e), 1986); and James Der Derian, *Anti-Diplomacy: Surveillance, Simulation, Espionage, and Speed in International Relations* (Oxford: Basil Blackwell, 1989).

12. See CBS production standards for coverage of terrorism; and see Jean Baudrillard on "the manipulation of a general terror of death," in Andre Frankowitz (ed.) *Seduced and Abandoned: The Baudrillard Scene* (Glebe, Australia: Stonemoss Services, 1984), p. 20.

13. These questions presuppose yet confirm a legitimacy crisis in international relations; or it would appear so, if we share a view of inquiry into legitimacy with "the owl of Minerva," whose wings stretch from Hegel to Habermas to Fredric Jameson who says in the Foreword to Lyotard's *Postmodern Condition* that "legitimation becomes visible as a problem and an object of study only at the point in which it is called into question" (p. viii).

14. For its narrative style and absence of scientific pretensions, Walter Laqueur's *Terrorism* (and his anthology on terrorism) stands out as an exception to the ruling policy-oriented rubbish on the subject. See in particular his preface to the Abacus Edition, where he stated that "the failure of political scientists to come to terms with the terrorist phenomenon cannot possibly be a matter of legitimate dispute . . . Historical experience, it is said, cannot teach us much about terrorism; but what else can?" From *Terrorism* (London: Sphere Books, 1978), pp. 7–8.

15. I wonder, after watching some of these pundits (like Michael Ledeen) who are wheeled out as impartial commentators on terrorism, whether the best counter-terrorism action would be a surgical airstrike on some of those institutes (but then again, they might miss and hit the Carnegie Endowment for International Peace).

16. For the transition of political representation to simulation, see Baudrillard's *Simulations*, pp. 11–13 ("Whereas representation tried to absorb simulation by interpreting it as false representation, simulation envelops the whole edifice of representation as itself a simulacrum"). For its elision through the balance of terror into a "mutual simulation," see Virilio's *Pure War*, pp. 159–172.

17. Michel Foucault, "Response au cercle d'epistemologie," *Cahiers pour l'analyse*, 9 (Summer 1968). This is of course only a sketch of Foucault's historiographical technique. On the difficult task of plumbing our own archive, "the general system of the formation and transformation of statements," see the introduction and chapter 5 of Foucault's *The Archaeology of Knowledge* (London: Tavistock Publications, 1972); and on his recuperation of the genealogical approach, "gray, meticulous, and patiently documentary," see his seminal essay, "Nietzsche, Genealogy, History," in *Language, Counter-Memory, Practice: Selected Essays and Interviews*, ed. D. F. Bouchard (Ithaca: Cornell University Press, 1977).

18. For an excellent introduction to the function of the promise in the international order, see chapters 1 and 2 of Hedley Bull's *The Anarchical Society* (London: Macmillan, 1977).

19. See Thomas Hobbes, *Leviathan*, ed. M. Oakeshott (Oxford: Blackwell, 1957), pp. 85–87 and 112; Hugo Grotius, "Of Promises," in *De jure belli ac pacis*, trans. W. Whewell (London: John Parker, 1835), Vol. II, pp. 35–36; and Samuel Pufendorf, "Of the Nature of Promises and Pacts in General," in *Of the Law of Nature and Nations* (Oxford: Clarendon, 1935), pp. 390–401.

20. For Sartre, then, terror is not an anomalous feature of modern society, but fundamental, as is scarcity, to the formation of societies: "The origin of the pledge, in effect, is fear (Both of the third party and of myself) . . . Terror . . . is common freedom violating necessity, in so far as necessity exists only through the alienation of some freedom" (Sartre, *Critique of Dialectical Reason* (London: Verso, 1976), pp. 430–431.

21. See Martin Wight, *Systems of States* (Leicester: Leicester University Press, 1977), and *Power Politics* (Middlesex: Penguin, 1979).

22. "By international legitimacy I mean the collective judgment of international society about rightful membership of the family of nations; how sovereignty may be transferred; and how state succession is to be regulated, when large states break up into smaller, or several states combine into one. Until the French Revolution, the principle of international legitimacy was *dynastic*, being concerned with the status and claims of rulers. Since then, dynasticism has been superseded by a *popular* principle, concerned with the claims and consent of the governed." From Wight, *System of States*, p. 153.

23. Wright, *Systems of State*, p. 160.

17. Television and Democracy

The theories and research findings discussed in this paper are derived from the work of the Cultural Indicators Project, directed by George Gerbner and Larry Gross (The Annenberg School of Communications, University of Pennsylvania), Michael Morgan (Department of Communication, University of Massachusetts), and Nancy Signorielli (Department of Communication, University of Delaware). See George Gerbner, Larry Gross, Michael Morgan, and Nancy Signorielli, "The Dynamics of the Cultivation Process," in J. Bryant and D. Zillman, eds., *Perspective on Media Effects* (Hillsdale, NJ: Erlbaum, 1986), pp. 17–40; "Political Correlates of Television Viewing," *Public Opinion Quarterly*, 48 (Spring 1984), 283–300; "Charting the Mainstream: Television's Contributions to Political Orientations," *Journal of Communication*, 32:2 (Spring 1982), 100–127; "The 'Mainstreaming' of America: Violence Profile No. 11," *Journal of Communication*, 30:3 (Summer 1980), 10–29; "Television Violence, Victimization, and Power," *American Behavioral Scientists*, 23:5 (1980), 705–716; Larry Gross, "The Cultivation of Intolerance: Television, Blacks, and Gays," in G. Melischek, K. E. Rosengren, and J. Stappers, eds., *Cultural Indicators: An International Symposium* (Vienna: Austrian Academy of Sciences, 1984), pp. 345–364; Larry Gross and Michael Morgan, "Television and Enculturation," in J. Dominick and J. Fletcher, eds., *Broadcasting Research Methods* (Boston: Allyn and Bacon, 1985), pp. 221–234; Michael Morgan, "Television and the Erosion of Regional Diversity," *Journal of Broadcasting and Electronic Media*, 30:2 (Spring 1986), 123–139; and Michael Morgan, "Symbolic Victimization and Real-World Fear," *Human Communication Research*, 9:2 (1983), 146–157.

18. MTV: Swinging on the (Postmodern) Star

1. For example, see E. Ann Kaplan, *Rocking Around the Clock: Music Television, Post Modernism and Consumer Culture* (New York: Methuen, 1984); and the issue devoted to MTV of *Journal of Communication Inquiry*, 10 (Winter 1986).

2. This is not to deny that there are other musical forms involved in music television, including country and western and various forms of black music, but rock and roll is clearly the dominant and most influential form, not only in terms of its presence on the screen and its economics, but also in terms of its leading position in defining the forms and formats of music television.

3. Andrew Goodwin, "From Anarchy to Chromakey: Music, Media, Video," *One Two Three Four (A Rock 'n' Roll Quarterly)*, No. 5 (Spring 1987), pp. 16–32.

4. The following discussion draws heavily upon Goodwin, "From Anarchy"; Simon

Frith, "Making Sense of Videos," and Will Straw, "Music Videos in its Contexts: Popular Music and Postmodernism in the 1980s." The latter two articles appear in Simon Frith, Andrew Goodwin, and Lawrence Grossberg, eds., *Sound and Vision: The Music Video Reader* (forthcoming).

5. Academics would do well to remember that we are also implicated in capitalist relations, and produce knowledge as commodities: whether in the form of books, journals, discourses with limited intelligibility to broader audiences, or educational apparatuses increasingly defined by limited access.

6. The following argument is an abbreviated version of my "Music Television and the Production of Postmodern Difference," in Frith, Goodwin, and Grossberg, *Sound and Vision*. A fuller reading of Springsteen is offered in my "Pedagogy in the Age of Reagan: Politics, Postmodernity and the Popular," in Henry A. Giroux and Roger Simon, eds., *Critical Pedagogy and Popular Culture* (New York: Bergin and Garvey, forthcoming).

7. This paper has benefited from conversations with my graduate students. I would particularly like to thank Charles Acland, Jon Crane, and Phil Gordon for their comments and suggestions.

19. The Decline of American Intellectuals

1. This essay is based on my talk at the conference "Wars of Persuasion: Gramsci, Intellectuals and Mass Culture" (University of Massachusetts, Amherst, April, 1987) and my book, *The Last Intellectuals: American Culture in the Age of Academe* (New York: Basic Books, 1987).

2. C. Wright Mills, "The Social role of the Intellectual," in his *Power, Politics and People*, ed. I. L. Horowitz (New York: Balantine, 1963), pp. 292–304.

3. Ferdinand Brunetière cited by Victor Brombert, *The Intellectual Hero: Studies in the French Novel, 1880–1955* (New York: Lippincott, 1961), p. 23.

4. H. Stuart Hughes, "Is the Intellectual Obsolete?" *Commentary*, 22 (1956), pp. 313–319.

5. See John P. Diggins, "The New Republic and its Times," *The New Republic* (December 10, 1984), p. 58.

6. Arthur Schlesinger, Jr., "The Highbrow in American Politics" (1953) reprinted in *The Scene Before You*, ed. Chandler Brossard (New York: Rinehart, 1955), p. 263.

7. John W. Aldridge, *In Search of Heresy: American Literature in the Age of Conformity* [1956] (Port Washington, NY: Kennikat Press, 1976), p. 5.

8. Merle King, "The Intellectual: Will He Wither Away?" *The New Republic* (April 8, 1957), pp. 14–15.

9. J. F. Wolpert, "Notes on the American Intelligentsia," originally *Partisan Review* (1947), reprinted in *The Scene Before You*, ed. Brossard, pp. 241–243.

10. Editorial Statement, "Our Country and our Culture," *Partisan Review*, 19 (1952), pp. 283–284.

11. Philip Rahv in "Our Country and Our Culture," *Partisan Review*, 19 (1952), p. 306.

12. David Riesman in "Our Country and Our Culture," *Partisan Review*, 19 (1952), pp. 311–312.

13. Max Lerner in "Our Country and Our Culture," *Partisan Review*, 19 (1952), p. 582.

14. Lionel Trilling, "The Situation of the American Intellectual at the Present Time," *Perspectives USA*, No. 3 (Spring 1953), pp. 29–30. This is an expansion of his comments that appeared in the *Partisan Review* symposium.

15. C. Wright Mills, "On Knowledge and Power," (1955) in his *Power, Politics and People*, pp. 599.

16. Alfred Kazin, *New York Jew* (New York: Vintage Books, 1979), p. 7.

17. Malcolm Cowley, "Limousines on Grub Street" (1946), reprinted in his *The Flower and the Leaf*, ed. D. W. Faulkner (New York: Viking, 1985), pp. 95–96.

18. See Kenneth C. Davis, *Two-Bit Culture: The Paperbacking of America* (Boston: Houghton Mifflin, 1984), pp. 190–202.

19. Isaac Rosenfeld, "On the Role of the Writer and the Little Magazine," (1956) reprinted in *Chicago Review Anthology*, ed. David Ray (Chicago: University of Chicago Press, 1959), pp. 6, 4.

20. Richard Rorty, *Consequences of Pragmatism* (Minneapolis: University of Minnesota Press, 1982, p. 227.

21. Charles Kadushin, *The American Intellectual Elite* (Boston: Little, Brown, 1974), pp. 26, 32.

22. Robert A. McCaughey, *International Studies and Academic Enterprise: A Chapter in the Enclosure of American Learning* (New York: Columbia University Press, 1984), pp. xiv., 227, 254, 232–233.

23. *Paul A. Baran (1910–1964): A Collective Portrait*, ed. Paul M. Sweezy and Leo Huberman (New York: Monthly Review Press, 1965).

20. The Myth of the Information Society

1. William Leiss, *The Domination of Nature* (New York: George Braziller, 1972), ch. 3.

2. Robert E. Lane, "The Decline of Politics and Ideology in a Knowledgeable Society," *American Sociological Review*, 31 (1968), pp. 649–662.

3. S. Serafini and M. Andrieu, Department of Communications, Government of Canada, *The Information Revolution and its Implications for Canada* (Ottawa: Supply and Services Canada, 1981), p. 13.

4. Arthur Cordell (Science Council of Canada), *The Uneasy Eighties: The Transition to an Information Society* (Ottawa: Supply and Services Canada, 1985), p. 3.

5. E. G. Mesthene, *Technological Change* (Cambridge, Mass.: Harvard University Press, 1970); J. K. Galbraith, *The New Industrial State* (Boston: Houghton Mifflin, 1967); Jacques Ellul, *The Technological Society* (New York: Knopf, 1964).

6. E. G. Mesthene, "Technology and Wisdom," in *Technology and Social Change*, ed. Mesthene (Indianapolis: Bobbs-Merrill, 1967), p. 59.

7. D. Bell, *The Coming of post-Industrial Society* (New York: Basic Books, 1973), xii. His later essay, "The Social Framework of the Information Society," in Tom Forrester, ed., *The Microelectronics Revolution* (Oxford: Basil Blackwell, 1980), 500–576, added nothing new.

8. Donald Schon, *Technology and Change* (New York: Delacorte, 1967), xiii.

9. Kimon Valaskakis, *Information Society Project* (Ottawa: Supply and Services Canada, 1979, 4 vols.), I, 40.

10. Marc Uri Porat, *The Information Economy* (Washington, D.C.: Office of Telecommunications, Special Publication 77–12, 1977, 9 vols.).

11. Bell, *The Coming of Post-Industrial Society*, p. 14.

12. Compare what follows with the brilliant commentary on Bell's work in Krishan Kumar's *Prophecy and Progress* (Harmondsworth: Penguin, 1978), ch. 6.

13. Bell, *The Coming of Post-Industrial Society*, p. 137.

14. Bell, *The Coming of Post-Industrial Society*, p. 43.

15. Serafini and Andrieu, *The Information Revolution*, p. 19.

16. Valaskakis, *Information Society*, p. 40; Serafini and Andrieu, *The Information Revolution*, p. 8.

17. See generally Jonathan Kozol, *Illiterate America* (New York: New American Library, 1984).

18. Edwin Diamond and Stephen Bates, *The Spot: The Rise of Political Advertising on Television* (Cambridge, Mass.: MIT Press, 1984).

19 *Newsweek* (10 August 1987), p. 17.

20. Lester Thurow, *The Zero-Sum Society* (New York: Basic Books, 1980).

21. Limits to the Imagination: Marketing and Children's Culture

1. This essay is based on a research project entitled "Technicians of the Imagination" supported by a grant from SSHRC, Canada.

2. Lloyd deMause, *The Evolution of Childhood* (New York: Harper and Row, 1974), pp. 1, 54.

3. David Riesman, N. Glazer and R. Denney, *The Lonely Crowd* (New York: Doubleday, 1956).

4. William Leiss, Stephen Kline, and Sut Jhally, *Social Communication in Advertising* (Toronto: Methuen, 1986).

5. Marie Winn, *The Plug-in Drug* (New York: Penguin, 1977); and George Comstock, S. Chaffee, N. Katzman, M. McCombs, and D. Roberts, *Television and Human Behavior* (New York: Columbia University Press, 1978).

6. Donald Roberts, "Children and Commercials: Issues, Evidence, Interventions in Rx Television," *Prevention in the Human Services*, Vol. 2, Nos. 1/2 (1983), p. 28.

7. James McNeal, *Children as Consumers: Insights and Implications* (Lexington: Lexington Books, 1987).

8. Brenda Dailey, Manager, "Product Testing at Milton Bradley," in *Communicating to the Youth Market: A Child's Perspective*, RC–7 from TVB, undated.

9. McNeal, *Children as Consumers*, 1987.

10. Peter Francese, *Trends and Opportunities in the Children's Market* (Des Moines: People Patterns, American Demographics, 1985).

11. McCollum/Spielman, *Topline Report*, Vol. 2, No. 2 (1983).

12. See McNeal, *Children as Consumers*; William Wells, "Communicating with Children," *Journal of Advertising Research* (1966), pp. 1–4; Ellen Wartella, D. Wackman, S. Ward, J. Shamir, and A. Alexander, "The Young Child as Consumer," chap. 9 in E. Wartella, ed., *Children Communicating* (Beverly Hills, Sage, 1979).

13. S. Ward, and D. Wackman, "Television advertising and intrafamily influence: Children's Purchase influence attempts and parental yielding," in E. A. Rubenstein, G. A. Comstock, and J. P. Murray, eds., *Television and Social Behavior*, Vol. 4, *Television in day-to-day life: Patterns of use* (Washington, DC: US Printing Office, 1972).

14. Felice Kincannon, "Now Billy Age Six Picks Brands," in *Marketing and Media Decisions* (March 1983), p. 68.

15. Laura Jereski, "Advertisers woo kids with a different game," *Marketing and Decisions* (September 1983), p. 72, 73, 126–130.

16. Kincannon, "Now Billy Age Six Picks Brands."

17. Television Bureau of Advertising, "Target Selling the Children's Market," (1986).

18. Tom Englehart, "The Strawberry Shortcake Strategy," in Todd Gitlin, ed., *Watching Television* (New York: Pantheon Books, 1986), pp. 74–108.

19. Cy Schneider, *Children's Television: The Art, the Business, How it Works* (Chicago: NTC Business Books, 1987), p. 125.

20. M. Grove, "Special Report: Licensing and Merchandising," *Hollywood Reporter*, Weekly International Edition (June 2, 1987).

21. B. Lowry, "Tie-ins: Raising the Bottom Line in Kidvid," *Hollywood Reporter* (June 2, 1987).

22. Schneider, *Children's Television*, pp. 24–27.

23. Schneider, *Children's Television*, p. 157.

24. Schneider, *Children's Television*, p. 33.

25. Bruno Bettleheim, *The Uses of Enchantment: The Meaning and Importance of Fairytales* (New York: Vintage Books, 1977).

26. Jane Rae, "If you are going to advertise to kids on television do it right," *Stimulus* (May/June 1985), pp. 24–25; and Wartella, *Children Communicating*, pp. 256–259.

27. Celia Anderson, "The Saturday Morning Survival Kit," *Journal of Popular Culture*, Vol. 17, No. 4 (1984), pp. 155–161.

28. Schneider, *Children's Television*, p. 23.

29. Sut Jhally, *The Codes of Advertising* (New York: St. Martins Press, 1987).

30. The research referred to here is being carried out by the author at York University, Toronto, and will be more fully reported in a forthcoming book entitled *Technicians of the Imagination*.

22. The Privatization and Transnationalization of Culture

1. Neu P. Eurich and Ernest L. Boyer, *Corporate Classrooms: The Learning Business* (Princeton, New Jersey: The Carnegie Foundation for the Advancement of Teaching, 1985).

2. The English go a step further. A new IT (Information Technology) Institute, scheduled to open in September, 1986, is financed directly by industry, and will be run as a business, "with the Institute's principal acting as managing director, reporting to a board of directors. Staff will be employed on a contract basis and will be offered high wages to tempt them away from universities and colleges." *Computer* (May 1, 1986).

3. Richard W. Stevenson, "An Industry Turns Volume Up," The *New York Times* (January 18, 1986).

4. "TV Programs That Play," *Business Week* (December 9, 1985), p. 72.

5. Thomas Morgan, "Is Public TV Becoming Overly Commercial?," The *New York Times* (April 9, 1986).

6. "The Public Service Idea in British Broadcasting: Main Principles," British Broadcasting Research Unit, London (1985), pp. 7–8.

7. Andy Chetley, "The Lessons from the Baby Food Campaign," *IFDA Dossier* 52 (March/April, 1986), pp. 45–46.

8. "Cigarette Ad Ban Recommended," The *New York Times* (March 24, 1986).

9. Irvin Molotsky, "A.M.A. Expected to Call for Ban on Cigarettes," The *New York Times* (December 5, 1985).

10. Elhanan C. Stone, "Ads have First Amendment Rights," letter to the *New York Times* (January 9, 1986).

11. Kevin Robbins, and Frank Webster, "Television and Consumer Capitalism," *Screen* (Summer/Autumn, 1986).

12. David Margolick, "New York Court lets Malls Limit Pamphleteering," The *New York Times* (December 20, 1985).

13. Stafford, Beer, "The Preposterous Inference," *Computer Networks and ISDN System*, 9 (1985), pp. 11–20, North-Holland, Elsevier.

14. "International Information Flow: A Plan for Action," A Statement by the *Business Roundtable*, New York (January 1985), p. 3.

15. "From Now to the Twenty-First Century," Global Media Commission, International Advertising Association, undated.

16. Philip H. Dougherty, "3-Way Merger to Create Largest Ad Agency," The *New York Times* (April 28, 1986).

17. "From Now to the Twenty-First Century."

18. Roger, Watkins, "Europe is Facing Commercial TV," *Variety* (April 23, 1986), p. 1. 17th International Television Annual.

19. "International Information Flow: A Plan for Action," p. 6.

20. Walter B. Wriston, "Economic Freedom Receives a Boost," The *New York Times* (April 15, 1986).

21. Interview with Peter Hall, The *New York Times* (February 16, 1986).

23. Media Beyond Representation

1. Friedrich Pollock, "State Capitalism: Its Possibilities and Limitations," in *The Essential Frankfurt School Reader*, ed. Andrew Arato and Eike Gebhardt (Oxford: Blackwell, 1978), p. 73.

2. Jean Baudrillard, *The Mirror of Production*, trans. Mark Poster (St. Louis: Telos Press, 1975), pp. 121, 127.

3. Henri Lefebvre, *Everyday Life in the Modern World*, trans. Sacha Rabinovitch (New York: Harper and Row, 1971), pp. 111, 112, 116–117. From this perspective, Saussure's insistence on the "arbitrariness of the sign" and its immense influence on subsequent linguistics takes on more of the character of a symptom than an unquestionable first principle of language. Ferdinand de Saussure, *Course in General Linguistics*, trans. Wade Baskin (New York: McGraw-Hill, 1966), p. 67f. See on this point Walter Benjamin, "Doctrine of the Similar," trans. Knut Tarnowski, *New German Critique*, No. 17 (Spring 1979). Also, Ian H. Angus, *Technique and Enlightenment: Limits of Instrumental Reason* (Washington: University Press of America and Centre for Advanced Research in Phenomenology, 1984), pp. 19–41.

4. Claude E. Shannon and Warren Weaver, *The Mathematical Theory of Communication* (Urbana: The University of Illinois Press, 1962), p. 5. David K. Berlo, *The Process of Communication* (New York: Holt, Rinehart and Winston, 1960), p. 72. Roman Jakobson, "Closing Statement: Linguistics and Poetics" in *Style in Language*, ed. Thomas A. Sebeok (New York: The Technology Press of MIT and John Wiley and Sons, 1960), p. 353.

5. Marshall McLuhan, *Understanding Media* (New York: Mentor, 1964), pp. 49, 294ff.

6. McLuhan, *Understanding Media*, p. 47.

7. It is rarely acknowledged, however, that this central utopian theme in McLuhan is a specific, polemical denial of the center/margin dependency theory from which Harold Innis developed his communication theory. See Harold Innis, *Empire and Communication* (Toronto: University of Toronto Press, 1972) and *The Bias of Communication* (Toronto: University of Toronto Press, 1951). These are two characteristic gestures of colonial intellectuals — criticizing and embracing empire. One of the few accounts which situates McLuhan in this context is Arthur Kroker, *Technology and the Canadian Mind* (New York: St. Martin's Press, 1984).

8. McLuhan, *Understanding Media*, p. 52.

9. McLuhan, *Understanding Media*, p. 64.

10. Jean Baudrillard, *Simulations* trans. Paul Foss, Paul Patton, and Philip Beitchman (New York: *Semiotext(e)*, 1983), p. 119f.

11. Jean Baudrillard, *In the Shadow of the Silent Majorities* trans. Paul Foss, Paul Patton, and John Johnston (New York: *Semiotext(e)*, 1983), p. 6.

12. See my discussion of "image-sets" in "Circumscribing Postmodern Culture," in this volume.

13. Shannon and Weaver, *Mathematical Theory*, p. 109.

14. Baudrillard, *In the Shadow of the Silent Majorities*, p. 43f.

15. I have developed this strategy in more detail in my essay "Oral Tradition as Resistance" in *Continuity and Change: The Cultural Life of Alberta's First Ukrainians*, ed. Manoly, R. Lupul (Edmonton: Canadian Institute of Ukrainian Studies, 1988).

24. Postmodernism: Roots and Politics

1. Raymond Williams, *Marxism and Literature* (New York: Oxford University Press, 1977), pp. 128–35, and *Politics and Letters* (London: New Left Books, 1979), pp. 156–66.

2. Serge Guilbaut, *How New York Stole the Idea of Modern Art*, trans. Arthur Goldhammer (Chicago: University of Chicago Press, 1983).

3. See in particular John Berger, "The Moment of Cubism," in *The Moment of Cubism and Other Essays* (New York: Pantheon, 1969), pp. 1–32; Steven Kern, *The Culture of Time and Space, 1880–1918* (Cambridge Mass.: Harvard University Press, 1983); Marjorie Perloff, *The Futurist Moment* (Chicago: University of Chicago Press, 1987).

4. I am triangulating among several writers' versions of postmodernism, particularly those of Susan Sontag, Fredric Jameson, Andreas Huyssen, and Sven Birkerts. Discussions of the interpenetration of high and popular culture are indebted to Sontag's "One Culture and The New Sensibility" (originally published 1965, reprinted in *Against Interpretation* [New York: Dell, 1969], pp. 294–304). See also Jameson, "Postmodernism, or The Cultural Logic of Late Capitalism," *New Left Review*, No. 146 (July–August 1984), pp. 53–92; Huyssen, *After the Great Divide:*

Modernism, Mass Culture, Postmodernism (Bloomington: Indiana University Press, 1986); Birkerts, *An Artificial Wilderness: Essays in Twentieth-Century Literature* (New York: Morrow, 1987); and my own discussion of recombinant culture in *Inside Prime Time* (New York: Pantheon, 1983), extended in " 'We Build Excitement,' " in Todd Gitlin, ed., *Watching Television* (New York: Pantheon, 1987), pp. 136–61.

5. Huyssen, *After the Great Divide*, chaps. 9, 10. The idea of modernism as a permanent revolution runs through Marshall Berman, *All That Is Solid Melts Into Air* (New York: Simon and Schuster, 1982).

6. Roger Shattuck, "Pre-Postmodernism," *The New Republic* (July 17, 1987), p. 32.

7. Quoted from the program of the London International Festival of Theatre (Summer 1987), p. 20.

8. Jameson, "Postmodernism," cited above, and "Postmodernism and Consumer Society," in Hal Foster, ed., *The Anti-Aesthetic* (Port Townsend, Washington: Bay Press, 1984).

9. Here I take some cues from Andreas Huyssen's *After the Great Divide*, but diverge from him in important respects — probably because I am focusing on the blank postmodernism of the 1970s and '80s than the more exuberant one — McLuhan, Warhol, and the Living Theatre — of the 1960s.

10. Mark Miller, "Deride and Conquer," in Todd Gitlin, ed., *Watching Television* (New York: Pantheon, 1987), pp. 183–228.

11. "Video Novels," *Boston Review* (June 1987), pp. 12–14. See also comments by Sven Birkerts, Rosellen Brown, and this writer in *Boston Review* (August 1987), pp. 2, 27.

12. Huyssen, *After the Great Divide*, pp. 188-91.

13. Bourne hoped for a "Trans-National America" — the title of his essay. Cited in Nicholas Xenos, "Uncommon Ground," a review of Paul Buhle, *Marxism in the U.S.A.*, *The Nation* (June 27, 1987), p. 895.

14. Diane Macdonell, *Theories of Discourse: An Introduction* (London: Basil Blackwell, 1986), p. 5.

15. The important prefiguration of this understanding that "superstructural" culture interpenetrates economic "base" is Marshall Sahlins, *Culture and Practical Reason* (Chicago: University of Chicago Press, 1976).

16. On the decomposition of the standard ideological configurations in popular sensibility, see Craig Reinarman, *American States of Mind: Visions of Capitalism and Democracy among Private and Public Workers* (New Haven: Yale University Press, 1987), chap. 9. Robert N. Bellah et al. (*Habits of the Heart* [Berkeley: University of California Press, 1985]) argue that the present-day middle-class language of political and moral life has become colonized by the self-centered assumptions of "expressive individualism"; but it remains possible that people are, to some extent, living in the light of some (residual? emergent?) communitarian goals although the fact is masked by their resort to an impoverished language.

17. See J. Hoberman, "What's Stranger than Paradise? Or, How We Stopped Worrying and Learned to Love the 'Burbs,' " and Katherine Dieckmann, "Stupid People Tricks: Making Fun of the Folks at Home," *Village Voice* Film Special (June 30, 1987), pp. 3–8 and 11–15. Hoberman offers the pointed observation that "AmeriKitsch, perhaps much of postmodernism itself, is the culture of suburban baby-boomers" (p. 8); also that "[t]he apparent impossibility of fully imagining [an interracial, cross-cultural, class-effacing] alternative is what accounts for the uncanny hermeticism, if not solipsism, of . . . all Americanarama."

Contributors

GORE VIDAL, novelist and commentator, has published many books on American history and on the American Empire. Among his works are *Burr*, *The Second American Revolution*, *Duluth*, *Lincoln*, and *Empire*. He lives in Los Angeles and Rome.

EILEEN MAHONEY is Assistant Professor of Communications at the City College of New York and Visiting Scholar at the Center for Telecommunications and Information Studies at the Graduate School of Business, Columbia University.

IAN H. ANGUS teaches in the Department of Communication at the University of Massachusetts at Amherst. He is the author of *Technique and Enlightenment: Limits of Instrumental Reason*.

STANLEY ARONOWITZ teaches sociology at the Graduate Center of the City University of New York. He is the author of *The Crisis in Historical Materialism*, *Education under Siege* (with Henry Giroux), *False Promises*, *Food, Shelter and the American Dream*, and *Working Class Hero: A New Strategy for Labor*. He has written widely for *The Nation*, *Social Policy*, the *VLS*, and *The Los Angeles Times*, as well as for numerous academic journals.

STEPHEN KLINE teaches at York University in Toronto. His publications reflect research interests in comparative cultural analysis, values, and attitude change, and in the news and advertising. He is coauthor of *Social Communication in Advertising* (also available from Routledge).

LAWRENCE GROSSBERG teaches at the University of Illinois, Urbana-Champaign. He is the editor of several volumes on Marxist cultural theory, communication theory, and popular music. He is coauthor, with Stuart Hall and Jennifer Daryl Slack, of *Cultural Studies*.

RUSSELL JACOBY is the author of several books, most recently *The Last Intellectuals: American Culture in the Age of Academe*.

WILLIAM LEISS is Professor of Communication at Simon Fraser University. He is the author of *The Domination of Nature, The Limits of Satisfaction, C.B. Macpherson*, and *Under Technology's Thumb* (forthcoming).

SUT JHALLY is Associate Professor of Communication at the University of Massachusetts at Amherst. He is coauthor of *Social Communication in Advertising*, also available from Routledge.

STUART EWEN is Chair and Professor of Communication at Hunter College, City University of New York, and Professor in the doctoral program in sociology at the University Center and Graduate School of CUNY. He is the author of *Allconsuming Images: The Politics of Style in Contemporary Culture* and *Captains of Consciousness: Advertising and the Social Roots of the Consumer Culture*.

LESLIE T. GOOD is Assistant Professor of Communication at the University of Massachusetts at Amherst, where she specializes in critical social theory.

ELLEN WILLIS is a staff writer at the *Village Voice* and the author of *Beginning to See the Light*. She has been a feminist activist since 1968 and was a cofounder of the original Redstockings.

NEIL EVERNDEN is an associate professor at York University, Toronto. He is a "human ecologist" whose work centres on the role of cultural influences in the understanding of nature, and on the consequences of this for the environmental movement. He is the author of *The Natural Alien* and *The Social Construction of Nature* (forthcoming).

MICHAEL OMI is a sociologist who teaches in the Asian American Studies Program at the University of California, Berkeley. He is coauthor, with Howard Winant, of *Racial Formation in the United States: From the 1960s to the 1980s*, available from Routledge.

HERBERT SCHILLER is Professor of Communication at the University of California, San Diego. Among his books are *Mass Communication and American Empire, Who Knows: Information in the Age of the Fortune 500*, and *Information and the Crisis Economy*.

GINA MARCHETTI teaches in the Department of Communication Arts and Theatre, Radio-Television-Film Division, University of Maryland, College Park. She has published articles in *Jump Cut, Journal of Communication Inquiry*, and other journals.

MICHAEL MORGAN is Associate Professor of Communication at the University of Massachusetts at Amherst. His research centers on the contributions of mass communication to audience conceptions of social reality.

BILL LIVANT teaches psychology at the University of Regina, Saskatchewan. He has published articles on social and developmental psychology, evolutionary biology, and (with Sut Jhally) mass communications.

JEAN BETHKE ELSHTAIN is Professor of Political Science, University of Massachusetts at Amherst. She is the author of several books, including *Public Man, Private Woman: Women in Social and Political Thought* and *Women and War*. Her writings on culture and politics have appeared in *The Nation, The New Republic,* and *Harpers*.

TODD GITLIN is Professor of Sociology and Director of the Mass Communications program at the University of California, Berkeley. He is the editor of *Watching Television* and the author of *The Whole World is Watching, Inside Prime-Time,* and *The Sixties: Years of Hope, Days of Rage*.

JAMES DER DERIAN is Assistant Professor of Political Science at the University of Massachusetts at Amherst. He is the author of *On Diplomacy: A Genealogy of Western Estrangement*.

ANDREW WERNICK is Professor of Sociology and Cultural Studies at Trent University, Ontario, where he is also Director of the Institute for the Study of Popular Culture.